Library of Congress Cataloging in Publication Data

Main entry under title:

Cultural politics.

   Includes bibliographies and index.
   1. Arts and society—United States—Addresses,
essays, lectures. 2. Radicalism in art—Addresses,
essays, lectures. 3. Dissident art—United States—
Addresses, essays, lectures. I. Starr, Jerold M.,
1941—
NX180.S6C855   1985   700′1′030973   84-26326
ISBN 0-03-062522-X (alk. paper)

NX
180
.S6
C855
1985

Published in 1985 by Praeger Publishers
CBS Educational and Professional Publishing
a Division of CBS Inc.
521 Fifth Avenue, New York, NY 10175 USA
© 1985 by Praeger Publishers

56789 052 987654321

Printed in the United States of America
on acid-free paper

Foreword

Alfred McClung Lee

With increasing diversity and rapidity, social change has in recent centuries disrupted the life-styles of millions. Technological innovations, migrations, and wars often weaken or destroy whatever security may be provided by family, employment, church, and community. So much is in flux. This has cast doubt upon the representativeness and integrity of political, business, and religious leaders. Where can one now turn for guidance?

As change spreads its impact outward from urban centers throughout the world, it gives increasing urgency to the search for credible answers to the questions Who am I? Why do I live? How can I live? In what can I believe? Upon what and upon whom can I depend? The old answers are fraught with doubt.

Humanity fumbles for new concepts with which to make old symbols viable, for ways to try to ignore or to cope with novelty. In this fumbling, reactionary cults compete with innovative artists and agitators in the offering of both useful and destructive services. As Walt Whitman put it, "The eager and often inconsiderate appeals of reformers and revolutionists are indispensable, to counterbalance the inertness and fossilism making so large a part of human institutions" (1870, p. 383). He lamented that prestigious literary products have "never recognized the people" (1870, p. 376). Even the "great poems, Shakspere [*sic*] included, are poisonous to the idea of the pride and dignity of the common people, the life-blood of democracy" (Whitman 1870, p. 388). But, as this book's studies make clear, growing popular literacy and revolt are creating both radical art forms and modified concepts of what is prestigious and notable in the art of our changing society.

In his social history of American literature, Parrington points out that his predecessors typically "labored under too heavy a handicap of the genteel tradition." They tried to find "daintier fare than polemics" even though the "foundations of a later America were laid in vigorous polemics, and the rough stone was plentifully mortared with idealism" (1930, I, pp. vi–vii). He placed his hope for society in people of letters who are "free souls, and in the measure of their abilities, free thinkers." He was concerned with the struggles between such innovators and the academic intellectuals whose theories are so largely "in charge of paymasters and . . . content with the drab rim of the familiar landscape." Creative spirits "become the authentic voice of this great shapeless America that means so much to western civilization" (1930, III, p. xxvii).

The growing intellectual domination of American life by an institutionalized middle class accompanied the rising tide of literacy. That meant an abundant supply of people trained to rationalize the tightening plutocratic control of society. In opposition, as Starr analyzes those confrontations in Chapter 9, radical artists are able to reveal "social conditions normally hidden from view" and to help "individuals to perceive what were thought to be their own personal troubles as shared social problems"; they thus help to "create community." In other words, radical artists can be "whistle-blowers" on social abuses and clarifiers of the nature of many other social problems. They can be therapeutic aids who can stimulate social consciousness and concern, and depictors of possible alternative courses of action. In spite of wide variations among their products, radical artists may reach mutually reinforcing perceptions. These perceptions can facilitate potentially useful efforts of social actionists trying to modify institutions through organization, confrontation, and negotiation. To have political influence, perceptions offered by artists must come to be shared by actionists and publics, or the artists must contribute directly to the work of actionists. Thus do contradictory products of free spirits undergo social selection and implementation.

Confusion arises in considering possible relations among radical artistic, social scientific, and social actionist efforts. This reflects conflicts among the ideals that are said to be necessary for artists and scientists to hold in order to do creative work.

Members of social elites typically prefer artists and scientists who comfort and support them, who add to their prestige and power. They want specialists who are either political lackeys or politically noncontroversial. They want technicians whose novelty exploits form or rhetoric, not content. They give lip tribute to the ideal that artists should dedicate themselves to the true, the beautiful, the ugly, and that social scientists should try to be dominated in their thoughts by observations of what they take to be reality. Therewith, they insist that the value commitments of these specialists should be un-critically and even unconsciously congruent with theirs.

But this elitist conception of art, science, and action does not work. It does not fit the facts of creative experience. "Fieldwork" among creative artists and social scientists—whether or not they may be called "radical"—drives them away from elitism and toward democratic values, toward humanist concerns. Their work cannot be freed from value implications. Their quests make them question. Their probes for new perceptions take them beyond superficialities. Their selfless struggles give them human rather than just personal concerns.

"Positivists" have successfully seized control of the public image of social science, but this situation needs to be recognized as a per-version of traditional and useful scientific ideals (Lee 1973, 1978). The complex methodological games they play provide the basis for what Roszak (1969) calls the "paternalism of expertise." The positiv-ists do this by erecting barriers against the kind of free-ranging and radical (that is, cause-seeking) investigation that respects only evi-dence and rejects professional expediencies that are intellectually damaging.

The true, the beautiful, and the ugly exist in human contexts. Artists produce conceptions and objects out of their own experiences and usually try to place them in a social context. Similarly, scientists probe for what can be taken to be a better understanding of reality, even in astronomy and physics, through observations by themselves and by other human beings. Curious scientists cannot avoid seeing and questioning relations of their data to the fate of the human lot. Thus both artists and scientists create conceptions and symbols they hope other humans will accept and employ. They do not find humanist ideals irrelevant; verifiable perceptions of realities help people. Especially in the cases of radical artists and radical social scientists, their creations can be meant to serve the same interests as do those of radical social actionists. As Starr and others demonstrate, such innovations can have social effect only through the organiza-tional work of social actionists.

Edgar notes in Chapter 1 that literary artistry and social action-ism "are rooted in symbolism. Meeting to this extent on common ground, they serve—not consistently, but on occasion—as catalysts to stir and stimulate each other." What radical artists and scientists portray can give substance to the propaganda of social actionists, whether or not it is produced for such a purpose. Quite frequently, however, as Marcus points out in Chapter 2, cultural radicalism avoids "movements designed to change the political and economic apparatus." It focuses on "new forms and means of expression in art, literature, and theater, and a popular culture expressed in changing modes of living, values, and sensibilities fostering personal growth and new programmatic means of change." Myers's essay on those "a little hipped on the subject of Trotsky" (Chapter 5) indicates how that interest enabled radical culturalists to continue their experimentation in spite of Red scares directed at political radicals.

In this anthology the participants analyze choice examples from a century and a half of radical artistic and activist attempts to counteract fossilized unrepresentativeness in American institutions, in American social control mechanisms. This book is a testimonial to the virtues of interdisciplinary discussion and exchange. In reading these pages, I am impressed by the continuing contributions to American life and thought that can be traced—positively and negatively—to the Greenwich Village revolt of 1910–20, to the Dadaists and Leninists of 1916–23, to Marcus Garvey's Pan-Africanism of 1916–25, and to the more recent movements. As Gutknecht says in Chapter 4, Garvey "created a collective conscience that still lives in the hearts and minds of those contemplating new ways of building social movements."

The posc of some artists of being nonpolitical is a fascinating aspect of movements discussed here. "Despite the separation of literature and politics in our everyday consciousness," in Chapter 6 Ferrari illustrates how the two are related. For example, as George and Starr state in Chapter 7, "Ironically, the retreatist, apolitical Beats played a critical role in the rise of both the hippies and the New Left, movements that together altered significantly a society most Beats believed was beyond redemption."

In the last two chapters, Starr deals with contributions to political awareness in a broader sense. He discusses black, feminist, Yippie, and mass media actions from the 1960s on. "Certainly," he observes in Chapter 8, "concerns at the heart of the women's movement—for life, health, and community—can provide the moral basis for any future opposition to the excesses of capitalism and its amoral rationality." He sees, as did the Dadaists, political theater as a critical art form, with scenarios being concocted by a wide range of artists and actionists from radical ranks to the public relations specialists of

Madison Avenue. In Chapter 9 Starr is especially concerned with finding ways to stimulate individual creative freedom in personal relationships and modes of expression in a setting that will also provide opportunities for effective collective action. This freedom cannot come from "the imposition of authoritarian discipline and antiquated dogma" or "the euphoria of Romantic fantasy." He sees it coming from "a concerted application of value-committed humanist reason."

This is an encouraging book. It portrays and analyzes how generations of more or less "free" minds have tried to come to grips with the growing disruption, anonymity, and intimations of pointlessness of American existence. It shows how radical artists and activists are able to lead satisfying lives. They do not, like others of their time and place, try merely to secede from society through joining futile and degrading cults. They do not, like so many, permit themselves to be merely willing and unobtrusive tools.

A society in which radicalism can flourish is not sick. It is permitting experimentation in art and action that can help make necessary adaptations to changed life conditions.

REFERENCES

Lee, Alfred McClung. 1978. *Sociology for Whom?* New York: Oxford University Press.

———. 1973. *Toward Humanist Sociology.* Englewood Cliffs, N.J.: Prentice-Hall.

Parrington, Vernon L. 1930. *Main Currents in American Thought.* 3 vols. New York: Harcourt, Brace and Co.

Roszak, Theodore. 1969. *The Making of a Counterculture.* Garden City, N.Y.: Doubleday/Anchor.

Whitman, Walt. 1870. "Democratic Vistas." In his *Prose Works 1892*, vol. II, edited by Floyd Stovall, pp. 361–426. New York: New York University Press, 1964.

Acknowledgments

We are indebted to Bennett Berger, University of California, La Jolla campus, for making this collection possible. He convinced the National Endowment for the Humanities that it was an idea worth supporting, and he generously shared his knowledge with us through the summer of 1979 and, informally, for some time afterward. In 1981 he turned his attention to other matters. With the unanimous consent of the group, Jerold Starr assumed editorial leadership and brought this anthology to completion. Bennett will be surprised to see this book in print. We accept full responsibility for what is here, and we do hope he appreciates our effort.

Contents

Introduction

Jerold M. Starr

This collection of studies has been contributed by a group of sociologists and historians who are commonly concerned with contributing an understanding of the past to the creation of the future. The modern age was launched with the promise of the Enlightenment—liberty, equality, fraternity. The diffusion and frustration of these values have produced their own discontents—repression, exploitation, alienation. These discontents, in turn, have fostered their own movements for change. Radical political movements have aimed at democratizing the dominant institutions of the political economy. Radical cultural movements have aimed at democratizing people's life-styles, personal relationships, and forms of aesthetic expression.

Despite important gains, such movements have failed to produce the deep and lasting transformation needed. It has become apparent that the complete revolution must be one that takes place both in the sphere of culture and in the sphere of politics, one that is concerned with personal relationships and morals as well as power and wealth. Movements that have aimed for only cultural change have been vulnerable to co-optation by the corporations or repression by the state. Movements that have aimed for only political change have sometimes seized power, but have failed the revolution by reproducing the established culture of domination.

Is a synthesis of the cultural and the political, the personal and the collective, the expressive and the instrumental possible? If so, how is it to be achieved? What can we learn from past movements that have featured some convergence between cultural and political radicalism? Under what historical conditions have cultural and political radicals been able to make common cause (sharing people, settings, resources, and/or symbols), and under what conditions have they become competitors, even enemies?

In our attempts to answer these questions, we were compelled to distinguish further between radical movements according to the means they have employed. Such means have included conventional political strategies in which people have been mobilized to influence institutional authorities (such as bloc voting, lawsuits, and demonstrations), strategies of cultural subversion in which individuals intentionally have violated norms and asserted new rights in their everyday relationships, and strategies in which radical groups have utilized art and literature to change people's political orientations.

There have been many movements in modern history that have used conventional political strategies to achieve radical political change. This has been characteristic of most Socialist International parties since the late nineteenth century. Also, there have been many radical cultural movements in which unconventional personal relationships and innovative styles of aesthetic expression have been ends in themselves. This has been characteristic of Romantic bohemian movements from the early nineteenth-century French Romantics to most of the counterculture of the 1950s and 1960s.

The focus of this collection is on those historical movements that combined both radical political and radical cultural elements in their choice of means and ends. This includes cases where conventional political strategies were adopted to protect or advance radical cultural change, as with the Beats in the late 1950s and early 1960s and the "women's liberation" movement of the late 1960s. It also includes cases where radical cultural practices were employed to promote radical political change, as with the Berlin Dadaists at the end of World War I and the Yippies of the late 1960s.

The cases in this anthology are in the mode of the new social history. While traditional narrative history concentrates on individual elites and political and military events, the new social history concentrates on the relations between material conditions, socialization and popular culture, mass movements and social change (Stone 1982). Our treatment of these cases also is sympathetic to "mentalité" history with its emphasis on the relative autonomy of culture from material conditions, the power of ideology to move people to action, and the capacity of individuals and groups at critical historical moments to be agents of social change.

Our discussion of such cases includes analyses of those moments when political and cultural radicals have been able to sustain a creative alliance based on their mutual opposition to the puritanism and privilege of the bourgeoisie, the confrontations between them over issues such as individual freedom versus organizational solidarity, the debates between radical artists and writers over whether to seek change in the political arena, and the controversy over whether and how radical art and literature can move people to political action.

Such controversies about cultural politics have a rich history in Europe and America. They have been at the center of the revolutionary ferment in Greenwich Village in the period leading up to World War I (Chapter 2), in Europe during and after World War I (Chapter 3), among American novelists during the Depression (Chapters 5 and 6), and as recently as the 1960s (Chapter 8). We must study these past movements, which can teach and inspire us for today's struggles.

THE DIALECTIC OF CULTURE AND POLITICS

In the course of our study, it became apparent that radical cultural movements have played an essential role in the dialectic of modern history. All of the authors in this volume see their movements as arising out of a need to preserve old or advance new cultural values in response to the social upheaval of urban industrial development. For the English Romantics, the despised "machine in the garden" symbolized the commercial technology that threatened the old "way of life that had sustained art" (Chapter 1). The denizens of Greenwich Village stressed "creativity and self-expression" as a form of resistance to "a bureaucratized order operated by dull, faceless men" who administered the affairs of people who worshipped "the machine and materialism" (Chapter 2). The Dadaists sought to sabotage "the culture of industrial capitalism, which, collapsing under the weight of its own contradictions, had degenerated into wholesale human slaughter" (Chapter 3). The residents of Harlem in the 1920s saw their indigenous culture undermined by the "penetration" of outside political and economic forces, and searched for a new "basis of solidarity" to overcome their vulnerability (Chapter 4). In the 1930s, artists and writers struggled to come to terms with the collapse of Western capitalism and the historical meaning of the Soviet revolution (Chapters 5 and 6). And in the late 1950s and the 1960s millions of blacks, youth, and women protested being left out of or subjugated by the patriarchal consumerism of corporate, suburban life (Chapters 7 and 8).

This sense of rupture with the past often led to a belief in cultural renewal through generational rebellion. In varying degrees the generational idea gripped artists and writers in all these movements.

Edgar proposes that, despite many differences, the English Romantics were bound by a common generational sensibility that pivoted around the French Revolution of 1789. In pre-World War I Greenwich Village, Randolph Bourne dreamed of revitalizing American culture through a multinational fellowship of young intellectuals. Marcus also cites "generational conflict" as the basis for the establishment of the new Liberal Club in 1915. Inspired by the personal charisma of Socialist feminist Henrietta Rodman, the new Liberal Club, together with such kindred institutions as Polly's Restaurant, the Washington Square Bookstore, and Provincetown Playhouse, formed "a mecca for radicals and bohemians." The Dadaists advocated the rebellion of the youthful and modern against the old and decadent. Ferrari reports a split among proletarian novelists between the "older New Men," who stayed with the Communist Party-sponsored John Reed Clubs and *The New Masses*, and the "younger New Men," who sympathized with Trotsky and founded the *Partisan Review.* Kerouac, Ginsberg, and their friends often referred to themselves as "a new beat generation." And, by the 1960s, the student movement made "generation gap" a household term.

This generational vision typically was part of a larger complex of Romantic values that expressed the alienation and rebellion of these cultural radicals. From the early nineteenth century through the mid-twentieth, the English Romantics, the Greenwich Village rebels, the Dadaists, the Beats, the hippies, and the Yippies all advocated a cultural alternative to the values of industrial capitalism. They criticized materialism and utilitarianism as alien to the human spirit and advocated creativity and self-expression.

The collective and personal dimensions of this opposition were joined for many artists and writers because the Industrial Revolution made them a "status group in decline" (Chapter 1) whose work was being "proletarianized" (Chapter 2). During World War I and the later Depression, they faced a situation of "blocked ascendance" (Chapters 3 and 6) and advocated state support without political constraints for all artists (Chapters 3 and 5).

Throughout modern history, political radicals also opposed this new industrial order by urging those whose labor was being exploited and traditional human rights repressed to organize themselves for revolt against the industrialists and the state. These were periods of widespread social dislocation in which both material interests and cultural values were disturbed significantly. As such, these were periods of ideological ferment for both political and cultural radicals.

THE STRUCTURE OF IDEOLOGICAL CONFLICT

The systematic examination of political and cultural elements in these cases finally led us to new insights into the sources of ideological tension between activists and artists in the past. In terms of political content, radical ideologies share an emphasis on social causes, political cures, and democratic participation in social affairs. Conservative ideologies, in contrast, hold that behavior is determined by heredity and/or inherent sin, call for elite control of social institutions, and advocate little political program beyond military defense of the marketplace.

In terms of cultural content, Romantic ideologies place high value on the individual. They may be contrasted to rationalist ideologies in terms of personal intuition vs. objective calculation, creative self-expression vs. technical discipline, craftsmanship vs. routine work procedures, expressive norms vs. instrumental norms, the exotic vs. the uniform, heroic individuality vs. organizational conformity, spontaneity vs. planning, and localism vs. centralization.

When both cultural and political dimensions are considered, four familiar types stand out: rational conservativism, Romantic conservatism, rational radicalism, and Romantic radicalism. Of course, such types do not fully represent all concrete historical occurrences. Rather, they are conceptual models that codify the complex diversity of our cases to enable comparison. While this focus on uniformities necessarily exaggerates aspects of the empirical phenomena, it does help us to understand the essential dynamics of these cases (McKinney 1954; Hempel 1963).

Moreover, I propose that historically these types have functioned as deep structures in cultural thought. Each has its own distinctive logic and has exerted a powerful attraction for different groups and individuals. Each also is flawed in some critical way, so none, in itself offers the radical transformation we seek. That transformation, I hope to demonstrate, would require a more self-conscious attempt to synthesize certain principles of each into a new whole. Whether and how that might be possible will be the subject of my final reflections in Chapter 9.

From Adam Smith to Milton Friedman, rational conservatism has been represented by the free agent, marketplace ideology of modern capitalism. In its earliest formulation this Enlightenment doctrine constituted a radical critique of monarchy and colonialism. However, by the early nineteenth century, this bourgeois ideology was out-flanked on the left by more democratic varieties of socialism and anarchism. And today the ideology of corporate capitalism is the dominant orthodoxy of the ruling classes in many countries of the world. Rational conservatives oppose state regulation of the econ-omy or of matters of personal conscience. They advocate protection of individual liberty and reject attempts to rectify inequality. They believe in the logic of the marketplace.

Romantic conservatism is elitist in orientation and can take either a reactionary or a quietistic political direction. The earliest expression of reactionary Romantic conservatism emerged imme-diately after the French Revolution in the writings of Burke, de Maistre, Bonald, Gentz, Friedrich, Schlegel, and Muller, among others. The main theme of this counterrevolutionary theory of the state was an attack on the capacity of reason to serve as the basis of social order. Instead, there was advanced a theologically rooted justification of authority as, by nature, centered on the infallible monarch—the one master capable of keeping all men from destroy-ing each other.

Recalling the terror of the French Revolution, the Romantic conservatives denigrated the idea of a secular public and idealized the natural, "organic" feudal community. They charged that, since men were naturally weak and wicked, any large assembly inevitably degenerated into a destructive mob. They insisted that a stable society must be founded on the cornerstones of religion, patriotism, and the patriarchal family. They held that property also should be based on authority and not on individual achievement. They asserted that any abdication of these principles in favor of attempts at rational self-rule could only destroy those natural institutions vital to the welfare of all men (Walter 1964; Marcuse 1972).

Over the century and a half between then and now, Romantic conservative movements have flared up in those social strata ad-versely affected by the growth of industrial capitalism. In Germany in the 1930s, lower-middle-class tradesmen, shopkeepers, and artisans felt their economic position deteriorating relative to the trade unions, on the one hand, and to the large corporations and department stores on the other hand (Gerth 1940). Anxious about their declining status, many threw their support behind Hitler and the Nazis, who promised to take command of these modern forces and restore the old Germany.

In the United States in the early 1950s, it was this same small business class who reacted to "the steady growth and concentration of government, labor organizations, and business enterprises" (Trow 1958, p. 273). Members mourned the passing of the "golden age of small farmers and businessmen" and found an outlet for their hostility and resentment in Senator Joseph McCarthy's attacks on "the 'big shots,' the 'stuffed shirts,' the 'bureaucrats'" (Trow 1958, pp. 273, 274).

In the late 1960s this class found a similar champion in Alabama Governor George Wallace, whose presidential platform promised revenge against urban minorities, hippies, labor unions, big business, and, especially, "pointy headed" Washington bureaucrats. In the late 1970s the New Christian Right, including the Moral Majority, emerged as a political force drawing on the same Romantic conservative opposition to modernization. Strongly patriarchal, this movement seeks to restore the influence of family and church. Members are strongly opposed to pornography, premarital sex, abortion, divorce, and the rights of women, youth, and homosexuals generally. They strongly favor prayer in the schools, tuition tax credits for religious schools, the teaching of "creationism," the death penalty, and increased military spending (Yinger and Cutler 1982; Gordon and Hunter 1977-78, p. 7). They differ profoundly from the rational conservatives in their advocacy of state regulation of morals.

Like all anti-modernist Romantic conservative movements of the past half century, the New Right is strongest among small businessmen, politicians, and churchmen, who are able to integrate their wives into their careers and create "a functional basis for wifely subordination and an organic image of an integrated family" (Gordon and Hunter 1977-78, p. 7). Surveys also show the movement to be concentrated in those strata marginal to the domain of industrial capitalism—older Americans, women, those from small towns, especially in the South and West, and those with little education and low income who are from a conservative and religious background.

Stressing the importance of nature over nurture, "The New Right wants to raise a new generation on the idea that inherent sin, rather than a brutal environment, is the source of the world's troubles"

(Viviano 1981, p. 56). For them, President Reagan is "the latest Romantic Hero who tells us his magic is simpler and stronger . . . than logic and intellect." Reagan exalts the myth of "woman" and wages a holy crusade against the evil of godless Communism to the adulation of his following (Wolfe 1981).

The contemporary intellectual expression of such reactionary Romantic conservatism can be found in the politics of the "Libertarian Right," including William F. Buckley, Jr., the *National Review* magazine, and the Young Americans for Freedom. Their position includes a belief in the "great man" theory of history, support for a strong chief executive and militaristic foreign policy, an attack on the bureaucratic welfare state, especially any attempts to regulate competition (such as affirmative action quotas, voter registration enforcement, and unionism), and a celebration of the heroic entrepreneur, the "captain of industry" who risks battle and tastes triumph in the marketplace.

The earliest expression of quietistic Romantic conservatism can be found in Hugo, Flaubert, and the French Romantics of the early nineteenth century. These men of letters thought of themselves as a "natural elite," "geniuses" born to a world "hostile to talent and sensitivity" who sought to transcend their "horror of daily life" through "cosmic self assertion" (Grana 1967). In England, Scott and Carlyle shared this orientation (Chapter 1). While such men desired social change, they really didn't think it possible. In their view, the bourgeoisie were too corrupt and timid to be reformed. They believed that all public efforts to change society were doomed to fail until each individual's heart and mind were changed through the power of example or personal experience. Consequently, they asserted, a true artist should concentrate on saving his or her own soul by shunning business and making art for its own sake.

More contemporary expressions of Romantic quietism can be found in this volume in the Beat suspicion of "representative" politics, Kerouac's celebration of the social outlaw, the rebel without a cause, Timothy Leary's invitation to "turn on, tune in and drop out," and *Rolling Stone* magazine's "politics of rock."

Since Lenin, a common expression of rational radicalism has been the centralized planning, collective-welfare orientation of communism or state socialism. Like rational conservatism, this approach is oriented to the market rather than the community. Unlike the latter, rational radicalism features state-level economic regulation by bureaucratic managers to reduce inequality and foster collective development. Throughout its history and especially in the 1960s, this approach was outflanked on the left by efforts to develop more decentralized and democratic forms of organization, forms that would permit both individual freedom and community solidarity. Most of these attempts were influenced by concurrent experiments in Romantic radicalism.

The modern tradition of Romantic radicalism extends from Blake and Shelley through John Reed and Berlin Dada to Ginsberg and some of the Beats, Abbie Hoffman, and the Yippies. While Romantic conservatives have avoided rational conservatives as philistine conformists, Romantic radicals have challenged them as oppressors and exploiters. Romantic radicals reject the organizational conformity of the rational radicals and the quietistic elitism of the Romantic conservatives in the name of individual freedom. If they espouse a doctrine, it is that of anarchy. They believe it is both desirable and possible to create a society of freely choosing individuals who are not constrained by economic necessity or political coercion. When they are forced by circumstances to take an overtly political stand, they oppose the state (sometimes violently) and all social organization that represses individual self-expression.

Sometimes such opposition to the bourgeois state has complemented the work of socialist organizers. At those times they have acknowledged each other as radical spirits in revolt against a common enemy. Sometimes, however, Marxist-Leninists have attacked such anarchists as "bourgeois individualists" unconcerned with defending the revolution and feeding the population. In turn, the anarchists have attacked the socialists as dogmatic authoritarians, insensitive to human potential. Is such conflict inevitable? Is some kind of ideological or practical accommodation possible? Is a revolution in both culture and politics possible in our time? These are the questions that guided our study.

THE CRAFT OF INTERDISCIPLINARY RESEARCH

The framework for these social histories of radical movements represents an attempt to achieve another kind of synthesis: history and sociology. All seven contributors were fellows in a National Endowment for the Humanities seminar in the summer of 1979.

Directed by Bennett Berger of the University of California, the seminar brought together six members of each discipline to study the traffic between political and cultural radicalism in modern history. Berger understood clearly that the scope and complexity of this topic demanded a fresh perspective.

Developing this fresh perspective was another matter, however. In the past competition between the disciplines, sociologists criticized traditional narrative history as atheoretical, unsystematic, and speculative. Historians, on the other hand, criticized sociology as static, dehumanized, and inattentive to the facts. We had many of those biases to overcome.

What we sought to develop that summer and in the years since then is an "analytic historiography" (Zaret 1978) that would resolve this nomothetic/ideographic polarity and combine the best elements of both disciplines, the systematic theorizing of sociology with the drama and factual basis of history. We sought to do this by applying a common conceptual framework to a range of historical cases in order to establish an empirical base from which we could make theoretical inferences. A true synthesis also demanded that the concepts used emerge from the concrete particularity of each case.

It is only the fact that we all lived together for three months and remained in communication for years afterward that encouraged us to consider such a goal possible. In the final analysis, however, we cannot claim to have used a standard methodology. Scholarship such as this is still much more a craft than a science. However, we do feel that we succeeded in developing a sufficiently common conceptual focus to make these cases comparable. Perhaps that is all one can reasonably hope for in attempting a form that Hofstadter (1968, p. 18) has called "part narrative, part personal essay, part systematic empirical inquiry, part speculative philosophy."

Taken together, the cases in this anthology cover the past century and a half: from the English Romantics of the early nineteenth century through the early twentieth-century Greenwich Village revolt, the Dadaists and the Leninists of World War I, the Garveyites of the 1920s, proletarian novelists of the Depression era, and the emergence of the Beat generation in the aftermath of World War II to the New Left, civil rights, and hippie movements of the 1960s, finally transformed into Left Leninist, Black Power, and New Age movements by the end of that decade. The book concludes with a discussion of cultural politics, social movements, and the prospects for radical change in the 1980s.

Along the way, the reader will encounter a colorful parade of the most committed radical activists and creative artists in modern history: from William Blake to Allen Ginsberg, Mary Shelley to Mary McCarthy, Tristan Tzara to Abbie Hoffman, Emma Goldman to Bernardine Dohrn, Marcus Garvey to Stokely Carmichael, James Farrell to Jack Kerouac. We will follow the action from the Cabaret Voltaire to Mabel Dodge's salon to the Coexistence Bagel Shop; from Gallery 291 to Gallery Dada to the Six Gallery. And we'll read about it through the pages of *The Masses* to *The New Masses* to *The Berkeley Barb*, the *Seven Arts* to *Partisan Review* to the *Village Voice*.

Each of these case studies is in some ways distinctive, featuring different characters and settings, and illuminating different aspects of the dynamic relationship between art and politics. However, all these cases are presented and analyzed in such a way as to generate more global insights into the complex dialectic of social movement, social control, and social change as we strive to understand our past, to evaluate our present, and to propose our future.

REFERENCES

Gerth, Hans. 1940. "The Nazi Party: Its Leadership and Composition." *American Journal of Sociology* 44 (Jan.): 517-41.

Gordon, Linda, and Allen Hunter. 1977-78. "Sex, Family and the New Right." *Radical America* (Nov.-Dec.): 9-25.

Grana, Cesar. 1967. *Modernity and Its Discontents*. New York: Free Press.

Hempel, Carl G. 1963. "Typological Methods in the Social Sciences." In *Philosophy of the Social Sciences*, edited by Maurice Natanson, pp. 210-30. New York: Random House.

Hofstadter, Richard. 1968. "History and Sociology in the United States." In *Sociology and History*, edited by Seymour Lipset and Richard Hofstadter, pp. 3-19. New York: Basic Books.

McKinney, John C. 1967. "Constructive Typology: Structure and Function." In *An Introduction to Social Research*, edited by John F. Doby: 230–43.

Marcuse, Herbert. 1972. "Counterrevolution and Revolt." In *Studies in Critical Philosophy*, translated by Joris De Bres, pp. 111–27. Boston: Beacon.

Stone, Lawrence. 1982. *The Past and the Present.* Boston: Routledge and Kegan Paul.

Trow, Martin. 1958. "Small Businessmen, Political Tolerance, and Support for McCarthy." *American Journal of Sociology* 64, no. 3 (Nov.): 270–81.

Viviano, Frank. 1981. "The Crucifixion of Evolution: What Your Kids Will Be Unlearning This Fall." *Mother Jones*, Sept./Oct., pp. 22–30, 56–59.

Walter, E. V. 1964. "'Mass Society': The Late Stages of an Idea." *Social Research* 31 (Winter): 398–410.

Wolfe, Alan. 1981. "Ronald, the Romantic Radical: The Age of Reagan vs. the Age of Reason." *Mother Jones*, Dec., pp. 37–39.

Yinger, Milton, and Stephen Cutler. 1982. "The Moral Majority Viewed Sociologically." *Sociological Focus* 15 (Oct.): 289–306.

Zaret, David. 1978. "Sociological Theory and Historical Scholarship." *The American Sociologist* 13 (May): 114–21.

1 Romantic Writers Confront the "Machine in the Garden": Symbol Production, Life Ways, and Political Expression

Frank T. Edgar

In exploring connections between English Romanticism and politics, literature and public affairs, life ways and ideology, poetry and history, a complete and rational structuring of the argument might include municipal and regional geography, demographic stratification, religious affiliations, nationalist aspirations and morale, and generational responses. But the main trend and approach are personal.[1]

The gist of the argument is that both literary romanticism and sociopolitical awareness or activism are rooted in symbolism. Meeting to this extent on common ground, they serve—not consistently, but on occasion—as catalysts to stir and stimulate each other. Symbolism, the stock-in-trade of politicians and statesmen, is also the productive raison d'être of poets, sometimes visible in their life ways as well as in their works. In a sense, symbol production is the vocational purpose for which poets live.

For the first generations of pioneering English Romantics—William Blake (1757–1827), William Wordsworth (1770–1850), Samuel Taylor Coleridge (1772–1834), Percy Bysshe Shelley (1792–1822), and others, including George Gordon, Lord Byron (1788–1824)—reacting to political oppression and social blight in the earlier stages of the Industrial Revolution, it may be said that a grand negative symbol was the Machine in the Garden: whether identified as a textile factory ("dark Satanic mills"), a steam locomotive ("a giant with one idea"), or scales of living and modes of government wholly geared to material conditions, sanctioned by an economic ideology based on pure calculation.

This symbol, with its destructive implications in regard to nature and organic life, begat in the poets countersymbols and values evoking the personal-individualist attributes of humanity that, as it appeared to them, the Machine was out to destroy. In some measure the poets lived, or tried to live, according to these symbols of value, as well as developing them in their art. In them from time to time the Word became flesh, the argument structured in explicit frameworks of living habits: food, clothing, exercise and recreation, households, circles of friendship-love. And political action.

ROMANTICISM AND REVOLUTION

What are the effects of revolution, war, and industrialism on the cultures, particularly the literary culture, of a pluralistic society? Thematic links among English Romantic writers of the first modern revolutionary era may connect ultimately with later generations of neo-Romantic writers, including Americans of the Cold War and Vietnam eras, to supply an answer.[2]

A generation consists of individuals who participate in the same psychologically decisive events in the historical process (Wohl 1979, p. 210). They shape their ideas and definitions, and seek their identity, in the light of these common experiences. Often they do so in reaction against the generations that immediately precede them. So it was for Englishmen in their prime between the fall of the Bastille (1789) and the first Reform Bill (1832):

> The new generation was tired to death of the eighteenth century tradition, and profoundly disgusted with the intellectual and spiritual patrimony which they had inherited from it. They were sick of its sandy Utilitarianism, its cast-iron economics, its uninspired and uninspiring theology, the flat and deadly prose of its theory of life. They were ripe . . . for rebellion against a system which . . . had no word of response to utter, no shred of satisfaction to offer . . . the energies and the emotions. The new generation was crying out for at least a religion of action if they could hold no longer by any religion of speculative

belief. They wanted a political-social creed which would find room
for the new ideas and aspirations rejected or coldly viewed by the
politicians of the old order.... They were unutterably weary of contemplating the world as a mere storehouse of facts and figures, or as a
mechanical creation of laws, forces and formulae; and they were eager
to realize it once more as the scene of the endless drama of human
action and passion, of struggle and triumph and defeat. (Carlyle 1896,
pp. xii–xiii)

In brief, "Romanticism," says W. Jackson Bate, biographer of
Coleridge, "is one of the products that grew out of . . . rebellion
against . . . detachment from life" (*Christian Science Monitor*, Apr. 8,
1980, p. 20, col. 4).

Romantic symbolism's many meanings include movements,
moods, tones, styles, and tendencies. For our purposes it may be
appropriate to dwell not on Romanticism but on the Romantic. The
archetype is a person who rejects manipulation by impersonal forces
and who seeks to translate moral values and ideals into action (including creative acts) in order to make his or her own life (and perhaps the lives of others) more complete, fruitful, and interesting.
This kind of person can assume at will a creative role or stance, become voluntarily engagé. Such people believe, all dialectic and
naturalistic forces aside, that their individual work or contribution
really counts.

Romanticism is a matter of nuance and resonance, which must be
expressed and felt rather than defined. The problem of selection and
priority can be approached only through increasing specification.

The first principle of romanticism is the liberation of consciousness in life and work. It follows that

> The private conscience must be free.
> Privilege is opposed to progress.
> As a revolt from reason: too much analysis corrupts.
> Encroaching technology is a threat.
> Destroy the machine: wipe the slate clean.[3]
> Justification for anarchy: No society at all is better than a sham society.
> A lie cannot endure forever.

Once rid of sham, human society can simplify its life and liberate
its consciousness. Wordsworth demonstrated this in *The Prelude* with
his view that cities are evil and corrupting. By contrast, the land is

sacred. This pastoral dream reaches a climax with Blake's "Beulah," a symbolic idealization of the peasant past: a primitive classless society, a state of social, sexual, and intellectual simplicity, blessed anarchy. Small wonder that poet-journalist James Agee, muckraking among Southern tenant farmers in the 1930s, listed Blake among his "unpaid agitators" (1941, p. xxii) and included Shelley in his pantheon of antiauthoritarian demigods.

It may be conjectured that the English Romantic movement was launched when Blake and Wordsworth, having been seduced by the principles of William Godwin's *Political Justice* (1793) and the works of democracy's evangelist, Thomas Paine, revolted against reified Reason as a preliminary to their questioning the premises and pragmatic consequences of the French Revolution. Like their contemporaries and successors—Coleridge, Shelley, William Morris (1834–1896)—they could accept neither traditional Christianity nor materialism in its British form of Utilitarianism. Each tried to work out another ideology, a combination of ethical and political theories, that could be used to organize their lives and their literary work—and as a basis for occasional traffic with public affairs. The impact of industrialism—acquisitive, competitive, and secular—on the national culture was repugnant to them, and one clue to what motivated all of them is the social relevance of fantasy to bolster the self against vulnerability and alienation.

At certain points of change in social stratification, men of letters may be regarded as a class or status group in decline, threatened by the machine and by a new class or status group of managers, technicians, and "servicers" of various kinds, including civil servants. Both these groups are likely to be linked by a web of personal relationships and influences. The literary men, mostly nonaffluent, are generally autonomous, though they share common social circumstances and situations, if not common backgrounds, locations, and life ways. Dislocated, if not annihilated by a new order of technology and careerism engulfing their autonomy, overturning their values, they brace themselves to resist, to devise ways and means of survival.

In tracing connections between symbolic concept and concrete fact, between culture and politics—the conflicts and ambiguities that lie between circumstances and vocational commitment—it is necessary to note a radical change in sensibility brought about by frustration. This took place in the years following 1792 when the British royal proclamation of May 21 against "'divers wicked and seditious

writings'" ushered in the "'black era of reaction and coercion'"
(Erdman 1954, pp. 197, 198, citing C. Grant Robertson, *England
Under the Hanoverians* [London: Methuen, 1930], p. 363), extending into the post-Napoleonic era. True, the proclamation (as, from
1815, the Holy Alliance) could no more restrain revolt than Wordsworth's sonnet against a projected railroad could stop railroad building. But it seemed at that time impossible, in Blake's defiant words,
to "build Jerusalem in England's green and pleasant land." From repressive measures in Britain to the Congress of Vienna some 20 years
later, this atmosphere damped or diverted for a time the minds of
ardent youth and others in their prime who were weary of both
military and social conflict. One, William Blake, the petit-bourgeois
artisans' soul, eventually managed to rework his religious legacies
from the seventeenth century into literary and moral weapons of
formidable power. Some, like William and Dorothy Wordsworth and
Samuel Coleridge, deriving some status and income from the professional middle classes but inclined to wander, went abroad, and, returning, adjusted their value systems, their ideologies. Others, like
Shelley and Lord Byron, went abroad into permanent exile, continuing in Italy and Greece, respectively, to support radical and
revolutionary causes.

Returning to the Romantic writers' and rebels' anchoring argument: machine, slow down, let be. Making all reasonable concessions
to economic development, to legitimate industry and commerce, let
us continue to nourish the primal, the simple, the natural—or leave
them alone. This was the common value that gave some unity to
these writers' diversity.

The social backgrounds and characters, identities, and reputations of these literary symbolmakers, social critics, and political dissenters cut through the principal strata of England's preindustrial
society: from Blake's little world of the London artisans to Byron's
great world of peers in Parliament. Their respective radicalisms and
romanticisms are as various as their origins.

The Ecstatic Radical

The only native Londoner among the greatest English Romantics,
the son of a hosier, Blake had the "little tradesman's look": the
sober, industrious traits of the petit bourgeoisie. Living "bitterly in

the decay of his engraver's craft," he understood all too well that "a man's thinking must depend on his social position" (Morton 1958, pp. 19, 23). His sociology of knowledge was complex: artisan and artist, he was a radical in both roles, as an artistic innovator and the representative of a class. The mood, style, and ideology of mid-twentieth-century Beats and hipsters has been described as a "run-back" to his "ecstatic radicalism" (Roszak 1969, p. 126), recoiling and rebelling against the whole rationalist frame of the eighteenth century. Of all the group of Romantic symbolmakers, Blake is the most complete and cosmic in his Utopian mentality and vision. He has been called the "greatest English antinomian" (Morton 1958, p. 36), heir to a tradition of doctrines that had crystallized in the seventeenth-century millenarian movement, with its expectations of happiness, holiness, freedom, and justice in a new order of things. These doctrines held a radical belief with respect to the nature of God and His relations with man: God exists in man and in all created things. Many believed He had no other existence. This pantheistic belief Blake accepted: "God only acts and is in existing beings or men" (Blake, "A Memorable Fancy"). With this, moral and cere-monial law were no longer binding, having been the result of a curse now lifted, though orthodoxy still imposed it on institutional Chris-tianity. The nucleus of these doctrines was a cluster of ideas asso-ciated with the "Everlasting Gospel," the title of Blake's last great poem, and a certain symbolism relating to the destruction of Babylon and the building of a new Jerusalem, directly relevant to the Age of Revolutions (Morton 1958, pp. 36, 37).

These political ideas in religious form went underground from about 1660 to 1789, with cryptoradicals "treasuring subversive pamphlets" (Morton 1958, p. 14) in old cupboards, a legacy from the millenarians, Ranters (who practiced nudism), Muggletonians, and other sects who, with the Quakers, shared "a common body of ideas, a common language" (Morton 1958, p. 35), artisans and tradesmen inhabiting the same social circles and geographic areas around London, where Blake was born (1757) and spent his whole life. When he and his wife Catherine became foundation members of the Swedenborgian Congress in London (1788), one year before the fall of the Bastille, this was the last link in a chain of antinomian influences that gave Blake his general framework of ideas: "first of all, it was a tradition of revolution" (Morton 1958, p. 36). He alone of all great English poets remained a manual worker all his life, so he saw the development of industrial capitalism in England from the "craftsman's special viewpoint" (Morton 1958, p. 50). He was 32 when the French Revolution came as a catalyst to release some of his best work.

Symbolmaking, he was the only one of his political group, which included the Girondist sympathizer Tom Paine, to wear the red cap of the Jacobins and walk the streets in it. His productions included engravings for the works of a female member of the same group— women's liberationist Mary Wollstonecraft (*Dictionary of National Biography*, II, p. 644). When he ceased to be revolutionary in the political sense after Britain went to war with France (1793), his romantic, apolitical radicalism fitted him for a unique place in the history of culture and, indirectly, in the sphere of public affairs. His radicalism was even more extreme and, in some ways, consistent than Shelley's: all things were possible to the human mind; as a symbolizer he could define "Prudence" as a "rich, ugly old maid courted by Incapacity" (*Prophetic Books*, "The Marriage of Heaven and Hell—Proverbs of Hell").

Whiggish Radicals

A wound-up character in Lawrence Lipton's *The Holy Barbarians* sounds off:

> The body finds the food it needs, . . . and so does the soul. Coleridge needed opium and Wordsworth needed Nature. Nature would not have written *Kubla Khan* for Coleridge and opium would not have written the *Intimations of Immortality* for Wordsworth. They found what they needed. Now, what made them need these things and at what point in their development it could have been changed—that I don't know. (Lipton 1959, p. 19)

Answers must be sought, if not found, in the historical conflicts of "idealism followed by disillusionment, the young rebelling against authority, the struggle between liberals and conservatives, the Negro question . . . wars and the threat of wars, the campaign against poverty" (Ellis 1967, p. xi). It must be looked for also in the milieus of English provincial middle-class families, such as those of Coleridge, son of a clergyman; Robert Southey, whose father was a draper; William and Dorothy Wordsworth, children of a country attorney.

Compared with Blake, Wordsworth, with well-to-do relatives and connections and a university education, was solidly middle-class, in some ways the most stable of this group, though his political consistency, from radical to liberal to conservative, may be questioned. His maternal uncle, William Cookson, was an abolitionist who knew the great leader of the anti-slavery forces, William Wilberforce (Manley 1974, p. 160). The families on the whole, however, were conventional. Wordsworth, when he came to the university, was not really identified with Cambridge radicalism, itself a residue of political puritanism newly fired by Enlightenment ideals. He was at first unimpressed by the French Revolution, and it is suggested that he took freedom too much for granted: "Anyone who walked through the dales of the Lake District knew that every individual should have his rights and his independence" (Manley 1974, p. 40). Then, in the summer of 1790, in France, he was caught up in the joyous madness of the French Revolution, still in its first moderate phase. Later, under the influence of Captain Michel Beaupuy, a descendant of the Renaissance humanist philosopher and essayist Montaigne, Wordsworth espoused the abolition of hereditary rights (Manley 1974, pp. 41, 53). Back from France in 1793, he could excuse the execution of Louis XVI thus:

> I am so strongly impressed with the baleful influence of aristocracy and nobility upon human happiness and virtue that if, as I am persuaded, monarchy cannot exist without such supporters, I think that reason sufficient for the preference I have given to the republic system. (Owen and Smyser, eds. 1974, I, p. 46)

Like Thomas Paine, Wordsworth identified closely with the cause of the more moderate Girondins, beginning to shift ideological ground with the mass executions of members of that group by the extremist Jacobins (Manley 1974, p. 47). His initial sympathy for the French Revolution can perhaps be described as a kind of flirtation, or at least as an emotion falling somewhat short of complete, committed love, bearing some relation to his lingering affection for his French sweetheart Annette Vallon, left behind when he returned home: or to his fluency in the French language, lost after years of disuse (Manley 1974, pp. 101, 133). With his friend and associate Coleridge he can be depicted as a young Whiggish radical, inheriting many of the ideals and principles of the English Whig Revolution of

1688–89 and its American analogue in the century following, which he saw at first as being realized again in France. His advocacy of universal and equal manhood suffrage as late as 1809, when he was 39, shows that the transition was a slow one. Again, in contrast with Blake, the Londoner and urban radical, Wordsworth, perhaps always a congenital conservative, was ever at heart the countryman. Having known the Paris of 1792 and the Revolution of the guillotine, he tended to see the city, realistically and symbolically, as a potential peril (*The Prelude*, VII, ll. 671–75), with the corresponding inclination to exalt rural virtues as paramount.

As Wordsworth was the countryman, so Coleridge, son of a vicar who died early, leaving him to grow up a virtual orphan, was by nature (that pivotal word) the city dweller, though by no means a typical burgher any more than he was like the Londoner Blake. As Wordsworth was devoted in his art to the poetry of common life, sometimes to the point of banality and bathos, so Coleridge was devoted in his to the fantastic, the magical, and the marvelous. Both tried to actualize their ideals in their lives, Wordsworth substituting his own "dear native regions" for Utopia with some success. Coleridge's failure to find Utopia, either by founding, with his brother-in-law Robert Southey, a democratic commune or pantisocracy ("power of all") in western Pennsylvania or by farming in the west of England, has been dramatized and distorted for posterity by his addiction to opium. Having lost his hold on the future, he groped with nostalgic yearning backward toward the grandeur of an irrecoverable but imaginable past and created Kubla Khan's pleasure dome as its symbol. Losing Utopia, he found Xanadu. But his magnificent failure initially was a failure of perception with respect to his own origins, nurture, and tastes. His affinity for the country was no more than his friendship for Wordsworth and Wordsworth's sister Dorothy, whose unspoken love for Coleridge is one of the binding ties in this circle of friends. Intellectually, he belonged with another kind of circle, more urban and urbane, such as the one with which he spent his later years at Highgate, in North London.

Whatever their differences—rather, because of these differences— the collaboration of these two poets in *Lyrical Ballads* (1798) traditionally is taken to mark the beginning of the Romantic epoch in English literature, in scope and elevation, intensity and power, second only to the Elizabethan.

Aristocratic Radicals

If Blake, artisan and semiproletarian, is the ecstatic radical, with his roots deep in seventeenth-century millenarian expectations of radical religious sects; if Wordsworth and Coleridge are the quintessence of middle-class, college-bred liberal or Whiggish radicalism, almost predestined to become disillusioned and revert to a conservative stance—then Shelley and Byron are the aristocratic radicals (though the term with respect to Byron must be severely qualified), representing, respectively, the new county gentry of the 1700s and the older peerage. Byron, if not positively a radical (though an associate of political radicals in several lands), is surely the aristocratic rebel par excellence; Shelley, a kind of angelic anarchist, is the true poet of radicalism, as it was crystallizing in the late eighteenth century, the unqualified, the consistent radical of his generation, and legitimately the ancestor of succeeding radical generations in both politics and literature. Political radicals have recognized him as being only secondarily a poet and primarily the prophet of a new era and a new order of things. The supreme thesis of Shelleyan ideology represents the poet as the true trafficker and mediator between the realms of literary inspiration and the political culture.

The year of Shelley's birth (1792) punctuates a time frame in which Blake was still associated with London radicals, the young Wordsworth was observing the political fevers and passions of Revolutionary Paris, and "[r]efugees from France were landing on the Sussex coast from every sort of boat, many of them passing within a mile or two of the Shelley home on their way to London" (White 1940, II, p. 421). Yet the death throes of the old feudal order, lamented by the conservative Whig statesman Edmund Burke, and the birth of a new age of freedom, heralded by Tom Paine, William Godwin, and Mary Wollstonecraft (and for a while by Blake), stirred no more than a ripple in Shelley's native county, as in Wordsworth's Cumberland. Sussex at that time showed "a determined conservatism"; there was a saying among Sussex countrymen: "We won't be druv" (White 1940, I, p. 4, II, p. 422). The poet's forebears, in the main, showed the mettle of their posture.

> Shelley's eight male ancestors in the direct line are all described as squires or gentlemen. At the time of Shelley's birth no one of them had won national or even local distinction as a public servant or in any pro-

fession. Their wives were all of good, undistinguished county families. (White 1940, I, p. 6)

They professed a "probable connection with the more distinguished Michelgrove Shelleys, landholders under Edward I, producing a Knight of Rhodes and a Judge of Common Pleas" (White 1940, I, p. 6). Their political connections were Whig aristocrats, but the family had been neither Whig nor aristocrat until its fortunes were established by Percy's grandfather through two marriages that enabled Shelley's father to enter Parliament. Hence, it is fair to say that Shelley was not born "into an old aristocratic family, but a *nouveau riche* 'county' family . . ." (Cameron 1950, p. 2). Parvenus may adopt any political creed from radical to Tory; the Whiggism of the Shelleys was liberal in regard to the principles of the American and French revolutions, at least before the Terror. The significant fact is that Shelley's views, particularly his religious views, were not the result of "rebellion against a conservative home. On the contrary, the basis for them was laid in that home" (Cameron 1973, p. 4).

It was, rather, his early persecution at school that "laid the psychological basis for that hatred of tyranny which Shelley later integrated—using the Whig outlook of his family as intellectual foundation—into his political philosophy." The French Revolution, though, had little influence on him until he prepared to enter college, when he decided to devote his life to fighting tyranny (White 1947, II, p. 423). At Oxford he devoted himself to freedom and republican ideas, yet he was still very aristocratic in feeling and behavior, and offended by the crudities of democracy (White, 1940, I, p. 107). Finally, under the influence of the rationalist philosopher Godwin, he passed beyond Whiggery and republicanism, beyond his own family tradition, to the egalitarianism of the complete radical and anarchist: "He wished to sit in Parliament but to reform it, and ultimately to do away with it" (White 1940, I, p. 107). He went beyond his mentor and father-in-law, Godwin, who affirmed a duty to argue about perfection in "select circles of friends who meet for debate, but never (virtue forbids) for action. . . ." For the romantic Shelley, this "cold precept" of eighteenth-century rationalism became a "zealous missionary call" (Brailsford 1913, p. 165).

As for Byron, Pilgrim of Eternity, in his pattern of aristocratic stratification a lingering feudal element was as strong as the nouveau element in Shelley. "I was born of the aristocracy . . . and am sprung, by my mother, from . . . kings . . ." (Cameron 1973, p. 162). He was proud of his "high blood . . . I have still a few Norman and Scotch inherited prejudices on the last score. . . ." (Cameron 1973, p. 179). Yet he was "an up-to-date 'Revolutionist'" an Englishman "too sensitive to what monarchs are doing to rustics, citizens to bulls, Turkish chains to Greek helots. . . ." (Cameron 1973, p. 172)—a mere sojourner in the great world he despised. Byron's struggle to maintain his legal heritage was modified by revolutionary events that produced "puzzling inner tensions between radical aristocrat and aristocratic radical. . . ." (Cameron 1973, p. 163). On his Eastern journey he was "piqued by the Turks' refusal to recognize his rank in official processions" (Cameron 1973, p. 171). Closer to home, he owned coal mines in Rochdale and estates supporting cottage industries, though the stocking weavers were being ruined by inflation. His traffic with the deprived and rebellious poor was no missionary endeavor, as it was with Shelley, but a practical matter of rents (Cameron 1973, p. 162).

Byron no more than lingered on the fringes of Shelley's circle of intellectuals, bluestockings, free-love advocates and experimenters, vegetarians, and bohemians. Loving and admiring Shelley, whom he acknowledged as one of the most unselfish persons he had ever known, he could not accept or abide the ways of Shelley's more advanced friends. Byron's liaison with Shelley's sister-in-law, Claire Clairmont, with a daughter as its fruit, was no free-love affair but an old-style seduction.

Like Wordsworth, whom he could not admire, Byron tended to favor simple societies; and, more remotely from "dear native regions," he fancied sensuous pagan, or semipagan, types: Malay and Mediterranean, a preference that partly explains his commitment to the cause of Greek independence. When in 1824 he gave his life for that cause, the noble gesture was a consummation of Romantic symbolism: the individual who vainly had sought freedom and happiness for himself voluntarily subordinating personal goals to a national cause.

Yet with all his gifts—courage, fundamental honesty, and hatred of cant—Byron remains in some degree a grand poseur (though this has become somewhat a cliché), what in great measure a club foot, frustrated love, and traumatic relations with his mother had made him: a libertine manqué, a Calvinist pagan incapable of pagan spontaneity and naturalness, slave both of a disappointing morality and of his own passions. A cryptoevangelical puritan (he objected to mixed bathing on the beaches), he could never, unfortunately, repudiate puritanism, but could repudiate the ill effects of its economic instrument, the machine—as he did, a peer of the realm, defending the Luddite frame breakers in public debate.

These aristocrats in rebellion, Byron and Shelley, must be looked at against the background of their youth: the reactionary morality of Regency England during the Napoleonic wars; the severe discipline and homogeneous culture promoted at their elite preparatory schools, Harrow and Eton; the character and mentality of people like Eton's headmaster, Dr. John Keate, who knew beyond doubt and question that boys could, and should, be flogged into a state of purity and grace. Harsh facts falling on sensitive natures may supply a partial answer to the question of what shapes patrician rebels—in Shelley's case, the question of how the grandson of a wealthy baronet became a thorough egalitarian. But then the old man, the baronet-grandfather, had been born in New Jersey of an American mother, and was atheistic as well as democratic. Can one altogether discount geographic and generational influences, no matter how remote and indirect? Shelley's American ancestor as well as Byron's Normans?

Tyranny's Symbolic Archetypes: Dungeon, Engine

The differences between Byron and Shelley are pointed up by their reactions to one facet of their Swiss sojourn, the castle of Chillon. For Byron, recalling its prisoner, it was the "eternal spirit of the chainless mind." For Shelley: "I never saw a monument more terrible of that cold and inhuman tyranny which it had been the delight of man to exercise over man" (White 1940, II, p. 446). The reactions of the two poets define their respective ideological roles: Byron, aristocratic rebel, jealous of his own freedom and honor, dreaming of an upheaval that will destroy the corrupt system; Shelley, infinitely more the radical idealist, seeing the corruption in cosmic terms, as a sickness of soul stemming from the prime foundation. For both, however, the fortress was a monstrous symbol of the old oppressive order, a man-eating monster like the Bastille that swallowed Dickens's doctor of Beauvais.

If, in the category of symbolic monsters, the feudal lord's dungeon was one of the old type, hence perhaps less fear-inspiring through being more familiar, the steam engine, still a novelty, could be taken as a more ominous, more sinister, and more subversive enemy, an even more lethal threat.

Looking at a locomotive in Scotland about 1820, Wordsworth imagined it had a life of its own. "Yes," Coleridge replied, "it is a giant with one idea,"[4] an insightful comment on the acquisitive state comparable with Carlyle's *Sartor Resartus* on the engine threatening to tear him limb from limb (Manley 1974, p. 197)—and with Blake hurling his gage at the arid cycles of a mechanistic universe, complex patterns of machines within machines, "intricate wheels" to "perplex youth" and the "myriads of eternity . . . Kept ignorant . . . to view a small portion & think that All," the whole man reduced to a hand, the shame of "unnecessary and man-made poverty," in which ancient harmonies and simplicities are despised or destroyed (Blake, "The Sons of Urizen").

The "cold and inhuman" with a will of its own: no wonder Romantic poets, then as now, felt a chill. With industrial cities already "on fire," human culture must gird itself to stop the "reckless destruction of the land" (Manley 1974, p. 197), aroused and goaded in different generations by Oliver Goldsmith (1728–1744), William Cobbett (1763–1835)—or Wordsworth in opposition (1844) to the intrusion of the Kendal and Windermere Railway into the Lake District.

Wordsworth wished that region to preserve its natural beauty and "pointed out that there was already transportation." A railroad would ruin the countryside. He noted the alleged benevolent motives of manufacturers and capitalists backing the railway, who declared that they would send hundreds of their employees "by car loads to Grasmere for the vacations," and answered that "these employers would do well to pay their workers a living wage and give them a decent working day so that they could pay to go on vacation where they chose, not where their employers dictated."

Is this assertion self-interested? Certainly. Is the self-interest legitimate? Probably. Wordsworth pointed out that "a valid perception of romantic scenery is neither inherent in mankind, nor a necessary consequence of even a comprehensive education." Rather, it stemmed from "processes of culture or opportunities of observation in some degree habitual." He recalled a keen assessment by a "shrewd and sensible woman" of his native region: "Bless me! folk are always talking about prospects: when I was young there was never sic [such] a thing neamed [named]." The large majority of mankind cannot grasp the pleasure that some take in romantic scenery: "That is a fact." Open Windermere to railways and you will have, to the profit of shareholders and the lower class of innkeepers, "wrestling matches, horses and boat races . . . and pot houses and beershops. . . ."

Is this "selfishness"? To the charge that it is, Wordsworth answers that the charge should cease. The cry of "selfishness" has been raised by three sorts: "they who wish to bring into discredit all such as stand in the way of their gains. . . ."; "they who are dazzled by the application of physical science. . . ."; and liberal do-gooders, always ready to stand up in the cause of the poor against tradition, but who ignore specifics (Owen and Smyser 1974, III, p. 339). The railway power, of course, cannot be swayed by sentiment. Its interest is understood where legitimate issues of trade and agriculture are concerned. But the staple of the Lake Region is its beauty: let be (Ellis 1967, pp. xi–xii).

THE SYMBOLMAKING COUNTERATTACK

In reviewing who these radical writers were, what they are best known for, and how they fit into groups, the ties with women, each of whom deserves notice in her own right, must not be forgotten. There was Dorothy Wordsworth (1771–1855), William's beloved sister and Coleridge's friend, neither a feminist nor a bluestocking, but a sensitive observer of nature whose perceptions contributed directly to the poets' work. There was Mary Wollstonecraft (1759–1797), who opened doors to modern feminism, whose writings Blake embellished with his engravings, and who was a pivotal member of that radical group including Thomas Paine with which Blake was associated for a time. And there was her daughter by William Godwin, Mary Wollstonecraft Godwin (1797–1851), who married Percy Bysshe Shelley and wrote the classic prototype of modern horror tales, *Frankenstein* (1818), its theme being technological man as the creator of synthetic monsters. From Blake's lament of the "dark Satanic mills" we have come full circle: from man becoming a machine to a machine becoming man.

We shall look next, more categorically, at some specific ways in which the poets, symbolmaking, counterattacked.

In analyzing their efforts, it is useful to consider the social dropout, name changes, the threesome (as a deviation from the conventional couple), pastoralism and the gypsy motif (wanderlust: long walks by night, extended Continental journeys) as examples of symbol production representing forms of ideological work, conscious or unconscious, that can be related to writers' material circumstances, as well as to their self-conceptions and the requirements of their chosen careers. Other symbolic categories include diet, drugs, and dress—nudity may be a sign of innocence. Love, comradeship, and religion may cohere in a house of friends.

Diet and Drugs

Wordsworth and his sister Dorothy set the model for simple life ways complementary to poetry (and as a relief from politics). Sojourning at Windy Brow Farm, near Keswick in the Lake District, they practiced strict economy: no tea; bread and milk for breakfast and supper; for dinner, mostly potatoes (Ellis 1967, pp. 67, 68). At Racedown in Dorset they ate out of the garden: "essence of carrots, cabbage, turnips, parsley . . . living on air"[5] (Ellis 1967, p. 80). At Stowey in Somerset, their friend and neighbor Coleridge, though mentally feeding on "honey-dew" and the "milk of Paradise," grew grain, potatoes, and other vegetables, and kept ducks, geese, and two pigs (Ellis 1967, p. 105).

Shelley's diet was Spartan. He drank "distilled water, tea or coffee, and ate bread-cakes with little or no butter, fruits, vegetables, and possibly honey." The menus of his friend J. T. Newton tell the story:

> Breakfast—dried fruits, toast or biscuits, weak tea made with distilled water and with a small portion of milk. No butter on toast, or very scanty.

> Dinner—potatoes, with some other vegetables in season; macaroni, tart or pudding, with only a few eggs. Sauce made from onions (especially those imported from Portugal), stewed with walnut pickle.

The imported Portuguese onions are worthy of comment: the exotic side of simplicity.

For Shelley vegetarian habits went along with a tendency to avoid regular, sit-down meals and to snatch food and drink at odd moments (White 1940, I, p. 302; R. M. Smith 1945, p. 4). This restlessness was due not so much to dislike of food as from impatience; absorbed in a book, Shelley ignored meals altogether (White 1940, I, pp. 85–86, II, p. 445). At Oxford he had questioned in theory the right of human beings to take animal life, but had not given up hunting or eating meat (White 1940, I, p. 107). Introduced to the philosophy of vegetarianism by a Mr. Turner (whose wife Cornelia became for a while an intimate friend), he accepted the basic dietary of the Newtons, arguing that

> eating animal flesh was the basis not only of human disease, but of human vices as well. Man had only to confine himself to a harmless Newtonian diet in order to free himself from disease and from the various social and political evils to which he is at present addicted through his predatory, carnivorous habits. (White 1940, I, p. 303)

Thus, finding a connection between meat eating and warfare, he shaped an ideology; but in practice he was a strict vegetarian only with other vegetarians, and as compensation developed a "decided sweet tooth" (White 1940, I, pp. 85–86). Nor did he give up pistol practice.

Blake's diet was less subject to ideological definition and rationalization—perhaps because there was even less of it. There were days when his wife put an empty plate on the table, an eloquent symbol of destitution. Blake, withdrawing from politics and, in his later days, almost from the mundane world, found his own "milk of paradise" to feed on:

> For years together he never left his rooms, except to fetch his daily pint of porter from a neighboring public house; and then there is the charming story which Gilchrist tells, how a nobleman once sent Blake some spirit distilled from walnuts for artistic uses, which Blake, on tasting, found so good that he continued, absent-mindedly, to apply it to his lips instead of to his canvas.... One can see the far-away expression of his eye as the aroma mingled with his meditations. (De Sélincourt 1971, pp. 21–22)

The conjunction of spare diet with the use of elixirs and anodynes to allay pain through fantasy is not uncommon for romantic spirits. The case of Coleridge is pivotal. At one point his neuralgic pains were running from his right temple to his right shoulder. He took 25 drops of laudanum every five hours for relief. The doctor thought the disease might be due to anxiety or nervousness. Maybe so. He was living with an epileptic; the baby cried a good deal; and Mrs. Fricker, his mother-in-law, proved irritating. He wrote to Charles Lamb: "O my God! my God! when am I to find rest."

Shelley sometimes took laudanum to relax his mind (G. B. Smith 1877, p. 131). Once, developing a passion for Mary Godwin though still wed to his first wife, Harriet, he caught up a bottle of the drug, saying, "I never part from this." He recommended laudanum to Mary—it would rescue her from the tyranny of her family—but Mary refused. Once, in the midst of his crisis with the two women, the poet took poison, but the dose did not prove fatal (Hotson 1930, pp. 22, 23).

Dress and Undress

The upheaval of the English Civil War in the seventeenth century spawned various sects, including Baptists, Quakers, and the Fifth Monarchy Men (millenarians), the group that, at long range, most influenced the moral growth, insight, and advocacy of Blake. Another group, the Ranters, may be interpreted as an example of how cultural eccentricities can limit political effectiveness. The ideology of this sect may have included a justification of ritual nudism. Clothes were taken as a sign of lost innocence, a token and a symbol of the knowledge of good and evil, and the curse that accompanied this knowledge. "A return to nakedness was symbolic of the lifting of the curse," and the naked human form "was the supreme symbol of the divine in man and of the liberation of the spirit" (Morton 1958, pp. 53–54). But the good intentions and resources of the Ranters were wasted on "crazy extravagances which exposed them to police action and alienated many possible supporters" (Morton 1958, p. 63, and note 2).

These views surfaced again, on a more limited scale, with a later generation of reformers. Shelley's ingenious friend Newton, a man of never-ending theories, also found a focus in an ideology, which never quite became a cult, of innocent nudism. Wearing clothes was unnatural, a bad habit, and, like meat eating, the source of many woes. Shelley's old friend Thomas Jefferson Hogg wrote of the nude little Newtons:

"Except on my first visit, the dear children never appeared naked before me; before Bysshe [Shelley] they often did. It is for his credit's
sake that I state it. I was of the earth, earthy; he was of the heaven,
heavenly;—I was a worldling; he had already returned to nature, or
rather he had never quitted her." (R. M. Smith 1945, p. 175)

At Casa Magni during Shelley's last days, the three women of the
household were entertaining a male visitor when the poet came in
from a swim and, caring nothing for convention, oblivious to the outside world, walked stark naked across the room. Becoming aware of
the setting, he tried to hide behind a maidservant. Reproached by
wife Mary, he came up to explain, seaweed in his hair and scented
with salt, good to look at, a pagan symbol of youthful innocence.
The ladies covered their faces. Mary Shelley, daughter of Godwin, he
who had once been an advocate of free love, was horrified (Maurois
1924, p. 310).

The whole psychology of dress, or undress, is full of examples
from radical cultures. Coleridge as "Silas Tomkyn Comberback"
(1793) wore the dragoon's red coat as part of his disguise. Blake
about the same time flaunted the Jacobin's red cap, the only one of
his group to do so. Or take the feminine bonnet as a symbol of
materialism and vanity. Here Shelley in his relations with his two
wives made a clear-cut distinction, condemning Harriet, who bought
bonnets with innocent hedonism and "rapture," while condoning the
"fault" in Mary, who bought them with a philosophical and "lofty
condescension . . ." (Maurois 1924, p. 176).

Problems in Identity: Dropouts, Name Changes

Coleridge's agricultural philosophy perhaps was not too novel for
a Romantic poet. "Who am I," he asked, "to decide whether a weed
should grow or not?" The same philosophy kept him from setting
mousetraps. He thought it unchivalrous (Ellis 1967, p. 105). Here
are some affinities with the more rabid, if not radical, ecologists of
the late twentieth century.

"Who am I?" A fundamental question, going back to the original
egg and sperm. Wordsworth and Coleridge were complementary.
Wordsworth, though brooding, had a serenity and confidence Coleridge never knew. The latter, from the time of his first miseries at

Christ's Hospital, half-starved and sometimes whipped, had gone through more than one identity crisis: from the child role, acting out a dream-wish of Leander swimming the Hellespont (which brought him close to arrest for pickpocketing when he swam up against a gentleman's coat) to the tragifarce of "Private Silas T. Comberback" when, a temporary dropout from Cambridge in rebellion against mathematics and other complexities, he joined the dragoons, his true identity revealed when he scrawled a Latin lament on a saddle.

The whole question of name changes is an interesting one and is a significant micro-theme of Romantic ideology.

Among the many moods and meanings of Romanticism is the lure of the exotic. Is this one reason why some Romantic rebels and radicals change their names? What problem of identity is involved, for example, for unemployed, or underemployed, intellectuals? Does it tie in with the Romantic principle and premise concerning the vindication and value of the individual as against class and society, justifying rebellion, asserting the intrinsic worth of the autonomous (or anonymous) person? Is such a move necessary to reify a new role? to burn bridges?

Samuel Taylor Coleridge, running away to join the army, takes the nom de guerre of "Silas Tomkyn Comberback." Is there in the last name the implied significance of "coming back" to something?[6]

Clara Mary Jane Clairmont, running away to the Continent as part of a "threesome" with Percy Shelley and Mary Godwin, becomes Claire Clairmont—more succinct and sophisticated, more French?—shedding the plain and childish connotations of the middle names?[7]

A name change, indeed, is like slipping on a mask. More than symbolic, it can facilitate a change in character and new beginnings.

Walking and the Gypsy Motif

For Blake, long walks were a habit; with his wife Catherine, in his prime he could pace off 40 miles at a stretch (De Sélincourt 1971, p. 8). The young Wordsworths likewise were ambulatory, and so, from a conventional point of view, set a trend of Romantic eccentricity. As their middle-class relatives were baffled by William's having fathered an illegitimate child by a French Catholic girl, Annette Vallon, so they failed to comprehend Dorothy's "unladylike conduct in wandering around the country[side] unprotected" (Ellis 1967, p. 65). Justifying her conduct, she thought it would have given her friends pleasure "that I had the courage to make use of the strength with which nature has endowed me. . . ." Not only was walking more fun than riding in a post chaise, but it saved 30 shillings. Is there a bit of ideology here? Save money; besides, using your legs is more enjoyable than being moved by wheels. One can almost hear an echo from Bunyan's Valley of Humiliation: "I love to be in such places where there is no rattling with coaches, nor rumbling with wheels," a place where one may be thinking "what he is, whence he came, what he has done . . ." (Bunyan 1678–84, pt. II, ch. VI). Windy Brow Farm, Keswick, was such a place, given to William rent-free by a friend. He and Dorothy walked to it, in two days, from the coach stop. For six weeks they walked, read, studied.

Despite the seeming regularity of a pattern imposed by farming and philosophy, reading and writing, there is a kind of gypsy motif that plays through this circle's life, at least compared with the staid deportment of those who never rove or ramble at all. William and Dorothy and Coleridge were indeed walkers who came and went as they pleased. Coleridge's wife, Sarah, more conventional, took a dim view of these jaunts, inclined to be jealous of a style in which three were company—not "crazies" or "zanies" or "wild ones" exactly, but a little strange: "those who loved each other with a terrible intensity, who did not care what other people thought, who often arrived as the moon came over the cottage, who departed who knew when?" (Manley 1974, p. 131).

Following their epoch-making collaboration in *Lyrical Ballads*, published in 1798, William, Dorothy, and Samuel—a "merging of earth, sky, sea" (Manley 1974, p. 86)—were wandering "gipsy fashion" through the German lands, the journey that was to prove an opening wedge in the future (1810) rift between the two poets. Their motives were cheaper living and learning the language. Coleridge, more sociable, more the cosmopolite, learned German well. Wordsworth, who had learned French easily for love of the Revolution and Annette, found German something else. It forced him "to withdraw into himself, into his own language, his own past" (Manley 1974, pp. 100, 102, 101). It tended, we may assume, to make him more conservative. Yearning for stability, he was carried back in nostalgia to his birthplace, his "dear native regions" (*The Prelude*, VIII, l. 468). The ideal is the real, and the old ways are good.

22 / F. T. Edgar

The Free-Love Ideology and the Threesome as a Life Way

The trio of Wordsworth, his sister Dorothy, and Coleridge was in a sense the residue of Samuel's scheme with his fellow poet and brother-in-law, Robert Southey, to go as pioneers to Pennsylvania and plant a commune by the Susquehanna. In retrospect, this plan is amusing, almost laughable, in the light of Coleridge's character. As has been said, he was as natural to the urban scene as his friend and peer from the Lake Region was to the rural. Wordsworth never quite understood Samuel's style of life, but easily succumbed to his amazing gift for friendship. Dorothy was certainly in love with him, if the interpretation of Amanda Ellis is correct in asserting that Dorothy's diaries corroborate the view that she was in love with Coleridge, and that he loved her for a while. "The fact that she suppressed her love accounts, in part, for her premature senility" (Ellis 1967, p. xii). If this is true, it is sufficient justification for the free-love doctrine proclaimed by Godwin and applied by Shelley, though in the event the pitfalls of expression proved at least as disastrous as the perils of repression.

Perhaps the most radical and romantic ideology to come out of resistance to the industrializing-acquisitive state and its adjunct, the respectable middle-class family, was the free-love concept, which included, and vindicated, many of the themes that make up the Romantic complex of ideas: liberation of the consciousness in life and work, freedom of the private conscience, vindication and value of the individual, a return to emotionalism, a return to earlier traditions (romantic love in the Middle Ages), love of the exotic, revolt against society as convention and mechanism, and a fervent belief shared by writers as different as Byron and Thomas Carlyle (though both were Calvinists) that no society at all is better than a sham society.

Free love was the Garden of Eden; monogamous, monopolistic marriage was the machine in the garden.

In his great seminal tract *Political Justice* (1793)—in some measure a Bible for Blake, Wordsworth, and Shelley, until they went beyond it—William Godwin, moral philosopher and for a time a philosophical anarchist, Rousseau's disciple, laid down the tenets of his creed: law and government, property and marriage are outmoded, tyrannical institutions and should be abolished. Above all, love should be free, because it is absurd to expect the inclinations and wishes of two human beings to coincide, through any long period of time. To oblige them to act and live together, is to subject them to some inevitable portion of thwarting, bickering and unhappiness. . . .

The subject of cohabitation is particularly interesting, as it includes the subject of marriage. . . . The evil of marriage, as it is practised in European countries, extends further than we have yet described. The method is, for a thoughtless and romantic youth of each sex, to come together, to see each other for a few times, and under circumstances of delusion, and then to vow eternal attachment. (Godwin [1793] 1971, p. 302)

The couple find themselves deceived. They try to make the best of things. Closing their eyes to the truth, they try to talk themselves into believing that they were right in their "first crude opinion of each other. Thus the institution of marriage is made a system of fraud. . . ." This blindness and hypocrisy make for faulty judgments in every aspect of life.

So much for sentimentality and boy-meets-girl. Further:

[M]arriage, as now understood, is a monopoly, and the worst of monopolies.[8] So long as two human beings are forbidden, by positive institution, to follow the dictates of their own mind, prejudice will be alive and vigorous. So long as I seek, by despotic and artificial means, to maintain my possession of a woman, I am guilty of the most odious selfishness. (Godwin [1793] 1971, pp. 302–03)

Interpreting and embellishing his father-in-law's gospel, Percy Shelley—though an arch-Romanticist flaying calculators, mechanists, and Utilitarians who subordinate love, friendship, nature, and the poetry of life to security—nonetheless shows a kind of rationalist Benthamite bias. Holding that marriage is not intrinsically an honorable estate, he believed that the union of a woman and a man may retain a sacramental character so long as it makes them both happy. Dissolution is automatic, however, from the time its pains and miseries exceed the good in it. Constancy in itself is no virtue.[9]

On the whole, the theme of sexual liberation was limited to a small coterie of middle-class intellectuals, among them Blake, Mary Wollstonecraft, and Godwin himself.

Wollstonecraft was no Romantic and, though beautiful, in no way representative of the feminine mystique. Fully eighteenth-century, her lights were reason and experience. When women achieved liberty and equality, they would prove their full worth as human beings. Living up to her beliefs, she became the mistress of an American captain, Gilbert Imlay; produced a daughter, Fanny; traveled to Scandinavia and became intimate with Helen Maria Williams, a friend of the French Girondins, the party of the moderate left. Deserted by Imlay, and after attempting suicide, she threw in her lot with Godwin. Once their "equal partners" relationship was consummated, they adjusted principles to circumstances and married—she to protect the coming child, the future Mary Shelley; he out of regard for her happiness—though each preserved autonomy by keeping a separate establishment (H. M. Jones 1954, pp. 252–53). But the author of the *Vindication of the Rights of Women* died (1797) 11 days after the birth of her child.

Though in reality only one, Shelley, would stay the course, Godwin and Wollstonecraft, in more than a procreative sense, were the parents of a generation of Romantic radicals and rebels. Shelley took the fruit of their union, Mary Godwin, as his second wife. Godwin the widower married the ogling widow Mrs. Clairmont, becoming stepfather to her daughter Clara Mary Jane (first known as Jane, then Claire); and this young woman became the mother of Allegra, a natural child begotten by Byron.

These intricate family relationships represent a divergence between a rationalist older generation and a more romantic younger generation; the ideas of feminism and free love coming out of Wollstonecraft's *Vindication* and Godwin's *Political Justice* are two of the ideological strands that unite them. Feminism is really the rationalists' counterpart of the free love of the Romantics.

In Shelley's circle the life way of the threesome, occasionally a foursome, became almost a cult, representing a partial reconciliation of ideals with circumstances. The shifting, sometimes confusing, patterns of relationship—Shelley, Harriet, and Thomas Jefferson Hogg; Shelley, Harriet, and Eliza Westbrook; Shelley, Harriet, and Elizabeth Hitchener; Shelley, Harriet, and Mary Godwin; Shelley, Mary, and Claire Clairmont—all represent, to varying degrees, phases on the evolutionary path to creating a "house of friends," though seldom with any real degree of stability.

Shelley's ideal household would have been a threesome: himself, Harriet as the "sister of his soul," and Mary as his wife. He could not be persuaded of the absurdity of trying to shelter two incompatible women (Hotson 1930, pp. 23, 29–30). Yet he came to doubt that Harriet was suited to her role: "Are you above the world, and to what extent?" Never affecting "what I did not feel," he could assert with complete sincerity that his "attachment to Mary neither could nor ought to be overcome" (Hotson 1930, p. 31). His desertion of Harriet and elopement with Mary were part of his plan and purpose (White 1940, II, p. 427), a matter of ideological work in which dream, thought, and sentiment were combined in his attempt to reify an idea. No doubt there was someone in the world who could be Harriet's soul brother; but he, Shelley, was not that one. He could be only her protector, as it were, her parent (Hotson 1930, p. 43). One critic supports the view that Harriet was essentially a child dependent on big sister Eliza, remaining the "little sister" to the end (Hotson 1930, p. 57).

It is true that the presence of the prosaic spinster Eliza West-brook as one of the trio in Ireland lent a stability to that venture that had been missing at the time of Shelley's first Continental exile in the summer of 1814. When he, still married to Harriet, and Mary eloped to the Continent, they took her stepsister Claire along. For one thing, she knew French; also, as Hogg shrewdly noted, Shelley always needed to have a third party, man or woman, around as a prop (R. M. Smith 1945, p. 9). This combination held for the second Continental visit in 1816.

In the right setting, the ambiance of a threesome[10] was balm to Shelley's wounds, ballast for hope in his last days, as when he sailed his boat by moonlight off the Italian coast, Mary at his feet and their friend Jane Williams in the stern, playing her guitar.

Pastoralism and the Gypsy Motif

The rationalism and skepticism of the Age of Reason were alien to Blake's most cherished beliefs. In the net result, he returned to the innocence of his earliest self and the quiet ecstasy of the pastoral life (Hagstrum 1966, p. 150). In Blake's Romantic ideology the pastoral myth as antithesis and antidote to Reason and Revolution gains poignant reality both at the beginning and at the end of his life.

One scholar has observed that "It is often those who live between town and country, or for whom country scenes are a memory of childhood, a symbol of the lost Eden, who have the keenest and

most poignant sense of pastoral beauty" (Raine 1951, p. 10). Wordsworth felt the depths of his relationship with lakes and mountains
only after he had left them for the first time. In *Songs of Innocence*
Blake opens up a pastoral world that "has the double intensity of the
natural world" and of a "lost Paradise, radiant in the golden visionary distance of memory, in which Wordsworth [saw] the tree he
loved in boyhood." Blake from infancy knew the two worlds of the
city and the countryside. From the print shops of the city he could
wander into the country lanes on the outskirts. "It is a great thing
for a boy to have his freedom, as Wordsworth also had his, during
those years in which poets gather the impressions and sensations
upon which they draw, to the end of their lives" (Raine 1951, pp.
10–11).

With this linking of Blake and Wordsworth in boyhood we have
in the making a wedge in the door leading into the world of the
Romantic imagination in the first English Romantic generation. But
it is emphatically the world of the child, soon outgrown (Frye 1947,
p. 237). The "Arcadian illusion" (Pfaff 1980, p. 72) has been perpetuated into the suburban myth of the twentieth century; but by
the very nature of its association with childhood and innocence, it is
a transient thing. Nature has her limits; a simplified rural life is, in a
way, the antithesis of civilization. Urban decadence confronts rural
"idiocy" across the middle zone of suburban sterility. Notwithstanding the decay of the metropolis in our time, and a general feeling of
"impending doom for the cities," it has been argued that the real
image and archetype of the "unfallen" state is not Arcadia, but
Utopia, though even Utopia "means nothing unless it is conceived
in the apocalyptic terms of a New Jerusalem . . ." (Frye 1947,
p. 238; see also Berger 1979, p. 64 and Berger 1981, passim).

Thus, in historical reality the city is the goal: Blake's London,
not Wordsworth's Grasmere. The wanderlust of gypsy and pastoralist
life ways represents a kind of freedom, but not civic freedom. As
Thomas Mann, epitome of the burgher spirit, noted, we are not
gypsies living in a green wagon. Every rational being desires a home
of some kind. Yet how can a human being feel at home in a universe
of vast elemental forces? How can a culture simultaneously enrich
the lonely individual and "renew the forwardness which was the best
part of the [American and French] political revolutions?" (Jones
1954, p. 412). That is the problem, perhaps the central problem,
that the world has yet to recognize. In the early 1800s it was still

comparatively new and a leading question for Western intellectuals: philosophers, artists, men of letters—religionists, rationalists, humanists, freethinkers—and more than any, perhaps, the Romantics.

Friendship House

A central and recurrent theme in Shelley's circle is the idea of a "house of friends,"[11] a kind of continuance of Coleridge's pantisocratic creed, which points toward the Red House of William Morris (begun 1859). It is perhaps a microversion of Shelley's pure and austere Spartan republic, another version, secularized, of Bunyan's House Beautiful. Such a house, in prospect, was one at Nangtwillt, Wales—a region of "wildness and beauty" with a "mountain torrent," a Romantic poet's dream. Shelley hoped the property of 130 acres could be farmed by Elizabeth Hitchener's father, a retired public-house keeper. But the house cost too much, and Mr. Hitchener, prudent man, would not let his daughter go (Maurois 1924, pp. 107–08).

They tried again at a cottage above a wooded gorge, looking down on the sea, in the "very picturesque" hamlet of Lynmouth in north Devon. A threesome was established with the arrival of Miss Hitchener, the "spiritual sister." The housing arrangements met with some admonition from Shelley's mentor Godwin, who thought the domicile too large and expensive. In a starchy note he let Shelley know that a small, modest house ought to be good enough for any of Godwin's disciples. Shelley replied respectfully that there was not enough room in a small house. Though he hated to admit it, there might be a problem of moral propriety if two unmarried people of different sexes occupied the same bedroom.[12] Again he had to make an ideological shift: "He knew that in a regenerated society this prejudice would disappear, but in the present state of things, promiscuity appeared to him imprudent. However, he advanced this opinion—which he feared was rather reactionary—with precaution" (Maurois 1924, pp. 109–10).

The domestic problems of idealistic philosophers were compounded in 1816 when Shelley, Mary, and Claire Clairmont fled to Switzerland, their second expedition to the Continent. Settling at Brunnen, they found a deserted, tumbledown chateau, hired two rooms for six months, and "bought furniture, beds, chairs, wardrobes and a stove." Again, as in Wales and Lynmouth, they thought that in this "house of friends" they had found a new life. But the new stove did not work very well, and the poet lacked manual skills.[13]

One wonders, indeed, whether ideologies can be domesticated without strain. In the last exile at Casa Magni, though the "wild scenery and primitive people were most congenial to Shelley (D.N.B. 1973, XVIII, p. 37), housekeeping problems marred concord in the "house of friends." Mary Shelley and Jane Williams got on each other's nerves (R. M. Smith 1945, p. 11), as Harriet Westbrook Shelley and Elizabeth Hitchener had at Lynmouth. "Housekeeping in common is for women the acid test. There were stupid quarrels over servants and frying pans" (Maurois 1924, p. 308).

POLITICS: GROUPINGS AND TRAFFIC

There may be some question as to whether Blake—ultimately a solitary, an isolate in the absolute sense (Kazin 1946, pp. 2–3), a man of unique and transcendent vision, supreme symbolmaker—can be readily identified with any specific group beyond the broad setting of the artisans' London and the world of dissenting radicalism. In the years immediately following his marriage, he was taken up by the Reverend Henry Mathew, who helped defray the printing costs of *Poetical Sketches*, and by Mrs. Mathew, an accomplished lady who led a literary salon (Raine 1951, p. 13). For a time in the immediate wake of 1789 he was associated with a radical group in London whose center was his publisher, Joseph Johnson, and which included Dr. Richard Price, Joseph Priestley, William Godwin, Mary Wollstonecraft, and Thomas Paine, all of whom Blake met at Johnson's weekly dinners. Paine, particularly, linked this circle with a movement: that of the London Corresponding Society, which has been claimed, none too accurately, as the "first definitely working-class political organization formed in Britain." Influenced by French Jacobinism, it promoted a "propaganda of ideas" that helped London radicalism to acquire "a greater sophistication . . . from the need to knit diverse agitations into a common movement" (Thompson 1963, pp. 20–21).

Beginning in 1793, there came a series of arrests, trials, transportations, and penal acts that broke up the society, driving Tom Paine (Blake aiding his flight) into exile. Five years later, when Bishop Watson published a book attacking Paine, Blake wrote on the title page, "To defend the Bible in this year of 1798 would cost a man his life. The Beast & the Whore rule without control" (Morton 1958, p. 17). The state and the established Church were in process of creating hell on earth, and what is hell but "being shut up in the possession of corporeal desires which shortly weary the man"[14] (Morton 1958, p. 44). As with the crushing of the Levelers by Cromwell, so in the crushing of the Jacobins the revolutionary order awoke to the realization that victory would have to be deferred.

The war with France brought both high taxes and depression: low wages and unemployment, pauperism and crime. The protective tariff made food dear. Reformers preached manhood suffrage and universal education.

The Somerset community where the Wordsworths and Coleridge lived was shocked when it learned that an advocate of these reforms, John Thelwall, was going to visit the poets. A former servant in the manor house where the Wordsworths were staying told a woman at Bath of "suspicious" people now there. This woman gave a more elaborate account to her employer, who wrote to the Home Secretary. The substance of the charge was as follows:

> The Wordsworths were an "emigrant" family from France. (William *had* spent some time there.)

> The master Wordsworth had no wife, but was cohabiting with a woman who passed as his sister (Dorothy, and she was).

> These people carried camp stools on their walks and a "Portfolio" to record observations. They had been heard to say that they would be "rewarded" for them.

> They were "very attentive to the river." Moreover, these "French people" had been asking whether the brook was navigable to the sea. When told it was not, they were later seen examining the brook "quite down to the Sea."

> Conjecture was made that they might possibly be agents for "some principal in Bristol."

More suspicious yet, the honest villagers reported that the "French couple" had been seen, of all things, "washing and mending their clothes all day Sunday"[15] —an antinomian gesture, surely—and wandering "frequently out upon the heights most part of the night"— the gypsy motif again.

The visible facts were true enough: Wordsworth was tracing the source of the brook as a possible subject for a poem Coleridge had in mind.

The plot thickened. Honest Tom Poole, a native of the region, was rumored to be "protecting a mischievous gang of disaffected Englishmen." Coleridge met a woman from a nearby village who told how a "Mr. Coleridge" at Stowey was a "vile Jacobin villain" who had "seduced a young woman in our parish." No doubt about it: associate with people who wash clothes on Sunday and walk with them by night, and lo! you will turn ultimately to treason and seduction.[16]

The matter did not end there. A detective, one Walsh, was sent down from London to investigate. He would hide behind sand dunes and listen to the poets discuss Spinoza; he reported suspicious references to "Spy Nozy." He added that the people at Alfoxden manor house were not French, but could do as "much harm as all the French can do. . . ." He thought it, indeed, no French affair, "but a gang of disaffected Englishmen." A waiter named Jones reported that the Wordsworths gave a dinner with 14 people, and there was "a little Stout Man with dark cropt Hair and . . . a White Hat and Glasses got up and talked so loud and with such a passion that Jones was frightened and has not gone near them since."[17] The man with the white hat was Thelwall; the Coleridges and the Pooles were among the Wordsworths' other guests.

Thelwall wanted to settle in the neighborhood, but Coleridge warned him not to: it would not be fair to Tom Poole. It was bad enough for Poole to sponsor Coleridge himself. "My peaceable manners and known attachment to Christianity [he was then a Unitarian] had almost worn it [local mistrust] away when Wordsworth came. . . ." The poets occasioned only threats; Thelwall would bring riots. Tom Poole would lose business and credit, his tranquillity would be disturbed, his ties of kinship weakened or broken, "and lastly, his poor old mother made miserable." Ideologies and reforms must yield to filial piety and solicitude. It was the combination of Wordsworth, Coleridge, and Thelwall that threatened the peace of the village: "Either of us separately would perhaps be tolerated; but *all three* together—what could it be less than plot and damned conspiracy? a school for the propagation of Demagogy and Atheism?" (Ellis 1967, pp. 120ff.).

In other words, a romantic, eccentric way of life can be construed as representing a radical movement; from the viewpoint of conventional wisdom, culture and politics conjoin.

Thelwall's temporary association with the poets illustrates well the overlapping of political and literary cultures, and helps to show why they are often tenuous. Thelwall was the son of a silk mercer and thus "straddled the world of Wordsworth and of Coleridge"—offspring of the professional classes—and the artisan world of the Spitalfields weavers (Thompson 1963, p. 157). When Coleridge had lectured on pantisocracy at Bristol in 1796, Thelwall had started a correspondence, and Coleridge's responses had been favorable. He saw Thelwall as "'intrepid, eloquent, and honest,'" and thought it likely that his influence on the working classes would be great. During the summer of Thelwall's visit, however, the generally idyllic nature of the poets' lives, despite government surveillance, persuaded Thelwall to opt out of public affairs (Thompson 1963, p. 164). The pantisocratic vision was still intact and tempting.

But the pastoral dream began to dissolve in the course of a walk that took the poets and the radical politician into a lovely retired vale.

> "Citizen John," said Coleridge, "this is a fine place to talk treason in." "Nay, Citizen Samuel," replied Thelwall, "it is rather a place to make a man forget that there is any necessity for treason." The anecdote foreshadows the decline of the first Romantics into political "apostasy"—most abject in Southey, most complex in Coleridge, most agonizing and self-questioning in Wordsworth. "I wish you would write a poem. . . ." Coleridge wrote to Wordsworth in 1799, "addressed to those who, in consequence of the complete failure of the French Revolution, have thrown up all hopes for the amelioration of mankind. . . ." (Thompson 1963, p. 176).

Thelwall by then had withdrawn to a remote farm in south Wales; in this pastoral retreat and semiretirement Wordsworth saw him for the last time, and "it was in such isolated surroundings as these that he was to depict the Solitary in *The Excursion*, meditating upon the delusions of those millennarial years." For Thelwall it was a process of withdrawal and return: He stayed in radical politics and joined the Reform Bill movement of 1831–32, though without his old vigor—time had passed him by (Thompson 1963, p. 176, and note).

Pantisocracy had been blown away by hard facts and by new winds of doctrine. Coleridge, reworking his ideology, was beginning to see the weakness of "democratic reason." He had come to think that Thelwall perhaps was the only "acting democrat that is honest," the rest "a most execrable herd. Arrogant because they are ignorant, and boastful of the strength of reason, because they never tried it enough to know its weakness" (Ellis 1967, pp. 123–24). With the French armies invading Switzerland and instituting military dictatorships in some cantons, "Coleridge's faith in the French Revolution vanished." As demonstrated in his ode "Recantation," he now thought aristocrats might govern better for the general benefit. He still opposed Pitt's government, which he thought had forced the war on France. He thought with agony of the maimed and wounded," of broken homes, frightened and starving children." All he had now was his religion, moving from Unitarianism back toward traditional Anglicanism, which he thought the one "'universally efficient,' cure" for social troubles (Ellis 1967, pp. 129–30).

By the time *The Prelude* was completed (1805), Wordsworth had long been confronting the need to conquer the French Revolution in his own mind by taking all mankind as his subject (Van Doren 1950, p. xviii). The revolution and Napoleonic despotism convinced him that preparation was needed for freedom. Calling himself a "liberal conservative" (like Tocqueville, like Trollope?), he argued that he always supported the weaker side, the "cottage hearth rather than the palace," but in democratic days, the crown.

With respect to social and political issues, in 1809 Wordsworth advocated universal and equal (manhood) suffrage, which puts him squarely in the radical camp. Presumably Englishmen, if not Englishwomen and the French, were ready for this right. But he was emphatically a Tory democrat. In 1817 he noted that, in the past 30 years the organic ties of the agrarian communities had loosened: "Everything has been put up to market, and sold for the highest price. . . . [A]ll the moral cement is dissolved . . . nothing being substituted . . . but a quickened self-interest." Was it this opinion and settlement that made him stand up for the landed interest and a particular noble house in a parliamentary election the following year? In addressing the voters of Westmorland, he referred to the

> independent and judicious House of Lowther: [and] men who are happy and proud to rally round the nobleman who is the head of that

house, in defence of rational liberty . . . a tried enemy to dangerous innovations—a condemner of fantastic theories . . . a Lover of the People, but one who despises . . . the false arts by which the plaudits of the multitude are won. . . . (Owen and Smyser 1974, III, pp. 155-56).

Wordsworth was convinced that human passions make a landed aristocracy necessary. The flaw in his reasoning lies in the implication that landed aristocrats are disinterested and exempt from human passions. He overlooked the fact that by the end of the Napoleonic Wars, the aristocratic system of society and government had become weak, having in great measure "outlived the loyalty that produced it" (Ellis 1967, pp. 334–37).

Wordsworth, then, was looking back to a benign feudalism, not forward to Utopia. His earlier musing on a "republic of peasants and shepherds" (Briggs 1959, p. 40) in Cumberland is perhaps more the stuff of pastoral poetry than of real life. But he was not altogether rooted in the past. More than most of his contemporaries, he had, with Coleridge, a true perception of the trends of his time, with portents full of foreboding for the future, writing in *The Excursion*: "continuous and compact . . . the smoke of unremitting fire hangs permanent . . ." (Briggs 1959, p. 54).

Why did the pantisocratic dream of Coleridge and Southey begin to fail within a year after it was born—that Utopian dream of equal rights, representative government, individualism, and communal ownership on the banks of the Susquehanna? The incompatibility of the last two principles suggests one reason. All these elements of social and political democracy were soon to be qualified, if not rejected.

Robert Southey, least-known of the "Lakers," was not least in sensitivity and humility—or honesty. Reworking his ideology, having defected from pantisocracy, he went to Portugal for six months to make money and do research. His uncle now found him "perfectly correct in behavior, of the most exemplary morals"—this young man who, in a mood of rebellion at Westminster School, had written an essay against flogging, which got him promptly expelled from the institution. Southey now wanted to study law. He wrote: "How does time mellow down our opinions. Little of that ardent enthusiasm which so lately fevered my whole character remains. I have contracted my sphere of action within the little circle of my friends . . ." (Ellis 1967, p. 129).

No doubt patriotism played a part, particularly once insurgent French democracy was swallowed up in Bonapartist imperialism (though even earlier). For Wordsworth, one turning point was the executions of his Girondist friends, though his radicalism continued for several years, perhaps directed less against the Terror than against Burke and the "Beast and the Whore" of the British oligarchy. Along with this, William and Dorothy were setting examples of compensation with simple life ways: living off the land, growing their own vegetables, rambling and night-walking at Windy Brow Farm near Keswick in the North, at Race Down and Alfoxden in the West Country, later at Dove Cottage, Grasmere. The "circle of friends" did not materialize for a while: the Wordsworths were at Grasmere, the Coleridges, Southeys, and Lovells, thirteen miles away at Greta Hall, Keswick (Manley 1974, p. 160). But the term "Lake Poets" is a misnomer. Coleridge lived in the region only now and then; Southey used Keswick as a base from which to write on subjects not connected with the lakes. Thomas De Quincey, essayist and opium eater, was there long enough to note Dorothy's "gipsy" turn, but stayed at Dove Cottage a comparatively brief time. Significantly, Charles Lamb "after a visit to Grasmere"—like Blake after Flipham or Samuel Johnson after the Hebrides—"found himself a more passionate lover of the city" (Ellis 1967, p. xii).

These facts raise the problem posed by Coleridge's distinction between "cultivation" (culture) and "civilization" (Briggs 1959, p. 477), the one more individual and personal, the other more institutional, collective, and political. Perhaps the traffic between them can be defined partly in terms of the relation between technology and the arts, between commerce and poetry. This generation of Romantic poets saw technology at least as a potential threat to the way of life that sustained their art. They came to see revolutionary politics the same way. The closest community and traffic of literary and political interests probably came with the visit (1797) of John Thelwall; but local peace, as Coleridge pointed out, was more important than radical insurgency.

The local, the immediate, the personal: church, soil, country. For Wordsworth's circle the ideological need was served by a thing called Nature, not only reified but deified. Calling attention to the yeomanry's attachment to their small holdings, Wordsworth reported one who had been advised by a neighbor to cut down a tree for profit: "Fell it . . . I had rather fall on my knees and worship it"

(Owen and Smyser 1974, III, p. 339). An atavistic reversion to Druidism? No, just devotion to permanent things.

Once Wordsworth pulled some berries from a holly tree and carried them to a barren patch of soil to plant them there, a "greening" gesture Charles Reich would approve. The pastoral myth is rooted in sound native soil. The ideal is the real. Notwithstanding dislocations caused by revolutions and industrialism, "there is always another tomorrow, almost a new season, when daffodils will grow again . . ." (Manley 1974, p. 198).

For Shelley, flowers, trees, clouds—women—could all be symbols of beauty; but a beautiful idea was just as exciting as a beautiful woman, and he "spent vastly more time and thoughts upon questions of practical politics" then on dreams and fancies (Cameron 1973, p. 8). Furthermore, he has been called, of all great poets of the past, not excluding Blake or Byron, the "most modern in his social thinking." And surely among the most radical. "He questioned everything: political and parental authority, marriage and divorce laws, Christian theology, the relation of sex to love, the nature of the self" (Cameron 1973, p. 16). He is primarily not a lyrical, but an intellectual and philosophical, poet, a fact obscured by neglect of his prose works, such as *A Philosophical View of Reform*, in which he elaborates on the theme of Rousseau and Godwin that evil is a product of social causes (Cameron 1973, p. 10).

Even in his student days at Oxford, Shelley was

> alive to the passing political events of the day, writing to the editors of newspapers, identifying himself with their opinions, congratulating them on their triumphs, indignant at their persecution, and, stranger than all, publishing a poem for the sustainment in prison of one of them who was considered by the leading Liberals of the day, as well as by Shelley, a martyr for the liberty of the Press. (G. B. Smith 1877, p. 78)

This "martyr" was the Irish journalist Peter Finnerty, sentenced to 18 months imprisonment for "libel" of Lord Castlereagh in a candid letter to the *Morning Chronicle*. Shelley subscribed a guinea for his defense (White 1940, I, pp. 107–08). Between the ages of 19 and 22, prior to the elopement with Mary Godwin, he also defended the radical publications of Daniel Isaac Eaton and helped take up a public subscription for the Hunt brothers, John and Leigh, in their confrontation with the Prince Regent (White 1940, II, p. 427). His championship of Leigh Hunt, thrice prosecuted for outspoken editorials in the radical *Examiner* (White 1940, I, p. 108), culminated in 1822 with Shelley's helping Hunt to start a new publication, the *Libberal*, against the Tory *Quarterly Review*. It was while returning from their last editorial conference that Shelley was drowned (Cameron 1973, p. 7).

Shelley's support of Finnerty extended to the whole Irish nation. Byron referred to the Union of Great Britain and Ireland as the "'union of the shark with his prey'" (Cameron 1973, p. 6). Shelley favored repeal of that union, retaining the kingship for a while to curtail warfare (White 1940, II, p. 437). The most amusingly bizarre instance of Shelley's polemical fervor is his Irish campaign. In Dublin he and Harriet tried a crusade of pamphlets to promote morality, sobriety, and philanthropy among the Irish, more or less according to English Puritan precepts. The sobering fact was that on St. Patrick's Night the great majority of the Dubliners got roaring drunk. Not only that, but the "proletariat" of that time and place seemed by no means disposed to rebel against their lot. Starveling paupers crowded around the coaches to admire the fine clothes of the rich. Such was Ireland the absurd: "wretched but jeering, suffering but garrulous, discontented, and rejoicing in her discontent" (Maurois 1924, pp. 104–05). Such was Dublin, that paranoid, yet complacent, city.

Shelley did address a large public meeting at which Ireland's rebel leader, Daniel O'Connell, was chief speaker. He established contacts with several Irish nationalists. In *An Address to the Irish People* (1812) Shelley moved ideologically from anticlericalism to reform (Cameron 1973, pp. 6–7). Under the goad of Godwin, however, who dourly predicted a bloodbath (G. B. Smith, 1877, p. 64), his "spiritual son" decided to give up his rescue mission to aid a people who, it appeared, could not care less about being saved. This renunciation took place in a setting somehow emblematic of missionary, and ideological, work in general: Shelley composing "Proposal for an Association for the Good of Mankind" while his wife Harriet's elder sister Eliza was sewing a red cloak[18] and Harriet herself was setting up a meal of bread and honey (Maurois 1924, p. 105).

The Irish venture, which barely touched the surface of the real problem, and perhaps was doomed from the start because of Shelley's hostility to Catholicism, is in marked contrast with Shelley's proposals for English parliamentary reforms. He wanted to liberalize the suffrage laws but, still the aristocratic radical, not yet for women—or even all men. More emphatically, he desired to abolish civil disabilities for religious reasons and to do away with tithes. He believed in the liquidation of the national debt by assessments on all physical property (White 1940, II, pp. 436–37).

Going beyond the political, Shelley led off with a £100 subscription to construct an embankment that would help the Welsh at Tremadoc reclaim land from the sea. And he raised money to aid the families of the executed Luddite frame breakers in Yorkshire (White 1940, II, p. 427).

But here his brother-poet, Byron, whom he had yet to meet, was far more deeply and publicly involved. Byron has been seen as "among the most essentially political" of English poets (Morley 1921, VI, p. 107), and his reactions to the Luddite risings show a remarkable capacity to shift ground in a comparatively brief time. At first he took note of the "desperate plight of his weaver tenants, resorting to the illicit strike action called Luddism against the merchants who owned the stocking frames in their houses." Facing insolvency from encumbered estates, he imagined himself joining the "broken shopkeepers" in rebellion against the strikers. As the weavers, sick with famine, resorted more and more to violence, he let his agents double the rents. "I must rebel, too," Byron wrote, just before his speech in the House of Lords on the Frame Act, which would have made frame breaking a capital offense. Here his humanity triumphed. His vehement disapproval of that measure was diametrically opposed to the vindictive stance of the Hunts' radical *Examiner*, which proclaimed that Luddism should be crushed by violence (Cameron 1973, pp. 173, 174–75). In his maiden speech (February 27, 1812) on the Frame Act, two days before the publication of *Childe Harold* (Cameron 1973, p. 176), he declared:

> I have traversed the seat of war in the Peninsula, I have been in some of the most oppressed provinces of Turkey; but never under the most despotic of infidel governments did I behold such squalid wretchedness as I have seen since my return in the very heart of a Christian country. (Borst 1948, p. 152)

Byron sat on a committee that replaced the death penalty with fine or imprisonment, but the death clause was restored when the bill was sent back to the Commons (Cameron 1973, p. 175).

Byron's second speech in the session of 1812, on behalf of both the Nottingham artisans and the Irish peasants, was even more radical. At this time he could be called a radical in the reformist sense: going to the root of corruption (Cameron 1973, p. 176). That same year he enrolled in a "new caucus of Whig and independent reformers called the Hampden Club." The "tutelary genius" of this group was Lady Oxford; her country house in Herefordshire was a setting for instigating radical action (Cameron 1973, p. 179). In the following year (June 1, 1813) Byron made his third and last speech, under wholly radical auspices and with only one supporter. He made it in connection with reform petitions, including one censuring magistrates who were attacking the right to petition in Luddite regions.

This was the end of Byron's active parliamentary career. Although three years later, with the Nottingham weavers rising again, he could still write, in a jesting mood, about joining the reformers, he was now convinced that parliamentary tactics were useless, that revolution might be the only answer. Mixed government was futile. If a republic were not possible, then a despotism of one man might serve: "the leader in talent and truth—is next to the Divinity!" (Cameron 1973, p. 175), a curious prelude to Carlyle's thesis of the Great Man.

Shelley, too, by this time (ca. 1815) was "no longer inspired to enter personally into political agitation" (D.N.B. 1973, XVIII, p. 34, col. 2), yielding to Godwin's curb on the spirit of English radicalism, pivoting from direct action to a more historical view of human change and progress (White 1940, II, pp. 430, 431). If politics lost by this quietism, literature gained. When Godwin talked him into giving up his "missionary" activities, as in Ireland," Shelley "pursued the ideal in his poems" (Brailsford 1913, pp. 166–67), content "to work upon the world by his writings" (D.N.B. 1973, XVIII, p. 34, col. 2), as in his Address to the People on the Death of the Princess Charlotte, protesting the execution of three workmen "incited to Luddite violence" by a government spy (Cameron 1973, p. 14). In the year following his first meeting with Byron, he published his Proposal for Putting Reform to the Vote Throughout the Kingdom and began writing The Revolt of Islam, "a poet's impassioned vision of the French revolution and the succeeding reaction." When not writing, he was "much engaged in relieving the distress of the cottagers in his neighbourhood" and publishing political tracts (D.N.B. 1973, XVIII,

p. 35, col. 2; p. 36, col. 1). Yet as late as 1818–19 he could say: "My purpose has hitherto been simply to familiarize the highly refined imagination of the more select classes of poetical readers with beautiful idealisms of moral excellence." (Preface to *Prometheus Unbound*)

The important fact is that Shelley received attention from the working classes, both conservative and radical. In the latter group Richard Carlile in the 1820s published several editions of *Queen Mab* and laudatory remarks on Shelley in his *Republican.* When Carlile was in jail, eight fellow radicals tried to carry on. They were arrested and sent to Newgate, whence they published Shelley items in the *Newgate Magazine* (White 1940, II, pp. 404–06). Shelley might just possibly have known Robert Owen, mill owner and founder of New Lanark, perhaps more influential than Carlile in spreading information about Shelley among working-class radicals. The Owenites regarded *Queen Mab* almost as a Bible (White 1940, II, pp. 406–08). If Robert Owen was the father of British socialism, Shelley in a sense was its grandfather; both influenced Bernard Shaw and the Fabians (White 1940, II, pp. 404–08, 420). Another class of radicals influenced by Shelley were men who fought for the Chartist cause: Henry Hetherington, James Watson, William James Linton, J. G. Holyoake (White 1940, II, p. 407). Between 1825–26 and 1835–41, three working-class radical periodicals published 39 Shelley items. To one scholar it is clear that "Shelley's most ardent and devoted admirers were to be found among the readers and editors of these journals (White 1940, II, p. 409).

With the failure of the Chartists in the 1840s, a cycle ended; there was to be little important popular agitation in England for 50 years. Yet the resonance of Shelley's Romantic radicalism influenced "Young Germany in the abortive revolution of 1848 and the Italian patriots of the Risorgimento." In the 1930s a "group of Communists in a Milwaukee jail were reported to have attempted to convert fellow prisoners by reading *Queen Mab* aloud" (White 1940, II, pp. 416–17). Somehow the conjunction of Shelley with jailed Marxists in bland Milwaukee in hardheaded Wisconsin epitomizes all the ambiguities of symbolmaking Romantic poets' traffic with ideologies and politics. But then the English Romantic movement was another conjunction of poetry with history.

CONCLUSION: THE GENERATION OF 1914
AND THE GENERATION OF 1789

Fernand Braudel's structural approach to history, with its divisions into geographical time, social time (groups and generations), and individual time (personalities and events) (Braudel 1966, p. xxii) might be used as a paradigm for some inductions on the England of the French Revolutionary Wars and the 1832 Reform Bill in the areas of regional geographies, socioeconomic backgrounds (including religion and education), political affiliations, and rivalries.

Another approach, expanding on the second of Braudel's classifications and taking up a thesis recently explored by Robert Wohl, is generational: "All suffer from the general confusion as to what a generation is" (Wohl 1979, p. 2). Is it those "sharing a common sensibility and fate" (Piazza 1979, p. 10)? Is it Ortega y Gasset's "dynamic compromise between a minority and a mass" (Wohl 1979, p. 139)? Is it rather "like a magnetic field 'at the center of which lies an experience or a series of experiences'" (Wohl 1979, p. 209)? How long is a generation? What is the distinction between a "long" one and a "short" one? In what sense is a generation "lost" or "silent"? What is the actual difference between a generation to whom much is given and one from whom much is expected?

A "generation" may be defined as an aggregate of human beings conditioned for a time toward a common viewpoint through sharing the same processes of enculturation or education, or through having their individual developments shaped by the same historical events: examples are those who fight in a war, join in a revolution, or endure any crisis in common.

> It is a system of references and identifications that gives priority to some kinds of experiences and devalues others—hence, it is relatively independent of age. The chronological center of this experiential field need not be stable; it may shift with time. What is essential to the formation of a generational consciousness is some common frame of reference that provides a sense of rupture with the past and that will later distinguish the members of the generation from those who follow them in time. The frame of reference is always derived from great historical events like wars, revolutions, plagues, famines, and economic crises, because it is great historical events like these that supply the markers and signposts with which people impose order on the past and link their individual fates with those of the communities in which they live. (Wohl 1979, p. 210)

The generation, then, is bound by experience more than by time. "Historical generation is not defined by its chronological limits or its borders. It is not a zone of dates; nor is it an army of contemporaries making its way across a territory of time" (Wohl 1979, p. 210). Nonetheless, with respect to the pivotal events that shape generations, dates are of some symbolic value.

Take, as representative of his generation's creative minority, Rupert Brooke, born "during the second half of the 1880s into the educated, professional middle class", going up to King's College, Cambridge, in 1906, where he met some of his generation's elite, in rebellion "against the nineteenth century and Victorianism." What did they want instead?

> They wanted to be modern. [So did Abelard and other *moderni* of the twelfth century.] To be modern, they thought, meant to be socialist, feminist, indifferent if not hostile to religion, irreverent about conventions and traditions, and in favor of natural as opposed to formal manners. It meant to prefer the country to the city and the company of simple people to society; to live chastely while unmarried, but to talk freely and even obsessively about sex; and not necessarily to rise when a lady entered the room. It required being candid even at the risk of seeming rude. (Wohl 1979, pp. 86–87)

Their mentors and models were George Edward Moore, Henrik Ibsen, H. G. Wells, Roger Fry, E. M. Forster, Sidney and Beatrice Webb, and George Bernard Shaw (Wohl 1979, p. 86).

To that extent, then, they were also disciples of Shelley, Blake, and Wordsworth; and Brooke's generation of 1914 was in touch through symbol with the generation of 1789.

Perhaps Brooke's "return to nature" was more sophisticated, more self-conscious than Wordsworth's:

> Under this influence the country near Cambridge was full of young men and women walking barefoot, sharing his passion for bathing and fish diet, disdaining book learning, and proclaiming that there was something deep and wonderful in the man who brought the milk and the woman who watched the cows. (Wohl 1979, p. 87, quoting Virginia Woolf)

An abortive love affair with a woman he met through the Fabian Society turned Brooke against modernism, feminism, and the rest.

The magnificent immensity of Niagara Falls convinced him that he was still a romantic Victorian at heart. He wrote to a friend: "'I sit and stare at the thing and have the purest nineteenth century thoughts, about the Destiny of Man, the Irreversibility of Fate, the Doom of Nations, the fact that Death awaits us All. . . . Wordsworth Redivivus. Oh dear! Oh dear!'" (Wohl 1979, p. 87, quoting Brooke).

Brooke revolted against the "sandier" aspects of Fabian socialism, as the original Romantics had revolted against the aridity of Godwin's rationalism or Bentham's utility. Like them, he was "fascinated by the vagabond and the wanderer as human types"; the intellectuals of his war generation were "fascinated by the image of the traveller," their souls skewed to the tramp, the gypsy, the hobo, or the way-farer. They were

> "always wandering, always pursuing something, always fleeing some-thing. . . ." They were people, like Nikos Kazantzakis, who "longed for flight." They delighted in the wanderings and adventures of Charlot, "the tramp," "the vagabond," "the emigrant," and "the gold pros-pector". . . . And they were fascinated by the story of Ulysses. . . . Like Ulysses, they wandered without real hope that they would ever again find the shores from which they had departed. (Wohl 1979, p. 226)

Wohl offers an explanation:

> . . . traveling offered nourishment to a spiritual life that was unable to sustain itself on its own resources and that was constantly on the verge of dissolving into suicidal despair. It was a liberation from the self for young men overwhelmed by the weight of their egos [self-awareness?] and the hopelessness of their time. If one kept going one could forever be in flux. . . . The essential thing about this kind of travel was not the destination, but the fact of the departure.[19] (Wohl 1979, p. 228)

Citing Teilhard de Chardin, Wohl notes a more vital point: ". . . spatial and geographical exoticism was nothing but a metaphor for something deeper and more universal: the longing for renewal. The equation of traveling with spiritual rebirth was an old theme in Western culture" (Wohl 1979, p. 228).

Belief in the eternal cycles of creation sustained the Romantic writer in his life ways, as it inspired symbol creation in both his life and his art—"another tomorrow . . . when daffodils will grow again." In their traffic with war and revolution on several fronts—technological, sociopolitical, ideological—that was the hope of Wordsworth, the prophecy of Blake, the dream of Shelley. Their response to 1789—a seminal, symbolic year—made them pivots of a literary and political generation, for "[h]istorical generations are not born; they are made" (Wohl 1979, p. 5). As members of a creative minority, their ideological work, in the form of symbol production, was to shape or sharpen in some measure the mood, thought, and style of later Romantic or radical generations—so diversely stratified as the generations of 1848 (Young Germany, Young Italy), 1914 (Bloomsbury and Greenwich Village), 1917 or 1929 (the Milwaukee Marxists), and 1945 (the Beats).

Despite adjustments to conventions, lapses into conformity, and changing with circumstances, the elite among these generations, eye to eye with the onrushing "machine" threatening to rend them, clung to the Romantics' first principle: that the individual person and experience are the ultimate object of concern and study (Hughes 1958, pp. 24, 23). Says the romantic, fantasizing Cecilia Jupe, epitome of anti-authoritarian individual consciousness, pondering hard times: "I thought I couldn't know whether it was a prosperous nation or not, and whether I was in a thriving state or not, unless I knew who had got the money, and whether any of it was mine" (Dickens, *Hard Times*, bk. I, ch. IX).

NOTES

1 Such a study logically "begins with the individual, his hopes, fears, problems, solutions, and habitual associations of his daily round of life . . ." (Thoman and Corbin 1974, p. 141, citing Rex A. Lucas, *Minetown, Milltown, Railtown: Life in Canadian Communities of Single Industry* [Toronto: University of Toronto Press, 1971], p. x).

2. "The romantic rebels of the past speak more directly to the rebels of today than any other group of writers in the past" (Cameron 1973, pp. vi). In what sense is it true that the earlier period anticipated the more recent past? What might be the affinities between a Blake and a Ginsberg, a Shelley and a Robert Lowell, a Coleridge and a Kerouac—between any of the three English Romantics and a Mario Savio of Berkeley?

3 Mario Savio, student activist leader at the University of California, Berkeley, ca. 1965: "Stop the [academic] machine! I want to get off."

4 The "fixed glare" of international banker J. P. Morgan has been compared to the "onrushing headlight of a locomotive" (Miller 1979, p. 251).

5 The problem of money was not acute: William had a legacy of £400.

6   The theme of wanderlust and identity is illustrated by Jack Kerouac, apostle of the Beats in the 1940s and 1950s, who went south to Virginia to become a "big poet," then enlisted briefly in the U.S. Navy. After two months he was given a psychiatric discharge (*Current Biography*, November 1959, p. 19, col. 2).

7   In Berkeley, California, in the 1960s, as his popular legend maintains, Robert Savio becomes Mario (masculine form of Maria or Mary, ever pure). Was this for romantic reasons, including greater euphony? On one occasion, by report, he entered a bank, seeking a loan, and was refused. "But I'm Mario!" he replied. Savio was an angel-faced hipster standing on street corners, a profile like that of John the Apostle. Seek and ye shall find; ask and it shall be given unto you. But the greatest of these is love. No wonder the Judeo-Christianity religious-ethical system is sometimes disappointing.

8   It is interesting to note Godwin's use of an economic term. His work followed Adam Smith's *Wealth of Nations* (1776) by 17 years. What monopoly is in the economic sphere, monogamous marriage may be in male-female relationships. In a sense free trade is the economic equivalent of free love.

9   Echoes of this theme, questioning monogamous values, appear in Lawrence Lipton's *The Holy Barbarians*.

10   The threesome was part of the youthful life ways that evolved in the liberated decade of the 1960s: whether as two single women and one single man (as in the television program "Three's Company"), or, as it took hold for a time in Britain, one married couple and one single man. The motive seems to have been, as in Shelley's case, a broader basis of association, security, sharing, and companionship. This writer has observed, however, that the third party can become the scapegoat, or lightning rod, in the relationship.

11   Jack Kerouac, guru of the Beat Generation, from about 1942 maintained an apartment near the Columbia University campus as a gathering place for young intellectuals, including poet Allen Ginsberg (*Current Biography*, November 1959, p. 20, col. 1).

12   This problem was overcome in the Israeli kibbutz of the later twentieth century by having a young man and a young woman assume a sibling relationship.

13   Compare the commune in Mendocino County, California, of the 1970s, where the development of manual skills was a point of pride and ensured independence (Berger 1981, pp. 19, 106–09).

14   "[C]orporeal" not meaning sexual, but "merely physical or material" (Hagstrum 1966, p. 145, n. 10).

15   The persistence of English Sabbatarian attitudes is indicated by the assertion, undocumented, that in the early part of the nineteenth century it was illegal to make arrests on Sunday (Maurois 1924, p. 152).

16   Or, as essayist Thomas De Quincey reversed the proposition: He who starts off committing murder, regarded as one of the "fine arts," will end up guilty of Sabbath breaking and procrastination.

17   Note changing patterns in the images of subversion. In mid-twentieth-century America, as in early-nineteenth-century Europe, long hair was a sign of unconventionality. Was Thelwall's "cropt" hair too out of line with the old-style conformists' tie wigs, his "dark" hair too deviant from their powder? But styles were changing fast about 1796, as Bonaparte's star began to rise.

During World War I, in a rural setting near the English coast, Duncan Grant of the Bloomsbury Group was suspected of being a spy because of his "dark complexion and quiet manners . . ." (Edel 1979, p. 215).
18 Note the symbolic dress and diet in connection with ideological work. Is this symbol production? Compare Blake's red liberty cap and Coleridge's red coat when he joined the dragoons as "Comberback."
19 This theme is novelized by Jack Kerouac in *On the Road* (1955).

REFERENCES

Agee, James. 1941. *Let Us Now Praise Famous Men.* Boston: Houghton Mifflin.

Bate, Walter Jackson. 1968. *Coleridge.* New York: Macmillan.

Berger, Bennett M. 1981. *The Survival of a Counterculture: Ideological Work and Everyday Life Among Rural Communards.* Berkeley and Los Angeles: University of California Press.

——. 1979. "American Pastoralism, Suburbia, and the Commune Movement." *Society*, July-Aug., pp. 64–69.

Borst, William A. 1948. *Lord Byron's First Pilgrimage.* New Haven, Conn.: Yale University Press.

Brailsford, H. N. 1913. *Shelley, Godwin, and Their Circle.* New York and London: Oxford University Press. Reprinted Hamden, Conn.: Shoestring Press, Archon, 1969.

Braudel, Fernand. 1966, 1972. *The Mediterranean World in the Age of Philip II.* 2nd ed., 2 vols. New York: Harper & Row.

Briggs, Asa. 1959. *The Age of Improvement 1783-1867.* New York: David McKay.

Brinton, Crane. 1926. *The Political Ideas of the English Romanticists.* Oxford University Press. Paperback ed., Ann Arbor: University of Michigan Press, 1966.

Brown, Nathaniel. 1979. *Sexuality and Feminism in Shelley.* Cambridge, Mass., and London: Harvard University Press.

Bunyan, John. [1678-1684]. *Pilgrim's Progress.* Pt. II, ch. VI.

Butler, Marilyn. 1982. *Romantic Rebels and Reactionaries.* New York: Oxford University Press.

Cameron, Kenneth Neill. 1950. *The Young Shelley: Genesis of a Radical.* New York: Macmillan. Reprinted New York: Octagon, 1973.

———. ed. 1973. *Romantic Rebels: Essays on Shelley and His Circle.* Cambridge, Mass.: Harvard University Press.

Carlyle, Thomas. 1896. *Collected Works.* Vol. I, *Sartor Resartus.* London and New York: Chapman and Hall.

Chard, Leslie F. 1972. *Dissenting Republican: Wordsworth's Early Life and Thought in Their Political Context.* The Hague and Paris: Mouton.

Christian Science Monitor. 1980. Apr. 8, p. 20, col. 1. Quoting Walter Jackson Bate, *Coleridge.*

Current Biography. November 1959. Article on Jack Kerouac, pp. 19-21. New York: H. W. Wilson.

Dawson, P. M. S. 1980. *The Unacknowledged Legislator: Shelley and Politics.* Oxford: Clarendon Press.

De Sélincourt, Basil. [1909] 1971. *William Blake.* New York: Scribner's.

Dickens, Charles. [1854]. *Hard Times.* Bk. I, ch. IX.

Dictionary of National Biography (D.N.B.). 1917. Edited by Sir Leslie Stephen and Sir Sidney Lee. London and New York: Oxford University Press. Reprinted London and New York: Oxford University Press, 1973. Vols. II, III, IV, XI, XVIII.

Edel, Leon. 1979. *Bloomsbury: A House of Lions.* New York: Harper & Row.

Ellis, Amanda M. 1967. *Rebels and Conservatives: Dorothy and William Wordsworth and Their Circle.* Bloomington: Indiana University Press.

Engell, James. 1981. *The Creative Imagination: Enlightenment to Romanticism.* Cambridge, Mass.: Harvard University Press.

Erdman, David V. 1954. *William Blake: Prophet Against Empire.* Princeton, N.J.: Princeton University Press. Revised ed. 1969 and paper ed. 1976 by Princeton University Press.

Frye, Northrop. 1947. *Fearful Symmetry: A Study of William Blake.* Princeton, N.J.: Princeton University Press.

Godwin, William. [1793] 1971. *Enquiry Concerning Political Justice*, edited by K. C. Carter. Oxford: Oxford University Press.

Gouldner, Alvin. 1976. *The Dialectic of Ideology and Technology.* New York: Seabury Press.

Gutknecht, Douglas. 1982. "The Rise and Fall of the Garvey Movement, 1916–1925: Cultural-Expressive Versus Instrumental-Political Dimensions." MS.

Hagstrum, Jean H. 1966. "William Blake Rejects the Enlightenment." In *Twentieth Century Views of Blake: A Collection of Critical Essays*, edited by Northrop Frye, pp. 142–55. Englewood Cliffs, N.J.: Prentice-Hall.

Hayter, Alethea. 1968. *Opium and the Romantic Imagination.* Berkeley and Los Angeles: University of California Press.

Hotson, Leslie, ed. 1930. *Shelley's Lost Letters to Harriet.* London: Faber and Faber.

Hughes, H. Stuart. 1958. *Consciousness and Society.* New York: Vintage. Reprinted New York: Octagon, 1976.

Jones, Howard Mumford. 1954. *Revolution and Romanticism.* Cambridge, Mass.: Harvard University Press.

Kazin, Alfred. 1946. *The Portable Blake.* New York: Viking Press. Baltimore: Penguin Books, 1977.

Levine, George, and U. C. Knoepflmacher, eds. 1979. *The Endurance of Frankenstein.* Berkeley, Los Angeles and London: University of California Press.

Lipton, Lawrence. 1959. *The Holy Barbarians.* New York: Julian Messner.

McGann, Jerome. 1976. *Don Juan in Context.* Chicago and London: University of Chicago Press.

McNiece, Gerald. 1969. *Shelley and the Revolutionary Idea.* Cambridge, Mass.: Harvard University Press.

Manley, Seon. 1974. *Dorothy and William Wordsworth, the Heart of a Circle of Friends.* New York: Vanguard Press.

Marchand, Leslie A., ed. 1973–82. *Byron's Letters and Journals.* 12 vols. London: John Murray.

——. ed. 1957. *Life of Byron.* 3 vols. London: John Murray.

Maurois, André. 1924. *Ariel: The Life of Shelley.* Translated by Ella D'Arcy. New York: Appleton. Less a biography than a romantic caricature, but useful and evocative within limits. Reprinted 1936.

Miller, Nathan. 1979. *The Roosevelt Chronicles.* Garden City, N.Y.: Doubleday.

Morley, John. 1921. *Collected Works.* 12 vols. London: Macmillan.

Morton, A. L. 1958. *The Everlasting Gospel: A Study in the Sources of William Blake.* London: Lawrence and Wishart.

Owen, W. J. B., and Jane Worthington Smyser, eds. 1974. *Prose Works of William Wordsworth.* 3 vols. Oxford: Oxford University Press.

Pfaff, William. 1980. "Reflections: Aristocracies." *The New Yorker.* Jan. 14, pp. 70–78.

Piazza, Paul. 1979. Review in *Fortnightly*, "Books and Arts," Oct. 12, pp. 10–12.

Prothero, Rowland E., ed. 1901. *The Works of Lord Byron: Letters and Journals.* 13 vols. London: John Murray.

Raine, Kathleen. 1951. *William Blake.* New York: Oxford University Press.

Rand, Ayn. 1971. *The Romantic Manifesto: A Philosophy of Literature.* New York: New American Library.

Roszak, Theodore. 1969. *The Making of a Counterculture.* Garden City, N.Y.: Doubleday.

Schorske, Carl E. 1981. *Fin-de-Siècle: Politics and Culture.* New York: Random House/Vintage.

Smith, George Barnett. 1877. *Shelley: A Critical Biography.* Edinburgh: Douglas. This work, reflecting the biases of Mary Shelley and her daughter-in-law, and Victorian biases in general, must be used with caution. Perhaps the facts are more supportable than the interpretations. For comment, see R. M. Smith, below.

Smith, Robert Metcalf, in collaboration with M. M. Schlegel, T. G. Ehrsam, and L. A. Waters. 1945. *The Shelley Legend.* New York: Scribner's.

St. Clair, William. 1972. *That Greece Might Still Be Free: The Philhellenes in the War for Independence.* Oxford: Oxford University Press.

Stern, Michael. 1979. Review of Dee Garrison, *Apostles of Cultures. Los Angeles Times*, July 8, Book Review section, p. 13.

Stoddard, Richard Henry. 1877. *Anecdote Biography of Percy Bysshe Shelley.* New York: Scribner, Armstrong. Combines accounts by Denis F. MacCarthy, Thomas Jefferson Hogg, Thomas Love Peacock, Edward John Trelawney. R. M. Smith, in *The Shelley Legend* (above), calls this "useful" and "For the beginner, perhaps the best brief one volume account of Shelley that can be had. . . ."

Thoman, Richard S., and Peter B. Corbin. 1974. *The Geography of Economic Activity.* New York: McGraw-Hill.

Thompson, E. P. 1963. *The Making of the English Working Class.* New York: Random House.

Van Doren, Mark, ed. 1950. *William Wordsworth: Selected Poetry.* New York: Random House/Modern Library.

White, Newman I. 1940. *Shelley.* 2 vols. New York: Knopf. Revised ed. by Knopf, 1947. Reprinted New York: Octagon, 1972.

White, Reginald J. 1953. *Political Tracts of Wordsworth, Coleridge, and Shelley.* Cambridge: Cambridge University Press.

Wohl, Robert. 1979. *The Generation of 1914.* Cambridge, Mass.: Harvard University Press.

2 The Interaction between Political and Cultural Radicalism: The Greenwich Village Revolt, 1910–20

Irwin Marcus

Nineteenth-century America experienced relatively few movements that achieved the viable traffic between cultural and political radicalism. Using the wealth and power generated by society, defenders of the established order both enticed and overawed its citizens. Population diversity, including ethnic, religious, racial, gender, and class cleavages, undermined efforts to form and maintain broad-based, social-action movements. Internal fragmentation also afflicted American radicalism and weakened it as an instrument for change. Ideological differences, personality conflicts, and power struggles often superseded the imperative of unified action for fundamental social change. Compounding the effects of splintering within political radicalism, cultural and political radicals usually followed divergent and even conflicting paths. On rare occasions, however, major social problems led to the emergence of interconnected groups of able dissidents who initiated traffic and ephemeral alliances between political and cultural radicalism.

In the early twentieth century the United States experienced unusual growth and dislocation as the combination of industrialism, urbanism, and immigration catapulted the nation into a position of world leadership. This transformation generated substantial benefits and exacted high costs that America distributed inequitably. The major institutions of the society, such as the family and the school, offered insufficient solace to the traumatized and deprived, and little inspiration to the idealistic. Aware of these defects, some idealistic youth sought a setting where they could live in accordance with their values, engage in creative work, and do the vital spadework required for the emergence of a new and better society. In Greenwich Village, a special enclave in New York City, dissidents created an exciting experiment. They formed their own settings for interaction, such as restaurants, clubs, and salons, and forged an informal, personal communications network that linked cultural and political radicals in an innovative manner. Their political and economic critiques and affirmations, cultural activities, and way of living made Greenwich Village in 1910–20 the site of a major movement in the traffic between cultural and political radicalism. However, the combination of internal defects and the detrimental effects of the government repression associated with World War I and the Red Scare destroyed the experiment.

A few movements achieved ephemeral interaction and cooperation between cultural and political radicalism. Cultural radicalism involves a higher culture embodied in new forms and means of expression in art, literature, and theater, as well as a popular culture expressed in changing modes of living, values, and sensibilities fostering personal growth and new, programmatic means of change. In most cases it avoids involvement in movements designed to change the political and economic apparatus. Political radicalism, on the other hand, combines a critique of the existing political, economic, and social systems with advocacy of a society based on liberty, equality, and fraternity. This approach concentrates on the issues of wealth and power and the need to overthrow the existing regime. Cultural radicals emphasize form in the way of living and in the creative process; political radicals focus on changing the dominant institutions. Under most circumstances their differing orientations lead cultural and political radicals to follow divergent and even opposing paths. However, special circumstances sometimes occasion an unusual alliance focused on introducing new ways into both cultural and political spheres.

Youthful rebels confronted an adversary that entered the twentieth century as a rich and powerful nation buttressed by industrialization, immigration, and urbanization. This status provided additional reinforcement for the long-standing optimism of the national rhetoric. Nevertheless, old problems continued and new ones emerged.

Many Americans remained immersed in poverty and powerlessness. The urban condition spanned the unprecedented wealth and splendor of the elite and the squalor of the unemployed, the unskilled, and minorities. A well-entrenched leadership commanded political, economic, and cultural power, and imposed a restrictive code of living.

Some youth, aware of the lack of collective spirit and purpose of the society, withheld their full allegiance. They saw a bureaucratized order operated by dull, faceless men determined to perpetuate an unjust order. Reinforcement of their critique came from other advocates of change who gained public attention and achieved a measure of political power. *McClure's* and other muckraking periodicals exposed political and economic corruption while the Progressives implemented business regulation, consumer legislation, and conservation measures. In a more radical vein, the Socialist Party of America built a mass movement dedicated to the achievement of a socialist democracy. Socialists exerted influence and provided success in Oklahoma, Milwaukee, and the Lower East Side of New York City. On the far left, the Industrial Workers of the World proclaimed labor solidarity, direct action, and the goal of a just society. It also conducted mass strikes in Lawrence, Massachusetts, and Paterson, New Jersey, led by Bill Haywood and Elizabeth Gurley Flynn, that inspired workers and youthful rebels.

Energized by this ferment, some middle-class youth searched for a setting where they could achieve self-realization and contribute to the formation of a society fulfilling their dreams. Their special place—incubator of change, excitement, and vitality—needed accessibility to dynamic international currents, a cultural tradition, and a hospitable attitude to experimentation. A bohemia in a metropolis provided the social space and cultural freedom for maintaining a way of life based on creative expression and espousal of unpopular causes. Greenwich Village offered a special refuge for young dissidents as a modern village in the midst of America's economic and urban colossus.

In the era of industrial and finance capitalism, New York City occupied the unique position of national and international leadership in population, economic activities, and cultural affairs. Its growing population included the wealthy and professionals, employees in garment factories and printing shops, and marginals who struggled for survival. Their ways of life coexisted uneasily, merging only in a common interest in the wealth produced by the factories and docks that undergirded the life of the city. Greenwich Village combined the population diversity of the metropolis with a quiet and individualistic atmosphere resulting from relative isolation and distinctive streets. A combination of historic tradition, available space, and low rents attracted writers, artists, social workers, reformers, and crusaders to become villagers in 1910–20.

The Greenwich Villagers, many of them transplanted from towns and small cities in the East and Middle West, viewed mainstream society as a denial of what they held precious. They desired to live in an environment stressing creativity and self-expression. Their credo included liberty, living for the moment, and paganism. The society that they projected featured female equality and an educational system encouraging the flowering of children. American society, ugly and unfair, repudiated these ideals with its dehumanized economic system and its worship of the machine and materialism. They found confirmation of their perspective not only in the hopeful and democratic words and life of Walt Whitman but also in the pool of ideas developed in Europe. In the writings of Karl Marx they encountered the themes of exploitation, class struggle, and the just society. The recently translated works of Sigmund Freud aided those seeking sexual freedom and a new sense of personal identity.

The dehumanized economic system, which alienated and crushed the worker, symbolized American society. Not only did manual and craft workers experience the degrading effects of extensive division of labor and scientific management, but the cultural workers—journalists, authors, cartoonists, and artists—faced the dangers of proletarianization. Many cultural workers were employed by large organizations that used modern technology to enhance circulation and profitability. Many writers and artists, no longer craftsmen and independent operators, found themselves separated from their audience and from the right to decide about the form and substance of their work. Some of them perceived themselves as members of a "cultural proletariat" sharing the grievances of other wage workers and as their natural allies in the struggle against the capitalist oppressors. This viewpoint received classic expression in the experiences and writing of Randolph Bourne, a hero of the Greenwich Village Rebellion.

RANDOLPH BOURNE

Bourne, a man with a brilliant mind and a crippled body, experienced a stifling middle-class life in a small New Jersey town around the turn of the twentieth century. Bloomfield had shifted from a country town to a small cog in the Northeastern urban industrial complex as new factories sparked population growth, which created conflicts between the small elite and the growing working class. Family financial difficulties forced Bourne, despite his proven academic abilities, to endure six years of oppressive manual labor before he matriculated at Columbia University. After facing many bitter struggles obtaining employment, he secured a job working for a musician who owned a machine that cut perforated music rolls for player pianos. After he learned the operation and became more proficient, his employer reduced the piece rate. Bourne rebelled against this injustice, but his employer remained unmoved and circumstances forced him to remain at work on the terms set by his employer. This personal experience provided him with a special insight into the nature of the class struggle.

Exposure to systematic exploitation united Bourne's experience with those of other members of the working class, including coal and iron miners. The Colorado labor war of 1913–14 offered Bourne an opportunity to express his views about the class struggle and his solidarity with the coal miners. He applauded a demonstration against John D. Rockefeller and declared that he had the psychology of a twelfth-century baron. Bourne noted that with adequate socialist representation in Congress, these bloody wars wouldn't occur, because public opinion could be mobilized against them. He resonated with emotion when he heard an organizer of the Industrial Workers of the World read a pamphlet depicting the oppression of striking iron ore miners on the Mesabi Range. Bourne's emotions found voice in the ringing words of his poem "Sabotage":

> Into your machines, O my masters, you have knotted and kneaded our lives . . . We are the cogs, we are the levers, we are the machines, at which these metal monsters work . . . But see! now as the dim confused cry of revolt sounds far within the factory walls . . . We are men again, we strain to tear ourselves from the suffocating embrace . . . but

in us dawns the mad hope, the wild certainty of the day . . . when new
free sweet moralities shall arise, and in the healing touch of brotherhood, the machines into which, O my masters—you have knotted and
kneaded our lives—shall be not flesh of our body, but docile nerves and
sinews of our will! (Randolph Bourne Papers, box 8, 1912)

Serious reading in radical thought, including socialism, reinforced
the lesson of his work experience and prepared Bourne for the next
stage of his life, when he won a scholarship to Columbia University
and joined the student body as a mature freshman in 1909. His
period at Columbia widened and deepened his understanding of the
world as he met and impressed notable professors, such as Charles
Beard and John Dewey, who led the revolt against formalism. Bourne
embraced their relativistic and activistic posture, and he became a
disciple of Dewey's pragmatism. Intellectual growth didn't stifle his
sense of rage against injustice, and he conducted a single-handed war
in behalf of the university's underpaid and overworked scrubwomen.
The university offered recognition and financial aid that contributed
to his self-development, as did a tour of Europe, during which he
witnessed socialism and feminism in action as well as absorbing a
cultural tradition. Columbia supplied friendships, conversations, and
a sense of community that Bourne treasured and tried to duplicate,
without complete success, in his later life.

At the conclusion of his formal education, Bourne embarked on
a career as a journalist and author that was highlighted by the publication of books on education and war, and articles in *The New
Republic*, *The Dial*, *The Seven Arts*, and *The Masses*. In these publications he presented his dream of a fellowship of youth creating a
finer cultural order based on a new national consciousness. He hoped
for an alliance of workers and intellectuals to forge a society that was
democratic in economics and aristocratic in culture. The United
States, according to Bourne, had many elements of a great society
but lacked a guiding spirit. The absence of a national fabric of
spiritual experience allowed the possessive impulses to triumph over
the creative impulses, leading to the decay of the society and the inability to harness science and democracy. The role of education
loomed large in Bourne's conception of a cultural revival forged by
young intellectuals.

Critical of the obsolete ideas and methods, the stultifying regimentation, and the hierarchic form of the educational system,

Bourne looked to Dewey's ideas and their implementation in the Gary, Indiana, school system. This approach included a variety of activities, an expanded role for the manual arts, and the opportunity for self-expression by the pupils. Broadening his perspective to society, Bourne again noticed the dominance of conformity, as expressed in the "melting pot" theory. To this exaltation of the Anglo-Saxon he counterposed his concept of a transnational America in which new peoples would save the nation from stagnation and foster the emergence of the first international nation. Bourne offered a new ideal of weaving diverse peoples from other lands into a nation capable of offering a new spiritual citizenship such as Zionism offered Jews. The younger American intelligentsia would play a key role in achieving a new form of society with dual citizenship and free, mobile passage of immigrants between the United States and their native lands. To improve society in the near future, Bourne proposed a national educational service that would provide youth with training for work and the opportunity for service. Their activities would improve social services and tone up moral life by offering a moral equivalent for universal military service for the young seeking nonmilitary action.

The coming of World War I, however, produced a climate favoring the channeling of all energies into patriotism and military service. The temper of the times induced the editors of *The New Republic* and the publisher of *The Dial* to join John Dewey in supporting the military intervention of the United States. Interventionists saw an opportunity to infuse the national government with the right personnel and ideas, and to affect the future of the world by influencing the provisions of the peace treaty. Bourne demurred from this stand in a series of notable essays in which he condemned American intellectuals. He berated them for their failure to create a new synthesis, their willingness to ally with the least democratic elements of society, and their call for the subordination of all elements of life to the single purpose of victory by means of total mobilization. He predicted that the war would leave the nation spiritually impoverished, and implored youth to build a wider consciousness of the personal, social, and artistic ideals that American civilization needed to undergird the good society.

Bourne criticized American intellectuals, especially pragmatists, for their lack of poetic vision and their exaggerated emphasis on the mechanics of life at the expense of the quality of living. Malcontents,

noteworthy for their creative skepticism, must project the democratic goals needed by society. *The New Republic* closed its pages to
his articles, and *The Dial* removed him from its editorial board. These
developments jeopardized his income and forced him to prepare
translations and write hack reviews to earn a living. Bourne also suffered the loss of friendships and the alienation of his sister Margaret,
who almost put him out of the house in Bloomfield and declared
she'd cheerfully have used a gun on him if she had one. In these
trying days he turned inward and to a few close friends who came to
his bedside when he contracted pneumonia and died in December
1918. His death robbed the nation of an incisive critic, herald of a
new age, and unifier of political and cultural radicalism.

JOHN REED

John Reed, whose message bore a stronger imprint of political
radicalism, also served the dual function of hero and unifier of political and cultural radicalism. A transplant from Portland, Oregon, he
received his education in the East at a private school and at Harvard,
where he made a name for himself by his journalism, club activities,
and cheerleading. After graduation he left for New York and Greenwich Village, where, with the aid of Lincoln Steffens, he secured a
position as a journalist. The color and excitement of the city fascinated him, and he explored both its underside and its high life.
Reed's joy in living, his presence in the right place, and his writing
style secured his reputation as a talented and promising journalist.
This growing reputation offered him access to leading publications
and a livelihood. However, radicalization, resulting from personal
experience, conversations, and reading, led him to seek an outlet for
material unsuitable for mainstream publications that would contribute to social change and satisfy a growing personal need.

The Masses, a magazine supporting cultural and political radicalism, provided a vehicle for the publication of Reed's pieces about the
struggle against an unjust society. After hearing Bill Haywood describe the mistreatment of Paterson, New Jersey, strikers by city
officials, Reed went to the city to publicize the repression and help
lift the virtual news blackout. In the course of his investigation, an
altercation with a policeman led to his jailing along with hundreds
of strikers. The courage, warmth, and humanity of the strikers

moved him, and he later expressed his feelings in "The War in Paterson." He declared that the mill owners controlled the police, the press, and the courts, and that the Paterson establishment, rather than the Industrial Workers of the World, acted contrary to the American ideals and used violence. In other memorable articles Reed depicted the struggles of Pancho Villa in behalf of the Mexican people and the battle waged by Colorado coal miners, Mother Jones, and the United Mine Workers against Rockefeller and his cohorts.

Although *The Masses* served as his focal point, Reed also spent time at the Liberal Club, where he saw avant-garde posters and paintings, heard lectures on birth control and anarchism, and talked and danced. He went to Polly's Village Restaurant for good food, card games, and conversation. At Mabel Dodge's salon he met and conversed with the leading lights of the Village and radicalism, and began a love affair with Mabel Dodge. The conjunction of the Paterson strike and the presence of Bill Haywood at one of Mabel Dodge's evenings led him to stage the Paterson Pageant. The pageant, which depicted the major events of the strike, with the strikers as cast members, won acclaim for its artistry. Reed found the perfect subject for his talent when he went to Russia to witness and report the ferment of 1917. Using a vast accumulation of proclamations, posters, and official documents, he wrote *Ten Days That Shook the World*, a memorable book that captured the confusion of the Russian Revolution while doing justice to the record, Reed's support of the Bolsheviks, and his activist proclivity. However, he contracted typhus and died in the Soviet Union in 1920, before his final phase of political radicalism had a full opportunity to unfold.

PLACES FOR INTERACTION

Greenwich Village included places for interaction as well as notable and dynamic personalities. Villagers needed comfortable and stimulating settings for the exchange of ideas and personal interactions that they prized as hallmarks of community and the good life. The Liberal Club offered a forum and clearinghouse for new ideas, and provided a social center that attracted radicals and bohemians to a little theater, exhibitions of Cubist paintings, debates about free verse, and dances and annual balls. It emerged from a generational conflict in which the younger, more radical wing left the old club headquarters off Gramercy Square for a more hospitable setting on Macdougal Street. In conjunction with Polly's Restaurant, the Washington Square Bookstore, and the Provincetown Playhouse, it formed a mecca for radicals and bohemians. Henrietta Rodman, a socialist-feminist high school teacher whose ideas and activities polarized the original organization, became the moving spirit of the new Liberal Club. A charismatic personality who openly lived with many men and had a preference for sandals, loose-flowing gowns, and smoking in public, she attracted attention and strong responses. While her demeanor alienated the founders of the old club, the New Women, who comprised a major segment of the new club, supported her and her advocacy of sexual equality. She forced the New York City Board of Education to grant maternity leaves to married women teachers and advocated a socialistic society with cooperative nurseries and communization of the home.

The Liberal Club offered sanctuary, sympathetic companionship, and intellectual challenge for a diverse membership that included rebels and bohemians. The club at 137 Macdougal Street consisted of two large parlors and a sunroom, and had a piano in the front parlor, sparse furniture, and modern art. Polly's Restaurant, in the basement, supplemented these facilities with its simple, cheap, and satisfying food. The Washington Square Bookstore, at 135 Macdougal Street, became an informal lending library for Max Eastman, John Reed, Floyd Dell, Art Young, George C. Cook, and other prominent cultural and political radicals who belonged to the Liberal Club.

The Liberal Club planted the seed of the new theater in New York City. Its Dramatic Group staged a number of satirical one-act plays by Floyd Dell, but some of its members, finding these productions too amateurish and insufficiently ambitious, formed the Washington Square Players. It produced plays by Eugene O'Neill and George C. Cook, as well as Henrik Ibsen and George Bernard Shaw, and competed with commercial theaters. In addition, Cook worked out most of his plans for the Provincetown Playhouse at the Liberal Club, and many members of the club served in his casts.

The Liberal Club also provided a forum for airing the ideas of cultural and political radicalism. It publicized Freudianism and gave Margaret Sanger one of her major platforms. Bill Haywood preached his message of radical unionism, and Emma Goldman offered a holistic view of society that incorporated political and cultural elements. A sense of fraternity resulted from the dances and the wine-and-talk parties. However, U.S. entry into World War I brought the threat of censorship and a more restrictive national mood that contributed to personal animosity and institutional changes. The Liberal Club disintegrated as members dispersed and its financial condition became precarious. In an increasingly martial society an institutional meeting place for open discussions of art and revolution became a dispensable luxury. Invasions of tourists and the relocation of Polly's made the course of decline irreversible. Nevertheless, in its heyday the Liberal Club served as a setting for community and an incubator of ferment essential to the traffic between cultural and political radicalism.

Mabel Dodge's salon, which lasted from 1912 to 1915, featured the interplays of stimulating ideas and fertile minds in a special setting provided by a dynamic woman. In many ways she seemed to be an unlikely candidate for the role of hostess of a controversial salon because of her self-centered attitude, lack of competence in dealing with ideas, and preoccupation with sexual relationships. Nevertheless, her charisma, energy, and wealth enabled her to construct a temporary stage for the movers and shakers of New York.

Her spacious apartment at 23 Fifth Avenue reflected her distinctiveness in its white decor and Continental furnishings. After completing its interior decoration, Mabel Dodge sought companionship and the opportunity for new experience. Hutchins Hapgood, an author and social critic, introduced her to John Reed, Max Eastman, and Alfred Stieglitz, and contributed the idea of "evenings" that consisted of stimulating conversations and good food and drink in a suitable atmosphere. This concept appealed to Mabel Dodge, who loved to match guests in startling new combinations. Her salon became a leading meeting ground for artists, intellectuals, seekers, and radicals. She possessed a definite and unique style reflected in her long robes, floppy hats, huge turbans, and flowing scarves. Although she said little, she had a faculty for attracting prominent individuals who responded to her setting by speaking with emotion and conviction.

The unpredictable quality that characterized Mabel Dodge's evenings is illustrated by the failure of the heralded confrontation between the socialists and the anarchists and the surprising success of the less promising battle between Bill Haywood and a group of artists about the nature of art and the role of the artist. Other sessions centered on politics, sex, and art, as well as such diverse topics as birth control, feminism, poverty, and the Mexican Revolution. At midnight the focus of the participants shifted as the doors of the dining room opened for a feast: tables laden with plates of ham, turkey, cheese, and salads, and bottles of Scotch, wine, and other liquor. Small-group conversation and departures followed this phase of the evening.

At one of the evenings, Mabel Dodge met John Reed, who incarnated Greenwich Village radicalism; they collaborated in staging the Paterson Pageant and began an affair. They went to Europe together, but their relationship deteriorated when Reed refused her demand to be the sole focus of his life. When they returned to the United States, the evenings resumed but the old spirit couldn't be recaptured. By 1915 Mabel Dodge had retreated from the daily issues of the world, and the doors of the salon closed. The salon served as an outlet for the ferment of the prewar years, when its participants saw no conflict between the struggle to shape the social order and the struggle to enhance oneself.

Although centered on the evenings in this period, Mabel Dodge saw revolutionary developments in literature and the visual arts, and intuitively sensed the importance of these changes. She became involved in the creative spirit of the new movement, although her fundamental interest remained the effect of people on her and her effect on them. Her frequent visits to Stieglitz's Gallery 291 excited her. She donated time and money to the preparation of the Armory Show and helped introduce Gertrude Stein to the American public. Dodge's salon and Gallery 291 offered Greenwich Villagers major sites for thoughtful and lively discussions.

Gallery 291 focused on the legendary Alfred Stieglitz, a herald and sponsor of modern art in America, the father of modern photography, and the hub of a group of important cultural figures. He fought formalism and indifference to aesthetic standards by battling for the highest level of craftsmanship in art and welcoming newness in every field of human endeavor. Stieglitz condemned the rampant commercialism of American society and counterposed the standard of uncomprising purity in art and theater without regard for pecuniary factors. A philosophical anarchist, he sought to create a climate conducive to free disclosure and discovery. Gallery 291 welcomed all comers and featured spontaneous and animated conversation; it constituted a forum and laboratory where new artistic expressions could be examined and evaluated.

However, Stieglitz experienced a growing sense of personal alienation that his work illustrated. The early pictures, warm with human life, gave way to nature scenes generally denuded of man as his work moved from a focus on the social to abstraction and concern for form. Stieglitz displayed and explained European avant-garde painting in a series of pioneering shows and in *Camera Work*, and also sponsored progressive American painters when other art dealers in New York ignored them. After 1913 Stieglitz played a more passive role in the New York art world as a result of the emergence of new galleries and periodicals, but especially because of the challenge of Mabel Dodge's salon and the dramatic effects of the Armory Show. Although recognized as the spiritual father of the progressive artists, he played no direct role in organizing the show that nevertheless conformed to many principles.

Other artists also fought the academic approach that focused on the value of inherited tradition rather than the forthright depiction of nature or the inner emotional world of the artist. As exemplifed in the National Academy of Design, most American art at the turn of the twentieth century had a sentimental and uninspired character. Led by Robert Henri, a countermovement emerged that opposed blind obedience to established standards and favored more freedom, greater emphasis on American art, and depiction of the life of the common people. The activities of Henri and his followers led to the exhibit of "The Eight," followed by the Exhibition of Independent Artists in 1910, in which Henri and John Sloan played prominent roles. Concurrently, although with different orientations, Henri and Sloan, along with Stieglitz and his Gallery 291 and *Camera Work*, helped to pave the way for the Armory Show.

The fledgling Association of American Painters and Sculptors, which drew membership from "The Eight" and the Exhibit of Independent Artists, undertook the massive assignment of sponsoring and assembling this major international exhibit. Arthur Davies and Walter Kuhn assembled 1,300 major works of modern European and American art for the purpose of presenting a coherent exposition of modern art to educate the American people. European avant-garde forms, from Post-Impressionism to Cubism, received most of the attention as the show provided Americans with an opportunity to view the works of Cézanne, Gauguin, and Van Gogh. Exhibits in New York, Chicago, and Boston drew an aggregate attendance of almost 300,000 and stimulated the sale of modern paintings.

Most of the press responded critically, especially to the newest manifestations of the artistic revolution, with their sharpest shafts aimed at Matisse. Their critique focused on the immorality of the artwork and the incompetence of the artists. In their opinion, European culture posed a danger to the wholesome, youthful culture of America. Some critics drew parallels between artistic insurgency and political radicalism, viewing both phenomena as harbingers of anarchy and part of a global movement to degrade and destroy. The *New York Times*, for example, described the Cubists and Futurists as cousins to the anarchists in politics who, by speaking in a special language understood by themselves, became as anarchistic as those who would overthrow all social laws.

Although hailed as a path-breaking event in twentieth-century American art, the Armory Show made little money and set the stage for a split between realists and modernists that destroyed the Association of American Artists and Sculptors. Nevertheless, it introduced a whole generation of American artists to modern art, fostered the emergence of new galleries open to the exhibits of progressive American artists, and helped to sensitize American collectors to the importance of this new realm of art. After the Armory Show the art establishment no longer exercised uncontested dominance over the art world.

The Paterson Pageant, a form of "social art," arose from the conjunction of a strike by silk workers, supported by the Industrial Workers of the World, in Paterson, New Jersey, and efforts by John Reed. The Industrial Workers of the World, a radical industrial union, conducted a successful textile strike in Lawrence, Massachusetts, in 1912 that catapulted the organization to public attention and into the hearts of the Greenwich Villagers. The following year immigrant silk workers struck against oppressive working conditions in Paterson, and Reed, already sympathetic to underdogs, heard Bill Haywood discuss the strike at a Mabel Dodge evening. Impressed and aroused by Haywood's depiction, he traveled to Paterson to witness the strike. While in the city he was arrested and jailed for failing to move when ordered to do so by a policeman. This experience gave Reed the opportunity to observe the courage, warmth, and humanity of the strikers, and the impressive qualities of Haywood and the other leaders. After his release from jail he published an angry article in *The Masses* critical of the violence of mill owners and their supporters.

The Villagers attended mass meetings in support of the Industrial Workers of the World, but they wanted to increase their contribution. The idea of a Paterson Pageant, to be staged in Madison Square Garden, emerged. The basic concept consisted of a dramatization of the main events of the strike, with the workers as the actresses and actors. Reed immersed himself in writing and staging the production, assisted by Robert Jones, who designed the stage setting, and John Sloan, who painted the scenery. Aided by spectacular sets, the pageant achieved instant success and established an intense rapport between the performers and the audience, composed largely of New York workers with a sprinkling of bohemians. The play depicted the strike, the funeral of a striker, mass meetings, processions, speaking, singing, and the dispatch of the children of the strikers to the homes of supporters in other cities. Although a moving, evocative work of art, it couldn't banish the world of exploitation, and the mill owners triumphed in the strike. It failed as a fund raiser, but, as Randolph Bourne phrased it, ". . . it stamped into one's mind the idea that a new social art was in the American world, something genuinely and excitingly new."

The Provincetown Playhouse, a result of the joint efforts of George Cram Cook and Eugene O'Neill, with help from John Reed, gave the Villagers an opportunity to participate in the theater as writers, performers, and audience. Cook, a product of the Middle West, grew up with a sense of high expectation that he interpreted as a mission to nurture a community of artists who could re-create the glories of Periclean Athens. He went to Chicago and New York, searching for freedom and outlets for creative self-expression. Disdaining the artificiality and standardization of Broadway and the American theater in general, he sought the opportunity to stage plays of a realist and experimental character. A mercurial and undisciplined person, his initial excitement with the Washington Square Players turned to disdain when they rejected one of his plays. He formed the Provincetown Playhouse to bring the European tradition of "free theater"—social criticism and psychological drama—to the United States. Provincetown, the summer enclave of the Greenwich Villagers in Massachusetts, offered a setting for experimentation. John Reed, who had earlier influenced Cook with the Paterson Pageant and his enthusiasm for an ancient miracle play, now contributed his energy and plays to the early efforts of the players. The discovery of Eugene O'Neill made the first season a success and provided glowing prospects for the future.

However, while Cook saw the Playhouse as a potential catalyst of an American renaissance and a means of individual achievement, most Villagers had a more restricted conception of its nature. Their partial commitment, in contrast with the total immersion of Cook, involved authorship of one-act plays, some amateurish acting, and having a good time. Light, satirical plays focused on life in Greenwich Village, such as the love affair between Mabel Dodge and John Reed, pleased the performers and the audiences, but left Cook dissatisfied. The production of Eugene O'Neill's plays in Provincetown and New York offered Cook a mission, O'Neill an audience, and the Playhouse a destiny. After a successful production of *Bound East for Cardiff*, the Players staged *Emperor Jones* in 1920. This event brought national recognition to Eugene O'Neill and the Provincetown Playhouse. However, the war undermined the mood of fun and experimentation, O'Neill and Cook quarreled, and Cook abandoned the Playhouse and went to Greece. The Provincetown Playhouse left a mark on the history of the American theater by launching the career of Eugene O'Neill and influencing the direction of Broadway.

PUBLICATIONS

The Masses, as the fullest expression of the mood of freedom and creativity, provided a major rallying point for the interaction of cultural and political radicals. It tried to harness energy, youth, and hope to a vehicle of change, and it stood for fun, truth, beauty, and freedom as well as peace, feminism, and revolution. Its editors, contributors, and readers yearned for changes in tastes, habits, and morals. A bright and bold publication, it featured a beautifully designed format that appealed to a readership including most progressive intellectuals in the United States and important European writers. The editors viewed their publication as a popular socialist magazine, and filled its pages with provocative cartoons and lively writing. They rallied to the defense of the birth control crusade and published many articles about the class struggle. John Reed's "War in Paterson" depicted a labor war between mill owners and workers in which the exploitative capitalists used violence against the gentle, alert, and brave strikers. An article on the Wheatland Riot in California described a scene in which the sheriff and his deputies, acting in behalf of the owners of a ranch, opened fire on a peaceable crowd;

the strike leaders were imprisoned and the sheriff and the ranch owners were exonerated. *The Masses* also featured articles on the labor struggle in Colorado in which the money interests, led by Rockefeller, attempted to crush the United Mine Workers in a struggle climaxed by the Ludlow Massacre, in which the militia destroyed a tent colony, killing and wounding the children and wives of the miners in the process.

The nature and success of *The Masses* owed much to its editor in chief, Max Eastman. Handsome of face and figure and gifted of mind, he combined romanticism as an attitude toward life with the scientific method as a way of thinking. After completing his education at Williams and Columbia, he settled in New York and became a feminist who spoke frequently for equal rights for women. As editor of *The Masses* from 1912 to 1917, Eastman brought strength of character, great charm, and organizational ability to the twin tasks of organizing and financing the periodical. He espoused Marxism, supported the working class, and admired the Industrial Workers of the World. He viewed Freudianism as a new faith that could change bourgeois social conventions by liberating the emotions. Eastman strongly supported birth control and linked it with socialism by declaring that the population explosion caused poverty and undermined worker militancy.

Floyd Dell, associate editor, exerted an influence second only to Eastman's. He presented a rationale for the magazine's position on sexual freedom, birth control, and feminism. In Dell's view, socialism and feminism operated as equal partners in the struggle for the economic and social changes needed to produce a society with justice and freedom for all. Feminism would liberate men by introducing the economic independence of women and would make it possible for love relationships to supersede marriage. Sexual freedom and the possible ephemerality of love made birth control essential. Dell and Eastman also used the pages of *The Masses* to condemn the double standard, criticize antiquated divorce laws, and characterize prostitution as an outgrowth of the capitalist system.

The euphoric era of *The Masses* drew to a close as the United States drifted into military involvement in World War I. War ended the honeymoon period for political and cultural radicals that had rested on the struggle against a common enemy, the latitudinarianism of the Socialist Party of America, and an optimistic mood. It produced a major dilemma for radicals that they handled in different ways. Some responded by taking an anti-war stand as an essential posture for fostering the emergence of a democratic and creative society. Others, mostly cultural in their basic orientation, saw the increasing preoccupation with the war as undermining the mood of fun and joy, and threatening the balance and interchange between the cultural and political realms. From a cultural perspective they could be somewhat sanguine about the results of their rebellion and fearful about setbacks. Book and periodical publishers had opened their pages to new writers and their modern forms and subjects.

The contrast between the seventy-fifth birthday celebration for William Dean Howells in 1912 and the response to his eightieth birthday symbolized the transformation of the literary realm. The former occasion drew 400 members of the national elite, including President Taft, and received extensive press coverage; the latter event received passing mention. In the art world the rise of "The Eight" and especially the Armory Show undermined the establishment and opened opportunities for younger, more innovative artists to exhibit and sell their work, and gain recognition from galleries and collectors. The theater also changed as the Provincetown Playhouse and other new theaters emerged, European playwrights became more popular, and Eugene O'Neill received increasing acclaim.

The political realm, on the other hand, looked much less promising. With the outbreak of World War I, almost all European socialist parties abandoned international working-class solidarity to champion the war aims of their homelands. The carnage of the battlefield boded ill for the dreams of the socialist commonwealth. On the home fronts, governments established machines of national conformity. The United States passed legislation that restricted civil liberties and inaugurated a draft. Many cultural radicals, taking pride in the changes in their realm, viewed the opportunities for immediate, fundamental political transformation as negligible and feared that they would be victims in a war between the government and increasingly sectarian political leaders. They could recall that some of the critics of the Armory Show linked modern European art and anarchy. A perception by political leaders of a bond between political and cultural radicalism in a time of national emergency could lead to a political and popular "backlash" that would deprive cultural radicals of hard-won gains on the cultural front. Moreover, some cultural radicals began to focus on changes in the form of expression, rather than the subject matter or the political posture of the artist, as the real measure of cultural radicalism. This perspective provided less common ground for solidarity with political radicals.

The war, while stimulating solidarity in some circles, undermined the convergence of cultural and political radicalism in general and in *The Masses* in particular. The special character of *The Masses* resulted from its combination of good reportage and excellent graphics. It attracted talented cartoonists, not only because of its stance on issues and the freedom that it granted to its contributors, but also because of the increasing reliance of the press on photographers, which led to the technological obsolescence of newspaper illustrators and the migration of many of them to New York. For a time the tolerant spirit of the era and the conciliatory talents of Max Eastman prevented the latent conflicts between contributors about the relationship between writers and artists and art and politics from becoming public and divisive issues. However, the 1916–17 crisis brought a stronger anti-war stance in editorials, articles, and cartoons, and shattered the tenuous unity. John Sloan and Art Young became the leaders of opposing factions of cartoonists.

The special nurturing character of the era and locale of the Greenwich Village Rebellion had encouraged their ephemeral collaboration until a time of crisis unlocked their latent differences and conflicts. John Sloan spent time as a journalist, but painting urban scenes became his primary interest. The successful struggle against the art establishment opened new opportunities for dissident artists. Sloan loved *The Masses* and spent much time working for it. However, his real work remained elsewhere. Although a democratic socialist for a time and an admirer of Eugene V. Debs and his humanism, he had a limited commitment to social change and wouldn't convert his art into a weapon for socialism. Human beings interested him more than schemes for human betterment. He presented a glimpse of daily life by drawing caricatures of social manners, and seldom conveyed a deep political point. When the war came, Sloan wanted *The Masses* to maintain a posture of good humor and opposed its decision to take a political position because he considered a balanced, nonpolitical approach more beneficial to the magazine and society.

Art Young, Sloan's chief adversary, worked as a journalist in Chicago in an era when technological and economic change transformed the world of journalism. Cartoonists, in particular, saw their position deteriorate as the use of photographs became more wide-spread. Moving to New York, Young became radicalized, and by 1910 he decided he belonged with the socialists in their fight against the capitalists. His cartoons and captions gave the viewer an inside picture of social relations characterized by hypocrisy and corruption. *The Masses* offered Young the major outlet for his politics and his talent.

Editorial discretion to caption cartoons precipitated the outbreak of the controversy. Sloan and his allies saw this function as usurpation by the editors that politicized their work and reduced its effectiveness. Behind the caption battle stood the issue of the philosophy of *The Masses*. Sloan focused on acute observations of situations with social importance, while Young advocated greater politicizing by direct attacks on capitalism in all its manifestations. World War I crystallized the issue of the proper means of promoting socialism in a magazine of politics and culture.

Other contributors split over the issue of American involvement, with the majority, led by Eastman, Dell, Reed, and Young, opposing intervention. By 1917 they lashed out at President Wilson and opposed conscription. Anti-war editorials, articles, and drawings dominated the publication. Its anti-war position led to *The Masses* being banned from the mails and newsstands, and the indictment of several editors and contributors. Eastman, Reed, Dell, and Young underwent two trials that ended in hung juries. However, by this time Sloan and his associates and the right-wing socialists had departed. The suppression undermined the magazine's financial position, and it expired with the November–December 1917 issue.

The demise of *The Masses* set the stage for *The Liberator*, also edited by Max Eastman, which followed some of the currents of its predecessor but took a more political turn. It operated in a less optimistic and tolerant era, and featured articles on major strikes, the suppression of radicals, and developments in Europe. Feminism and cultural radicalism faded as forces promoting fundamental change. No successor emerged to match the incisive reportage and memorable graphics of *The Masses*. Earnest and substantial as well as fun to look at and read, its anti-capitalistic ethic made it appealing to radicals and bohemians in Greenwich Village, whatever their particular orientation.

The inability of *The Liberator* to sustain effective political radicalism and traffic between cultural and political radicalism symbolized a general characteristic of the 1920s. The Greenwich Village organizations no longer performed a synthesizing function. The character of the area changed as the subway and widened streets made it more accessible to tourists and new residents. This shift undermined the Liberal Club, which also suffered from the increasing conservatism of feminism and the individualism of the 1920s. Mabel Dodge departed for the Southwest and her salon closed. The Provincetown Playhouse lost its experimental nature as personality conflicts, the lure of professionalism and publicity, and the changing nature of Broadway deprived it of its special mission. Gallery 291 no longer attracted radicals eager for exposure to modern art and conversation as Alfred Stieglitz retreated from the public arena to focus on himself, his friends, and art. The Association of American Painters and Sculptors disappeared after playing its historical role as sponsor of the Armory Show. The demise of *The Masses* and *The Seven Arts*, a leading organ of cultural radicalism, also took its toll.

THE DECLINE OF RADICALISM

The loss of key individuals played a crucial role in the divergence and decline of radicalism. Emma Goldman and Margaret Sanger followed divergent paths; the birth control movement lost its connection with radicalism and took a conservative turn. Political radicalism suffered a triple blow with the imprisonment of Eugene Debs and the exile of Bill Haywood and Emma Goldman. Some cultural radicals, such as John Sloan, lessened and moderated their political involvement. The deaths of John Reed and Randolph Bourne robbed the movement of two heroic, creative figures.

Major national movements that had interacted with the radicalism of Greenwich Village lost their vitality. Freudianism became the basis for cocktail party conversation and dream books rather than a force for social change. The form of the flapper and the freedom to consume embodied the popular mode of feminism. The Socialist Party of America fragmented and faded, the Industrial Workers of the World suffered from repression and a changing economy, and the Communist Party remained weak because of internal decay and dissension and strong societal opposition.

Uncomfortable with the weak and unpopular American left of the 1920s, many young artists went to Paris to escape the cultural conformity of the United States and become residents of the homeland of bohemia and modern European culture. These uprooted Americans thought that Europeans knew how to live; the trip to Europe would also expose them to the masters of literary and artistic modernism. Other cultural radicals followed the path to the small towns of Connecticut; Van Wyck Brooks, for instance, settled in Westport. Searching for the roots of American culture, he earlier had noted the deadlock in American minds between the highbrow, who prizes the sublime, and the lowbrow, who focuses on practicality and business, and offered a middle plan as the preferable level. It was necessary to create objects of loyalty capable of bringing the springs of creative energy into play. The younger generation, wandering in the wilderness and drifting into unproductive channels, needed a great corporate purpose to inspire—a poetic rather than a pragmatic approach to life. The nation needed a class of cultural pioneers to reforest its spiritual territory.

Brooks and Bourne, key figures on *The Seven Arts*, which became a casualty of the war in 1917, shared a cultural orientation critical of puritanism and the materialism of America, an optimism about the potential of young intellectuals to inaugurate change, and a hopefulness about creating a society with a positive common direction and purpose. However, while the war crisis and its aftermath radicalized Bourne, Brooks became increasingly conservative as an advocate of American nationalism and a critic of literary modernists.

Greenwich Village in 1910–20 provided one of the major examples of traffic between cultural and political radicalism in the history of the United States. Socialism, syndicalism, and anarchism had their Village adherents, and the institutions of Greenwich Village provided publicity and assistance for these movements. In the cultural sphere, Villagers played an important role as critics of middle-class life, especially its conformity, hypocrisy, and materialism. They viewed the cultures of Eastern and Southern European immigrants, Native Americans, and Afro-Americans more sympathetically. They experienced and publicized a way of life focused on comradeship, freedom, and joy. Viewing the body as a temple, they exalted sexual freedom, female equality, and birth control. Greenwich Village called for a new American culture, erected on the foundation laid by Walt Whitman, that would provide the spirit and undergirding of a new society. Villagers admired the works of modern European writers and publicized them. They praised and staged the plays of leading European dramatists and introduced Eugene O'Neill to the theatrical world and the American public. They published and publicized the work of Amy Lowell and other new poets. Initially with the work of "The Eight," and later by means of Gallery 291, Mabel Dodge's salon, and the Armory Show, Villagers played an important role in introducing modern art to the American public.

Their visionary orientation, while it undermined some opportunities for programmatic initiatives, gave a valuable breadth and spirit to radicalism. Nevertheless, their achievements fell short of their vast goals as the limitations of some of the participants undermined the effectiveness of the movement. The rebels saw a direct connection between the personal and social realms, and sometimes exaggerated the societal significance of their private lives. They aspired to be creators of a new culture and harbingers of revolution, but at times neglected the difficult tasks of formulating a coherent program and devising means to implement their ideas. Some radicals lacked depth and duration of commitment and belonged to the intellectual proletarians who, according to Emma Goldman, displayed an aloof sympathy for the working class and its oppression but wouldn't establish solidarity with the disinherited. As they hovered in a void outside the class relationships of society, they looked to friendships to supply the richness missing from the larger social and political life. However, their overemphasis on personal life placed an unsupportable burden on friendship. As a result, rivalries and splits emerged, and Greenwich Village developed some of the hierarchical features of mainstream society. Sometimes Villagers engaged in self-indulgence and romanticism while neglecting creativity and political organizing.

Radicals and radicalism found it difficult to do justice to both cultural and political spheres. Few individual radicals—Randolph Bourne was one major exception—achieved first rank in both domains. Even the most conscientious synthesizers usually gave clear priority to one sphere, especially when a time of crisis seemed to make a choice necessary. *The Masses*, the major formal effort to synthesize, illustrated both the extent and the limits of the traffic between cultural and political radicalism. It stood for socialism and the inauguration of the new society as well as advocating feminism, a focus on youth, and freer forms of sexual expression. Its editors saw much value in literary and artistic realism, and provided space and praise for American and European realistic writers. John Sloan and other realistic painters received recognition in its pages. However, those cultural products notable for new form rather than new content received much less attention. Eastman and Dell didn't appreciate the poems of Pound and Eliot or the paintings of the Armory Show, However, they did publish a few drawings by Arthur Davies, who had coordinated the Armory Show. When World War I and the Bolshevik Revolution forced radicals to take a stand, some writers and artists turned to their cultural work, often focusing on form and technique, while most political radicals, notably journalists, authors, and cartoonists, centered on opposition to the war and fostering revolutionary change.

The Greenwich Village Rebellion, although it faded in the 1920s, left a valuable legacy to later radical movements. The New Left of the early and middle 1960s paralleled its predecessor in important ways. Both movements stressed the youth theme and bohemian elements. Success and conventional achievement seemed deadening and contemptible. An attempt to establish human relationships on the basis of love and spontaneous, "authentic" emotion received their approbation. They desired an environment with a sense of high purpose, a community with the opportunity for more interesting and meaningful life. Both movements criticized capitalism and opposed military intervention by the United States in a controversial war. They criticized the reigning sexual morality and emphasized love rather than marriage. In Greenwich Village and in the 1960s, women and their issues played important roles, but men retained control and sexual equality remained elusive.

For a time the New Left demonstrated some of the tolerance and openness of its predecessor, but in both cases the escalation of foreign conflict and the intensification of domestic suppression led to increasing dogmatism and sectarianism, and a decline in the traffic between political and cultural radicals. By the late 1960s the Students for a Democratic Society fragmented, the hippies aligned with the counterculture, and many radical women and blacks left the general movement to form more particularist organizations. In the 1920s and the 1970s mainstream society eschewed political radicalism, although some radicals operated in community groups and the anti-nuclear movement in the 1970s and in the Socialist and Communist parties in the 1920s. However, society accepted diluted versions of cultural radicalism devoid of its earlier political content. They embraced the flapper, birth control, and Freudianism in the 1920s and accepted new clothing styles, modern music, and drugs in the 1970s.

The Greenwich Village Rebellion formed a major part of the tradition of American cultural and political radicalism. It drew on the ideas of the Transcendentalists, Walt Whitman, and the Muckrakers, and provided a solid foundation for its twentieth-century successors. Although internal defects and powerful adversaries precluded the realization of its goals, it supported the underdog, presented the dream of a just society, and exhibited a joy in living. Its efforts contributed to the increased acceptance of the new art, theater, and literature. Richard Hofstadter, a skeptic about the compatibility of bohemian life and serious creative or political purposes, nevertheless praised it as "a bright movement in our own history before the First World War when esthetic experimentation, courageous social criticism, and the Bohemian life all seemed to converge . . ." (Hofstadter 1963, p. 426). For a brief time Greenwich Village hosted viable traffic between cultural and political radicalism.

REFERENCES

Aaron, Daniel. 1961. *Writers on the Left: Episodes in American Literary Communism.* New York: Harcourt, Brace and World.

Brooks, Van Wyck. 1955. *John Sloan; A Painter's Life.* New York: Sutton.

——. 1924. *America's Coming-of-Age.* New York: B. W. Huebsch.

Brown, Milton Wolf. 1963. *The Story of the Armory Show.* Greenwich, Conn.: Joseph H. Hirshorn Foundation.

Cheuse, Alan. 1982. *The Bohemians: John Reed and His Friends Who Shook the World.* Cambridge, Mass.: Apple-Wood Books.

Cowley, Malcolm. 1963. *Exile's Return, A Literary Odyssey of the 1920's.* New York: Viking Press.

Dell, Floyd. 1933. *Homecoming: An Autobiography.* New York: Farrar and Rinehart.

Eastman, Max. 1948. *Enjoyment of Living.* New York: Harper.

Filler, Louis. 1966. *Randolph Bourne.* New York: Citadel Press.

Fishbein, Leslie. 1982. *Rebels in Bohemia: The Radicals of the Masses, 1911–1917.* Chapel Hill: University of North Carolina Press.

Fitzgerald, Richard. 1973. *Art and Politics: Cartoonists of the Masses and Liberator.* Westport, Conn.: Greenwood Press.

Golin, Steven. 1983. "Defeat Becomes Disaster: The Paterson Strike of 1913 and the Decline of the I.W.W." *Labor History* 24 (Spring 1983): 223–48.

Hofstadter, Richard. 1963. *Anti-Intellectualism in American Life.* New York: Random House.

Humphrey, Robert. 1978. *Children of Fantasy: The First Rebels of Greenwich Village.* New York: Wiley.

John Reed Papers. Harvard University.

Lottman, Herbert R. 1982. *The Left Bank: Writers, Artists, and Politics from the Popular Front to the Cold War.* Boston: Houghton Mifflin.

Luhan Mabel (Ganson) Dodge. 1936. *Movers and Shakers.* New York: Harcourt, Brace and Co.

The Masses, 1912–18.

May, Henry F. 1959. *The End of American Innocence; A Study of the First Years of Our Own Time, 1912–1917.* New York: Knopf.

O'Neill, William. 1978. *The Lost Romantic: A Life of Max Eastman.* New York: Oxford University Press.

Osborne, James. 1980. "Paterson: Immigrant Strikers and the War of 1913." In *At the Point of Production: A Local History of the I.W.W.*, edited by Joseph R. Conlin, Westport, Conn.: Greenwood Books.

Randolph Bourne Papers. Columbia University.

Resek, Carl, ed. 1964. *War and the Intellectuals: Essays by Randolph S. Bourne 1915–1919.* New York: Harper & Row.

Richwine, Keith Norton. 1968. "The Liberal Club: Bohemia and Resurgence in Greenwich Village, 1912-1918." Ph.D. dissertation, University of Pennsylvania.

Rosenstone, Robert A. 1980. "Mabel Dodge: Evenings in New York." In *Affairs of the Mind: The Salon in Europe and America from the 18th to the 20th Century*, edited by Peter Quennell, pp. 131-50. Washington, D.C.: New Republic Books.

———. 1975. *Romantic Revolutionary: A Biography of John Reed.* New York: Knopf.

The Seven Arts. 1917.

Sochen, June. 1972. *The New Woman: Feminism in Greenwich Village, 1910-1920.* New York: Quadrangle Books.

Unger, Irwin. 1974. *The Movement: A History of the American New Left, 1959-1972.* New York: Dodd, Mead.

Ware, Caroline F. 1935. *Greenwich Village, 1920-1930; A Comment on the Civilization in the Post-War Years.* Boston: Houghton Mifflin.

Wertheim, Arthur Frank. 1976. *The New York Little Renaissance: Iconoclasm, Modernism, and Nationalism in American Culture, 1908-1917.* New York: New York University Press.

3 Revolutionary Art versus Art for the Revolution: Dadaists and Leninists, 1916–23

Jerold M. Starr

The half century or so from the 1870s into the 1920s was a period of tremendous upheaval in Europe. Most countries were being transformed by rapid industrialization, urbanization, and economic growth. The expansion of the state and the marketplace had the effect both of undermining traditional networks of social and economic security and of liberating many at the bottom from their conventional status obligations. Challenged from below by youth, women, workers, and ethnic minorities seeking greater participation, many governments responded with calls for increased productivity, heightened nationalism, and imperialist expansion—calls that brought all countries inexorably closer to world war.

As the modern nation-state and the corporate marketplace expanded, they extended their logic of instrumental rationality into more and more areas of traditional society. Calculation replaced custom in political and economic affairs. This new cultural hegemony was resisted by a great many artists and intellectuals, who advanced their own neo-Romantic visions of social life.

During the first quarter of the twentieth century, there was a veritable revolution in the arts. Innovation was especially dramatic in

I wish to express my personal gratitude to Jeff Halley, State University of New York at Purchase, who shared that wonderful summer of 1979 with us. Jeff is a colleague and a friend from whom I learned a great deal about the Dada movement and the sociology of art in general.

painting and sculpture, including the forms (surfaces, materials), contents (choice and representation of subject matter), and applications of art. Such innovations expressed deeper changes in the relationship of the artist to the public and to the art establishment that were intimately related to changes in the artist's view of self and of the social purpose of art.

Most of the developments of the period reached their climax in World War I and the movement called Dada (1916–23). During this historical moment of resistance to capitalist rationalization, many attempted to connect Dada's cultural radicalism to the Marxist-Leninist revolution that had toppled the Russian czar and was shaking liberal strongholds all over Weimar Germany. This period and the relationship between these movements are especially revealing subjects in the study of the historical experience and possibilities of cultural politics in modern society.

THE HISTORICAL CONTEXT

As mentioned, the period from 1870 until the outbreak of World War I was marked by the increasing dominance of the industrial nation-state. Subsistence agriculture, barter exchange, and reciprocity systems were replaced rapidly by wage labor, cash exchange, and private property. Regional and religious differences gave way to national languages, more uniform dress, large urban centers, mass public education, and mass-circulation newspapers, all contributing to the sense of a common nationality.

The extension of new technologies into all spheres of life raised expectations for a safer, cleaner, and more comfortable future. Advances in transportation and communication had a special impact on the spirit of the times. After 1880 distances were shortened and new worlds made more accessible by the development of the bicycle, the motorcycle, the high-speed railroad, and the steamship, and the building of new canals. By the 1920s automobiles and airplanes were moving large numbers in record time. Developments in mass communications further accelerated this "new rhythm of movement" and "new, more discontinuous and disjointed sense of space and time." These included the "fast-moving and jerky cinema," trans-atlantic telephone calls, oceanic cables, and radio broadcasts (Wohl 1979, p. 227).

The widespread political and economic changes taking place undermined the authority of traditional elites and moved large segments of the population to seek a better life:

> Oppressed peoples were clamoring for statehood. Workers were insisting on higher wages and shorter hours. Peasants were demanding land or more favorable sharecropping arrangements. Everywhere in Europe there was a movement to open political participation to larger groups of people. . . . Authority, whether exercised by landlords, factory owners, clergymen, or fathers within their own families, was being angrily disputed. (Wohl 1979, p. 211)

THE RISE OF THE AVANT-GARDE:
THE ARTIST AS REBEL PROPHET

This challenge to authority also took place in the world of ideas. During the fin de siècle many intellectuals staged a "revolt against positivism." Reacting against an overly rationalized model of man and an overdetermined conception of society and history, these young thinkers proposed new "philosophies of life" (Mannheim 1971, p. 220; Hughes 1961, p. 428). Such philosophies rejected all forms of bourgeois rationalism as inadequate to comprehend the complexity of modern man. The philosophies of life held that, beneath the reified categories of abstract reason, there breathed the "non-logical, the uncivilized, the inexplicable"; beyond the "iron determinism" of social Darwinism there reigned the "freely speculating mind" (Hughes 1961, pp. 36, 39). Such modern thinkers as Freud, Jung, Weber, Croce, Bergson, Pareto, Proust, and Gide led the challenge.

According to Hughes (1961, pp. 35–36), only a very few of these thinkers could be considered "neo-romantic . . . the truly great either were hostile to what they took to be neo-romantic tendencies or, like Freud and Weber, sought to curb the romanticism they discovered within themselves. . . . The social thinkers of the 1890s were concerned with the irrational only to exorcise it." However, the intellectual generation that succeeded them, "the young men of 1905 . . . became frankly irrationalist or even antirationalist."

The new machine age themes of speed, domination, power, and travel became equated with "spiritual rebirth," the widespread belief that "an entire world or culture was about to be renewed." Many looked for this cultural renewal from the growing legions of educated youth and in the concept of youth as "a state of mind, a style of life" destined to bring down the old and bring in the new (Wohl 1979, pp. 227–39).

The young men of 1905 "were no longer satisfied with the urbane detachment of their elders. Everywhere, they were in search of an ideal." Such thinkers as Stefan George in Germany and Gabriele d'Annunzio in Italy promoted a youthful spirit through a "cult of spontaneous creation." More frankly Romantic interpretations of Nietzsche and Bergson were used to justify "direct-action politics" in Germany and France. In this sense, the revolt against positivism of the fin de siècle planted the seeds of a new Romantic movement that was to last into the first few years of the 1920s, spanning over 30 years in all (Hughes 1961).

The Romantic challenge was especially pronounced in the arts and letters. Throughout Europe there arose bohemian colonies of painters and poets. They lived in the proletarian sections of modern cities where studio space was available at cheap rents. Because of lack of electricity, running water, heat, or furnishings, their social life was spent largely in public eating houses where the owners and even waiters occasionally accepted works of art as payment for food or drink.

These young artists challenged the authority of the art establishment (the museum directors, gallery owners, academy professors, and art critics) and rebelled against the conventional techniques. They rejected the mimetic tradition applied to portraits of the wealthy and powerful or religious themes. Instead, they painted natural scenes of simple laborers and peasants, frequently in the style of the African and Oceanic primitives. They spurned commercial success as corrupting of the creative spirit and came to think of themselves as rebel "prophets and esthetic law givers," identifying with "the poets and philosophers as intellectuals worthy of high social position." Influenced by historicism and Romanticism, many artists "came increasingly to see themselves as especially sensitive instruments of the Zeitgeist," an avant-garde on the frontier of its time (Shapiro 1976, p. 65).

In major cities throughout Europe the prewar period featured a continuous wave of new movements in art. The reigning Impressionists were challenged by the Postimpressionists, Expressionists, Fauves, Cubists, Futurists, and, finally, Dadaists and Surrealists. Giuliano (1968, p. 14) writes:

Each faction commanded its own cafe and social scene. They competed for the position of avant garde and often melded and changed as artists would switch allegiance from cubism to surrealism and back again. It was common to issue a manifesto and to seek the alliance of poets and intellectuals to help the generally non-verbal artists articulate their aims.

All of these movements encouraged the artist to "renounce all illusion of reality on principle," to give expression to his or her subjective perception of the world by deliberately distorting natural forms and colors to reveal a deeper truth (Hauser 1958, p. 229). Expressionist painter Emil Nolde explained:

> There are no firm esthetic rules. The artist creates a work according to his nature and instincts. He himself stands astonished before the result, and others with him, and only gradually does the new allow itself to be grasped rationally or put into esthetic rules. Art wants to give itself; it does not want to be dictated to, either by the will or by reason. (Shapiro 1976, p. 87)

Under the leadership of Kandinsky, the Expressionist Blaue Reiter (Blue Rider) group (1911–14) made the final break with representational art and entered completely into the realm of abstraction. Kramer (1981, p. 18) writes, "Under the influence of theosophical doctrines that looked upon the material universe as a snare and a delusion, Kandinsky turned to the realm of the 'spirit' as his artistic province, and thus initiated an artistic revolution that fatefully altered the whole course of modern art."

The Cubists extended the Blaue Reiter's experimentation with color to the investigation of form, but rejected the nostalgic Romanticism of their predecessors. Discovering the artistic possibilities of industrial images and materials, the Cubists promoted abstraction as the hallmark of the modern spirit. The Cubists and those who followed constituted a movement to create a modern art for the new machine age, to break down "the traditional division of fine art from the applied and commercial arts," and to produce "a new vision of an integrated modernist culture based on a creative alliance of aesthetics and technology" (Kramer 1979, p. 45). In this new vision the "avant-garde" would become the culture of the bourgeoisie.

Although sympathetic to the anarchist, socialist, and democratic movements of their day, the Expressionist artists chose to refrain from active participation in politics. Instead, they emphasized the cultural dimensions of their rebellion. For example, the Fauvist Maurice Vlaminck withdrew from anarchist politics to express revolt in his landscape paintings, which featured "violent brush strokes and heavy daubs of bright color." He explained:

> What I could have done only by throwing a bomb—which would have led me to the scaffold, I attempted to realize in my art, in painting, by using colors of maximum purity. Thus I satisfied my desire to destroy old conventions, to "disobey," in order to recreate a sensitive, living, and liberated world. (Shapiro 1976, p. 30)

While many in France and Germany reacted against rampant industrial capitalism and rising nationalism, young intellectuals in Italy deplored their country's backwardness and poverty, and were embarrassed by its failure to expand its empire to Ethiopia and surrounds. Moreover, the constitutional monarchy that ruled the country was notorious for its corruption. Italy was rife with political movements challenging the liberal bourgeois administration of Giovanni Giolitti.

In the first decade of the new century, this widespread discontent crystallized in a movement of painters and poets who celebrated industrialization, nationalism, and war. The movement was called Futurism, and its indomitable leader was a "dapper, mustachioed thirty-three year-old poet with a genius for polemic" named Filippo Tommaso Marinetti (Shapiro 1976, p. 106).

Those painters who were to join the Futurist movement under Marinetti's leadership first met as young workmen and art students in Milan and Rome. They all had experimented with left politics and, although they had withdrawn from active participation, still contributed drawings to socialist and anarchist publications.

Marinetti was able to weld these disparate elements into a programmatic movement through a posture of radical negation. By 1905 he had turned against the revisionism of Italian socialism, but stepped up the attack on all ideologies and institutions of the day: monarchism, clericalism, parliaments, bureaucracies, and, above all, gerontocracy. Youth was the constituency Marinetti sought to cultivate, and his utopian dreams rested on the boldness of a new generation of young Italians fed up with the old order and impatient for greatness.

On February 20, 1909, Marinetti published the "Foundation and Manifesto of Futurism" in the Paris newspaper *Le Figaro*, thus launching the movement. In this initial manifesto he "praised energy, danger, violence, war, militarism and patriotism and declared war on museums, libraries, and feminists as well as *passatisti* in general" (Shapiro 1976, p. 108). Over the next five years Marinetti and the Futurists published numerous manifestos, distributed thousands of handbills, made countless speeches, and "planned and staged flamboyant demonstrations in major Italian cities" (Shapiro 1976, p. 50). They wore dark suits that often were pelted with pasta and rotten tomatoes. The succès de scandale that they enjoyed through their many pranks and riots drew attention to their program and their art.

The technique of Futurist art was to employ abstraction in order to reveal essence, in a manner analogous to that of modern science. Breaking down objects in the style of the Cubists, the Futurists sought not simply to uncover basic structural form but also to identify "lines of force" that would "converge upon the sensation of the spectator, driving him into the center of action where simultaneity of movement overwhelms him—or is supposed to" (Newmeyer 1955, p. 100).

The Futurists were the "only group of the avant garde whose art was overtly political." They "grounded their esthetic in a comprehensive social and political program: the rejuvenation and modernization of Italy," enthusiastically espousing "modern life with its crowds, noises, and burgeoning technology" (Shapiro 1976, p. 103). Their favorite subjects included an airplane in flight, social clashes, and riots.

At Marinetti's prodding, the Futurists turned to painting war themes. In 1914 ex-Socialist Benito Mussolini turned interventionist, and in 1915 the Futurists joined forces with his Fasci di Azione Rivoluzionaria. Wohl (1979, p. 178) writes:

> With some reason, Marinetti later claimed that Fascism was a fulfillment of Futurism—or at least of Futurism's minimum program, which included, among other things, "the coming to power of youth against the parliamentary, bureaucratic, academic, and pessimistic spirit." Once in power. Mussolini encouraged the identification of Fascism with Futurism, pronouncing his regime to be one in which "daring" youth would always be preferred to "cowardly" age.

Of course, it was not only the Futurists' program but also their political practice that paved the way for Fascism. In 1924 Croce wrote:

> For anyone who has a sense of historical connections, the ideological origins of Fascism can be found in Futurism, in the determination to go down into the streets, to impose their own opinions, to stop the mouths of those who disagree, not to fear riots or fights, in this eagerness to break with all traditions, in this exultation of youth which was characteristic of Futurism. (Kramer 1980, p. D41)

Although Mussolini didn't reject Futurism until 1919, the decline of the movement was already apparent by 1916. Willet (1978, p. 25) comments: "Looking at Futurism's subsequent decline, it is difficult not to conclude that its grip, both on the most gifted Italians and on the outside world, was broken as soon as Marinetti's right-wing values and slogans could be tested against the realities of war."

THE GREAT WAR: THE GREAT DISILLUSIONMENT

For years a world war seemed both impossible and inevitable. The doctrines of competitive capitalism, utilitarianism, and Spencerian evolutionism held that war was part of the barbaric feudal past and not possible within the modern network of economic interdependence. Nevertheless, major European crises had erupted almost every year after 1895: the Boer War, Fashoda, the Russo-Japanese War, Agadir, the Balkan wars. Moreover, "Germany's determinism to dominate the continent and challenge England's control of the world's seas and markets" made war in Europe appear "inevitable" (Wohl 1979, p. 211).

Middle-class intellectuals, particularly educated youth, welcomed the war as the one "blow of fate" that could reconcile class conflict, mobilize the spiritual interests of the nation, and give birth to a "new, more ethical and less commercial man" to replace the mundane, interest-bound bourgeoisie and proletariat. Indeed, Wohl (1979, p. 217) reports, "When war did break over Europe, it was interpreted by intellectuals as an hour of redemption, a rite of purification, and a chance, perhaps the last, to escape from a sinking and declining civilization."

The reality of the war made a mockery of such hopes and dreams. Before long, the organized bloodbath drove many to disillusionment and despair. In England the "war poets provided the theme: doomed youth led blindly to the slaughter by cruel age" (Wohl 1979, p. 105).

Although the carnage was confined to the combatants, the suffering was widespread. Wohl (1979, p. 217) explains:

> All inhabitants of Europe were exposed to the militarization of life and language, the erosion of individual freedom and social differences, the disruption of economic life, the drain of wealth, the hardship caused by food shortages, the growth of collectivism and bureaucracies, the collapse of the international system and the release of huge reservoirs of aggressivity and violence.

The artistic world suffered serious disruption from the war: "During the first weeks of the war there was a rash of emigrations, voluntary and involuntary." The Germans had to leave France, the Russians had to leave Germany, and many pacifists left their own countries "to avoid conscription or escape the hysteria and suspicion at home" (Shapiro 1976, p. 133). Colonies of émigré artists, writers, and political activists grew up in the large cities of neutral countries: Amsterdam, Barcelona, Lisbon, New York, Geneva, and Zurich.

The art market stopped functioning, making it difficult for even the well-known to make a living. Schools and galleries were closed and publications were censored. Cultural radicalism generally was suppressed by the patriotic conformity demanded by the state in the name of the war effort. Shapiro (1976, p. 142), writes: "As the war ground on, the painters more and more frequently complained of their forced artistic inactivity." They kept in touch with each other by mail and an occasional intermediary, sharing their concerns.

For various reasons Zurich became "the meeting ground for exiles of all sorts—the safe, though scarcely calm, eye of the hurricane" (Shapiro 1976, p. 159). Because of its size, location, and ethnic diversity, Switzerland had an established policy of military neutrality. This allowed Zurich to serve as the unofficial capital of world capitalism, its international banking system preserving the assets of elites and the integrity of capitalist economic relations during periods of defeated diplomacy and military confrontation. As a consequence Zurich, paradoxically, also served as the center for radical refugees seeking asylum from the war. The Rumanian artist Marcel Janco (1957, p. 46), one of the original Dadaists and himself a Zurich refugee during the war, has written:

> Zurich was a haven of refuge amid the sea of fire, of iron and blood. It was not only a refuge but the trysting place for revolutionaries, an

oasis for the thinker, a spy exchange, a nursery of ideologies, and a home for poets and liberty-loving vagabonds. . . . It became a meeting place of the arts. Painters, students, revolutionaries, tourists, international crooks, psychiatrists, the demimonde, sculptors, and polite spies on the look out for information, all hobnobbed with one another.

DADA: THE FINAL NEGATION

It was in Zurich in 1916 that all the young century's trends and movements in art and politics climaxed in what came to be called Dada. Conceived in a spirit of artistic and political revolt, Dada was born into the horror of world war and, over the next seven years, grew to encompass three continents.

The Dadaists accepted the Marxist interpretation of the war as representing the greedy adventurism of a capitalist class grown fat with political power. In the words of the Dadaist Richard Huelsenbeck (1951b, p. 39), "In Zurich the international profiteers sat in the restaurants with well-filled wallets and rosy cheeks, ate with their knives and smacked their lips in a merry hurrah for the countries that were bashing each other's skulls in."

The essential spirit of Zurich Dada was protest. Its attitude was outrage at the destruction of beauty, goodness, and truth by the culture of industrial capitalism, which, collapsing under the weight of its own contradictions, had degenerated into wholesale human slaughter. Dada's artistic and political posture was radical negation, the complete destruction of all traces of the past in order to purify humanity and build a new society on the ruins of the old. Despite the positive affirmation implicit in their position, the Dadaists concentrated on negative action, practicing provocation, not contestation. Zurich Dada constituted a great refusal. It eschewed any desire to convince anybody of anything. Its goal was more direct and simple: to shock a bourgeois public out of its apathy. By unblocking communication and returning people to primary awareness, it hoped to overcome passivity and create movement (Willener 1970). In short, in the words of Hannover Dadaist Max Ernst, "Dada was like a bomb." Dada declared its own war on the smug bourgeoisie that was carrying on business as usual, safely behind the lines. It sought to blow middle-class cultural assumptions into little pieces, to bring the war home.

"The Dada Movement" (1953, p. 670) comments:

> It is true that the original adherents of the movement claimed to be pacifists, but they nevertheless took a paradoxical delight in destruction; they loathed, yet made capital out of, the battles of Verdun and the Somme because the war represented the triumph of chaos over law and order—all that the nineteenth century had most revered. It would have been cowardly and dishonourable, they felt, as well as being opposed to their inverted principles, to refrain from the holocaust. So they proceeded to contribute to it as effectively as possible in their own way. Art, religion, literature, politics, logic, "all social hierarchies" must be abolished they decreed, and Dada (i.e., the cult of negation and anarchy) set up in their stead.

THE ORIGINAL CAST

Those who came to launch Dada in Zurich in 1916 had been influenced by the various movements of the period preceding the war, especially Futurism. The founder of the Cabaret Voltaire, where Dada was born, was a 30-year-old German Catholic named Hugo Ball. Experienced in all aspects of stage work, Ball had come from Munich, where he had collaborated with Kandinsky in trying to found an Expressionist theater. Ball also had worked as a radical journalist, contributing to the pro-youth, anti-war, and graphically Expressionist review *Die Aktion*, and collaborating on a periodical entitled *Die Revolution.*

Appalled by his firsthand view of the war in Belgium, Ball had fled to Zurich with forged papers under an assumed name, accompanied by his mistress, Emmy Hennings, a 31-year-old cabaret singer. To make ends meet, Ball and Hennings took jobs as piano player and diseuse for a troupe of circus-style entertainers. They "then decided to open their own Zurich cabaret as a center for any performers who might care to volunteer" (Willet 1978, p. 26). For Ball, the aim of the cabaret was to "transcend the War and jingoism and recall the few independents who live for other ideals." In February 1916 the Cabaret Voltaire was opened with Ball as manager and Hennings as star (Verkauf 1957b, p. 156).

Also on hand was Ball's friend from Munich, 22-year-old Richard Huelsenbeck. Huelsenbeck was an Expressionist poet who also had written for *Die Aktion.* Ball and Huelsenbeck shared an interest in the Futurist "Marinetti's phonetic, telegraphic, typographic use of language, and had organized a reading in his honor in Berlin only two weeks before Italy's entry into the war" (Willet 1978, p. 26). Once the war broke out, Huelsenbeck found Germany "unbearable." He received permission from the army to study medicine in Switzerland and arrived in Zurich just six days before the opening of the Cabaret Voltaire.

Also in attendance that first evening of the Cabaret Voltaire was a small, monacled, dapperly dressed 20-year-old Rumanian named Sami Rosenstock. He had been studying mathematics at Zurich University and writing symbolist poetry under the name Tristan Tzara. Tzara joined the Dada group instantly, and became its strategist, publicity manager, and, in 1917, editor of the periodical *Dada*. Impudent, witty, and contentious, Tzara feuded with Huelsenbeck, André Breton, and others over the direction of Dada.

Marcel Janco was a 21-year-old countryman of Tzara's who had come to Zurich to study architecture. He created posters, decorations, and masks for the Cabaret Voltaire. Janco was a participant in many of the Dada exhibitions, and his woodcuts illustrated the first book of the *Collection Dada*, edited by Tzara.

The one major artist of the original Zurich group was 30-year-old Hans Arp. Born in Alsace, Arp moved in 1904, at the age of 18, to Paris, where he was greatly impressed by modern painting. Over the next four years he studied at the Weimar School of Applied Art and the Academy Julian. After working alone in Switzerland for three years, Arp emerged in 1911 as cofounder of Der Modern Bund. Arp then collaborated with Kandinsky on the book *Der Blau Reiter* and participated in several exhibitions. Arp's other pre-Dada acquaintances included Guillaume Apollinaire, Max Jacob, the Cubists Pablo Picasso and Georges Braque, and Amedeo Modigliani, who drew his portrait (Verkauf 1957b, p. 115).

At the outbreak of the war, Arp returned to Switzerland, where, in November 1915, he exhibited his first abstract collages, and tapestries at the Tanner Gallery in Zurich. It was at this exhibition that he met another artist, Sophie Taeuber, whom he was to marry in 1922. Between 1916 and 1919 Arp and Taeuber illustrated Dada journals and exhibited at the Dada "manifestations." Arp took little part in the soirées, but Taeuber frequently performed modern dance under a pseudonym at the Galerie Dada. In 1917 Arp made his first wood relief, initiating his distinctive style of unadorned, undulating, abstract forms.

Sophie Taeuber was born in Zurich in 1889 and studied art at the Technical School in St. Gall from 1908 to 1910, and with Wilhelm von Debschitz in Munich from 1911 to 1913. Active in the Dada movement from the beginning, she also taught at the School of Applied Arts from 1916 to 1929. Writing about those early years, Arp said, "The pictures she [Sophie] was doing at the time exercised a decisive influence on my work."

THE DADA BOMB EXPLODES

For the six months of its operation, the Cabaret Voltaire presented performances every evening that, in Janco's (1957, p. 78) words, were "pregnant with a spirit of protest." Janco's (1957, p. 36) account of the Dada ethos confirms Hauser's (1958, p. 235) claim that Dada represented "Romantic Rousseauism in the most extreme meaning of the term":

> We had lost confidence in our "culture." Everything had to be demolished. We would begin again after the tabula rasa. At the Cabaret Voltaire we began by shocking the bourgeoisie, demolishing his idea of art, attacking common sense, public opinion, education, institutions, museums, good taste, in short, the whole prevailing order.

The name Dada was taken to signify the new movement. One account attributes the find to Ball and Huelsenbeck; another to Tzara. In both cases the discovery occurred through a chance exploration of the French dictionary. The word, translated as "hobbyhorse," had instant appeal for everyone. Childlike, musical, and international, it seemed suspended between mystery and nonsense, a favorite position of the Dadaists.

The stylistic innovations of all of the modern art movements were assimilated into Dada's eclectic search for a new art. Huelsenbeck (1951a, p. 279) recalls:

> All of us were enemies of the old rationalistic art which we regarded as symptomatic of a culture about to crumble with the war. We loathed every form of an art that merely imitated nature and we admired, instead. The Cubists and Picasso. We agreed with the Futurists that most

public monuments should be smashed with a hammer, and we delighted in the nonrepresentational experiments of Arp, van Rees, and Marcel Janco.

From their friend Kandinsky and the Expressionists, the Dadaists adopted the free use of color. Janco's woodcuts and his personal view that "the sculptor must become an artisan" bring to mind the Expressionist group that called itself Die Brücke. From the human figures in Cubist paintings, especially those of Picasso, came the inspiration for "the grotesque cardboard costumes, used in Dada stage performances to create an alienation-effect" (Haftman 1960, p. 216). Dada also borrowed the collage form from the Cubists.

The movement with the largest impact on Dada was Futurism. From the Futurist Umberto Boccioni the Dadaists adopted the use of new materials, such as cardboard, wire, and pieces of wood, in constructing the collage. When the Cabaret Voltaire opened, it was decorated with Futurist posters that were characterized by "the free use of typography, in which the compositor moves over the page vertically, horizontally and diagonally, jumbles his type face and makes liberal use of his stock of pictorial blocks" (Richter 1965, p. 33). Dada borrowed this technique for its own posters, fly sheets, and periodicals, and improved on it by developing the photomontage, the intended effect of which was to give "to the individual letter, word or sentence a freedom it had never possessed" (Richter 1965, pp. 114–15).

In music and poetry the Futurists had pioneered what they called "bruitism." In 1911 Luigi Russolo built "a noise organ in which he could conjure up all the distracting sounds of everyday existence," modern sounds for modern times. Bruitistic poems alternated noises with words. The logical extension of these became Marinetti's and Kruchenykh's phonetic poems, consisting solely of nonsense syllables, a completely abstract and nonrepresentational poetry divorced from any association with established meaning.

The Dadaists adopted the idea of abstract and phonetic poetry, then developed it much further. Nonsense poems were composed by picking words out of a hat; static poems were made by rearranging chairs upon which posters, each with a word, had been placed; "gymnastic poems" were recited in which Tzara and Huelsenbeck did deep knee bends in between verses; "Ball composed 'sound poems' in which he did his best to avoid anything that sounded like any word in any language; and groups of Dadaists spoke and chanted simultaneous poems, each speaking a different language or saying different words," thus, in the words of Tzara, "showing the struggle of the human voice with a threatening, entangling, and destroying universe whose rhythmical sequence of noise is inescapable" (Shapiro 1976, p. 161; Esslin 1961, p. 262).

Esslin (1961, p. 264) describes Dada plays as "essentially nonsense poems in dialogue form . . . accompanied by equally nonsensical business and decorated with bizarre masks and costumes." Hugnet (1946, p. 17) comments:

> For these performances Janco designed paper costumes of every color, put together with pins and spontaneous in the extreme. Perishable, purposely ugly or absurd, these materials, chosen by the chance action of eye and mind, symbolized in showy rags the perpetual revolt, the despair which refuses to lose itself in despair.

Two longer plays by Georges Ribemont-Dessaignes were greatly admired by the Dadaists. The first, *L'empereur de Chine* (The Emperor of China), written in 1916, deals with the themes of sexuality, slavery, imperialism, war, rape, violence, and cannibalism. Its intention, according to Esslin, was "to shock a bourgeois public" as well as "create a poetic universe with validity on the stage." The second play, *Le bourreau du Pérou* (The Hangman of Peru), is concerned with the seduction of the state by the forces of destruction.

Most important, Dada took from Futurism its whole posture of provocation, including its improvisatory cabaret theater, with its shock effects, its literary and spoken manifestos, and its general emphasis on spontaneous action. When he took Dada with him to Berlin in 1918, Huelsenbeck credited Tzara with enunciating the principle of the literary manifesto in 1916 and explained: "The manifesto as a literary medium answered our need for directness. We had no time to lose; we wanted to incite our opponents to resistance, and, if necessary, to create new opponents for ourselves" (Richter, 1965, p. 103).

Despite its continuities with earlier movements, Dada represented something qualitatively new in the history of modern art. Haftman (1960, p. 103) states:

> Dada has its own place in history and its own originality. In Dada these isolated elements formed a unity for the first time. Dada took up all

these separate ideas, assembled them and established them as a unified expression of experiences and emotions that were wholly of the present. In this way, Dada finally cut the umbilical cord that bound us to history.

Despite its attacks on the past and present, Futurism worked to promote its program for the future. Dada completed Futurism's project of destruction by rejecting all programs for the future as well. Hans Richter (1965, p. 34), who joined Dada in its early years, writes:

> Dada not only had *no* programme, it was against all programmes. Dada's only programme was to have no programme . . . and, at that moment in history, it was just this that gave the movement its explosive power to unfold *in all directions*, free of aesthetic or social constraints . . . this freedom might (and did) lead either to a new art—or to nothing. Unhampered by tradition, unburdened by gratitude (a debt seldom paid by one generation to another), Dada expounded its theses, anti-theses and a-theses.

DADA'S CULTURAL POLITICS

The basic principles of Dada art—the core of its praxis—were chance creation and the particularization of elements. Richter (1965, p. 51) declares, "Chance became our trademark." He explains, "The official belief in the infallibility of reason, logic and causality seemed to us senseless—as senseless as the destruction of the world and the systematic elimination of every particle of feeling." Chance was adopted as "a protest against the rigidity of straight-line thinking" (Richter 1965, p. 58). For example, here is Tzara's (1951b, p. 92) prescription for making a Dada poem:

> To make a dadaist poem
> Take a newspaper.
> Take a pair of scissors.
> Choose an article as long as you are planning to
> make your poem. Cut out the article. Then cut
> out each of the words that make up this article
> and put them in a bag.
> Shake it gently.
> Then take out the scraps one after another in the

order in which
       they left the bag.
Copy conscientiously.
The poem will be like you.
And here you are a writer, infinitely original
and endowed with a
     sensibility that is charming though beyond
     the understanding of the vulgar.
               Tristan Tzara

As is apparent, the practice of chance creation subverted the bourgeois rationalistic value of utilitarian means-ends logic and expressed the bohemian Romantic values of spontaneous creation and presentness. The practice of chance creation, as in Tzara's poem, produced a random juxtaposition of dissimilar elements that dislocated the given frames of reference, exploded the reified categories of bourgeois thought, and aspired to shock the audience into a new awareness of the primary power of language and art.

Thus, the logic of chance creation also was integrally related to the other salient feature of Dada art, the particularization of elements. Such particularization was expressed visually in the photomontage. Richter (1965, p. 114) describes the process briefly: "They cut up photographs, stuck them together in provocative ways, added drawings, cut these up too, pasted in bits of newspaper, or old letters, or whatever happened to be lying around—to confront a crazy world with its own image." The photomontage did more than simply mirror the disintegration of the bourgeois order. By uprooting elements from their conventional contexts, it subverted their taken-for-granted meaning.

In speech the particularization of elements was expressed through a form of "chatter" dissociated from language. Discourse is constructed according to the rules of language, with the intention of meaningful communication. Chatter, on the other hand, is immediate, unplanned, and uncensored. "It can easily do without meaning: it need only be information, indication, or merely a means of relieving one's feelings, relaxing, or passing the time." As Tzara declared, "Thought is produced in the mouth."

The very idea of explanation was rejected, and contradictions were used as a way of "blowing up" the language of the bourgeoisie and, thus, of "destroying the main bridges between 'them' and 'us,' by incommunicability" (Willener 1970, pp. 204–07). Willener (1970,

p. 207) observes, "Having brushed aside all obstacles, all justifications and all obligations—including that of explaining oneself—they reached that vital level where joy, movement, spontaneity, and metamorphosis have their being; language is no longer a poor means, but a game, a celebration."

Through the use of chance and radical particularization the Dadaists sought to transcend the bourgeois image of society and history as mechanistic and determined. Their quest led in two directions. One was Freudian in thrust; chance construction was like the free association that emancipates feelings and unlocks the secrets of the unconscious mind. The other was Jungian in thrust, the search for the ineffable higher consciousness of the universe. Richter (1965, p. 51) reflects that the experience of chance creation

> . . . taught us that we were not so firmly rooted in the knowable world as people would have us believe. We felt that we were coming into contact with something different, something that surrounded and inter-penetrated *us* just as we overflowed into *it* . . . beneath it all lay a genuine mental and emotional experience that gave us wings to fly—and to look down upon the absurdities of the "real" and earnest world.

There was more than a little mysticism in the Dada attitude. Richter (1965, pp. 57, 59) refers to chance as "a magical procedure" whose "secret" purpose "was to restore to the work of art its primeval magic power. . . ." Ball urged all to "withdraw into the innermost alchemy of the word" (Motherwell 1951, pp. 8, xviii). This attitude was a current in the Romantic wave that flowed from avant-garde circles throughout the period. Artists and intellectuals aspired to initiate works that seemingly created themselves, developed their own independent life, and provoked onlookers into a qualitative transformation of consciousness. Such an epiphany was not possible within Rationalist thought. It was a celebration of the triumph of the spirit over its materialist adversaries.

The emphasis on presentness served to deny continuity in historical development. In contrast, it implied the power of individual acts to create unique moments or "free spaces" in time, in which the radically new might suddenly emerge. The Russian Suprematist painter Varvara Stepanova wrote in 1919: "Non-objective creation is still only the beginning of an unprecedented Great Creation, which is destined to open the doors to mysteries more profound than science and technology" (Rosenberg 1981, p. 20).

Max Ernst and Johannes Baargeld must have felt themselves close to such "Great Creation" when, as Hugnet (1946, p. 26) reports, they began to discover in their automatic drawing another drawing, the contours of which appeared "slowly out of the tangled lines—like an apparition, like a prophecy. . . ." Certainly, the Dadaists' posture of anti-art expressed the mystic attitude that seeks to explode all forms so as to be absorbed into the "all oneness" that lies beyond the cultural veil.

Since the basis for a technical elite lies in its mastery of the established rules, the rejection of such rules also constituted the rejection of such elites. The Dadaists were contemptuous of the art establishment and wished to elevate practicing artists to the level of aesthetic lawgivers, visionary prophets in an age of decadence. As Arp was to claim later, "At the time the action of opening a zip-fastener for a beautiful woman was called sculpture" (Willener 1970, p. 202). Within such a broad definition anything might be considered art.

No more graphic illustration of this idea can be found than Duchamp's submission of ordinary functional objects as works of art to be displayed in museum showings. From 1913 on, he submitted such objects as a bicycle wheel fastened to a kitchen stool (*Bicycle Wheel*), a snow shovel (*Shovel*), and a public urinal (*Fountain*). Only the latter was rejected. In 1915 he coined the term "ready-made" to refer to such works of art by decree.

At one New York showing the artist-photographer Man Ray exhibited a metronome with an eye on it, entitled *Object to Be Destroyed.* His stated intention was to show the visual in a sound-producing object. When the public responded by destroying his object, Ray filed a claim with the company insuring the exhibit, arguing that because he had signed it, the metronome was a work of art.

Of course, if anything can be considered a work of art, then any-one can be considered an artist. Consequently, there was no great need for "artists." Duchamp promptly retired from painting alto-gether and spent the rest of his life in various private activities, including playing chess with his friend Man Ray.

In June 1916 the Dadaists published the only issue of the period-ical *Cabaret Voltaire*, which included contributions by Apollinaire, Picasso, Modigliani, Kandinsky, Marinetti, and others in addition to the Dada nucleus of Arp, Ball, Huelsenbeck, Janco, and Tzara.

The Cabaret Voltaire closed in July 1916, forcing the Dadaists to find new settings for their evening performances. The "First Dada Evening" was held July 14, 1916, at the Wuag Hall and, according to Tzara's notes, featured numerous "demonstrations" (including Tzara's demand for "the right to piss in different colours"), Cubist dance, "gymnastic poem, concert of vowels, bruitist poem, static poem, chemical arrangement of ideas," and the African rhythmic pounding of Huelsenbeck's "big drum." The evening ended when the performers' cardboard costumes were torn off by the audience, windows were smashed, and the police were called in to restore order.

Ultimately this succès de scandale constituted the essential spirit of all Dada creativity. It made the movement truly public and provided the necessary social context within which their various artistic experiments could be understood. Hugnet (1946, p. 17) recalls the pandemonium of the Dada "manifestations":

> The Dada activities in Zurich from 1916 to 1918 shook off their literary character and directly attacked the conventions and stale responsibilities of a public which in the face of such effrontery wavered between rage and amazement. On the stage of the cabaret keys were jangled until the audience protested and went crazy. . . .

Shapiro (1976, p. 161) adds, "Another favorite technique in those days of hourly war bulletins was the fake news release in which true information about the far-flung members of the avant-garde was mixed with absurd or apocryphal reports." Although few would admit to any intentions, Dada's project was to deflate all pomposity, pull the rug out from under all pretensions, put a tack on the chair of decorum, and enjoy a collective belly laugh forceful enough to shake the rafters of the creaky establishment. The Dadaists worked in a spirit of subversion more akin to Groucho than to Karl Marx. For them, all society was Margaret Dumont.

In January and February 1917 the Dadaists staged their first exhibition at the Galerie Corray on Bahnhofstrasse, and on March 23 they held the "Grand Opening of Galerie Dada." Over the next two months they staged two more exhibitions and four evening events at the gallery, the most ambitious of which was a performance of the Expressionist play *Sphynx and Straw Man* by the Austrian painter Oscar Kokoschka. Janco directed the production and designed the masks.

Tzara took over the editorship of the periodical *Dada*, and in July the first issue appeared. Over the next few years several more followed (at the rate of about two a year), featuring the works of Braque, de Chirico, Duchamp, Ernst, Feininger, Klee, Laurens, Masson, Matisse, Miró, Picabia, Ray, and Tanguy, among others, in addition to the Dadaists themselves. Despite this prestigious assembly, Dada's proudest creation remained public chaos. Not content with their popular triumph at the Cabaret Voltaire and Galerie Dada, the Dadaists proceeded to spread their campaign of disorder into the streets of Zurich. "The Dada Movement" (1953, p. 670) reports: "Appalling rumors were circulated; fictitious reports were sent to the newspapers; entertainment innocently advertised to attract middle-brow aesthetes, lady water colourists and members of choral societies, would turn out to be obscene and blasphemous displays."

Dada's position that anyone can be an artist was radically democratic. If common people could create a new art, could they not also create a new reality? Did the Dadaists really believe in the creative potential of the common people? Probably not. Despite their anti-militarist, anti-capitalist, and radically democratic stance, the Zurich Dadaists did not make common cause with the political left. Shapiro (1976, p. 160) states: "They ignored Bolsheviks such as Lenin and pacifists such as Romain Rolland, or else ridiculed them; they mocked revolutionaries for assuming that people were capable of reason and worthy of salvation. All they were willing to concede was the absurdity of life."

Hugo Ball, the founder of the Cabaret Voltaire, was unable to reconcile himself to this position and took his leave of Dada around June 1917. He went to Bern, where he helped edit a democratic, anti-kaiser weekly. Within a year he retired to a Swiss village to write a biography of Bakunin and to study anarchism. Perhaps Ball was initially attracted to Dada because of his understanding of Bakunin's position that during the early stages of a revolution, destruction and construction are one and the same. It became apparent to him, however, that Dada represented "a new nihilism which not only questioned the value of art but of the whole human situation" (Hauser 1958, p. 235). This was too much for Ball, who explained, "I have examined myself carefully, and I could never bid chaos welcome" (Richter 1965, p. 43).

THE CHALLENGE OF REVOLUTION
AND THE SPREAD OF DADA

The political and economic deterioration associated with the war brought forth a storm of protest throughout Europe and Russia. Everywhere authority was under attack. Shortages and inflation provoked food riots in many cities. Soldiers mutinied and deserted in large numbers. The labor unions and left parties grew rapidly in size and militancy.

The most significant transformation occurred in Russia. In March 1917 the aristocracy was overthrown and replaced by a democratic republic. Eight months later the new government was overthrown by Lenin and the Bolsheviks in the name of socialism.

Europe was in turmoil by the end of the war. Peasants seized estates in Italy and Spain. Defeat brought the collapse of the Austro-Hungarian and Ottoman empires. In Germany, on November 9, 1918, Kaiser Wilhelm II abdicated his rule and Frederick Ebert became president of the new Weimar Republic. The new republic's Liberal/ Democratic Socialist ruling coalition continued to be challenged aggressively from both the right and the left. To many, the roaring cannons had sounded the death knell of liberal capitalism. The rise of the new Soviet state appeared like a harbinger of the new age, almost a historical imperative. In 1919 Soviets were set up in Berlin and Munich, as well as Vienna, Budapest, Turin, Fiume, and Glasgow.

The spirit of the revolution burned brightly in the arts as well. In Russia the Futurists had labored to advance the cause of modern art. With the triumph of the Bolsheviks in 1917, modern art suddenly achieved official support in Russia. Under the direction of Anatole Lunacharsky, director of the Commissariat of Enlightenment (Narkompros), the progressives sought to bring the best of art and science to the masses, to complete the political revolution by replacing the peasant culture of the czarist period with a new proletarian culture for industrial socialism.

Lunacharsky appointed David Petrovich Shterenberg, a progressive painter who had lived in Paris the last years before the war, to head the graphic arts division (IZO) of Narkompros. Between 1918 and 1921, IZO set up 36 museums around the country, 13 of which provided art education for the proletariat. Modernism in all the arts, abstract painting in particular, "established a virtual dictatorship over the museums, the art schools and the cultural bureaucracy. For the first time in history, the avant-garde was elevated to the position of power, charged with the task of remaking an entire civilization" (Kramer 1979, p. 44).

Three weeks after the establishment of the Weimar Republic, Shterenberg directed a manifesto at "progressive" German artists. He pointed to the Russian government's support of "the new tendencies" in art and declared that only "the new creations that came into being shortly before the world upheaval can be in step with the rhythm of the new life being created." Shterenberg called for intellectual exchanges leading to an international organization of Russian and German artists.

Greatly impressed with the openness of the Bolsheviks to modern art, "Western intellectuals replied to this manifesto with expressions of solidarity with Russian artists and the Russian people; many spoke out against the Allied anti-Bolshevik intervention in the Civil War in late 1918 and 1919" (Shapiro 1976, p. 179). Exhibitions of each other's art were organized in both Russia and Germany.

Three German editors/correspondents—Alfons Paguiet, Alfons Goldschmidt, and Arthur Holitscher—traveled often to Russia and reported on cultural-political relations between the two countries. The latter two, along with Ludwig Rubiner, went on to found the Berlin League for Proletarian Culture in 1919 and later the Proletarian Theater (Willet 1978, p. 56). By 1919 artists all over Germany, especially the young generation that had come of age during the war, had "embraced the Left, determined to have some say in the rebuilding of German society. In a spate of manifestoes, painters and writers proclaimed their adherence to the proletariat, and then to the Spartacists, as the government brought in the counter-revolutionary Freikorps to crush them" (Shapiro, 1976, p. 186–87).

Berlin was the center of this movement for a revolutionary art. In 1918 two new organizations were formed, the Arbeitsrat für Kunst (Works Council for Art) and the November gruppe. Both groups sought to overthrow the conservative art establishment and to bring modern art to the people through publications, exhibitions, and entertainments. The Arbeitsrat barely survived the brief revolutionary period, but the November-Gruppe lasted until 1932. The principal achievements of these movements were to liberalize museum leadership and to increase government support for teaching the new art and applying it to the design of buildings and tools.

The most famous experiment of this kind was the founding of the Staatliches Bauhaus in 1919 under the direction of the architect Walter Gropius. Organized like a medieval craft guild, instruction in the Bauhaus "sought to combine esthetics with practicality," training students in both manual labor and the "fine arts." "Everything from the theory of abstract art to the revival of crafts to the design of factories, office buildings and entire cities, was joined in a program to reform the look and feel and function of virtually every aspect of modern civilization" (Kramer 1979, p. 45).

The dominance of Expressionism in German popular art became a subject of debate. Supporters asserted that Expressionism was the broadest-based movement against nineteenth-century representational art and that its exhibition and impact still had a public character. Critics countered that the Expressionists' tendency to keep their art separate from their politics was no longer progressive. Many on the left now demanded an art explicitly committed to the aims of socialist revolution. They scoffed at Expressionist works like Ernst Kirchner's self-portrait of his personal war trauma. According to them, in the current revolutionary political climate, mere expression of the artist's feelings was no longer a sufficiently radical act. The historical possibilities of the moment demanded a more deliberately political art.

Some argued that art must be unionized and subsidized by the state, but remain free of political control in a manner comparable with academic science. They proposed that artists must develop their own revolutionary commitments freely in order to create anything with true artistic value. Allowing this to occur would protect the people from the implicit materialism of the socialist leaders and preserve the spirit of revolutionary freedom in the production of popular culture.

Still others rejected the very concept of proletarian art, on both practical and theoretical grounds. Practically, some pointed to the conservative tastes of the proletariat and proposed that, as a mass, it would never be responsive to the distinctively individualistic expression required of authentic modern art. Theoretically, some objected to art designed exclusively for any stratum in the class structure, arguing that true art must be rooted in the basic species/being of the whole human community.

Dada was perhaps the most incandescent of the revolutionary flames that burned across the continents. From 1918 to its self-willed demise in 1923, Dada spread to Germany, France, Spain, Italy, Holland, Yugoslavia, Czechoslovakia, as far west as the United States, and as far east as Russia. While communication, even collaboration, continued between artists in most of these Dada centers, Dada assumed a distinctive character in each location. In the process, breaches occurred between branches of the movement over its future direction. The critical issue was the relationship of art to politics, and the positions adopted clearly reflected the different sociopolitical contexts of the movement.

BERLIN DADA: RADICAL ART FOR THE REVOLUTION

The Original Cast

Dada began in Berlin in 1917, when Richard Huelsenbeck journeyed there from Zurich and joined up with the Austrian-born artist Raoul Hausmann. Hausmann had been contributing to the magazine *Freie Strasse*, started in 1915 by the Munich *Revolution* group, with which Ball had been involved. They were soon joined by the Herzfeld brothers, Wieland and Helmut, then publishing a youth-oriented, anti-war magazine called *Neue Jugend*. The magazine was distinguished principally by the lithographs of George Grosz, a young illustrator and cabaret entertainer, who also found a home in Dada. The other founding member of Berlin Dada was an architect named Johannes Baader, who alternated between Dada and the mental asylum. Protected by the law dealing with criminal responsibility, Baader was notorious for his outrageous pranks.

The core group was joined at different times by the poets Franz Jung, Carl Einstein, and Walter Mehring, the accomplished artist and only woman of the group, Hannah Hoech (who also was Hausmann's mistress), the anti-war painter Otto Dix, Grosz' brother-in-law Dr. Otto Schmalhausen, and the financier of the "Dada Fair" Dr. Otto Burchardt.

The first Dada evening, held at the I. B. Neumann Gallery on February 18, 1918, featured a lecture by Heulsenbeck. Over the next few weeks the founders organized themselves into Club Dada. Many of the members of Club Dada took movement names for themselves. Baader called himself Oberdada (prophet of Dada) and, sometimes, Superdada. Hausmann often signed his works Dadasoph (student of

Dada).. Helmut Herzfeld went under the name John Heartfield as a protest against rising German nationalism and, according to Richter (1965, p. 102), "out of love for his own romantic version of America." He also called himself Monteurdada (builder of Dada).

The first public meeting of Club Dada took place on April 12, 1918, at the Neumann Gallery. At this meeting Huelsenbeck launched the movement with a ringing manifesto against Expressionism, Futurism, and all other movements in modern art and a "battle cry" for "DADA!!!!" (Richter 1965, pp. 104-07). In his manifesto Huelsenbeck contends that artists must "hold fast to the intelligence of their times" and "the highest art will be that which in its conscious content presents the thousandfold problems of the day, the art which has been visibly shattered by the explosions of last week, which is forever trying to collect its limbs after yesterday's crash." Huelsenbeck accuses Expressionists of having sold out to respectability and comfort. However, he declares, Dada is a "new art," one that relates directly to the "new reality" and, thus, "leads to amazing new possibilities and forms of expression in all the arts."

True to Dada's nihilistic, self-mocking pose, Huelsenbeck's manifesto concludes with a negation of his affirmation: "Blast the aesthetic-ethical attitude! Blast the bloodless abstraction of expressionism! Blast the literary hollowheads and their theories for improving the world! For Dadaism in word and image, for all the Dada things that go on in the world! To be against this manifesto is to be a Dadaist!"

When they weren't engaging in provocative polemics, the Dadaists were willing to acknowledge that its spiritual anarchy and social alienation made the earlier avant-garde movement in art progressive in thrust, even a harbinger of the revolution. They argued, however, that the complacent bourgeois world view already had been torn apart. To persist in esoteric abstraction was to abandon social conscience and indulge in bourgeois individualism. The revolution of the present called for political commitment and a new objectivity (*neue Sachlichkeit*) in art, best represented by the works of Ernst, Picabia, Carrà, de Chirico and Grosz.

The Dadaists saw popular culture as the opium of the people. This humanist-Marxist interpretation was about to be developed by the Critical Theorists of the Frankfurt School of Sociology. The struggle for a new art was seen as the struggle for revolutionary consciousness. Grosz

... offered the artist two choices, either to become an engineer—a technician—or a creator of the new art of the masses, integrating "himself, as a propagandist and representative of the revolutionary idea and its adherents, into the army of the suppressed, who struggle for their rightful share of the world's goods and for a meaningful social organization of life." (Shapiro 1976, p. 264)

The Berlin Dadaists were furious over the government's brutal suppression of the Spartacist uprising and over the assassinations of the revolutionaries Karl Liebknecht, Rosa Luxemburg, and Eugen Levine. They no longer saw the bourgeoisie as just philistines, but as exploiters and oppressors as well. During the German revolution of 1918, Huelsenbeck was declared commissar of fine arts. Between 1918 and the late 1920s, Grosz, Herzfeld, Heartfield, and Hausmann all belonged to the Communist Party. For the Berlin Dadaists, true art must be art for the revolution. In 1920 Grosz and Heartfield declared, "The Red Soldier's cleaning of his gun is more important than the entire metaphysical work of all the painters. . . ."

Publications, Exhibitions, and Scandal

The Berlin Dadaists published and distributed numerous journals, anthologies, and political pamphlets during their active years, 1918–22. In 1919 the Malik Verlag house, founded by the brothers Herzfeld two years earlier, began publishing occasional issues of the magazine *Der Dada*, in addition to a series of satirical political journals that provoked constant harassment by the authorities (Willet 1978, p. 50). *Der blutige Ernst* (Deadly Earnest) was followed by the brilliant *Jederman sein eigner Fussball* (Every Man His Own Football) and *Die Rosa Brille* (Rose-Colored Spectacles). Walter Mehring says the Dadaists themselves sold *Jedermann sein eigner Fussball* on the streets of Berlin, wearing frock coats and top hats and following behind a little brass band. In the wealthier areas of the city they "earned more taunts than pennies," but in the working-class districts, still bullet-scarred from the government-Spartacist battles, "the band was greeted with cheers and applause" (Richter 1965, p. 111).

According to his attorney, Count Harry Kessler, Heartfield's intention in *Jedermann sein eigner Fussball* was "to drag through the mud everything that was previously dear to the Germans, that is, all

outworn 'ideals,'—even those of the Left if they were useless clichés—
in order to break a new path and find fresh air" (Shapiro 1976, p.
200). Mehring boasts that "Every man his own football soon entered
the Berlin language as an expression of contempt for authority and
humbug" (Richter 1965, pgs. 111–12).

All of these publications were quickly banned by the authorities.
In response, the Dadaists gave them new titles and put them out
again. During the state of siege brought on by the unsuccessful right-
wing Kapp Putsch, Mehring reports the Dadaists "were charged with
seeking to bring the Armed Forces into contempt and distributing
indecent publications" (Richter 1965, p. 112). Heartfield was given
a two-week jail sentence. Released after eight days, he quickly put
together an issue of *Die Pleite* entitled "Schutzhaft" (Protective
Custody), which charged soldiers and prison guards with abuses
against political prisoners.

After this experience the tone of *Die Pleite* became more seriously political. Six more issues followed, reaching a circulation of
10,000 to 12,000. Through the 1920s Malik-Verlag became a major
publisher of left-wing literature, starting with Zinovieff's short
biography of Lenin. Up until 1923, however, Heartfield's zeal was
all Dada, for which he published many works, including Huelsenbeck's *En avant dada* (1920) and Grosz's *Mit Pensel und Schere*
(1922).

As in Zurich, Dada's greatest passion was to shock the bourgeoisie; its greatest triumphs, succès de scandale. They alarmed the public
with enigmatic little stickers that they plastered all over the doors
and windows of Berlin shops. They lured audiences to their meetings
under innocent pretexts and then harangued them with insults. There
were frequent fistfights, even riots, until they had to get police permits to hold their meetings. Grosz (1946, p. 82) comments, "We
simply mocked everything. That was Dadaism. Nothing was holy
to us."

Heartfield "liked to dishonour the Army by parading in a particularly repulsive uniform with only one side of his face shaven"
("The Dada Movement" 1953, p. 670). Grosz urinated on the paintings at a Berlin exhibit. Baader was the most outrageous Dadaist of
them all. Diagnosed by state psychiatrists as a megalomaniac, he once
mounted the pulpit of the Berlin Cathedral unnoticed, excoriated the
congregation for not giving a damn about Christ, and announced
that Dada would save the world. At the ceremony inaugurating the

first German Republic in the Weimar State Theater, Baader showered the founding fathers with leaflets proclaiming himself president of the globe.

Sometimes non-Dadaists would share Baader's madness.

> Baader ... assembled a huge scrapbook that he called the *Dadacon* and claimed it was greater than the Bible, including the New Testament. ... He believed that in thumbing through the book as he arranged it, one was bound to develop a dizzying headache, and that only when one's mind was a complete whirl could one comprehend the *Dadacon*. (Grosz 1946, p. 184)

Baader announced that he was willing to sell the *Dadacon* for $35,000. U.S. war correspondent Ben Hecht actually offered Baader $18,000 for the book. They haggled over price and the deal fell through. Baader wound up burying the *Dadacon* in his garden.

The Politics of Art

In the final analysis, the Berlin Dadaists were only partially successful in creating new forms of artistic expression for the new reality. Richter (1965, pp. 125, 112) points out that Huelsenbeck "wrote poems which fitted just as well into the Expressionist tradition (on which he poured such scorn) as they did into everything that one could call 'typical' Dada"; most of Hausmann's "works were very close to the same 'abstract' art that Huelsenbeck and Grosz so despised."

Grosz's drawings were typically composed of savage caricatures of pompous German military officers, fat, greedy capitalists, and timid but cunning politicians consorting with plump, painted prostitutes—an unholy power elite in an age of decadence. Still obsessed with blowing apart the complacent bourgeois world view, however, such drawings lack any affirmation of the subjectively liberating force of the beautiful image to complete the dialectic and establish a principle for the new reality (Marcuse 1978).

The Berlin Dadaists' proudest innovation in "new art" was the photomontage. The photomontage was constructed by piecing together words and images cut from newspapers and magazines and assembled in such a way as to create, in Hausmann's words, "a new unity in which was revealed a visually and conceptually *new* image of the chaos of an age of war and revolution." Hausmann asserted that this method "possessed a power for propaganda purposes which their contemporaries had not the courage to exploit" (Richter 1965, p. 116). In Heartfield's hands the veracity of news photographs and the familiarity of popular images were exploited to make subversive political statements (De Coster 1983).

Marcuse (1978, p. 49) charges, however, that "Anti-art is self-defeating from the outset." First, he argues, it misrepresents the essence of the crisis: "We are experiencing, not the destruction of every whole, every unit or unity, every meaning, but rather the rule and power of the whole, the superimposed administered unification."

Second, this different diagnosis implies a different prescription. To be politically effective, art must "fight reification" and "transform subjectivity" by holding out hope for a "community of freedom." The aesthetic form is essential to the political value of art precisely because it embodies beauty and hope: "The qualities of the form negate those of the repressive society—the qualities of life, labor, and love" (Marcuse 1978, p. 53). In the final analysis, the judgment about whether and when to attack the present or build the future is a complex and ambiguous one. It is the choice between resistance and affirmation. In a period of changing public consciousness, the boundaries are rarely clear. The meanings typically vary according to social circle, the explicit and implicit poised in dialectical tension.

The Art of Politics

Despite their expressed commitment to the revolution, the Berlin Dadaists were not able to make common cause with the Communist Party. Between the German national elections for the Constituent Assembly of January 1919 and those of June 1920, the Communist Party (KPD) increased its share of the vote from 10 percent to 34 percent, raising hopes for a strong movement for change in the shaky republic.

At this very moment, the Dadaists staged the huge Berlin Dada Fair (Dada-Messe), which brought together about 175 items from Dadaists all over Germany. Its catalog declared "Dada is political" and included a manifesto entitled "What Is Dadaism and What Does

It Want in Germany?" written by Hausmann and Huelsenbeck under the name Revolutionary Dadaist Central Council. Among other things, the manifesto "called for nationalization of property, socialist construction projects, the increase of leisure time through mechanization" and "artists' adherence to communism" as well as numerous enactments that expressed the nonsense and nihilism that had become Dada's trademark—for instance, "compulsory attendance of all clergymen and teachers to the Dadaist articles of faith;" "introduction of the simultaneist poem as a communist state prayer"; "immediate organization of a large scale Dadaist propaganda campaign with 150 circuses for the enlightment of the proletariat"; and "immediate regulation of all sexual relations, according to the views of International Dadaism through establishment of a Dadaist sexual center" (Huelsenbeck 1951b, p. 41).

Hovering over the first of the two rooms of the exhibit, suspended from the ceiling, was a pig-faced dummy in an army uniform, bearing the placard "Hanged by the Revolution." Also featured was a series of anti-military drawings by Grosz, named after the motto stamped on Krupp's canons. "If drawings could kill," commented Kurt Tucholsky, no mean satirist himself, "the Prussian military would surely be dead" (Shapiro 1976, p. 198).

It took a few months, but the fair drew the expected official response. The police prosecuted Grosz and Heartfield for insulting the armed forces. In mid-1921 the Prussian Ministry of Culture banned paintings by Dix and Schlichter from a big exhibition in the Lehrter Bahnhof. When the November gruppe refused to protest, Grosz, Hausmann, and Hoech joined Georg Scholz, Dix, and Schlichter in resigning. They formed an "opposition" and declared their "solidarity with the proletariat."

While such quixotic radicalism placed Dada far to the left of any other movement of artists, it did not please the Communist Party. The KPD's daily newspaper, *Die rote Fahne*, "warned the workers against Dada's attacks on the 'cultural heritage,' saying that such people had no business to call themselves communists" (Willet 1978, p. 53). Dada's flamboyant attacks on all traditions, including those of the left, made it an unreliable comrade. Certainly, when measured against the party's standard of discipline, the Dadaists were individualistic, exhibitionistic, and deliberately inconsistent.

In Richter's (1965, p. 112) view, "The flirtation with communism was solely the product of this *anti-everything* mentality, not of any devotion to the doctrines of Karl Marx. . . ." Richter notes that, after his visit to the USSR in 1925, Grosz's views changed drastically. He referred to Lenin caustically as "a little chemist," that is, an unimaginative technician with an instant cure for everything. By 1928 Grosz was vehemently anti-Communist. When the Nazis came to power, he moved to the United States, taught at the Art Students' League in New York, and became one of the country's foremost slick magazine illustrators. In his autobiography Grosz (1946, p. 185) recalls Dada politics as being "enigmatic" and "wonderfully wild," but never politically programatic.

Huelsenbeck, who in 1920 declared that "Dada is German Bolshevism," also later turned against Communism. He left Dada in 1920 to complete his medical studies, changed his name to Charles R. Hulbeck, moved to New York, and, until his death in 1971, practiced Jungian psychoanalysis. Over the period he continued to paint and write poetry and expository articles, some about Dada. In an article published for the first time in Robert Motherwell's 1951 anthology on Dada, Huelsenbeck stated, "We were not politicians, but artists searching for an expression that would correspond to our demands for a new art."

In Richter's (1965, p. 113) analysis, Dada politics was essentially anarchistic:

> Most Dadaists reserved their enthusiasm for the SELF, working out its own laws, its own form and its own justification, free from guilt and remorse. . . . The idea of putting people in a position to exploit their mental and physical energies in a spirit of unbounded optimism and faith in themselves—this was the idea behind the wild and exuberant antics of Dada. "To hell with art, if it gets in the way! . . ." This anarchistic spirit enabled the Berlin Dada movement to live life to the full in its way.

DADA IN COLOGNE AND HANOVER:
RADICAL ART AND THE REVOLUTION

In contrast with the Berlin group, the Dadaists in Cologne considered the revolution in art of equal importance with the political revolution. Their position was that "artistic and political development should take place side by side without one suppressing or patronizing the other" (Richter 1965, p. 160).

The leaders of Cologne Dada were Max Ernst, Johannes Baargeld, and Hans Arp from the Zurich group. After the war they founded a radical periodical, *Der Ventilator*, which sold 20,000 copies in the streets and at factory gates. Full of criticism and mockery for all the established institutions, the periodical was banned as subversive by the British Army of Occupation in the Rhineland.

Although he shared their hostility to capitalism, Ernst charged that the Berlin Dadaists' conversion to Communism had influenced their work adversely. At the time he was engaged in his "automatic process" paintings of mechanical inventions, later celebrated by Breton as some of the first and finest examples of Surrealist art. Looking back, Ernst explained, "We wanted to keep away from all politics and keep on with the manifestations and declarations of principle. To us the poet was above the fray."

In 1920 Ernst and Arp were able to convince young Baargeld, then a leader of the Communist Party in Cologne, that "Dada went much farther than Communism and that its combinations of new found inner freedom and powerful external expression could set the world free: every man a personality through Dada!" (Richter 1965, p. 160). Baargeld's banker father was so delighted with his conversion that he put up the money for Ernst's 1920 issue of *Die Schamade*, a disturbingly critical magazine that included contributions from many of the Paris Dadaists. The following year Ernst moved to Paris, and in 1923 he became active in the Surrealist movement.

In Hanover, Kurt Schwitters renounced what the middle class called art and claimed to live only for Dada. Schwitters represented Dada with a new kind of junk art he called Merz, which he extracted from the word *Commerzbank*. Grosz (1946, p. 186) recalls Schwitters' technique:

> He gathered everything he could find on the streets when he went out for a walk. He would pick up rusty nails, old rags, a toothbrush without bristles, cigar-butts, a spoke of a bicycle wheel, a broken umbrella—in short, anything that had been discarded as useless. He would then put them together into a smaller junk heap, which he would proceed to paste on canvas or old boards, fastening them down firmly with wire and cord.

Schwitters believed that creating a work of art out of the waste of industrial society constituted its own social commentary. "One can shout through refuse," he wrote. "Merz was like an image of the revolution within me, not as it was, but as it should have been" ("The Happening" 1965).

Richter (1965) recalls that Schwitters sold these *merzbild* collages by the hundreds, for 20 marks each, out of two enormous portfolios that he carried on his chest and back wherever he went. A "born shopkeeper," Schwitters rented rooms in his house, traveled fourth class, and never hired a porter. When he applied for membership in the Club Dada, Huelsenbeck blackballed him with the epithet "bourgeois." Also ignoring him when invitations went out for the Berlin Dada Fair of 1920, Huelsenbeck (1957, p. 56) openly chastised Schwitters with the charge "The remodeling of life seemed to us to be of prime importance and made us take part in political movements. But Schwitters wanted to have it expressed only by means of artistic symbols." Schwitters (1951, p. 60) countered, "As a matter of principle, Merz aims only at art, because no man can serve two masters."

PARIS DADA: RADICAL ART FOR ITS OWN SAKE

Dada was active in Paris from 1919 through 1923. Many of its proponents then joined the Surrealist movement, which emerged in 1924 under the direction of André Breton. Paris Dada was at the opposite pole of Berlin Dada. "Although it caused much talk and agitation, it never even seriously entertained the idea of political engagement" ("The Dada Movement" 1953, p. 670).

This difference was due principally to the lack of a revolutionary political situation in postwar France. Much of the war had been fought on French soil and the French had emerged victorious, thus vindicating their political and military leadership. Georges Clemenceau was appointed premier in mid-1917 and won public favor by imposing a harsh peace treaty on the Germans at Versailles. The possibility of a new politics emerged briefly after the Armistice, culminating in 1920 in the establishment of a Communist Party affiliated with the Third International. Nevertheless, most French people sought relief from their ordeal by returning to business as usual. Dadaist Ribemont-Dessaignes wrote in his memoirs, "A pre-revolutionary fever was quite visibly seething; but it aborted. Society life went on" (Willet 1978, p. 57). Reflecting this broader quietism, many of the French painters abandoned their bohemian life-styles for bourgeois respectability. Few works of the period made any social comment. So, despite its absence of political content, Dada once again was able to outrage the bourgeoisie.

Breton, who edited the review *Littérature*, Tzara, and Picabia were feuding leaders in the Paris Dada group, which included Louis Aragon, Paul Durmée, Paul Eluard, Théodore Fraenkel, Benjamin Péret, Georges Ribemont-Dessaignes, and Philippe Soupault. Other artists who took part in Dada exhibitions and manifestations included Céline Arnauld, Jean Cocteau, Giorgio de Chirico, Emmanual Fay, Fernand Léger, Jacques Lipschitz, Clement Pansaers, Jacques Rigault, and Sonia Delaunay.

The Paris Dada group was composed largely of alienated youth from high bourgeois society. They considered themselves radical artists who were above class conflict. Although critical of capitalism, they refrained from overt political commentary. They scorned bourgeois rule more for its vulgar taste than for its exploitation of workers or its repression of political dissent. Although predominantly—and sometimes self-consciously—French, they thought of themselves as above nationalism as well. If there was any social category with which they identified, it was generation.

Between 1919 and 1923 Breton, Tzara, and Picabia published numerous issues of various Dada magazines, including *Littérature*, *391*, and *DADAphone*, featuring various "works that have great succès de scandale; the Mona Lisa with a mustache by Duchamp; the famous inkspot that Picabia entitled Sainte Vierge, and the toy monkey which he calls 'Portrait of Cézanne'" (Hugnet 1946, p. 31).

As in Zurich, however, the essential spirit of Dada in Paris was expressed through public performances. The first event featured such scenes as Tzara reading a newspaper article, accompanied by clangings, tinklings, and other noises, and Picabia drawing on a large slate, wiping out each section as he finished it before going on to the next. Unlike the patrons of Zurich, however, those of Paris proved to be considerably more volatile. The first event ended in a riot and, for the second event, held at the Salle Gaveau on May 26, 1920, many members of the audience arrived with rotten tomatoes and eggs.

The Beginning of the End of the Beginning

The Salle Gaveau was the beginning of the end of Paris Dada. It had lost the element of surprise and was in danger of losing the initiative. Differences over tactics were exacerbated by bitter personal rivalries: Picabia against Tzara, Picabia against Breton, Breton and Tzara against each other.

Breton had personal ambitions to lead the movement in a new direction. He felt that Dada's unrelenting assault on all means of communication confused shock tactics with art. He had grown weary of what he considered pointless demonstrations. In his view, the destruction of society and art had been completed, and a new plan of action was required. Over the course of the next year he met with several of the Dadaists in Picabia's studio every week to thrash out new ideas.

One plan to break the impasse was the mock trial of Maurice Barrés, held at the Salle de Sociétés Savantes on May 13, 1921. Both as an author and as an individual, Barrés had been an idol of many of the Dadaists in their youth. However, his youthful nihilism, which had evolved through personal struggle into a highly literate wartime nationalism, had subsequently degenerated into neofascism. At the time of the trial he was a writer for the reactionary Paris newspaper *L'Echo*. The Dadaists accused him of "crimes against culture."

The French Dadaists took the trial very seriously. Not having grown up in France, however, neither Picabia nor Tzara shared their youthful admiration for, and sense of betrayal by, Barrés. Moreover, the "excessively serious" tone of the occasion contradicted the "angry nihilism" of Picabia and the "practical synicism" of Tzara. Both opposed the idea. Two days before the performance, Picabia published an article in *Comoedia* under the title "Picabia Breaks with Dada," in which he attacked Tzara and announced his withdrawal from the movement. He still came to the Barrés trial, but left early, complaining of being bored. Tzara took part as a witness, but his performance provoked Breton to criticize him for persisting in "Dadaist buffoonery" (Richter 1965, pp. 184–86).

In the analysis of Ribemont-Dessaignes, the Barrés trial was "not much like Dada" and left an "unpleasant taste" in the mouths of the participants: "Dada could be a criminal, a coward, a destroyer or a thief, but not a judge." Moreover, he sensed that the movement was dangerously close to being co-opted by its bourgeois audience and, thus, losing its radical thrust:

The audience was numerous and tumultuous, for by then it was understood that every Dada demonstration involved a certain amount of
obligatory uproar.... Scenes had become an amusement; to make a
noise had become a method of being a Dadaist oneself. Serious and
benevolent citizens defended "these young people" who were offering
an inimitable spectacle of intellectual justice. (Ribemont-Dessaignes
1951, p. 116)

In response to the crisis, Breton called for a "Congress of Intellectuals" that would "distill and unify the essential principles of
modernism." He was joined in this mission by a prestigious coalition
of artists and writers outside of Dada. Many Dadaists opposed the
proposition. Such a codification of principles appeared to violate the
essential spirit of Dada. The idea of congressional resolutions on
innovation struck these celebrants of spontaneous individual creation
as a contradiction in terms. Tzara ridiculed the idea, suggesting that
the congress would meet to decide "whether a railway engine was
more modern than a top-hat." Nevertheless, he and his friends
accepted the invitation, figuring that Breton "as a good Dadaist
would take on the role of a detonator to blow the Congress sky
high" (Richter 1965, p. 187). When they learned of Breton's "treach-
erous" attitude, however, they threatened either to boycott the
affair or to come with the express intention of sabotaging it.

In reaction to "Tzara's inevitable opposition, and the insidious
ways in which it operated," Breton issued a press statement, picked
up by a large daily, that warned the world against "the actions of a
character known to be a promoter of a so-called movement originating
in Zurich" and condemning Tzara as a "publicity-seeking imposter"
(Willet 1978, p. 93). This, Breton was willing to admit later, was "an
error of judgement." Richter (1965, p. 188) comments, "Among
those outraged by such apparent xenophobia were Satie, Eluard, and
Ribemont-Dessaignes, who joined Tzara in summoning a meeting at
which over forty signatures, including Brancusi and many other
foreign-born artists or writers, protested at the phrase 'originating in
Zurich' and formally withdrew their confidence from the Congress."
The petition was presented in the form of a countermanifesto,
entitled *Le coeur à barbe* (The bearded heart), written collectively.
Breton was then informed by his cosponsors that the plan was off.

No more Dada events took place in Paris that year. However,
several Dadaists—Tzara, Arp, Schwitters, Doesberg, and Richter

among them—met at the *Bauhausfest* in Weimar to bid Dada farewell. Tzara delivered funeral orations in Weimar, Jena, and Hanover, and Schwitters printed them in his periodical *Merz* under the title "Conférence sur la fin de Dada."

Meanwhile, Breton was preparing a new attack. In September he issued *Littérature no. 4*, calling it the first Surrealist number. Early in 1923 Breton attended the opening of a Picabia exhibition in Barcelona, where "he made a policy speech on the character (and the characters) of the evolution of modern art," omitting any reference to Tzara and his friends (Richter 1965, p. 191).

All of these mounting ambitions and seething rivalries built to a climax the evening of July 7, 1923—by all accounts the last Dada evening. Organized by Ilya Zdanevitch, a Russian émigré, the manifestation was held at the Théâtre Michel and featured short films by Richter, Man Ray, and Charles Sheeler, poems by Cocteau, and Tzara's short play *Le coeur à gaz*. The manifestation was called "Soirée du coeur à barbe," the title of the countermanifesto that had scuttled Breton's plans for the Congress of Intellectuals. Eluard refused to take part because of the inclusion of Cocteau.

During the performance of *Le coeur à gaz*, the rage of Breton and his colleagues finally broke loose. Hugnet (1951, p. 193) recalls that Breton, Aragon, and Peret climbed on stage and "started to belabor the actors. The latter, hampered by Sonia Delaunay's solid cardboard costumes, were unable to protect themselves and made efforts to flee with tiny steps. Breton boxed Crevel's ears soundly and broke Pierre de Massot's arm with his walking stick." Members of the audience brought the three intruders down from the stage. All three "were shaken, dragged away and forcibly expelled, their jackets torn apart. Hardly had order been restored when Eluard climbed onto the stage in his turn" to assault the actors. "Inflamed by the preceding rough and tumble, several members of the audience overwhelmed Eluard who fell violently against the footlights, a few of which were shattered. Eluard's friends sprang to his defense, while others called for the police to restore order." Hugnet recalls, "I can still hear the director of the Théâtre Michel, tearing his hair at the sight of the rows of seats hanging loose or torn apart and the devastated stage, and lamenting, 'My lovely little theatre'." The next day Eluard received "an official looking paper ordering him to pay 8,000 francs damages for offense against public morals. This is what Dada had come to."

Transition to Surrealism

Surrealism rose from the ruins of Dada in 1924. Under the direction of Breton at *Littérature*, the Surrealists built on the innovations of Dada, such as spontaneous creation (as in "automatic drawing and writing"), but developed a "far more systematic and serious experimental attitude toward the subconscious as the essential source of art" (Barr 1946, p. 11). Influenced by psychoanalysis, they studied dreams and visions, and the art of children and the insane. The surrealists also carried on the Dada élan of black humor to sabotage authority and convention.

The Surrealist method of "attentive receptivity" bore striking resemblance both to Freud's psychotherapy and Husserl's phenomenology. It guided a process of personal liberation in which the individual expressed himself or herself through uncensored creative activity and then drew back to gain reflected illumination of the possible meanings of the preceding action. Through such interpretation the individual gained in knowledge, imagination, and the capacity for change.

The political project of the Surrealists was to "sabotage" rational and "civilized" man in order to deliver him up to pure desire. This was to be accomplished by a process of "derealization," in which the reified categories of perception that formed the bourgeois culture of domination would be permanently shattered by the eruption of wild images from an unconscious mind free of such conditioning. Such images would transcend the artificial boundaries of the taken-for-granted world to reveal the infinity of possible relations. Willener (1970, p. 215) concludes: "From this to a belief that it is possible to transform the world is but a step."

Believing in the efficacy of their method, the Surrealists offered their services to the Communist Party on several occasions. Like the Berlin Dadaists, they were rejected. They "soon became disenchanted with all meetings in which workers criticized them as elitist and bourgeois and their works as unreal, and dropped out of the Party within a few years" (Shapiro 1976, p. 210).

By the mid-1920s the Soviet regime repudiated modern, nonrepresentational art "in favor of conventional styles of greater appeal to the masses that were therefore more useful as vehicles of propaganda and coercion" (Kramer 1979, p. 45). With this turn toward sentimentalized Socialist Realism, the regression to the narcissism of power became complete. Modernism survived only in architecture, where ultrafunctional high-rise buildings symbolized the authority and efficiency of the state while trivializing individual sensibilities. The revolutionary situation of infinite possibilities clearly was over, and in 1932 Stalin imposed complete state control over artistic creativity. By then Aragon was the only one of the original group to abandon Surrealism for Communism.

In the West, however, the modern art movement became enormously popular. Dada has been credited with reviving the tradition of spoken poetry and advancing the tradition of symbolist poetry, with theatrical experiments that presage the "theater of the absurd," with pioneering assemblage and collage techniques generally and with inventing the photomontage specifically, and with redefining painting as an activity rather than a making; this was an attitude inherited by the Abstract Expressionists of the post-World War II period. Through the years of anti-culture of the Dadaists has become the counterculture of the Surrealists and, finally, the established culture of contemporary capitalism.

In fact, the modern art movement generally, once the adversary of all establishments, has become an integral feature of Western industrial society. In the process, of course, it has lost its revolutionary spirit. Kramer (1979, p. 43) comments:

> Moving from the margin into the mainstream of our culture, modernism has . . . become expansive and imperious. No longer does it have any radical functions to perform. On the contrary, its own vested interests require that it become vigilant in conserving both its past achievements and its present prerogatives at which moment, of course, the revolution is spiritually dead.

In 1966 the Museum of Modern Art staged a fiftieth anniversary exhibit of Dada. Max Ernst commented, "If Tristan Tzara could hear that the museums are about to celebrate the fiftieth anniversary of Dada, he would turn over in his grave." Tzara's postmortem discomfort doubtless would reflect his recognition that his cultural revolution had been co-opted by the bourgeoisie he so despised, assimilated into the corporate marketplace like any other fashion.

TOWARD AN UNDERSTANDING OF CULTURAL
POLITICS: LIMITATIONS AND POSSIBILITIES

It seems clear in retrospect that Dada and early Surrealism were the climactic stage in a Romantic movement that began near the end of the nineteenth century and extended well into the 1920s. From the early nineteenth century on, Romantic movements flared up every 20 years or so in France, Germany, England, or the United States. The most daring synthesis of cultural and political radicalism was snuffed out at the barricades of the Paris Commune in 1871.

In the analysis of Caesar Grana (1967), this ideological posture was grounded in the changes in the economic condition of artists and writers. In the transition to capitalist industrial society, artists and writers lost the patron class of church, crown, and aristocracy as well as the protection of the guild, and had to create independently for later sale in the middle-class market. This "absence of obligation to the standards of a specific social environment had made originality not only possible but also, in a sense, the sole point and foundation of literary creation" (Grana 1967, p. 41).

This "freedom to experiment with new artistic manners and subjects" fostered a "widened sense of self importance" and self-discovery in the new man of letters. However, dependence on the unpredictable vicissitudes of the marketplace caused feelings of anxiety and suspicion. This situation

> ... bred in many writers a tendency to grow touchy concerning the momentousness and dignity of their trade, and one after another fell to speaking reverentially of the natural gap between the creator and the layman, between the imposing reach of the literary spirit and the small-minded tyranny of social demands. (Grana 1967, pp. 41–42)

In this way "arrogance and almost utopian self-confidence" were intimately connected to "fear, impotence and martyrdom," frequently resulting in "suspicion, anger and contempt" for the bourgeoisie (Grana 1967, p. 55).

A major reason the German Dadaists and French Surrealists were attracted to Communism was their mutual opposition to the bourgeoisie and the culture of industrial capitalism. Janco referred to the bourgeoisie as "our mortal enemy." Tzara (1951a, p. 80) boasted that artists and poets "rejoice at the venom of the masses," and

Huelsenbeck (1951c, p. 36) stated flatly, "Art was just there—there were artists and bourgeoisie, you had to love one and hate the other."

The attraction of the radical artists to Communism was based on epistemological grounds as well. They resonated with the Romantic elements in Marxist thought. Although, on the surface, the attempt to deduce all of historical development from a single logical formula appears to be very rationalist, Marx's concept of the dialectic also can be interpreted as continuous with German Romantic idealism. Mannheim (1971, p. 151) points out that the dialectical approach restores the historically unique individual "as a component part of a unique process of historical growth and development." This process includes a radical discontinuity in which quantitative changes in social conditions lead to a qualitative transformation of class consciousness and social structure. This transformation becomes possible only because of an irrational self-reversing tendency in capitalism. Since it doesn't fall into the linear causal logic of bourgeois rationality, the attempt at proletarian revolution, "however planned and 'scientific' it may be, inevitably produces an irrational 'chiliastic' element." In this context, revolutionary spirit must be considered a decisive but incalculable factor. I believe it is this quasi-religious, millennial character of Marxism that has made it so attractive to peasants in rebellion against oligarchy. Also, as Bamber (1982, p. 14) observes, Marxism "is based on a grand romantic myth—that we fell from and eventually will return to a classless society."

Finally, even Marx's brief vision of the Utopian, postcapitalist future is one that rejects the mechanical specialization of industrial society in favor of pastoral quiet and the many-sided development of the individual—a society that allows a person to "hunt in the morning, fish in the afternoon, rear cattle in the evening, criticise after dinner . . . without ever becoming hunter, fisherman, shepherd or critic." Looking at the situation in this way, we can see how the Dadaists and Surrealists could imagine their experiments in changing consciousness could contribute to the Communists' program for revolution.

The historical situation of the Soviet Communists dictated quite another strategy, however. They were faced with the challenges of modernizing an illiterate, superstitious peasantry, of disciplining labor for industrial and collective agricultural development, of forging a common national identity for an ethnically diverse population, and of defending their government against counterrevolutionary forces aided by the Western capitalist nations. At the same time, the Bolsheviks had no real knowledge of or sympathy for peasant communalism. As educated, middle-class intellectuals "who had themselves broken with friends, family and social class to join the revolutionary cause," the Russian Marxists saw peasant institutions as backward and inferior to economically rational enterprise (Kingston-Mann 1982).

Their solution was to destroy peasant institutions and values and to build a national culture around the principles of secular science. They buried the humanism of the young Marx and proposed a mechanistic model of society, a deterministic theory of history, and a materialist doctrine of causality. The new "scientific socialism" held that only the "objective structures" of political economy (such as technology and property ownership) were of any consequence, that socialism was historically inevitable, and that the realm of the spirit was merely "epiphenomenal."

Drawing on Marx's German Protestant reverence for the virtue of work, the Russian Marxists' policies rewarded labor productivity. Needing to concentrate their resources on building an industrial infrastructure and wishing to maintain a favorable balance of trade, they discouraged private consumption. Anxious about subversion and demanding ideological conformity, they dismissed any concern with the spiritual development of the individual as "bourgeois." By this they meant unconcerned with essential matters like property relations, exploitation, and inequality—asocial and self-indulgent.

Indeed, by many criteria the Dadaists and Surrealists were bourgeois. All were educated youth from bourgeois family backgrounds. Janco admits that "some of us even had governesses to bring us up" (Willet 1978, p. 28). Although they had chosen a bohemian life-style, they dressed fashionably and, at least according to Grosz (1946, p. 186), were "financed by rich playboy admirers who found an amusing outlet in Dada."

Unlike workers, these radical artists were not alienated from the product of their labor; they sold their works in the marketplace—sometimes at high prices—and they shared in the profits. Although they sympathized with the proletariat, many of the Dadaists' antics were offensive to working-class morals. In Paris the Dadaists made only one attempt to persuade the working class. On this occasion, Richter (1965, p. 175) reports, "The audience clearly found difficulty in swallowing ideas that consigned Napoleon, Kant, Cézanne,

Marx and Lenin to the same scrap-heap." The Berlin Dadaists made a more concerted effort to reach the workers and the left, but they, too, offended working-class morals and mocked leftist clichés.

In turn, the Dadaists also accused the Communists of being "bourgeois." Picabia criticized "Mssrs. Revolutionaries" for having "ideas . . . as narrow as those of a petty bourgeois from Besançon." In 1923, the year of Trotsky's famous statement on the matter, Schwitters, Arp, and Tzara joined others in issuing a manifesto in which they rejected the idea of proletarian art in favor of artistic freedom. They pointed out the proletariat's conservative preference for bourgeois culture and concluded, "Communism is just as bourgeois an affair as is majority socialism, in other words capitalism in a new guise" (Willet 1978, pp. 79–80; Also see Shapiro 1976, p. 208). By this they meant unconcerned with personal liberty and human potential—vulgar, timid and conformist.

Obviously there is some truth in this point of view. Although they have vastly improved the material welfare of their citizens, the Soviets have uncritically adopted the logic of the bureaucratic welfare state at the cost of individual liberty. They seem to have forgotten that human beings are symbol-making as well as tool-making animals, that aesthetic creation is an important activity in most cultures, that beauty, truth, and goodness are basic human values.

THE DIALECTIC OF RADICAL POLITICAL
AND RADICAL CULTURAL MOVEMENTS

The ideological tensions between the Leninists and the Dadaists and Surrealists make it evident that opposition to capitalist organization and culture may spring from different strata and express different aspirations. In trying to understand this issue in larger historical context, we must distinguish between radical political movements and radical cultural movements. The former are concerned principally with changing the structure of institutions and distribution of power; the latter, with changing the norms of interpersonal relations, lifestyles, and aesthetic expression. Anarchism and Marxism are the two most coherent radical political ideologies in modern history; Romanticism, the most coherent radical cultural ideology. Each of these movements seeks to change society in order to fulfill one of the ideals of the Enlightenment: liberty, equality, and fraternity.

Anarchists see repression of individual liberty as the major problem of the modern order. They reject the very idea of legislating behavior and call upon people to smash the apparatus of the state. Anarchists seek to create a society of freely choosing individuals unconstrained by political coercion and economic necessity. Consistent with their ideal, anarchists typically reject leadership and organization for themselves. This leads to an emphasis on spontaneous, direct action. During times of violent confrontation, however, some anarchist movements have organized themselves into elaborate underground secret societies, often infused with ritual and mystery. Clearly within the Romantic mode, anarchism has been attractive to cultural radicals over the years. Its propensity for violence has limited its appeal, however, especially for those of middle-class upbringing.

Marxists see the exploitation of labor, inequality of classes, and poverty as the major problems of the modern order. They seek a society in which cooperation and sharing take precedence over competition and acquisition, exploitation is nonexistent, inequality is minimal, and everyone's basic needs are provided for. According to Marxism, the capitalists employ a divide-and-conquer strategy to prevent the workers from recognizing and acting on behalf of their class interest. In order to escape their plight, workers must reject the false consciousness of bourgeois individualism, embrace the ethical and political superiority of the collectivity, and submit themselves to the ideological and tactical discipline of the party organization. Although, as demonstrated, Marxism contains elements of Romantic thought, it has most frequently been given a Rationalist interpretation. Orthodox Marxism has rarely been attractive to cultural radicals because it suppresses the rights of the individual in the name of a higher principle and promotes conformity in thought and behavior.

In contrast with most political movements, radical cultural movements typically are Romantic in ideology. Romantics attack the reification and devitalization of life by bourgeois Rationalism, including unthinking social conformity, lack of supportive fraternity, alienation of the spirit, and stifling of creative self-expression. Like anarchists, Romantics value individual liberty and voluntary community. However, their focus is not on collectively combatting the coercive power of the state but on inspiring the rebellion of the individual. Unlike anarchists, Romantics are not overtly concerned with institutional relations and the distribution of official power.

Rather, they seek to release individuals from personal inhibitions, expand the norms of interpersonal relations, and support experiments with new forms of living. Amid the chaos of Berlin just after World War I, the Dadaists attempted to create their revolutionary soviet, which demanded political commitment and organization. That is the basis for Huelsenbeck's denunciation of "Romantic quiet" and his rejection of Schwitters. Unlike political radicals, cultural radicals don't distinguish between means and ends. They try to express their values in their everyday activities, believing that the personal is political and a true revolution must be lived in principle each moment of one's life.

It would seem that the very nature of art would express Romantic values not provided for by the narrow premises of bourgeois Rationalism—fantasy, desire, community. From the late nineteenth century, however, art had been reduced to simply imitating nature. The Impressionists studied the writings of the physicists on light in order to more faithfully reproduce reality on their canvases. There was no thought of repudiating or transcending the given. Moreover, the art establishment had tightened its control over the distribution system and imposed a highly rationalized set of technical norms on what could be considered legitimate artistic creation. Finally, works of art had become commodified within the capitalist system, not just secularized but reduced to the status of private property rather than public spectacle. Hans Arp (1951, p. 292) cried, "Today nothing is sacred to man. He seizes upon everything with his coarse senses. Everything can be bought and sold. His tumult and shouting stifle every poem, every prayer."

The first Romantic wave associated with significant political activism in Western history occurred over the period 1830–50. It was active throughout Western Europe and climaxed in the aborted rebellions of 1848, This was followed by almost half a century of capitalist expansion, accompanied by the spread of Rationalism, including Benthamite utilitarianism and Spencerian evolutionism. The most dramatic exception to this general trend was the short-lived Paris Commune of 1871, in which the bohemians became freedom fighters against the crown. The revolt against this positivism in the last decade of the nineteenth century represented the beginning of a Romantic reaction to this development. The Dadaists represented its culminating expression. The Dadaists responded to the grave calculations and "crackpot realism" of the generals, bankers, and politicians with joyous nonsense, a lively and passionate celebration of life's unpredictability, an exhibition of sheer vitality.

Paradoxically, the Dadaists found it necessary to preach and practice a doctrine of anti-art in order to recover the historic function of art itself, that of stirring human passions. In so doing, they restored to art its radical function in capitalist society.

The radical function of art lies in its capacity to shape the perceptions and, thus, the consciousness of its public. Radical art can provoke indignation by exposing social conditions normally hidden from view, including the contradictions of the ruling elites and the more subtle details of exploitation and domination. Radical art can ridicule authorities, debunk myths, and delegitimate the culture of domination. Radical art can give scope to imagination, stimulate fantasies, awaken latent desires, kindle hope, and, ultimately, inspire action by evoking the image of a more beautiful future. Because it is public, radical art can provoke discussion, help individuals to perceive what were thought to be their own personal troubles as shared social problems, and, ultimately, create community.

At the most fundamental level, radical art challenges the taken-for-granted world, renders it problematic (and thus changeable), and stimulates visions of new possibilities. Thus, radical art is not a mere reflection of structural relations, but a creative human intervention that calls into question those relations.

Radical cultural movements that are not explicitly related to radical political movements are especially vulnerable to repression (as was Dada in Berlin and Cologne) or co-optation (as was Dada in Paris and elsewhere in the West). Once co-opted, they are able to extend their influence, but at the cost of becoming rationalized as they are accommodated to the given system of production and exchange. As a final consequence they become institutionalized, thus losing their radical thrust completely (for instance, modern art in the West).

Because they are value-oriented rather than power-oriented, operating at the level of consciousness rather than organization, radical cultural movements are typically more salient in the awakening stage (for instance, Russian Futurism and Constructivism, Berlin Dada) or in the aftermath of the repression of radical political movements (for instance, Berlin Dada). In the former case they can set the stage for the emergence of organized collective action by changing people's perceptions and desires.

When Marxist-oriented political movements begin to succeed (as with the Bolsheviks in Russia or the KDP in Berlin in 1920), however, they must organize themselves for diplomatic and military confrontations, present themselves as a viable alternative to the existing power structure, and prepare themselves for political leadership. This typically leads to demands for greater organizational discipline and ideological conformity. At this point the cultural radicals' celebration of individual sensibilities is seen as more of a liability than an asset.

Cultural radicals, in turn, are likely to experience the imposition of political discipline as an insufferable constraint on their freedom of action. When political movements triumph, they are likely to purge or discipline cultural radicals who do not conform to the demands of the new order. The stormy marriage between the Leninists and modern artists in Russia between 1917 and the mid-1920s remains the longest and most productive union of such forces.

On the other hand, when such movements are militarily repressed, the people's revolutionary yearnings typically are displaced to the symbolic realm, where the work of cultural radicals keeps the spirit of resistance alive. Henri Murger's extremely popular play on Paris bohemian life was produced in 1849, the year after the bloody repression of the revolution. Although his characters were seldom inspired by politics, they remained hostile to respectable society. Thus, Murger's play gave comfort to those looking for relief from political confrontations and also to those who wished to remind bourgeois society that there were people who still rejected its contradictions and corruptions in favor of a "life of freedom, work, and pleasure" (Siegel 1983, pp. 25–26). Thus, radical political and radical cultural movements constitute their own dialectic of historical action within the larger dialectic of Rationalism and Romanticism as modern Western society struggles with its own contradictions while in search of social arrangements that reconcile the solidarity of community with the liberty of the marketplace and fulfill all of our human potential.

REFERENCES

Arp, Hans. 1951. "Dada Was not a Farce." In *The Dada Painters and Poets*, edited by Robert Motherwell. New York: Wittenborn, Schultz.

Bamber, Linda. 1982. "Seeing Reds." *Working Papers*, May/June, pp. 61-64.

Barr, Alfred H. Jr. 1946. "Introduction." In *Fantastic Art, Dada, Surrealism*, edited by Alfred H. Barr, Jr. New York: Museum of Modern Art.

Clark, Carroll D. 1933. "The Concept of Public Opinion." *Southwestern Social Science Quarterly* 13 (Mar.): 311-20.

"The Dada Movement." 1953. *London Times Literary Supplement*, Oct. 23, p. 670.

De Coster, Miles. 1983. "Heartfield: The Art of Photo-persuasion." *In These Times*, July 13-26, pp. 20-21.

Edman, Irwin. 1939. *Arts and the Man. A Short Introduction to Aesthetics.* New York: W. W. Norton.

Esslin, Martin. 1961. *The Theatre of the Absurd.* Garden City, N.Y.: Doubleday.

Giuliano, Charles. 1968. "Dada, Surrealism and Their Heritage." *Boston Sunday Globe*, May 26, pp. 14-18.

Gouldner, Alvin. 1973. "Romanticism and Classicism: Deep Structures in Social Science." In *For Sociology: Renewal and Critique in Sociology Today*, edited by Alvin Gouldner, pp. 324-53. New York: Basic Books.

Grana, Caesar. 1967. *Modernity and Its Discontents.* Glencoe, Ill.: Free Press.

Grosz, George. 1946. *A Little Yes and a Big No: The Autobiography of George Grosz*, translated by Lola Sachs Dorin. New York: Dial.

Habermas, Jurgen. 1975. *Legitimation Crisis.* Boston: Beacon.

Haftman, Werner. 1960. *Painting in the 20th Century*, 2 vols. London: Lund Humphries.

Hauser, Arnold. 1958. *The Social History of Art*, vol. IV. New York: Vintage.

Huelsenbeck, Richard. 1951a. "Dada Lives!" In *The Dada Painters and Poets: An Anthology*, edited by Robert Motherwell. New York: Wittenborn, Schultz.

——. 1951b. "En Avant Dada: A History of Dadaism." In ibid.

——. 1951c. "End of the World." In ibid.

——. 1957. "Dada and Existentalism." In *Dada: Monograph of a Movement*, edited by Willy Verkauf. New York: George Wittenborn.

Hughes, H. Stuart. 1961. *Consciousness and Society*. New York: Alfred A. Knopf.

Hugnet, Georges. 1946. "Dada." In *Fantastic Art, Dada, Surrealism*, edited by Alfred H. Barr, Jr. New York: Museum of Modern Art.

——. 1951. "The Dada Spirit in Painting, Cologne and Hanover." In *The Dada Painters and Poets*, edited by Robert Motherwell. New York: Wittenborn, Schultz.

Janco, Marcel. 1957. "Creative Dada." In *Dada: Monograph of a Movement*, edited by Willy Verkauf. New York: George Wittenborn.

Kingston-Mann, Esther. 1982. "The Majority as an Obstacle to Progress: Radicals, Peasants, and the Russian Revolution." *Radical America* 16, no. 4: 74–86.

Kisselgoff, Anna. 1981. "Avant-Garde in Russia, 1913." *New York Times*, Feb. 8, pp. D8–9.

Kramer, Hilton. 1975. "The Spiritual Yearnings of a Founder of Dadaism." *New York Times*, Sept. 7, p. D39.

——. 1979. "Beyond the Avant-Garde." *New York Times Magazine*, Nov. 4, pp. 43–60.

——. 1980. "The 'Brutal Ideology' at the Heart of Futurism." *New York Times*, Dec. 14, pp. D41, D48.

——. 1981. "Taeuber-Arp, a Neglected Abstractionist." *New York Times*, Oct. 4, pp. 18–19, 21–22.

Mannheim, Karl. 1971. "Conservative Thought." In *From Karl Mannheim*, edited by Kurt Wolff. New York: Oxford University Press.

Marcuse, Herbert. 1978. *The Aesthetic Dimension: Toward a Critique of Marxist Aesthetics*. Boston: Beacon.

Mills, C. Wright. 1956. *The Power Elite.* New York: Oxford University Press.

Motherwell, Robert, ed. 1951. *The Dada Painters and Poets: An Anthology.* New York: Wittenborn, Schultz.

Newmeyer, Sarah. 1955. *Enjoying Modern Art.* New York: New American Library.

Read, Herbert. 1959. *A Concise History of Modern Painting.* New York: Praeger.

Ribemont-Dessaignes, Georges. 1951. "History of Dada." In *The Dada Painters and Poets*, edited by Robert Motherwell. New York: Wittenborn, Schultz.

Richter, Hans. 1965. *Dada: Art and Anti-Art.* New York: Oxford University Press.

Rosenberg, Karen. 1981. "The Shock of the Old: The Avant-Garde of the Twenties Comes Back." *In These Times*, Dec. 9-15, pp. 20-21.

Schwitters, Kurt. 1951. "Merz." In *The Dada Painters and Poets*, edited by Robert Motherwell. New York: Wittenborn, Schultz.

Shapiro, Theda. 1976. *Painters and Politics: The European Avant-Garde and Society, 1900-1925.* New York: Elsevier.

Shroyer, Trent. 1973. *The Critique of Domination.* Boston: Beacon.

Siegel, Jerrold. 1983. "The Rise of Bohemia." *The New Republic*, vol. 188, no. 4, Issue 3, 550 (January 31): 15-28.

Speier, Hans. 1950. "Historical Development of Public Opinion." *American Journal of Sociology* 55, no. 4 (Jan.): 376-88.

"The Happening." 1965. *Time Magazine*, June 4, p. 26.

Tzara, Tristan. 1951a. "Dada Manifesto 1918." In *The Dada Painters and Poets*, edited by Robert Motherwell. New York: Wittenborn, Schultz.

——. 1951b. "Manifesto of mr. aa the anti-philosopher." In ibid.

Verkauf, Willy, ed. 1957a. *Dada: Monograph of a Movement.* New York: George Wittenborn.

——. 1957b. "A DADA Dictionary." In *Dada: Monograph of a Movement*. New York: Basic Books.

Weber, Max. 1930. *The Protestant Ethic and the Spirit of Capitalism*, translated by Talcott Parsons. New York: Charles Scribner's Sons.

Willener, Alfred. 1970. *The Action Image of Society: On Cultural Politicization*. New York: Pantheon.

Willet, John. 1978. *Art and Politics in the Weimar Period: The New Sobriety, 1917–1933*. New York: Pantheon.

Wohl, Robert. 1979. *The Generation of 1914*. Cambridge, Mass.: Harvard University Press.

4 The Rise and Fall of the Marcus Garvey Movement, 1916–25: The Uses and Abuses of Cultural-Expressive Dimensions for Social Change

Douglas B. Gutknecht

This chapter is about Marcus Garvey's movement for racial justice, the Universal Negro Improvement Association (UNIA). Today there is belated yet genuine interest in how Marcus Mosias Garvey captured the imagination of poor blacks in the 1920s and still retains a pivotal and revitalized stature as a black leader of the highest magnitude. The meteoric rise of the UNIA between 1916 and 1925 to the largest mass movement for racial protest in the history of the United States certainly merits more reflection than has been offered up to this time. Many make passing reference to Garvey, but few really understand what he was up against as he confronted the racial consciousness of the most powerful nation in the world, just emerging from turning the tide in World War I.

Garvey has long influenced those interested in black power, black nationalism, and black militancy in general. However, his ambiguous position, even among militants and radicals, results from his style of thinking: an expressive emotional attitude and strong ideological bent. Garvey's mixture of diverse styles of thinking and

---

I would like to thank Edgar W. Butler, University of California, Riverside, and Bennett M. Berger, University of California, San Diego, for their helpful comments. I take complete responsibility for any flaws.

of promoting his movement confounds rather than clarifies. In addition we find contradictory ideological elements inherent in Garvey's formal program. He was a believer in Booker T. Washington's program of economic self-help and small-scale capitalism. He read Marx, yet also made some questionable references that could be interpreted as an implicit endorsement of some Ku Klux Klan arguments about the United States as "a white man's country" (Bontemps and Conroy 1966). Garvey's movement and ideas provide symbolic affirmation for the hopes of all racially oppressed people everywhere yet, as Goldman (1953) points out, some semi-fascist organizations in the United States may have been working in behalf of Garvey's ideals.

Social movements and organizations sometimes utilize cultural and symbolic resources, particularly when material and technological resources are seriously lacking. The need for recognizing such dimensions of social-movement culture is compatible with the belief that movements are both constrained by and active participants in their internal and external struggles over power, resources, ideological hegemony, and the allegiance of potential recruits. However, Garvey's use of ritual and symbolic appeals turned off many potential supporters and sympathizers in the labor movement, the Socialist Party, and the black intelligentsia in general.

Social movements often fail to utilize the group-based emotional and expressive energies of their members as a social, and ultimately organizational, resource. However, expressive commitment and ritual expressions of belonging, commitment, or solidarity on the part of movement constituents cannot take the place of systematic energy devoted to ideological analysis or political strategy, and the mundane daily tasks of paying the bills, or bailing out movement leaders. The dimensions of both heart and mind are often present in movements that accomplish their goals. This study calls attention to Garvey's use of emotional and expressive resources to accomplish his artful style of politics. It also offers a brief discussion of why his dramatic successes with the most submerged segments of the black underclass scared off potential allies, strongly aroused enemies, and failed at the pragmatic organizational and instrumental tasks of building a long-term movement capable of institutionalizing its fundamental accomplishments.

Understanding Marcus Garvey's national movement for racial justice, which emerged out of the ashes of World War I in Harlem, provides an excellent opportunity to briefly examine select dimensions of the social change process within a concrete historical move-ment. It is hoped that this discussion will provide a different perspec-tive for understanding the historical past and ultimately point a way for avoiding the same pitfalls in the attempt to create a new just and participatory future through the strategic mobilization of expressive social movement dimensions in unison with instrumental and prag-matic demands and contigencies.

This analysis also points to the need for a more complex view of social movements that emphasizes political and cultural, personal and collective, expressive and instrumental dimensions. An understanding of how and why social movements succeed or fail requires some understanding of how both dimensions fit together. Successful social movements and their sponsors sometimes make use of expressive dimensions (texts, media, rituals, symbols, themes, myths, cere-monies, locales) while not forgetting the importance of more instru-mental dimensions and analysis regarding tactics, strategic interests, power, control, technology, and financial resources. The key factor in explaining the success or failure of Marcus Garvey becomes one of articulating how the critical dimensions of the style or the art of politics (the dramaturgical, symbolic, and cultural mode of political propaganda in its best sense, the art of mobilizing the masses), be-comes both an opportunity and a fetter or limitation to the success-ful long-run construction of a unique social change opportunity for racial justice. Modern social change movements may improve their opportunities for success by learning some lessons from the history of racial struggles in America.

THE STRUCTURAL AND CONTEXTUAL BACKGROUND

The World War I period was the dramatic culmination of several important historical events: the failure of the Reconstruction, the emergence of Jim Crow segregation in the urban South, the loss of romantic illusions and deflation of the Northern urban rhetoric that racism had been eradicated, and the miserable plight of black veter-ans as they tried to find work upon their return home. Such events urgently underscored the weakened psychological and cultural self-esteem that many rural blacks had brought to the crucible of North-ern urban ghetto life. The necessity for some emergent form of community-based religion or social solidarity to build self-esteem in the face of destructive urban forces became evident to black leaders, like Garvey, sensitive to racial humiliation and aware of nationalistic struggles.

Marcus Garvey articulated an urban-based expressive movement devoted to racial justice that had its roots in the self-help, church-related, rural Southern culture. Garvey's Jamaican background in labor organizing provided him with some early social-movement leadership experience and allowed him to perceive a link between the need for a new self-image for blacks, and a larger agenda of a collective struggle for resources, land, a place or home free of racial oppression, and assaults on one's dignity. Such a movement required more than a renaissance of black literary leaders or middle-class intellectual rhetoric or socialist slogans because many urban blacks were uneducated. In addition the white man's vision of the future had long failed to include a significant place for America's minority groups. Let me briefly outline the conditions leading to the situation in the urban North.

After the Civil War, Southern blacks gradually developed re-worked cultural patterns and responses to the breakup of the slave-based plantation. The question of the survival of African cultural elements is less important here than the growth of indigenous black cultural ideological adaptations that were capable of giving the black community the beginning of a cohesive sense of self-discipline for survival.

As black migrations increased throughout the decade of 1910–20, the tensions in large Northern urban centers also increased. Meier and Rudwick (1970) argue that Garvey's movement was part of a larger pattern associated with migration tendencies among Southern blacks. This relationship was not new, but the crucible of densely settled ghetto life increased Garvey's appeal as a compensatory escape. These problems were apparent to black leaders of all skin tones and class levels. The issue became how to protect these people from racism, increasing violence, institutional discrimination in schools and housing, overcrowding, and unemployment (Spear 1967; Ofsky 1966). Increasing violence against blacks, during and after the return of black veterans who were accustomed to more humane treatment in Europe, was the straw that broke the camel's back. Bonacich (1976) documents a split labor market where blacks were paid less for the same work, worked longer hours, were kept out of union jobs with union wages, were displaced by automation, were first to be fired, and were used as strikebreakers, causing a backlash among some potential allies in white unions.

Ofsky (1966, p. 13) documents how the black ghetto of Harlem centralized and expanded in one area, uptown Manhattan, at the expense of several decentralized black areas, which led to an intensification of segregation and exploitation: "The Negro remained and expanded as the other ethnic ghettos disintegrated: Harlem became a slum with all attending consequences."

This external penetration and exploitation led some critics to use the term nationalism by suggesting that the destruction of indigenous cultural support systems actually created an internal colonial status for ghetto blacks (Tabb 1970). Lasch (1974) suggests that cultural, political, and economic penetration of urban ghettos like Harlem in the 1920s not only caused a collapse of black culture but also created a dangerous vulnerability to divide-and-conquer strategies. In his wider scenario, disorganization, insecurity, and fear, created by such total, external penetration of the ghetto colony, escalated the potential for both external and internal exploitation. Lasch (1974, p. 196) aptly summarizes the modern yet perennial theme of the debilitating effects of exploitation and manipulation:

> Those who deny the pathological elements of the culture of poverty would do well to ponder Malcolm's account of his own degradation, in a world where high status meant light skin, straight hair, the company of white women, and flashy clothes manufactured by white merchants especially for the ghetto and sold at inflated prices. . . .

GARVEY AND THE UNIA MOVEMENT

Marcus Garvey's organization, the Universal Negro Improvement and Conservation Association and African Communities League (shortened to UNIA), which started in England in 1914 and was brought to the United States in 1916, "can no longer be considered an anomaly of American politics" (Huggins 1977, p. 41). In the years 1919–25, the time it took his movement to take effective form, Garvey had risen from obscurity to international recognition and, by 1926, to federal prison, charged with misusing the mails. Clarke (1974, p. iv) aptly summarizes the many paradoxes of Garveyism: ". . . the vast material forces, social conceptions, and imperial interests which automatically sought to destroy him, his achievement remains one of the great propaganda miracles of this century." Based in Harlem, Garvey turned Booker T. Washington's message of economic self-help and racial dignity into a more aggressive version of international black nationalism.

The UNIA encapsulated the formal ideological goals of the Garvey movement:

> To establish a Universal Co-Fraternity among the race; to promote the spirit of pride and love; to reclaim the fallen; to minister to and assist the needy; to assist in civilizing the backward tribes of Africa; to assist in the development of Independent Negro Nations and Communities; to establish a central nation for the race; to establish Commissionaries or Agencies in the principal countries and cities of the world for the representation of all Negroes. (Garvey 1963, p. iii)

Garvey's mixture of goals and ideals suggests that sometimes the expressive tail actually wagged the instrumental dog of his social movement: "The U.N.I.A. . . . is a social, friendship, humanitarian, charitable, educational, institutional, constructive, and expansive society . . . the motto of the organization is: One God! One Destiny!" (Garvey 1963, p. xiii). Garvey's wife, Amy, in her biographical account called his movement "glorious and romantic"; it exhorted the black people of the world and fixed their eyes upon the bright star of a future (Garvey 1963, p. xiii). Huggins (1977, p. 46) is more blunt, asserting that "Garvey was threatening to other Negro leaders. . . . His pandering to the superstitions and fantasies of the mob was exactly the kind of tactic that black and white progressives abhorred." Political abhorrence is seldom however a simple fact of establishing a higher ground of nationality.

Garvey's movement provided its first major success and momentum to build a broader-based movement during the first UNIA International Convention of Negro Peoples of the World at Madison Square Garden in 1920. The supportive theme "Africa for Africans" became a cultural icon inspiring a new energy and commitment to a new self-determination for independence and nationhood. Likewise, the vision of a new Negro with pride and dignity was elaborated in the Declaration of the Rights of the Negro Peoples of the World. Political rhetoric for building a viable social movement must focus on attracting a following. Otherwise instrumental activities are blowing in the wind.

The vision of returning to Africa became a symbolic and support-ive device used for recruitment because it allowed the opportunity to dream of a new beginning in a new land, free of white racism. Coming at the time of the post-World War I economic depression, the Red Scare and urban riots, lynchings and racial hostility, it found blacks ready for a new beginning. Garvey didn't discuss the practical difficulties of such a scheme, only the need to return to Africa. Garvey's symbolic appeals touched the heart and spirit, and won many new members, but his very success helped to create a backlash against the flamboyant tactics he used. Early success in the formula-tive process required knowledge of how to make the transition to a new more practical approach. Garvey's inability to make such a practical transition resulted from his assessment of the conditions operative at this juncture in American History.

Garvey's movement may be identified as a unique form of emerging nationalism supporting segregation and racial self-determi-nation in post-World War I urban America, but its particular direc-tion resulted from Garvey's analysis of the general racial conditions prevalent in America at that time. Garvey's ideas became part of a historical dialogue with these social conditions; such conditions helped account for the cultural and instrumental elements of Garvey's attempt to rally the migrating urban black masses. Garvey was essentially a cultural nationalist who followed in the tradition of teaching pride in race and blackness, racial solidarity, and respect for African heritage.

Nationalism had its roots in the earlier slave rebellions, petitions for liberating slaves during and after the Revolutionary War, and various programs for returning blacks to Africa (Pinkney 1976, pp. 16–19). In the nineteenth century, black nationalist leaders such as Paul Cuffee, Martin Delaney, and Bishop Turner advocated pro-grams of racial solidarity, political and economic autonomy, and return to Africa or the West Indies. Early nationalists operated from a mixture of motives, altering their strategies as the conditions war-ranted, often becoming, like Delaney, more interested in means than in ends. Forms of nationalism derived from a tradition of black separatism, religious, discipline, and self-help. Meier and Rudwick (1970, p. xxxvi) offer two themes common to all forms of national-ism; no programmatic ideology and a sense of racial solidarity. Pinkney (1976, pp. 6–7) identifies three themes: unity/solidarity, pride in cultural heritage and black consciousness, and autonomy.

Pinkney (1976, pp. 13–14) identifies the important ideological dimensions inherent in nationalism as being between a cultural (expressive) and a political (instrumental) or revolutionary version:

> Cultural nationalism holds that black people throughout the world possess a distinct culture and that before black liberation can be achieved in the U.S. Blacks must reassert their cultural heritage. . . . A cultural revolution in the black community is essential before Afro-Americans can command the unity necessary to revolt against their oppressors. One of the most controversial types of black nationalism is revolutionary nationalism . . . most maintain that Afro-Americans cannot achieve liberation in the U.S. within the existing political and economic system.

Garvey's version of cultural nationalism combined the expressive hopes and dreams of racial solidarity with a fantastic instrumental goal of nationhood in Africa. The basic flaw was not in the utilization of the symbol of independent nationhood but in the impracticality of a return of millions of blacks to Africa. The symbolic and expressive appeal of a return to a far away homeland and the inspiration of nationhood prevented Garvey from sustaining his focus on the more practical elements of his instrumental program, building economic cooperation through racial solidarity.

Garvey's ability to build such a large mass movement for racial justice attests to the expressive and symbolic power of these techniques and ideas that touched the lives of blacks in a very personal way. However, the diversity and short-run success of such a young social movement suggests that the experience and symbolic appeals that worked in the short run provided a diversionary alternative to the instrumental issues of building a solid organizational basis. The generality and range of issues that Garvey tried to bring under the umbrella of his movement actually detracted from recognition of the key links necessary for long-run success: a more limited yet efficient and practical, use of his material resources like the Black Star Steamship Line which could be used to accumulate additional economic resources that might have facilitated the accomplishment of more realistic instrumental goals.

One can see various strains of nationalistic ideas—political, instrumental, and expressive—waxing and waning, sometimes creating coalitions or splitting to highlight differences. These differences depend on both external structural conditions and the internal organizational issues, and conflicts. The internal struggles often degenerate, as they did in Garvey's movement, to the level of personal attack and character assassination. It is my belief that Garvey succeeded so rapidly because he understood the symbolic, expressive, and cultural needs of his lower-class black supporters—he spoke their language and provided an opportunity for ritual participation, pageantry, celebration, parades, and showing racial pride and dignity. However, such successes created blind spots, and a potential vulnerability to those many groups poised to descend upon his movement and win back its supporters.

THE FRAMEWORK: INSTRUMENTAL AND EXPRESSIVE DIMENSIONS

The form and functions of artful political expression provide a framework highlighting the links of instrumental and expressive activity in social movements. Social-movement research has recently focused on the importance of political, organizational, and economic resources (instrumental activity) in the success or failure of social movements (Bromley and Schupe 1979). This necessary change of direction in social-movement research resulted from the overplaying of the expressive and presumably irrational emotional forces of crowd behavior in much writing on collective behavior. The present analysis begins by recognizing the importance of the shifting alliances of symbolic expression in instrumental political action, particularly radical movements for social change like Marcus Garvey's.

This analysis builds upon the idea of a social phenomenology of ideological activity, artful political propaganda, or symbolic politics. For example, Geertz (1964) views ideology as a form of thought that relates to the task of formulating moral sentiment in order to motivate, ensure commitment, and semantically structure and guide action through appropriate meaning. Ideologies may blind and deceive, but they certainly build group solidarity and provide insight into how social reality is collectively built and maintained.

Gouldner (1976, p. 250) defines the roots of ideology as moral and integrative undertakings, the integration of fragmented beliefs and actions in order to guide the creation of human solidarity, joint action, and the attainment of a new vision. Such a view highlights positive cultural dimensions of ideology, in contrast with the predominantly negative view that reduces ideology to instrumental rationalizations of material class interests. Ideology serves both instrumental and expressive purposes: intensifying instrumental conflicts by emphasizing differences of group goals, interests, resources, class or racial makeup while also creating the possibilities for joint action, shared suffering, and long-run commitment. Berger (1981, p. 19) argues for a microsociology of knowledge to complement a macrosociology of knowledge.

> But I am not primarily interested either in "laying bare" that these ideas are "merely" self-serving or that they are compromised by the exigencies of circumstance. I take it as a matter of course that beliefs are likely to have a self-serving component for the individuals or groups who espouse them. . . . Ideas are human creations, so they are created for purposes, in context, and are definable in time and place, by living people who invest themselves in these (rather than those) ideas for discoverable reasons.

This analysis builds upon the ideas of expressive or symbolic ideology and Berger's idea of ideological work. Ideological adjustments may be defined as intellectual work necessary when discrepancies arise between what individuals and groups believe or assert they believe, and the practical circumstances that require sensemaking or meaningful responses. Ideological adjustments are necessitated by changing sociopolitical, ideational, and existential environments. Such manipulation of ideas and sentiments is carried on most vigorously when routine individual (e.g., narcissism) or group behavior is in apparent contradiction with professed beliefs and ideals of group members, when socialization fails, or when groups experience material or emotional resource scarcities, conscious or unconscious conflicts, external repression, or change of leadership.

Clearly, in most instances ideological adjustment is a complex, inchoate process, full of ambiguities and inward turns of logic. One might observe groups and intellectual sponsors of ideas who are often unaware of larger historical and situational factors leading to the necessity of some form of ideological monitoring and expressive activities. Radical groups, cut off from the mainstream activities of realistic social compromise and reconciliation of diverse interests, may fill the gaps between theory and practice with extensive symbolic and behavioral adjustments. These adjustments are sometimes devoid of conceptual rigor or consistency because they are cut off from the ability to stand the test of evaluative feedback, which is also a fundamental extremist problem for many ideologies both on the left and right. Recognition of the dialectic between expressive and cognitive dimensions of social movements must not be interpreted as impugning the diverse activities, interests or commitments of movement participants or leaders. In fact, the energizing force behind successful movements must be individuals and groups with enough individual and group energy or motivation to continue a struggle.

Thus, the idea of cultural symbols or metaphors provides the key link between the expressive and instrumental or cognitive dimensions of ideology. Language is the most complex form of cognitive and instrumental symbolic communication, but used for expression it also supports manipulation and domination. That which we are lead to deeply believe in can function to enslave us. Symbols liberate our energies and thus require discretion if we are to avoid addiction to their form devoid of substance. For example, Garvey often used the evocative symbol of the lost and promised kingdom to focus emotional energies of highly religious urban blacks on the feeling of past and future greatness for cognitively articulating a systematic program for returning blacks home to Africa.

Symbols refer to salient group experiences and possess the properties of emotionality, expressiveness, and sacredness. Deeply felt experiences become condensed into a single word, a ritual, an emblem, a ceremony, clothing, a building, music, or any representation that imparts a high emotional quality to the symbol. This emotion is stimulated upon contact with the symbol. Symbols call into focus highly valued ideals and goals that, because of their sacredness, increase the self-esteem and solidarity of those who revere them.

One of Garvey's strengths and, at the same time, limitations resulted from his strong use of an oral tradition and rich metaphors that struck a resonant chord with the migrating rural blacks who possessed little formal education. After all, rural blacks had thrived on creating folk forms of media and communication to outwit slave masters and assist in the maintenance of a culture of resistance. Levine (1972, p. 135) takes to task historians studying the urban migrants of the early twentieth century for ignoring styles of black protest and cultural resistance:

> On the whole, such discussions have ignored the evidence of black folk-lore, black music, and black humor with their array—such heroes and

models as tricksters, bad men, blues men and the evidence of lower class black culture in which entertainers, preachers and underworld hustlers often occupy central positions.

The fundamental appeal of Garvey was to those people existing in the social and cultural wastelands of the inner-city ghetto. Although black leaders like W. E. B. DuBois consistently criticized Garvey for his narrowness, chauvinism, and demagogic qualities, Garvey's appeal was immense (Vincent 1970). However, his symbolic and cultural appeals often took precedence over the need to create a wider base. One must be careful not to place all the blame on Garvey, for the failure to create political alliances in the black community also resulted from rigidity and inflexibility on the part of middle-class black intellectuals and artists, as well as from the political oppression of the U.S. government.

Garvey's program was a unique blend of cultural-expressive and instrumental-political themes. His cultural message, not surprisingly, was most convincing to his followers when it downplayed intellectual complexities and political and class realities while focusing on symbolic issues and values, such as heroism, African homeland, racial self-reliance, and racial pride. Garvey's political and cultural program resembled Booker T. Washington's economic program of building indigenous economic institutions in order to create a self-sustaining community (Clarke 1974, p. 6). Garvey exhorted his followers to join the UNIA, buy stock in the Black Star Steamship Line, participate in the UNIA religious ceremonies, pageantry, and cultural activities, and have faith in the dawn of freedom in a new land. However, the political realities of the times required more rigorous analysis and constant adjustment of strategy and ideology.

Instrumental clarification or expressive elaboration becomes a process of adjustment, changes, and compromise in the face of inevitable opposition forces, both internal and, more important, external. Ideological adjustments assume cultural or symbolic trappings because compromise and pragmatic survival often dictate the need to wait and rebuild forces, to energize the expressive forces of group solidarity, and to sacrifice for a greater good. However, actions out of line with their ideological foundations soon must be accommodated to the new realities of survival and the necessity for believing firmly in one's cause. It is this incessant adjustment—perhaps even more than its representative, accurate view of the world—that best explains the workings of ideas in the daily struggle to make sense of the world. Symbolic or expressive rituals thus become both supportive, in that the ideals and goals of the movement gain a new meaning and energized focus, and more radical, in that the contrast with other (outsider or enemy) ideals becomes more clearly etched.

Symbols can serve important supportive functions for protest and radical groups trying to establish their social and political credibility. Symbols may allow a more successful recruitment and socialization of new members who identify with the sacredness of their symbols. In fact, symbols expressed through rituals often attract more attention than dry, abstract, ideological arguments of the instrumental variety. Those symbols, rooted in rituals, customs, and ideologies of groups with previously developed historical legacies, become available for use in the mobilization of the new members to accomplish agreed-upon goals. Symbols may have extremely narrow referents, as in single words or signs, or they may involve multiple and potent meanings, as in social-movement or organizational ritual, ceremonies, folklore, and mythic stories. Such symbols compress many intense historical memories, emotions, and thoughts into unified and passionate displays of unity and sharing.

Symbolic, ideological, and cultural resources also have a radicalizing purpose or function. The dynamic and emotional qualities of salient symbols and their repetitive expression often heightens the rhetoric of social-movement ideology by unlocking expressive feelings of those oppressed and humiliated by dominant authorities. Feelings of hostility to dominant powers are enacted through sacred and emotional symbols that set the group apart from the "profane" and corrupting forces of society or smaller groups. A sense of in-group solidarity often builds upon increasingly more radical symbols in order to establish the legitimate domains of in-group loyalty, community of kind, and universe of radical discourse. A sense of socially constructed turf or territory often coexists with a sacredness of symbolism that must be defended from outside violations. Potent ideological symbols are required when a strong sense of community is threatened. Militant actions often follow in a self-fulfilling manner when radical symbols become dominant. For example, the I.R.A. in Ireland has used symbolism regarding the death of comrades to enhance a sense of solidarity and community that in turn requires more radical action to live up to its image of commitment and loyalty.

Social movements and organizations often utilize cultural and symbolic resources for building loyalty and commitment, particularly in the face of limited or diminished resources. Garvey's expressive style became a necessary resource for building intense feelings of pride, self-worth, and belonging in an oppressed people. However, this ritualistic and expressive style was not a sufficient resource to build a movement rooted in a cognitively accurate picture of the social and environmental events of the times.

THE EXPRESSIVE DIMENSIONS OF THE GARVEY MOVEMENT

The failed attempts by social-movement actors as leaders or members are seldom addressed as a rational outcome of modern organizational life. When we are speaking of institutionalized action in social movements, the complexities of organizing and changing institutions or environments in the face of contingencies and uncertainties, brought about by complex decisions and information needs, is awesome. It most certainly must have been so for Garvey and others trying to make sense of American race relations in the post-World War I era.

Ritual, myth, and symbols enlarge the discussion of instrumental-political action to include the important expressive dimensions. Cultural rituals allow political and social-movement organizations to rationalize collective distress, resource problems, and social conflicts at a level where intense and unpredictable emotions may be displayed and channeled into stylized, conventionalized, and safe expression: "Political rituals are drama. . . . They are a dramatic play in which a group ritually enacts its belief in its legitimate power: e.g., its internal cohesion, its differentiation from the rest of the world, its right to visit retribution" (Klapp 1979, p. 121).

Thus, we can see that political activities often have as much to do with dreams, myths, ideologies, and solidarity building as with changing the world. Such symbolic elements communicate historically important memories in dramatic displays of harmony and consensus. The formalized and stylized simplicity of expression in such symbolic forms permits ready emotional identification and support for the political and cultural myths that must be sustained. Such social-cultural-political dramas may reaffirm personal identity and communities of kind or meanings that provide a ready symbolic vehicle for the assertion of common ideologies, myths, and dreams. Here, one can see the enormous potential political gain available to those media spokespersons and gatekeepers capable of using symbolic manipulation in ritual, ceremony, and other cultural modes to further political programs.

Garvey appealed to more than the consciousness of formal and rational surface interests because he probed beneath the surface of self-interests, reaching the level of feeling and emotions that made marginal urban blacks feel good about themselves. For example, his UNIA marched under its own flag with colors of red, black, and green, and had the African National Anthem put in verse and set to martial music:

> Ethopia, thou land of our fathers, thou land where the gods love to be,
> As storm cloud at night sudden gathers,
> Our armies come rushing to thee.
> We must in the Fight be victorious,
> For us will the victory be glorious,
> When led by the red, black and green. (Garvey 1963, p. 31)

Utilizing music to inspire his followers, "Garvey outlined a set of meaningful hymns, and Burrell and For of the Music Department put them into proper verse and set them to music" (Garvey 1963, p. 47). Amy Garvey (ibid.) suggests that the music impressed listeners with the "intents and purposes of the organization," and could even control and sober "zealots and fanatics" who might arise in their "far-flung brotherhood."

The ritual used in the services included a prayer that everyone recited at the end of every service. It included the following call for:

> Wisdom and discretion in all our undertakings, patience under our difficulties, triumph over our enemies, and a happy issue out of our struggles. Save us, we pray thee, from the great danger of unhappy division. Take from us envy, hatred, malice, and whatever may hinder us from union and concord: that as there is but one body, and one spirit, and one "type" of our calling, One God: One Aim! One Destiny! So we may be all of one heart and of one mind. . . . (Garvey 1963, p. 48)

Followers overflowed Garvey's 6,000-seat Liberty Hut Tabernacle every Sunday evening. One evening in 1921 he crowned himself president-general of the UNIA and provisional president of Africa. Kelly Miller (1974, p. 243) lists some of the symbolic elements constituting this African ghetto nobility as "knights of the Nile," "knights of the distinguished service order of Ethiopia," and "dukes of Niger and of Uganda." The cultural, symbolic mode of Garvey's appeal led many black leaders and radicals to ignore its political substance.

Garvey's brand of symbolic and ritualistic politics appealed to "both protest and fellowship" (Clarke 1974, p. xxix). Garvey asked, "Where is the Black man's government? Where is his King and Kingdom? Where is his President, his country, his ambassadors, his army, his navy, his men of affairs?" (Clarke 1974, p. 8). Adopting a mixture of Catholic and other Christian ritual, African tribal lore, and official pageantry and titles, Garvey taught his people to dream of an emerging great race. Chronon (1955) appropriately titles his work *Black Moses*, for Garvey addressed the oppressive conditions and emerging cynicism of the postwar era with a religious fervor resembling Moses' appeal to the children of Israel. Franklin Frazier notes practical, ritualistic, and Utopian elements in Garvey's mass-based style:

> He not only promised the despised Negro a paradise on earth, but he made the Negro an important person in his immediate environment. He invented honors and social distinctions and converted every social invention to his use in his effort to make his followers feel important. While everyone was not a "knight or sir": all his followers were fellow-men of the Negro race. . . . The women were organized into Black Cross nurses and the men became uniformed members of the vanguard of the great African Army. A uniformed member of a Negro lodge paled in significance beside a soldier of the Army of Africa. (Clarke 1974, p. 238)

FINAL REFLECTIONS

Collins (1982, p. 24) affirms only part of the picture when he argues for the importance of nonrational and expressive dimensions in building common interests in political and protest groups: "This requires that somehow they share a new national sentiment that makes them want to contribute to the group instead of being free riders. It is for this reason that ideological symbols and emotions are so important in politics."

Focus on dimensions of formal rationality and formal interests assume that people always know precisely what is in their interests, who their allies are, how to calculate their interests, and that these known interests unify rather than divide. In fact, pursuing individual interests may actually detract from group goals or interests, because individuals who become free riders find that:

> Which interests win out, nonetheless, is not a matter of social calculation. It depends on something deeper or moral feelings . . . the procedures that produce their moral feelings, I am to argue, are social rituals. . . . The key point is that groups not only contend over competitive interests but they also see their own interests in moral terms. (Collins 1982, p. 28)

However, the very complexity of social environments in which organizations operate often requires the constant infusion of both expressive and instrumental resources in order to cope, in times of turbulence, with the cognitive limitations of our ideologies.

An excessive emphasis on group loyalty and the mobilization of group sentiment in the short run must allow for broader instrumental goals, mobilization of recruits, and routinization or institutionalization of instrumental and material resources. However, a movement will fail after a relatively brief time without the mobilized sentiments, emotions, and expressive loyalties of committed members:

> Rather than focusing exclusively on the movement's attempt to foster social change, the resource mobilization approach allows for the possibility that a variety of audiences in addition to formal authorities, may have to be influenced in some fashion (e.g., neutralized, transformed into supporters) in order for the movement to continue to work toward its goals. Mobilization becomes very much an interactive process in which the societal response to movement activities and policies modifies future exchanges. (Bromley and Schupe 1979. p. 20)

Garvey, a newcomer to hardball American racial politics, elevated the expressive dimensions of movement activity in order to win supporters. As a self-elevated charismatic spokesperson and gatekeeper of nationalistic racial self-determination and pride, he chose to mobilize and recruit by altering the previous racial agenda of ideas. Compromise with other "blue vein" elite black leaders, intellectuals, or artists was out of the question. In fact, Garvey appeared to resent the fact that white bohemians dominated movements such as the Harlem Renaissance. He mistrusted such potential allies as Communists, Socialists, and the white working class (Moore 1974). One line of reasoning might explain Garvey's failure as one of mistaken ideological assessment—his failure to understand fully the state of political and cultural confusion during the 1920s in newly emerging black urban ghettos such as Harlem:

> The political distinction between the radicals and the old crowd negroes reflected a power fight which found on the one hand, nationalists, socialists, communists, trying to build a new basis of power in the urban community; and on the other hand, the combined forces of the N.A.A.C.P. and the other civil rights groups, plus the old line approach of the late Booker T. Washington. (Nelson 1976, p. 69)

Such ideological struggles often occurred as concrete daily struggles for organizational direction within the UNIA. Numerous Garvey lieutenants, such as W. A. Domingo, were expelled from the UNIA because of their attempt to incorporate other ideological strains into the Garvey movement. How Garvey handled these disagreements indicates his inability to build the very organizational base he felt so important. Black Communist infiltrators of the UNIA certainly intensified the organizational paranoia and interpersonal hostility that prevented the execution of daily, necessary activities in an environment capable of nurture and support. Internal struggles spelled doom for a movement already harassed by numerous external opposition groups and a climate of racial fear and uncertainty.

The continued appeal of Garvey's UNIA, even when submerged during the New Deal and post-World War II prosperity, has been to both the cultural vacuum of the ghetto and the class vacuum attendant upon ignoring a disposable, marginal underclass of urban blacks. Black leaders in the 1970s, such as Martin Luther King, Jr., praised Garvey and his ideas of racial pride, solidarity, and economic self-help, particularly during his later years, when Dr. King became more radical. However, neither Garvey, Malcolm X, Dr. King, Stokely Carmichael nor Jesse Jackson could overcome the complexities of organizing for social change in a system built upon repression, co-optation, and the ability to use reform to quiet critics.

One facet of this analysis that is of great interest in this time of general political apathy, particularly among the poorest and most defeated in our midst, is Jesse Jackson's ability, like Garvey's, to temporarily organize an effective movement of people one would not expect could be mobilized—the so-called Rainbow Coalition. Most often Jackson, like Garvey, achieved his effect by recognizing the usefulness of symbolic and cultural modes of politics for those caught between contradictory informational racial, class, and cultural worlds. Both Garvey and Jackson have mobilized oppressed groups who responded to orchestrated images that transcended drab politics. Neither Garvey nor Jackson can be accused of falling prey to what has been called the "liberal imagination": the emphasis on non-political, psychological elements of individual lives, divorced from group solidarity and community action.

We shouldn't consider the issue of movement success or failure in black-and-white, win-or-lose terms. Social behavior and action, including the building of social movements, require an analysis of concrete relationships and possible future actions. Game terminology more appropriately captures the complexity and uncertainty of struggle. The games and rules of social life can be viewed as man-made ones that allow the struggle for human freedom to proceed. Social movements come to mediate our goals, and often contradict our hopes and dreams. We must not be too harsh, for the perverse effects of social life come back to us as a result of changing times and complexity of events: initial large successes can create bondage in the aggregate at some later time. Small successes can provide the threads for our visionary tapestry of a more humane and just future. Our inability to see the forces perched on the ledge above us, waiting to devour us, should cause thoughtful humility. One must be careful when placing blame. Garvey's failure to create political alliances in the black community also resulted from a dialectical and interpretive response to rigidity and inflexibility on the part of potential allies.

Today, long after Garvey's deportation in 1940, the Black Muslims in the United States, the Rastafarian Brethren in Jamaica, nationalistic leaders in sub-Sahara Africa, black nationalists in the United States, and even moderate black leaders refer to Garvey as the forerunner of Pan-Africanism. In fact, Martin Luther King, Jr., when visiting Jamaica in 1965, spoke at the Garvey Memorial Shrine in a Kingston public park. He tacitly suggested that Garvey's early successes laid the groundwork for the later successes of the civil rights movement. He praised Garvey for being the first leader of a truly mass movement among blacks for racial dignity and justice.

In the final analysis Garvey's movement proved unable to develop reflectiveness about its own identity and direction, or to comprehend the larger, complex cultural picture of common oppression facing blacks of all skin tone, as well as other minority groups, white labor, cultural intellectuals and other potential allies. Unable to perceive the complex historical limitations on his tactical choices, Garvey failed to build a more modest and long-term social movement. However, he brought dignity and communal struggle to the forefront of drab instrumental political action, and created a collective conscience that still lives in the hearts and minds of those contemplating new ways of building social movements. Garvey's movement also succeeded in providing an example of how cultural and symbolic dimensions may complement more traditional instrumental goals. The nature of social systems and complex interrelationships demands that social movements address this cultural underside of social and organizational life.

REFERENCES

Berger, Bennett M. 1981. *The Survival of a Counterculture: Ideological Work and Everyday Life Among Rural Communards.* Berkeley and Los Angeles: University of California Press.

Bonacich, Edna. 1976. "Advanced Capitalism and Black/White Race Relations in the U.S.: A Split Labor Market Interpretation." *American Sociological Review* 41 (Feb.): 34–51.

Bontemps, Arno, and Jack Conroy. 1966. *Anyplace but Here.* New York: Hill and Wang.

Bromley, D., and A. Schupe. 1979. *Moonies in America: Cult, Church, Crusade.* Beverly Hills, Calif.: Sage.

Burkett, Randall R. 1975. "Garveyism as a Religious Movement." Ph.D. dissertation, University of Southern California.

Chronon, Edmund David. 1955. *Black Moses.* New York: Random House.

Clarke, John Henrik, ed. 1974. *Marcus Garvey and the Vision of Africa.* New York: Vintage Books.

Collins, Randall. 1982. *Sociological Insight: An Introduction to Non-Obvious Sociology*. New York: Oxford University Press.

Combs, David E. 1980. *Dimensions of Political Drama*. Santa Monica, Calif.: Goodyear.

Davis, David Brian. 1966. *The Problems of Slavery in Western Culture*. Ithaca, N.Y.: Cornell University Press.

Edelman, Murray. 1966. *The Symbolic Uses of Politics*. Urbana: University of Illinois Press.

Feuer, Lewis S., ed. 1969. *The Conflict of Generations*. New York: Basic Books.

Garvey, Amy Jacques. 1963. *Garvey and Garveyism in New York*. New York: Collier Books.

Geertz, Clifford. 1972. *The Interpretation of Cultures*. New York: Basic Books.

Goldman, Morris. 1953. "The Garvey Movement: 1916-27." Master's thesis, New School for Social Research.

Gouldner, Alvin. 1976. *The Dialectic of Ideology and Technology*. New York: Seabury Press.

Gusfield, Joseph. 1966. *Symbolic Crusade*. Urbana: University of Illinois Press.

Huggins, Nathan Dewin. 1977. *Harlem Renaissance*. New York: Oxford University Press.

Keniston, Kenneth. 1968. *Young Radicals*. New York: Harcourt, Brace and World.

Klapp, Orin E. 1979. *Opening and Closing: Strategies of Information Adaptation in Society*. New York: Cambridge University Press.

Lacy, Dan. 1972. *The White Use of Blacks in America*. New York: McGraw-Hill.

Lasch, Christopher. 1974. *The World of Nations: Reflections on American History, Politics and Culture*. New York: Vintage Press.

Levine, David. 1972. *Internal Combustion: The Races in Detroit, 1915-1926*. Westport, Conn.: Greenwood Press.

Mason, Philip. 1970. *Race Relations.* New York: Oxford University Press.

Meier, August, and Eliot Rudwick. 1970. *From Plantation to Ghetto.* New York: Hill and Wang.

Miller, Kelly. 1974. "After Marcus Garvey—What of the Negro," in *Marcus Garvey and the Vision of Africa*, edited by John Henrik Clarke, pp. 242-246.

Moore, Richard B. 1974. "The Critics and Opponents of Marcus Garvey." In *Marcus Garvey and the Vision of Africa*, edited by John Henrik Clarke, pp. 242-46. New York: Vintage Books.

Nelson, David Gordon. 1976. *Black Ethos: Northern Urban Negro Life and Thought, 1890-1930.* Westport, Conn.: Greenwood Press.

Ofsky, Frank. 1966. *Harlem: The Making of a Ghetto.* Chicago: University of Chicago Press.

Pinkney, Alphonso. 1976. *Red, Black, and Green: Black Nationalism in the United States.* New York: Cambridge University Press.

Spear, Allan H. 1967. *Black Chicago, the Making of a Negro Ghetto.* Chicago: University of Chicago Press.

Tabb, William K. 1970. *The Political Economy of the Black Ghetto.* New York: W. W. Norton and Co.

Vincent, Edward. 1970. *Black Power and the Garvey Movement.* San Francisco: Ramparts Press.

5 "We Were a Little Hipped on the Subject of Trotsky": Literary Trotskyists in the 1930s

Constance Ashton Myers

The brush with Leon Trotsky's version of Marxism on the part of certain major figures in the world of literature and art during the Great Depression is a sterling example of traffic between cultural and political radicalism. Moreover, the contact ended in classic fashion. A volume centering on this theme must recount the episode for a complete picture. The rise of the Stalinist dictatorship in the Soviet Union had strong repercussions in the U.S. intellectual community. When Stalin ejected Trotsky from the Third International and sent him into exile, the repercussions for Bolshevik Communism were as strong, lasting into the final quarter of the twentieth century. The Trotsky question rent the radical literary community, but notable for this essay, some of its most successful and uniquely creative members were drawn to Trotsky's cause and therefore left the comfortable, even chic, fringe of official Communism in the United States. They found his aesthetic suited to their requirements: He insisted on the artist's right to absolute autonomy and freedom from state service. Additionally, they found the civil libertarian causes of an "open hearing in an open court" and asylum for Trotsky compelling. All of these "rights" were denied by the officialdom in the Communist "Workers Party of the United States."

Trotsky had made his views on artistic independence known in his 1923 essay "Literature and Revolution." At that time an official

Soviet approach to art had not congealed, although it appeared that the traditional Russian "schools" were not faring well under the new Revolutionary dispensation. The culture commissars were promoting Futurism and "proletcult," or "studios for proletarian culture." The party sponsored artists' and writers' congresses in the 1920s and 1930s, with the intent of capturing promising literary and artistic talent for state service, exactly what Trotsky decried. A special congress of revolutionary writers assembled at Kharkov in November 1930 to settle on literary policies; the meeting supplied a "program of action" to the delegates, six of whom, from the United States, expected to return home triumphantly with a fresh guide for using the talent of cultural workers to serve the coming revolution (Cowley 1980, p. 136). The party continued to tout proletarian writing and art while encouraging a style known as Socialist Realism, the portrayal of a glorious socialism rising from the ash heap of brutal capitalist realities. Such congresses, held in European countries and the United States, and the "Leagues of Writers" they established, were some of the Communist Party's numerous "front" operations (Struve 1944, intro. and pp. 220–29; Simmons 1958, passim; Caute 1973; Budenz 1948; Hart 1937).

In the 1920s the talented writers who would align with Trotsky were just beginning their careers or were still in college. Already Marxism attracted them. Some were gravitating toward leftist circles, particularly the Workers Party, the official Communist movement in the United States, affiliated with the Third International. But they tended not to join, although a very few did enroll. John Dos Passos had returned from World War I a radical, and was writing for *New Masses*, which he had helped revive from Marx Eastman's defunct publication, *The Masses*, as a literary outlet for the Communist movement.

Since 1923 in Baltimore, V. F. Calverton had been publishing *Modern Quarterly*, giving it an emphasis on Marxist social analysis but devoting considerable space to advocacy of sexual freedom. On the latter topic, in his way an early popular mouthpiece for Freudianism in America, he was a widely read and favorite authority of the liberated college generation of the 1920s. Prudery, in sexual matters was for Calverton a hated bourgeois anachronism. In 1928 he pulled up stakes and moved his publishing venture to New York, the undisputed center for new intellectual currents and Marxist activity (Dos Passos 1956, p. 7; Gnizi 1974, pp. 200–01; Fass 1977, p. 197). Art historian Wanda Corn writes that the intelligentsia of the 1920s believed that "if one could fathom the contradictions of New York . . . then one might comprehend modern America" (1982, p. 43). In this mecca for the creative and inquiring, Calverton continued with his quarterly, moving socially among radicals of all creeds—Socialists, Communists, labor intellectuals, the literary and philosophical intelligentsia—keeping the same eclectic spirit in his journal, but on a personal level drawn to the Workers Party.

James T. Farrell had made his mark with his trilogy *Studs Lonigan*, and had come back to the United States from France to find himself attracted to the radical set in New York, which, for literary intellectuals, seemed to mean this loose alliance with official Communism. His connection with it was unsteady from the start. Both Farrell and Calverton were writing for *New Masses* and other publications of the Communist and the liberal press (Wald 1978, pp. 82–84). Like Dos Passos a bit older than others in the group, the Mexican painter Diego Rivera had been led by an innate rebelliousness to join the Mexican Communist Party in 1921, to visit the USSR, to dedicate his talent to the cause of socialism by executing huge frescoes with revolutionary themes—his purpose, to bring an intense visual experience of the class struggle to the masses. In Mexico City he had begun this work on government commission, completing dramatic murals for the Secretariat of Education that depicted the life of the Mexican peasant and villager, and, in the National Palace, murals that portrayed the history of Mexico from pre-Columbian times to an envisioned socialist future, accentuating the brutalities of the Spanish conquest—the middle segment of the visual story. In the course of these commissions he met an 18-year-old Communist Youth League member, Frida Kahlo, who was to become his third wife and an exhibited painter in the Surrealist tradition (Wolfe 1963, pp. 150–54; Herrera 1978; Rivera 1960, pp. 169–71; Detroit Institute of Arts 1978, passim).

Edmund Wilson, literary editor of the *New Republic*, recalled that he was trying, in the early 1930s, to immerse himself in Marxist literature—including Trotsky's writings—and in American versions of the class struggle. He explained, "The place to study the present crisis and its causes and probable consequences is not in the charts of the compilers of statistics, but in one's self and the people one sees." Living in accordance with his convictions, he was present at "bloody Harlan" and Pikeville, Kentucky, and at the Chattanooga trials of the men accused in the Scottsboro cases. His reports are, perhaps, the best account of each. A colleague remembered that Wilson's writings "impressed me probably more than anything else I read at the time. That was partly because they were *written*, not hammered out to meet a deadline. . . . Dos Passos observed these events, too, and brought to light the testimonies of the striking Kentucky miners, an early oral history, in his book *Harlan Miners Speak.* Both appeared confident that Americans might now "be willing to put their idealism and genius for organization behind a radical social experiment," in Wilson's words (Wilson 1957–77, pp. 217, 221; Cowley 1980, pp. 15, 17).

Mary McCarthy, too, was in the leftist movement shortly after leaving her drama studies at Vassar, introduced to it while on her job writing book reviews for *The New Republic.* She later claimed that all her debating, marching, singing *The Internationale,* and attending Marxist classes never made her a thoroughgoing Marxist. "I got involved with politics because the men I was with were involved with politics and I was just there," she insisted. Sure enough, soon she was living with the keenly political Philip Rahv, editor, with William Phillips, of *Partisan Review,* the organ of the New York John Reed Club. John Reed Clubs had been established, around the time of the Wall Street crash, in several major cities that had thriving Marxist organizations, as adjuncts of these groups, and each club had its own separate publication. The clubs' function (spokesmen announced) was "to clarify the principles and purposes of revolutionary art and literature, to propagate them, to practice them." And it was from the John Reed Clubs that delegates went to Kharkov, to return with fresh dicta for artists in 1930.

But the editors of *Partisan Review* in New York gravitated in 1936 to Trotsky "as the only outstanding Marxist still alive." By then Rahv had recruited McCarthy to write for the *Review;* she brought to it her hard-hitting satires of the status quo, her targets being detective fiction, politics in her native state of Washington, the hypocritical intelligentsia, anti-Semitism, the foibles of males, fashion magazines, and playwrights lionized by the Communists and by American "establishment" tastemakers (McCarthy 1951, pp. 83, 158, 186–89; McCarthy 1956, pp. 53–54; Grumbach 1967, pp. 62, 68–69, 75; Cowley 1980, pp. 135–36).

For all of the above, official Communism in the early 1930s provided "what they believed were the necessary answers to most problems," loosely delineating "the coming order" for them, leaving only details to be filled in. Most were among the 53 intellectuals who called themselves the League of Professional Groups for Foster and Ford, and drafted a manifesto, "Culture and the Crisis," supporting Communist candidates in the presidential election of 1932, William Z. Foster and James W. Ford (Hicks 1954, pp. 38–39; Cowley 1980, p. 112; Pells 1973, p. 138; Wilson 1957–77, pp. 222–23). They had kicked over their middle- and upper-middle-class traces (Farrell alone came from a blue-collar family), repudiating American political leaders and the institutions in which they wielded power because of their inaction in the economic crisis.

All had vowed to use their talents to promote the class struggle. For Rivera this meant the revolutionary mural; for McCarthy, satire and the exposé novel; for Wilson, satire in the sociopolitical essay; for Calverton and Rahv, careful editorial choices of essays, short stories, and poems that pointed up the fundamentally opposed interests of the working masses—often extended to cover cultural workers as well—and the employing classes. Newcomer Dwight Macdonald, after Yale and time on Macy's executive training squad, and on Luce's *Fortune*, wrote exposés of business that revealed his mounting disgust with the corporate ethic. The orthodox Communist Party held irresistible appeal for these intellectuals "as the only radical thing going." It was "the party," "the pinnacle," in their judgment (Levy 1966, pp. 28, 34–35; Gilbert 1968, pp. 200–02). Ferrari (see Chapter 6) describes Communism as "an intellectual home, apparently the only one for those who liked their answers whole"; this remained true enough until they "discovered" Trotsky.

One by one they began to pull away from official Communism. Each had either a continuing area of friction with it or an alienating encounter. When reformist Popular Front policies replaced Third Period "no class collaboration," a strategy of the party's conspiratorial past that had so limited members' contact with the American mainstream, the party tried to enroll all writers, Communist or not, into the literature of protest. It should be mentioned that now the Workers Party had a new name, the Communist Party of the United States of America (CPUSA). Earl Browder's appointment as general secretary of the CPUSA brought with it the slogan "Communism is Twentieth Century Americanism" as well as party endorsement of a few New Deal projects that appeared to inch toward a modest redistribution of society's goods. The party thus moved out into the wider world of "liberal" politics, hoping to woo the disaffected but hesitant.

In response to party influences, Calverton dropped *Modern Quarterly*'s sex articles to stress Marxist social analysis, attracting so wide a readership that party intellectuals took alarm. Later, Sidney Hook said they resented a nonparty intellectual's gaining a name for Marxist scholarship, especially when that writer had so limited a talent. Hook's somewhat jaundiced elitism shows through: he had earned a doctorate under John Dewey at Columbia University, whereas the self-taught Calverton had no academic degree at all. Furthermore, the party published writers with a tenth of the skill Calverton possessed—and regularly, too, if they followed the line of the hour. Hook is wrong about the reason for Communist resentment of Calverton. These party leaders were "thought controllers," one writer observed while testifying in the 1950s (Rosenfeld 1981).

Actually, Calverton brought on himself the wrath of *New Masses* editor Joseph Freeman and others because he insisted on keeping *Modern Quarterly* an open forum, printing Socialists, Communists, liberals, Trotsky himself. He refused to take party direction in making editorial selections. Soon, "in a mean and ugly campaign" he was labeled "plagiarist" and "fascist" (Hook 1969, pp. 243, 246–47). Nor would Farrell heed party-imposed restrictions on his critical and literary freedom. The most pungent criticism flew from his pen, his targets frequently party scribes; at the same time he was studying Trotsky's *History of the Russian Revolution* and quite openly keeping company with young Trotskyist ideologue George Novack (Wald 1978, pp. 45–47, 53, 81; Rideout 1956, p. 232).

Farrell and Calverton, both rejecting "ready made slogans," were natural converts to the ranks of Trotsky's sympathizers when the Moscow show trials forced the issue. Staged in the Kremlin in 1936, 1937, and 1938, these trials implicated Trotsky (probably spuriously) with other "Old Bolshevik" leaders of the Revolution of 1917 and Lenin's final years in plots to sabotage the Soviet government and murder its chief. We can only conjecture the reasons for such action, but the Old Bolsheviks, innocent or not, "confessed" and were executed. Highly newsworthy affairs, the trials served to divide the radical community.

At a cocktail party honoring *The Masses* cartoonist Art Young, McCarthy had her attention brought abruptly to the trials, which, she assures us, had not attracted her immediate notice before. Farrell approached her, as he had approached others in the room, asking her views on Trotsky's right to a hearing on the Soviet accusations and his right to asylum. After a briefing by Farrell, a basic instinct for fairness drew an affirmative reply to both questions. Yes, Trotsky was entitled to a hearing. Of course, Trotsky should have the right to asylum. Satisfied with her part in the poll, she went home and forgot the episode. Four days later she saw her name on a list with others—a "committee"—demanding a hearing and asylum for Trotsky. Annoyed by the arrogance of "the Trotsky Defense Committee" for using her name without asking her, she intended to demand to have her name removed. But she put it off. Then came the telephone calls from party people advising her to recant publicly, at once. "Behind these phone calls," she reports, "there was a sense of the party wheeling its forces into would-be disciplined formations, like a fleet or an army maneuvering."

McCarthy decided to stay on the committee, read Trotsky to argue his defense herself, and so became "an anti-Communist," or rather an anti-Stalinist, quite by accident, subsequently convincing a few to adopt her position and developing a deep personal admiration for Trotsky's "wit, lucidity, and indignation." It changed her life, she recalls. Others did have their names dropped. Procrastination alone saved her from joining "this sorry band," she reflects. But now she had the reputation of being a "Trotskyite" although, like most of his other literary sympathizers, she never joined the growing Trotskyist party. About the official Communists she had said she could not be one; she was "not made that way" (McCarthy 1951, pp. 83–86, 95–98; Grumbach 1967, pp. 63–64; McKenzie 1966, p. 23).

Partisan Review had been a vehicle for proletarian literature while it served the New York John Reed Club. Alan Calmer, national secretary of the club, had boasted, "The Marxian movement has led the poet out of the corral of preciosity into the open spaces of human experience"; for five issues Farrell wrote criticism under that dispensation, boldly attacking pet writers and "proletcult" in general, naming names, declaring the objective validity of art, and pronouncing independence of art from anybody's dogma, points Trotsky made in *Literature and Revolution*. Editors Rahv and Phillips shut the *Review* down through the tense early months of the Moscow trials, then revived it in December 1937, dedicating it to the principle of artistic autonomy and to its own "unequivocal independence." Farrell's political biographer claims Farrell had pushed them to a vague Trotskyism. Proud and confident after its separation from the party line, *Partisan Review* declared the writer's duty to be skeptical, to destroy official prejudices, and to rise "in permanent mutiny against [any] petty regime or utility or conformity." It promoted the notion of "an international" of intellectuals to circumvent state tyrannies. It opposed Popular Front politics, Socialist Realism, and other Communist orthodoxies of the hour.

With its fresh orientation, the *Review* could take on the Communist Party itself, which had abandoned radicalism anyway, its editors argued, and could engage in U.S. literary and political establishments as well (*Partisan Review* 1936, pp. 19–21; Wald 1978, pp. 40–41, 53–54; Pells 1973, pp. 336–37; Hindus 1979, pp. 191–97). Rahv had McCarthy writing "Theatre Chronicle" once a month for the journal, lisping the Marxists' language and taking her line from them, she tells us (McCarthy 1956, pp. ix–xi; Grumbach 1967, pp. 74–75; McKenzie 1966, p. 23). Edmund Wilson wrote for both Calverton's magazine and *Partisan Review.* Then the *Review* gained another talented contributor in Dwight Macdonald. A pro-Stalinist book review by Malcolm Cowley published in *The New Republic* drew fire from Macdonald, who drafted a pro-Trotsky letter to the editor. Whether he was simply playing devil's advocate we cannot know, but his letter won him an invitation to join the Trotsky Defense Committee, which he did, and was consequently brought into contact with this radical literary milieu (Macdonald 1959, p. 3).

As for Diego Rivera, the party had already deplored his lack of discipline. He painted what and how he pleased: Mexican peasants rather than Futurist themes, people going about their labors on farm or in factory rather than glorified, bemedaled Lenins and Stalins. When the archcapitalist Rockefeller family hired him to do a mural for the lobby of the Radio Corporation of America building in the new Rockefeller Center in New York, it was the last straw. The party read him out for accepting the commission. Writer Albert Halper attended the Communist meeting at which a party leader railed at Rivera, calling him "effete intellectual" and "Trotskyite" for so truckling to the bourgeoisie (Halper 1970, pp. 89–97). Rivera tried to make amends and do propaganda service for Communism through the large fresco, but his decision to have Lenin's visage peer out from the building lobby was too much for the Rockefellers; they had his partially finished mural hammered into powder. As commissioned, it was to portray Man, a stylized archetype, as master in the industrial age, a plan Rivera carried through; but the work depicted as well the religious, military, and political leaders as villains in the piece, holding back scientific progress. The Rockefellers had viewed the preliminary layout; obviously they overlooked the presence of Lenin and failed to grasp Rivera's intent for the three representative figures. They paid the artist the contracted price but halted the work and ordered it destroyed (Rivera 1975, p. 238; Peña 1980, p. 45; Arquin 1971, p. 41).

Edsel Ford did not cancel his contract with the Mexican muralist to paint "Dynamic Detroit" in the Detroit Institute of Arts. Rivera moved to Detroit and carried the work through to completion (Detroit Institute of Arts 1978). But, expelled from the CPUSA, he recoiled for a few years to Trotskyism. He proceeded to obtain asylum for Trotsky in Mexico. Indeed, during Trotsky's first years in that country he and his family lived in Frida Kahlo Rivera's house in Coyoacán. The artist and the revolutionary respected each other's work, but Trotsky, like the Stalinists, bemoaned Rivera's lack of Marxist discipline (Heijenoort 1978, pp. 110–12).

Some of these literary radicals took the notion that the language of Communism was far too ponderously laced with jargon, making it alien to American ears. Moreover, policies dictated in Moscow for the American scene seldom suited it. We should "Americanize" Marxism, Calverton and Wilson urged in their publications. When in 1934 A. J. Muste and a small body of labor-oriented intellectuals formed the American Workers Party, bent on "Americanizing Marxism," Calverton rushed to join it. This brought him directly to Trotsky, because within a year the five-year-old Trotskyist organization, the Communist League of America, merged with the Muste group. In another year they fused with Norman Thomas' Socialists. While ostensibly committed to keeping *Modern Quarterly* politically independent, Calverton's changing editorial board reflected the gyrations. Rivera, Edmund Wilson, and Max Eastman (an early defender of Trotsky's cause) served on it until 1935, then departed, fearing the journal would take on a very political Trotskyist coloration, since its editor was a member of the Trotskyist party.

Generally the fear had little basis. However, two persons from the Socialist Party's militant faction, a pro-Trotsky wing, served on the board after Rivera, Wilson, and Eastman left. And during the time of the Moscow trials, Calverton's name was on the Defense Committee list, and he opened his journal to articles defending

Trotsky, once firing an editor (Carlton Beals) who refused to protest
Trotsky's innocence, pressured to that action by Max Eastman and
by Trotsky himself. *Modern Quarterly* was a monthly from February
1933 to October 1938 (Gnizi 1968, pp. 79–81, 107, 222, 238, 240–
50; Gnizi 1974, pp. 208–10).

Dos Passos, too, championed an American radicalism. "I don't
think there should be any more phrases, badges, opinions, banners,
imported from Russia or anywhere else. Ever since Columbus, imported systems have been the curse of this continent. Why not
develop our own brand?" Here is a beginning to the pessimism, and
even the anti-radicalism, that later became his trademark. Agreeing
with Trotsky's view of the artist's role, and admiring Trotsky's historical and literary acumen and style, Dos Passos nevertheless by the
mid-1930s declined to join the Defense Committee, or any cause
(Dos Passos 1956, pp. 7–10; Wilson 1957–77, p. 199; Rideout 1956,
p. 160). Still, despite the precocious defection of a few, the Trotsky
question galvanized a body of radical intellectuals for work in the
aging revolutionist's defense. Most were clinging to the periphery of
the Communist Party in the 1920s, as we have seen. By the mid-
1930s, however, repelled by calcifying Soviet dogma and rigid policies
that reached into their sacred preserve of art and literature, yet hovering on the fringes of official Communism, these creative, critical
spirits only needed a polarizing issue. Trotsky provided it. Like themselves a rebel intellectual, he defined the Soviet regime and declared
artistic independence to boot. They easily slipped into the new radical orbit.

The love affair between Trotsky and the artists had its moments
of greatest ardor in 1933–39. With anti-Stalinism and artistic freedom the common denominators, they protested mechanistic Communist and opportunistic capitalist politics at the same time. They
scorned any official "line" for their novels, drama, art. Nor would
they consciously write to please United States tastemakers. Repeat-
edly they chided themselves for failing to take more overt political
action, for simply writing (or painting), for keeping to Washington
Square, rebelling with caustic pen and bohemian living rather than
joining their political brothers and sisters in Union Square, making
firm and dangerous commitments. At once both bohemians and
politicos, yet not fully either, they "resisted" on two levels. The
furor over Trotsky's defense gave them the chance to continue
mingling in both worlds. They could champion the civil libertarian

"open hearing in open court," and still cater to radical sympathies through allying with a famed revolutionist to find him asylum.

Moreover, all of them at one time or another stated the belief that Trotsky was a far more compelling figure than the man heading the Soviet state. So the literary Trotskyists declared freedom from official Communism, staying comparatively free of the Trotskyist party but finding that harder to do, and affirming in books and in their two principal journals their radical critique of capitalism with its opportunistic politics and its wars. They wanted to "Americanize Marxism." They also wanted a hearing and asylum for Trotsky. The former was an unlikely project, made all the more unfeasible by the fact that they had adopted as a cultural leader a Russian of extraordinarily cosmopolitan background, living in Norway and soon to reside in Mexico, who viewed the world's events through a prism fashioned in Germany. In this desire they would not succeed. They were able, however, to obtain the hearing for Trotsky and asylum for him, but only through a concerted effort that involved the community of socialists and liberals in the United States.

American Writers' Congresses held in 1935, 1937, and 1939 were Soviet efforts to capture intellectuals for party service. The first of these met before the Trotsky question presented itself so urgently. Farrell had considerable to do with organizing the first one, even adding his name to the "League of American Writers" that supposedly sponsored the congress to rally writers against "war and fascism," and to try and preserve a climate in which cultural workers could function freely, a liberal goal. A party Central Committee member issued the conference "call" in the January issue of *New Masses* (Cowley 1980, pp. 269–79). The altercation with Rivera had occurred just three years before. To preclude a similar unpleasantness, and in accordance with the spirit of the Popular Front, the CPUSA called an "American Artists' Congress" in 1936; another, more loyal, Mexican muralist, José Clemente Orozco, addressed the assembled artists (Davis 1975, pp. 249–50; Rothschild 1975, pp. 250–52). Serving freedom and rallying intellectuals in an age of despair and rising European repression had such a fair, earnest, liberal, progressive ring to it. Both congresses were pledged to serve those ends, yet after the Writers' Congress the real purpose shone ever so clearly. Farrell said that during the sessions of the meeting, he discovered that its aim was to rally writers against Trotskyism and for Socialist Realism.

By the time of the second congress two years later, the literary Trotskyists were wise to the strategem, and planned disruptions in some of the workshops. When awards were made, those honored included one literary Trotskyist—John Dos Passos—a reward, perhaps, for his keeping his name off the Defense Committee roster. Farrell didn't even attend. The party was forbidding its faithful to read him now. Between the congresses he had helped organize the Defense Committee and the Committee to Find Asylum, and had gone to Mexico with John Dewey's Commission of Inquiry, the "open hearing in open court" that exonerated Trotsky of Soviet accusations. Moreover, he had ridiculed the League of American Writers (it was "the League Against American Writing," he said), and panned Communist writers in his *A Note on Literary Criticism* (Wald 1978, p. 30; Wilson 1957–77, pp. 255, 266, 285; Hart 1937, pp. 236–37, 253–55; Kempton 1955, p. 142; Roskolenko 1965, p. 159).

The solidarity among literary Trotskyists reached its greatest cohesion in 1938 and 1939; afterward the alignment crumbled. In 1938 *Partisan Review* seemed to draw closer to political Trotskyism when it published the manifesto "Toward a Free Revolutionary Art," written by the French intellectual and leader of the Surrealist school of painters, André Breton, by Diego Rivera, and by Trotsky in collaboration, ritualistically denouncing the Soviet bureaucracy and demanding its overthrow, complete freedom for the artist, and the creation of "an International Federation for Independent Revolutionary Art." In 1938 Trotsky wrote his "Art and Politics" for this magazine he had disdained initially. But Breton's subsequent effort to create that "International Federation" failed (*Partisan Review* 1938, p. 3; Gilbert 1968, p. 200; Deutscher 1963, pp. 430–31). Moreover, both *Partisan Review* and *Modern Monthly*—the *Quarterly* was a monthly for five years—kept refusing to be mouthpieces for any one view, even Trotsky's.

Another high-water mark of solidarity was reached in the summer of 1939 when 96 intellectuals, with Dwight Macdonald as acting secretary, formed out of the old Committee to Find Asylum for Trotsky the League of Cultural Freedom and Socialism dedicated to "independent creativity" and "revolutionary progress," thereby linking cultural and political radicalism. Calverton, among other literary Trotskyists, signed its manifesto. It was one of his final protests. He died in 1940, three months after Trotsky's death, already a bitter opponent of World War II (Banks 1980; Gnizi 1968, pp. 299–300; Gilbert 1968, pp. 201–02).

The literary Trotskyists had to adjust their ideology to "stay" with Trotsky on cultural philosophy, his right to a hearing, and other questions dividing radicals while rejecting interpretations of Marxist doctrine accepted as undeviatingly by Trotsky as by Stalin. The two Marxist antagonists were very close, when not identical, on certain points, points that would split the party Trotskyists themselves in early 1940. These were dialectical materialism, the necessary "dictatorship of the proletariat" after the coming revolution, even "the class struggle," and the central point of friction within the Trotskyist following: "unconditional defense of the Soviet Union as the only workers' state, however degenerated." Refusal to join Trotsky in the defense of the Soviet Union in the wake of the show trials and the Stalin-Hitler Pact of August 1939 kept literary Trotskyists in agreement with each other.

In Mexican exile and bitter, Trotsky stuck stubbornly with his "principles" and fought any kind of revision. He opposed any sort of reform in his political organization as well, which was now not only out of the Socialist Party and calling itself the Socialist Workers Party but also on the path toward rupture over a proposal for change in party structure. Invective flew from Trotsky in Coyoacán to his party factions in Chicago, in Berkeley, in New York, wherever they might be, and back again, to the dismay of literary Trotskyists disillusioned with the old man's intransigence. The exiled Trotsky, despised and hunted by Stalin's hit men, stood up for preservation of the great experiment in the USSR despite the truth (as he perceived it) that it had fallen under gravely mistaken, power-drunk leadership. Just as adamantly he waged a war of words against reform in the Trotskyist party. But the rupture took place. In four months he was dead, assassinated and fast losing a sizable part of his intellectual following, the literary Trotskyists.

In late 1939, James Burnham, Trotskyist editor and theoretician, had raised in print the first doubts about the "unconditional defense" doctrine—indeed, about dialectical materialism as a "science" (as Marxists proclaimed it to be), or even as a creditable philosophy. This was the Burnham who (like Hook) had been a philosophy student of Dewey's, and who would later manage and publish the conservative opinion journal *National Review*. While the quarrel raged, he ostensibly renounced Marxism in toto and left the Socialist Workers Party. His protégé Dwight Macdonald, one of the few literary Trotskyists who had joined the Trotskyist party, stayed in for another year, then defected. Disenchanted with *Partisan Review*'s new guidepost, a mere "cultural socialism," but keeping his own "revolutionary zeal" (as he explained it), Macdonald founded *Politics*, in which he could freely lash out at the USSR, World War II, the Roosevelt administration, the Trotskyists themselves.

Farrell's sympathies were with the dissidents after the split, but when the Socialist Workers Party leaders were tried, convicted, and sentenced under the Smith Act, he spurred civil libertarian consciences (and Dos Passos was with him in this commitment), working on a committee for their defense, then faithfully writing to all of them as they served out their time at Sandstone, Danbury, and Alderson (Levy 1966, p. 6; Myers 1977a; Myers 1977b, pp. 143–71). We know he was distressed about their ideological rigidity. His short stories about young men caught up in Marxist party membership show how party requirements woodenized, dehumanized, made a man go back on friendship "for the party"; take orders from tinhorn generals "for the party"; and submit to berating by such tinhorn generals "for the party." His idealistic novitiate characters end up questioning their allegiance, at last renouncing it (Wald 1978, p. 91; Farrell 1947; Farrell 1950).

A biographer says Mary McCarthy made a career "of candor and dissent." A playfulness, but a serious Marxist analysis, informed her "Theatre Chronicle" in *Partisan Review*. Also disenchanted with the Marxists—and the Trotskyist—milieu in this latter period of feuding, she too, melted away. With Macdonald, Farrell, and Wilson, she opposed World War II. Like both, she inserted anecdotes and personalities from her activist years in her later novels and essays. Her writing gradually took on a strong feminist coloration. It was as though her anti-Stalinism and concern for justice for Trotsky, along with other causes of the left, had blinded her to feminist issues in the 1930s (McCarthy 1949, passim; McCarthy 1964, passim; McCarthy 1956, pp. 39, 53–54, 133–35; Grumbach 1967, 135–39). Afterward, she tended to downplay the class and social analysis that had given her *Partisan Review* pieces their bite. Alerted to questions of the male-female relationship in a patriarchal society, she now turned her genius for satire toward episodes illustrating that eternal debate.

Dos Passos moved all the way across the political spectrum, as

Burnham would do. Diana Trilling asks, "We understand his dis-illusionment with the political left: all of us share it who went through it, but why hasn't he widened with the years to the compass of tragedy rather than narrowed to bitterness?" Showing "the frustra-tion of his old impulse to perfection," in 1952 (Trilling reminds us) he was signing as one of an Arts and Letters Committee for Taft (Trilling 1978, pp. 247–49). In this year of electoral victory for Republican presidential candidate Dwight D. Eisenhower, the con-servative Senator Robert Taft of Ohio—"Mr. Republican"—had sought the nomination of his party.

By August 1940, the month of Trotsky's assassination, Diego Rivera also had fallen away from Trotskyism. His Rockefeller Center mural design at last came to public view. An assistant had photo-graphed it on the sly before the Rockefellers ordered it pulverized. Then the new Workers' School on West 14th Street offered Rivera movable panels on which to reproduce it, and he did so. Once back in Mexico, he painted it yet again, this time in the Palace of Fine Arts in Mexico City, now adding Marx's and Trotsky's likenesses to the group that included Lenin's. This entire matter was reviewed when he applied for readmission into the Communist Party in 1954, abjectly humbling himself, allowing his wife's funeral to be used as a forum for disseminating party propaganda (Hicks 1954, pp. 182–83; Wolfe 1963, pp. 296, 337–39; Peña 1980, p. 12). Rivera was the sole literary Trotskyist to return to party Marxism, and this he did just three years before his death.

Rahv and Phillips took *Partisan Review* farther and farther away from practical politics to center its attention on "cultural socialism," although Macdonald continued to write political pieces for it until he left to publish his own journal. *Modern Monthly* returned to quarterly status in the fall of 1938. Calverton's break with Trotsky came when *Modern Quarterly* called for "a thorough examination of radical doctrine," its target Bolshevism itself. At this point, Trotsky de-manded that his name be struck from the contributors' roster. When Calverton died in November 1940, *Modern Quarterly* died with him (Gilbert 1968, p. 244; Gnizi 1968, pp. 293–94). Finally, Edmund Wilson's 1938 letters show him probing deeper and deeper into the mysteries of Marx, Engels, Lenin, and Trotsky for his book *To the Finland Station*; he devoted two chapters of it to Trotsky. In those years he was married to Mary McCarthy. Impending fatherhood made urgent the labors on the book. Although he had signed the

Foster-Ford Manifesto in 1932 and was on the Trotsky Defense Committee, he inclined thereafter to adhere to a standard he had announced in 1929: "Writers should not sign anything; they should merely write" (New International 1929; Wilson 1957–77, pp. 249, 304, 358).

So the brief passion between Trotsky and certain literary radicals in the United States ended. A shaky connection at its most ardent moments, it had been founded on Trotsky's liberal aesthetic, which afforded them a way to keep their radical outlook and still refuse to bend to state service, as the big, "official" Marxist organization expected them to do. All had experienced considerable success following their own radical muses; why surrender their autonomy to serve a party, a state, when the prescribed techniques delivered questionable results at best? As Ferrari suggests in his study (see Chapter 6), ample evidence of this existed in the literary product of the party loyal.

A fundamental sense of justice shared by these literary radicals pulled them to the civil libertarian causes of a hearing and asylum for the beleaguered, exiled revolutionist. Just as strong a sense of individual freedom, however, kept most of them out of the Trotskyist political organization. And, doubtless, a powerful component of the Romantic (as described in Chapter 1) in their essentially anarchistic temperaments operated to keep them independent of such a tie: "The Romantic's first principle [holds] that the individual person and experience is the ultimate object of concern and study."

With the onset of World War II, and a tightening of doctrinal and bureaucratic rigidity in the Soviet Union, followed by the Soviet pact with Nazi Germany, questions were raised that rent the Trotskyist party in two. Trotsky's doctrinal rigidity in dealing with the crisis in his party weaned his literary disciples from him by 1940. Finding their champion of artistic autonomy so unbending and unfree of dogma served to disenchant absolutely. Most of them came out of the 1930s sure that art and political life must stay apart, discrete commitments. Their concept of Marxism as guide to political understanding and choice making could never extend to life in a Marxist party.

In this instance of trafficking between political and cultural radicalism, the contacts usually episodic and very, very tenuous, the cultural easily won. Ferrari's study (see Chapter 6) and Marcus' work on the Greenwich Village radicals of an earlier decade (see Chapter 2) impress the reader that the cultural will predictably win. Temperaments attracted to bohemian living as a backdrop for creativity, however tinctured with philosophic rejection of the political and economic status quo in the philistine world, appear to be temperaments unsuited to the discipline exacted by non-mainstream political groupings. There seems to be an inverse relationship between adaptability to doctrine and discipline and stellar creative ability in the arts, and in the sciences as well. Some of the erstwhile literary Trotskyists left Marxism altogether to find fresh approaches to problems of liberty and the state. All of them were touched in important ways by their brief liaison with Trotsky, as their personal reflections attest.

REFERENCES

Arquin, Florence. 1971. *Diego Rivera: The Shaping of an Artist, 1889-1921.* Norman: University of Oklahoma Press.

Banks, Ann. 1980. "Bread and Song: federal writers' project and the Popular Front." Paper read at American Historical Association annual meeting, Washington, D.C., Dec. 28.

Brightman, Carol. 1984. "Mary, Still Contrary." *The Nation* 238 (May 19, 1984), p. 611-19.

Budenz, Louis. 1948. *Men Without Faces: The Communist Conspiracy in the U.S.A.* New York: Harper's.

Caute, David. 1973. *The Fellow Travelers: A Postscript to the Enlightenment.* New York: Macmillan.

Corn, Wanda. 1982. "In Detail: Joseph Stella and *New York Interpreted.*" *Portfolio: The Magazine of the Fine Arts* 4 (Jan.-Feb.): 40-45.

Cowley, Malcolm. 1980. *The Dream of the Golden Mountain: Remembering the 1930s.* New York: Viking Press.

Davis, Stuart. 1975. "American Artists' Congress." In *Art for the Millions: Essays from the 1930s by Artists and Administrators of the WPA Federal Art Project*, edited by Francis J. O'Connor. Boston: New York Graphic Society.

Detroit Institute of Arts. 1978. *The Rouge: The Image of Industry in the Art of Charles Sheeler and Diego Rivera.* Detroit: The Institute.

Deutscher, Isaac. 1963. *The Prophet Outcast: Trotsky, 1929–1940.* London: Oxford University Press.

Dos Passos, John. 1956. *The Theme Is Freedom.* New York: Dodd, Mead.

Farrell, James T. 1950. "The Renegade." In his *An American Dream Girl and Other Essays*, pp. 274–302. New York: Vanguard Press.

——. 1947. "Comrade Stanley." In his *The Life Adventurous and Other Stories*, pp. 228–265. New York: Vanguard Press.

Fass, Paula S. 1977. *The Damned and the Beautiful: American Youth in the 1920s.* New York: Oxford University Press.

Gilbert, James B. 1968. *Writers and Partisans: A History of Literary Radicalism in America.* New York: John Wiley.

Gnizi, Haim. 1974. "*The Modern Quarterly*, 1923–1940: An Independent Radical Magazine." *Labor History* 15 (Spring): 199–215.

——. 1968. "V. F. Calverton: Independent Radical." Ph.D. dissertation, New York University.

Grumbach, Doris. 1967. *The Company She Kept.* New York: Coward McCann.

Halper, Albert. 1970. *Goodbye, Union Square: A Writer's Memoir of the Thirties.* Chicago: Quadrangle Press.

Hart, Henry, ed. 1937. *The Writer in a Changing World: The Second American Writers' Congress.* New York: Equinox Cooperative Press.

Heijenoort, Jean van. 1978. *With Trotsky in Exile: From Prinkipo to Coyoacán.* Cambridge, Mass.: Harvard University Press.

Herrera, Hayden. 1978. *Frida Kahlo Exhibition Catalog.* Chicago: Museum of Contemporary Art.

Hicks, Granville. 1954. *Where We Came Out.* New York: Viking Press.

Hindus, Milton. 1979. "Philip Rahv." In *Images and Ideas in American Culture: The Function of Criticism. Essays in Honor of Philip Rahv*, edited by Arthur Edelstein. Waltham, Mass.: Brandeis University Press.

Hook, Sidney. 1969. *"The Modern Quarterly:* A Chapter in American Radical History. V. F. Calverton and His Periodicals." *Labor History* 10 (Spring): 241-49.

Kempton, Murray. 1955. *Part of Our Time: Some Ruins and Monuments of the Thirties.* New York: Simon and Shuster.

Levy, Norman. 1966. "The Radicalization of Dwight Macdonald." M.A. thesis, University of Wisconsin.

Macdonald, Dwight. 1957. *Memoirs of a Revolutionist: Essays in Political Criticism.* Cleveland: World Publishing Co.

McCarthy, Mary. 1964. *A Humanist in the Bathtub. Selected Essays from Mary McCarthy's "Theatre Chronicles, 1937-1962" and "On the Contrary."* New York: New American Library.

——. 1956. *Sights and Spectacles, 1937-1951.* New York: Farrar, Straus and Cudahy.

——. 1951. *On the Contrary.* New York: Farrar, Straus and Cudahy.

——. 1949. *The Oasis.* New York: Random House.

McKenzie, Barbara. 1966. *Mary McCarthy.* New Haven, Conn.: College and University Press.

Myers, Constance Ashton. 1977a. "American Trotskyists: The First Years." *Studies in Comparative Communism* 10 (Summer): 133-151.

——. 1977b. *The Prophet's Army, Trotskyists in America, 1928-1941.* Westport, Conn.: Greenwood Press.

New International. 1929. 5 (Jan.): 5.

Palace of Fine Arts, Mexico. 1978. *Catalog: Exposición nacionale de homenaje a Diego Rivera con motivo del XX aniversario de su fallecimiento.* Mexico City: Palace of Fine Arts.

Partisan Review. 3: May 1936 and 5: Aug.-Sept. 1938.

Pells, Richard H. 1973. *Radical Visions and American Dreams. Culture and Social Thought in the Depression Years.* New York: Harper & Row.

Peña, Alfredo Cardona. 1980. *El monstruo en su laberinto: Conversaciónes con Diego Rivera.* 2nd ed. Mexico City: Editorial Diana.

Rideout, Walter. 1956. *The Radical Novel in the United States, 1900–1954: Some Interrelations of Literature and Society.* Cambridge, Mass.: Harvard University Press.

Rivera, Diego. 1975. *Confesiónes de Diego Rivera: Nuestras cosas.* 2nd ed. Mexico City: Editorial Grijalbo.

——. 1960. *My Art, My Life: An Autobiography.* New York: Citadel Press.

Rosenfeld, Megan. 1981. "On the Trail of the Blacklist." *Washington Post*, Jan. 3, p. B-3.

Roskolenko, Harry. 1965. *When I Was Last on Cherry Street.* New York: Stein and Day.

Rothschild, Lincoln. 1975. "The American Artists' Congress." In *Art for the Millions: Essays from the 1930s by Artists and Administrators of the WPA Federal Art Project*, Francis J. O'Connor, ed. Boston: New York Graphic Society.

Simmons, Ernest J. 1958. *Russian Fiction and Soviet Ideology.* New York: Columbia University Press.

Struve, Gleb. 1944. *Twenty-five Years of Soviet Russian Literature (1918–1943).* London: George Routledge.

Trilling, Diana Rubin. 1978. *Reviewing the Forties.* New York: Harcourt, Brace, Jovanovich.

Wald, Alan M. 1978. *James T. Farrell: The Revolutionary Socialist Years.* New York: New York University Press.

Wilson, Elena, ed. 1957–77. *Edmund Wilson: Letters on Literature and Politics.* New York: Farrar, Straus and Giroux.

Wolfe, Bertram D. 1963. *The Fabulous Life of Diego Rivera.* New York: Stein and Day.

6 Proletarian Literature: A Case of Convergence of Political and Literary Radicalism

Arthur C. Ferrari

Politics and literature are ordinarily separate realms of activity in market-based, industrial societies, much as economy and polity are separate, at least in consciousness (Giddens 1973, p. 202). Some intellectual journals (such as *The Partisan Review*, *The Masses*, *The New York Review of Books*) have attempted to combine political and literary analysis, but generally politicians are not also writers and writers are not also politicians, in their own or in others' eyes.

Despite the separation of literature and politics in our everyday consciousness, the two are related. Different realms of social activity may be distinct in our minds and their connections may not always be obvious or desirable, but they can never be completely isolated from each other. Accordingly, intellectuals have devoted some attention to understanding the relationship of politics to the arts and

Grateful acknowledgments is expressed to the National Endowment for the Humanities for a summer study grant in 1979 to U.C. San Diego with Bennett M. Berger. His words both in person and in print have inspired me in this essay and in my teaching. My colleagues in the seminar, some of whom are authors in this volume, deserve thanks too. Small grants from and a supportive milieu at Connecticut College furthered this work, as did Anita Fernald's typing skills. Alida Ferrari's contributions are too numerous to list.

literature (for instance, Marcuse 1972; Trotsky 1957; Thompson 1967). Specifically sociological analysis of the convergence of cultural and political actions is provided by Alfred Willener (1970) in his study of the May Movement of 1968 in France. Willener's study focuses on the participant's "action-image" of society that integrates both the political and the cultural dimensions. While much of the students' action-images concerned everyday experience, their political sensibilities were also reflected in literary, dramatic, and artistic works. Willener suggests that the May Movement's fusion of political and cultural action is similar to other culturally radical movements: Dada, Surrealism, the Living Theater, and Free Jazz. The "happenings" of the 1960s and the early 1970s in the United States and the earthworks of Christo (Fineberg 1979) fall into this category, as do other movements chronicled in this book. All have in common an attempt to politicize culture at both the abstract and the personal levels while not compromising the artist's work.

Finally, Bennett Berger (1981) has suggested some of the practical sociological difficulties inherent in attempts of political and cultural radicals to make common cause. Noting that politically and culturally radical movements converge and then diverge in different historical and geographical circumstances, Berger's work suggests that a microsociology-of-knowledge perspective might illuminate the circumstances under which political and cultural radicals can make common cause.

I examine one case of radical political and literary convergence in order to suggest sociological factors conducive to both their convergence and their divergence. The fusion of Communist Party U.S.A. revolutionary policy with literary philosophy during the 1930s will be chronicled. This "proletarian literature" movement was a relatively small but important radical movement among writers, critics, and other intellectuals that sought to capture realism from the dominant modernists. It sought to replace the primarily psychologistic, "artsy" literary production of the time with a more "down-to-earth," socially oriented genre more appealing to a working-class audience; in fact, the working class would provide the subject matter. The revolutionary class conflict that the Communist Party saw itself leading in the political arena would be reflected in literature and, in good dialectical fashion, contribute to the political revolution as well.

The data for this analysis are, for the most part, statements of literary philosophy made by participants themselves. Some secondary analysts' works on the period are used as is a reading of the literature itself—especially that found in the Communist-dominated journal of politics and literature, *New Masses.*

THE PHILOSOPHY OF PROLETARIAN LITERATURE, 1929–34

Editor Michael Gold's "Go Left, Young Writers," in the January 1929 issue of *New Masses*, informed his readers that a new writer was appearing. The new writer, writing in an instinctual and unpolished style, was about 21 years old, of working-class origin, and himself a worker (Gold 1929). In that same issue Martin Russak, a young author, discussed Jack London as America's first proletarian writer and provided a partial definition of the proletarian writer: "A real proletarian writer must not only write about the working class, he must be read by the working class." Furthermore, a good proletarian writer must possess "bitter hatred, absolute class solidarity, and revolutionary passion" (Russak 1929).

In the October issue of *New Masses*, on the eve of the Great Crash, Henry George Weiss complained that much of the poetry in *New Masses* could not be understood by ordinary workers (1929). Perhaps a solution to the problem raised by Weiss would be provided by an organization that announced its founding in the following (November 1929) issue of the magazine. About 50 people had joined together to form the John Reed Club of New York. The announcement stated: that "The purpose of the club is to bring closer all creative workers; to maintain contact with the American labor movement," much as the club's namesake had in an earlier era.

The espousal by Gold and the others of a proletarian literature in 1929 and 1930 reflected a set of ideas that were to influence American intellectuals, literature, and literary criticism throughout the tumultuous decade that followed. *New Masses* reflected the ideology and fortunes of the U.S. Communist Party, as did the John Reed Clubs, the party's affiliated literary organizations. The Communist Party's political policy in 1930 was aimed at immediate revolution; literary policy said that the writer would aid the revolution by speaking to the proletariat, for it was the proletariat who would soon inherit the remains of decaying capitalist America and replace it with a Communist society. Of course, what seemed plausible or even probable in 1930, America's collapse as a result of the (then beginning)

Great Depression, failed to occur. To those entering adulthood at this time, many things were possible as solutions to what became one of the most traumatic and tortuous crises in American history.

Marxists and non-Marxists alike saw the increasing unemployment and protest, the Hoovervilles, labor union agitation, soup kitchens, bread lines, and the apple sellers. It could indeed be time for the demise of capitalism and the rise of the workers to replace the bourgeoisie, just as they understood Marx had predicted. These were heady times for members of the Communist Party; they, after all, would lead the revolution. The party's membership grew, as did its organizing efforts.

On the literary front, John Reed Clubs spread. By 1932 there were 12 clubs with a total membership of about 900 in Portland (Oregon), Detroit, Boston, Philadelphia, Newark, San Francisco, Hollywood, Seattle, Chicago, New York, Washington, D.C., and Cleveland (Aaron 1961, p. 426). One purpose of the clubs was to develop new talent among the proletariat. After all, if the proletariat was to replace the bourgeoisie and its culture with proletarian culture, members of the proletariat would have to write it.

Proletarian literature was, in part, a literature to be aimed at workers. It was to be about workers and to be read by workers. The writer was to be what some would call a propagandist. Further, recognizing that few young writers were from the working class, the John Reed Club report published in the January 1930 *New Masses* put forth "A New Program for Writers." Writers were to attach themselves to an industry and become thoroughly familiar with it, so that they could write "from inside."

In September 1930 editor Mike Gold spelled out in some detail the meaning of "proletarian realism," a type of literature that would reflect the life of the workers and have a clear revolutionary point. Literature would deal with real (social) conflicts, not mental anguish; it would have a social function (a point to make), not be "art for art's sake"; it would be written in as few words as possible; the action would be swift and honest; it would not be melodramatic or pessimistic; and it would reflect the courage of the proletarian experience (1930, p. 5). Here, then, were guidelines for a literature to mobilize the masses for revolution; sensitive to and reflecting their lives, it would be written so they could understand it and be moved to join the revolution against the evils of a decaying capitalism and its decadent bourgeois culture.

THE CONTEXT FOR WRITERS, 1929–34

Proletarian literature was not the preponderant literature of the 1930s. Of about 17,000 novels published during the decade, only about 70 were proletarian (Rideout 1956, p. 171). Few who wrote it are remembered today, but in its time the idea generated tremendous controversy among intellectuals. That it was taken so seriously affords the analyst an opportunity to probe the historical record for clues to the prospects and tensions of radical political and cultural convergence. Rather than asking, with Howe and Coser, "How then was it possible for writers of talent and training . . . to lend themselves to such intellectual buffoonery?" (1957, p. 288), we can ask how it was that serious writers, some talented and some not so talented, attempted to unite their literary and political sensibilities—two modes of human endeavor not often united?

To begin with, we must appreciate the impact of the Great Depression. This is no place for a lengthy catalog of its effects, but coming as it did on the heels of a decade of boom and optimism, the crash and its subsequent severe depression deeply affected all levels of society. The responses of individuals and groups varied. For some, suicide or crime or mental illness; others were forced to abandon their homes and families in search of work; and others rioted. Later would come federally sponsored jobs and expansion of welfare. Labor unions increased their organizing efforts and grew, as did the Communist Party. Most people lived a life of both resignation and quiet hope.

The impact of the Great Depression on intellectuals, artists, and writers was by no means uniform, but it is fair to say that most were upset about the collapse and beset with worry about the irrationality and chaos that it implied. For some, their 1920s-based view of middle-class philistinism was vindicated. For those who had become expatriates, it signaled an opportunity to come home and help rebuild American society and culture. And for those just entering the adult world of employment (or unemployment), what were their prospects for a career as writer or poet? These were anxious, confusing days. Traditional formulas for leading one's life provided little guidance under circumstances of the Great Depression. There were decreasing outlets for young authors' publications, especially for young authors of the left, and payments for articles in magazines became smaller after 1929. To make matters worse, "The younger writers discovered that the repatriated expatriates, because they were already established in their fame, were taking up much of the available magazine space" (Rideout 1956, p. 137).

Little opportunity to publish, unemployment, and disaffection from "mainstream" culture were part of the immediate context in which young would-be writers found themselves. They were troubled by problems unique to themselves as writers as well as participating in the general malaise. Writers (and intellectuals generally) searched for ideas that would solve their own and America's problems.

The solutions and the hope for a better tomorrow were provided for some by Marxism and its major vehicle in America at the time, the Communist Party U.S.A. Marxism was a coherent ideology, perhaps the only generally available coherent set of ideas in 1930, that explained the Great Depression and could provide a refuge, a sense of unity, and hope for the future (Rideout 1956, p. 139). At least it seemed so at the time. Here was an intellectual home, apparently the only one for those who liked their answers whole. Marxism explained the Great Depression and provided a basis for action: join with the rising proletariat, overthrow the existing order, and help build a new, superior society. The Soviet Union provided the model of a Communist-inspired system that was enjoying considerable economic success, in contrast with the apparent failure of the American system. And more practically, the Communist Party was seeking new members for its revolutionary movement. Intellectuals, including writers, were among the thousands who joined the party, whose membership increased steadily during the 1930s.

Interestingly, the turn to Marxism and the Communist Party by a small but noticeable percentage of intellectuals provided them with more than answers to abstract questions about the causes of the Great Depression. The party was offering them a role in building a new society and, at the same time, an audience for whom to write. The American author could solve two problems at once by "going Communist." He or she could end the traditional "outsider" status of the intellectual in America and at the same time have a ready-made audience, the proletariat. We can remember here the advice of Gold, Russak, and others that proletarian literature be written about the proletariat, for the proletariat. And we see in this convergence of political and cultural radicalism how ideas, interests, and human needs were blended and intertwined under crisis circumstances.

A SHIFT IN THE PHILOSOPHY OF
PROLETARIAN LITERATURE, 1934-35

The meaning of proletarian literature changed subtly between 1929 and 1935, from that of a literature by the proletariat, for the proletariat, to a literature written "from a revolutionary perspective" (Schachner 1934; Aaron 1961). This shift in emphasis to the writer's perspective, that it simply be sympathetic to the revolutionary destruction of capitalism, broadened the scope of what proletarian literature could be and who could write it. Under such a guideline middle-class authors could write it and the middle class might be more interested in reading it.

The importance of a middle-class readership is reflected in circulation figures for *New Masses* during the first half of the 1930s. In September 1933, when *New Masses* ceased publication as a monthly, its circulation was 6,000 copies a month. During the period 1929-33 it had stressed and contained examples of literature by and for the proletariat. When it reappeared as a weekly in January 1934, *New Masses* sold 9,500 copies; by December of that year it had increased its circulation to 25,000 copies (Rideout 1956, p. 149). Not only did *New Masses* begin to publish weekly, but it reflected the changed philosophy of literature written "from a revolutionary point of view" with no restrictions on form, subject matter, or the author's or subject's class membership. This change in literary philosophy in a revolutionary journal of politics and literature appealed to a broader, more middle-class audience, and boosted circulation.

The change in literary philosophy is exemplified further by the addition of Granville Hicks as literary editor when the magazine reappeared as a weekly. Hicks's discussions of literary history and criticism followed the form (if not the content) of "bourgeois" criticism that appeared in such establishment journals as *The Nation*, *Saturday Review of Literature*, and *The New Republic*. His writings presented a knowledge of literature and philosophy rarely found outside the college-educated, that is, middle-class, literati.

Both of these phases of proletarian literature were not simply written about in the pages of *New Masses*. The Communist Party matched its revolutionary ideology with organization; the John Reed Clubs brought artists and writers closer to the working class and provided a training ground for new talent. The clubs accomplished this for writers with workshops, and each club had at least one "little" magazine in which authors could publish.[1] That the John Reed Clubs had considerable impact there is no doubt. Reviewing their reports and schedules of events in *New Masses*, one finds classes and workshops in writing, graphics, photography, painting, cartooning, theater, and dance. To the young left-leaning authors or would-be authors who were up against constricted publishing opportunities for their work, the John Reed Clubs offered publishing outlets in their literary magazines.

A CLOSER LOOK AT PROLETARIAN AUTHORS

The proletarian-literature philosophy struck a chord with relatively young, unemployed, high-school graduates of working-class background.[2] A notable few were college-educated and wanted a career in journalism. Most were first- or second-generation Americans, a common characteristic of working-class people in the 1930s.

Other clues to the characteristics of proletarian authors (and the importance of the John Reed Clubs to their development) are provided by an analysis of authors who submitted works to a contest for the best proletarian novel published in 1934. Ninety authors, all previously unpublished, submitted works; 30 of these authors were women. The areas of the country that had the heaviest concentration of submissions were areas of active radical politics and John Reed Clubs (Rideout 1956, p. 238).[3]

The "generalizations" of the preceding two paragraphs can only summarize the scant evidence that is available. What little evidence there is, suggests that young, probably ambitious, would-be journalists, novelists, and poets from working-class backgrounds who were unemployed or unable to work in their craft were seeking whatever opportunities might appear. One admittedly self-selected sample of novelists was one-third women. It is difficult to imagine that one-third of the working novelists of the 1930s were women. Their overrepresentation among proletarian novelists indicates further the appeal of the proletarian literature philosophy to the unemployed, the young, the inexperienced, and the otherwise powerless.

Not all writers who appeared in *New Masses* or John Reed Club magazines, or who published proletarian novels, were working-class or party members. And proletarian literature was not the only manifestation of the influence of Marxism in the 1930s. Aaron cites

William Phillips' characterization of the movement, in which he differentiates "older" from "younger" New Men (1961, pp. 270–72). The older New Men consisted of such authors as Hemingway, Cowley, and Tate, and a "few confident pioneers"—Joseph Freeman, Michael Gold, and Joshua Kunitz. The younger New Men were "still in their teens or early twenties, they were idealistic and ambitious. Moreover, they considered themselves set apart by age and by cultural affiliations from the older generation of revolutionary writers" (Aaron 1961, p. 271). Phillips says, further, that the older group consisted of revolutionary pioneers who did not assimilate the literary heritage of the 1920s from its literary fathers James Joyce and T. S. Eliot, as well as Cowley, Hart Crane, Kenneth Burke, and John Dos Passos.

Phillips and his friend Philip Rahv were part of a loose network (the so-called literary Trotskyists) that included James T. Farrell, Dwight Macdonald, Mary McCarthy, Diego Rivera, Edmund Wilson, Sidney Hook, and James Burnham. As Chapter 5 shows in detail, most of these intellectuals were influenced by or sympathetic to Marxism at some time in their careers, but never joined the Communist Party or completely embraced the philosophy of proletarian literature. Their reputations (established prior to the 1930s), supported by secure literary, university, or journalistic positions, or jobs with the Federal Writer's Project, provided them with the sociological support necessary to maintain a literary-philosophical stance independent of the party's line. Aaron cites the example of Clifton Fadiman, sympathetic to the Communist Party in the early 1930s, joining the *New Yorker* as a book reviewer in 1933, which "permanently separated him from the young Marxists" (1961, p. 245). It was those having lesser security, repute, training, and perhaps talent who were most involved with the John Reed Club magazines and the party's ideology of proletarian literature.

By 1934, when the philosophy of proletarian literature had been broadened to include much more than that written by the proletariat, for the proletariat, it became obvious that proletarian novels, at least, were not selling well.[4] Moreover, there was tension over proletarian literature between the Communist Party-John Reed Clubs-*New Masses* (older New Men) camp and the *Partisan Review*-fellow travelers (young New Men) camp, as well as criticism of the proletarian literature philosophy from independent radicals, liberals, conservatives, and socialists. This tension from within and attack from without contributed to the transformation of the party's proletarian literature philosophy to one of literature written "from a revolutionary point of view."

The ideological revision was reflected in the words of poet-critic Stanley Burnshaw, who remarked that the Communist editors of *New Masses* wanted "to drive away no one who can be turned into a friend of the revolutionary movement" (quoted in Aaron 1961, p. 275). Referring to earlier party doctrine that "pure" art was a reflection of incipient fascism, Burnshaw defended the new policy of literature from a revolutionary perspective by suggesting that "so long as he is true to himself as a writer honestly struggling to find a way out of the crisis," his work would not amount "objectively to quiescence to the process of fascization [*sic*] now going on" (quoted in Aaron 1961, p. 275). Now (by 1934), good art was not necessarily incipient fascism. The "literature from a revolutionary perspective" viewpoint was reiterated by Alexander Trachtenberg, a member of the Central Committee of the Communist Party, who spoke to the New York John Reed Club in October 1934. He reminded the membership that the purpose of the clubs was to win artists and writers to the revolution, and that the party did not want to interfere with the free exercise of people's talents or absorb talented people in other kinds of work, to the neglect of their craft (Aaron 1961, p. 281). This speech was a straightforward response to some of the younger New Men and fellow travelers who felt straitjacketed by the party's literary philosophy.

Both phases of the proletarian literature era were abetted by the John Reed Clubs. They brought young authors into contact with each other and with party ideology; their magazines provided training and publishing outlets; they stimulated and sustained writers' and other artists' work while providing a setting in which radical ideologues and producers of culture could commingle. But the John Reed Clubs could not overcome social and ideological differences between party and nonparty writers.

THE END OF PROLETARIAN LITERATURE, 1935-39

The Communist Party's change in literary policy was part of a change in broader political policy that became explicit after the Writers' Congress in April 1935. The call issued by Trachtenberg was announced in *New Masses* (Jan. 22, 1935) for the purpose of fighting the "twin menaces of war and fascism" and discussion of writers' problems. The announcement stated that "to this Congress shall be invited all writers who have achieved some standing in their respective fields. . . . " Noticeably absent from this invitation were young writers who had not achieved "some standing" in their respective fields.

The party was shifting its official political strategy from revolutionary to reformist, a move presaged by the second-phase shift in literary philosophy that attempted to broaden the appeal of proletarian literature to the middle class. The party was jumping on the Roosevelt bandwagon, supporting reformist measures, and, in general, seeking to enlarge its constituency. This was the party's Popular Front stage, dedicated to fighting fascism wherever and however necessary. One group from whom it hoped to gain adherents, and whose reputations would attract others, was writers and intellectuals. The Communist Party became interested in attracting writers, not in developing writing.

To facilitate its political goals, the party established the League of American Writers, a centralized organization run by a 17-member central committee of party members and close fellow travelers. The party was trying to attract prestigious authors such as Hemingway, Dos Passos, and Archibald MacLeish rather than to train new talent. The league's membership was open only to published professional writers, not to writers just beginning to learn their craft. In fact, the John Reed Clubs were dissolved.

The establishment of the League of American Writers ended the magazines and writing classes of the Reed Club period. Authors were asked to join hands with those whom they had previously denounced or seen denounced on the pages of *New Masses*. One case is particularly striking. In Granville Hicks's review of MacLeish's *Poems, 1924–1933* in the January 16, 1934, issue of *New Masses*, Hicks denounced MacLeish as a Nazi. In December 1935, after the policy change, MacLeish contributed to the *New Masses* antifascism issue. In March 1935, MacLeish's *Public Speech* was praised by Isidor Schneider on the pages of *New Masses* "as a 'beautiful and moving collection of poems'" (Rideout 1956, p. 242). Either MacLeish changed dramatically in a short period of time, and there is no reason to believe that he did, or party political and literary policy had changed, requiring some "ideological work" on the part of true believers.

The antifascism of the Popular Front and Spanish Civil War period diverted the attention of many intellectuals from the Moscow trials. and purges, and perhaps explains why there was so little controversy over the party's change in literary philosophy (cf. Miller, quoted in Aaron 1961, pp. 294–97). It was not until the Nazi-Soviet Nonaggression Pact of 1939 that most intellectuals left the Communist Party.

This review of convergence and then divergence of Communist Party political radicalism and the radical proletarian literati has ignored until now an important strand of developments. The evolution of the *Partisan Review* from the New York John Reed Club's magazine to a more broadly based journal of politics and literature represents a schism within the proletarian literary movement that might have ended proletarian literature even if the party had not scuttled it.

I mentioned earlier the older New Men/younger New Men differences within the left. Philip Rahv and William Phillips, both younger New Men and members of the John Reed Club of New York City, founded *Partisan Review* in 1934. Ostensibly an organ of the John Reed Club, the magazine was devoted to "quality" writing, an idea that saw Marxism as a method of analysis and opposed to the party's idea of art as political propaganda (Aaron 1961, p. 297). By 1936 the magazine was in the camp of the literary Trotskyites and its views were captured best by James T. Farrell's scathing attack on the party's and *New Masses'* views in his *A Note on Literary Criticism* (1936). Farrell's book-length "note" crystallized what was soon to become both an anti-Stalinist and an anti-party aesthetic position with roots in the 1920s.

Farrell denounced Michael Gold and Granville Hicks, then accused Russian and American Marxist critics of introducing extraliterary criteria into criticism, ignoring the persistence value of art, oversimplifying art, confusing art and propaganda, stigmatizing individualism, and making foolish or irrelevant judgments because they did not take their Marxism seriously (Farrell 1936).

Granville Hicks acknowledged that Farrell had "performed some valuable services" by pointing to constricting elements in Marxist (that is, party) criticism, but argued that he should understand the sectarianism of Marxist critics as an "unfortunate but excusable reaction to the aestheticism of the bourgeois critics who had rejected 'working class experience' as 'a fit subject for literature'" (Aaron 1961, p. 302). (Chapter 5 provides a more detailed description of the younger New Men viewpoint.) Farrell and the editors of *Partisan Review* come to form a "camp" when *Partisan Review* resumed publication in December 1937, after a period of cessation and a break from party influence. Their camp was anti-Stalinist politically and anti-party aesthetically (Aaron 1961, p. 302), and it formally marked the end of the convergence on the left of radical political ideology and a revolutionary aesthetics.

CONCLUSION

The convergence of literary philosophy and Communist Party revolutionary politics in Depression-torn American society was facilitated by a number of factors: a major domestic economic crisis at a time when an alternative model of society was enjoying success, and a well-organized political party was providing answers to major questions (ideology) and concrete opportunities to learn the writer's craft (clubs), outlets for work (magazines and audience), and general support to young writers that eased their "blocked ascendency" (Gouldner 1979). The strain of blocked ascendency is often cited as a structural inducement for individuals to join a movement (Brinton 1938; Oberschall 1973). This "package" of ideological, material, and sociological factors facilitated the convergence of political and literary ideas at both the cultural and the personal levels. And it was changes in these factors that led to the divergence of the political and literary movements of the 1930s.

The international situation changed with the spread of Nazism and the Moscow purge trials. Domestically, the reform programs of the Roosevelt administration tempered the worst effects of the Great Depression. The most direct impact of these reforms on the proletarian literature movement was the Federal Writers' Project, which employed writers and gave them alternatives to the John Reed Clubs, thereby providing the opportunity to write ("unblocked ascendency") in more "establishment" or "legitimate" forums. Communist Party strategy—the movement from a revolutionary to a reformist stance—in an effort to increase its constituency among the middle class and in the face of a nonrevolutionary working class, further encouraged a modification of literary ideals.

The ideological and aesthetic division among intellectuals over the propagandist nature of proletarian literature was itself an important source of divergence. Under crisis circumstances it was possible for some (especially those unemployed and unestablished) to combine literary and political ideals; the differences between literature and politics are not so "inherent" that they cannot be overcome. However, under less extreme circumstances (at least in capitalist societies and probably in Communist ones as well) the writer needs "bourgeois" freedom to seek the truth within the canons of his or her craft. Politics is about both more and less than the truth, and therefore conflicts with artistic endeavor. Perhaps politics and literature are ultimately assimilable to each other, but that awaits new developments in society and literature.

NOTES

1 There were nearly 30 John Reed Clubs around the country in 1934. Some cities and their magazines were New York (*Partisan Review*), Boston (*Leftward*), Hollywood (*Partisan*), Grand Rapids (*Cauldron*), Chicago (*Left Front*), Detroit (*New Force*), Hartford (*The Hammer*), and Philadelphia (*Left Review*) (Aaron 1961, p. 431).

2 The characteristics mentioned in this paragraph were gleaned from occasional brief sketches of authors, graphic artists, cartoonists, and poets who published in *New Masses*. Systematic, detailed information that one might find in biographical dictionaries was unavailable. Writers who remained would-be writers or who published but one novel are not included in biographical dictionaries. I know, because I searched in vain for information on them.

3 Midwest (23), New York City (20), California (16).

4 Henry Hart reported in a paper read to the Writers' Congress in 1935 that Cantwell's *Land of Plenty* sold 3,000; Conroy's *The Disinherited*, 2,700; and Rollins' *The Shadow Before*, 1,200. At that time it took sales of 2,000 copies for the publisher to break even on a novel (Rideout 1956, p. 235).

REFERENCES

Aaron, Daniel. 1961. *Writers on the Left.* New York: Harcourt, Brace and World.

Allen, Charles. 1943. "The Advance Guard." *Sewanee Review* 51: 410-29.

Berger, Bennett M. 1981. *The Survival of a Counterculture: Ideological Work and Everyday Life Among Rural Communards.* Berkeley and Los Angeles: University of California Press.

Brinton, Crane. 1938. *The Anatomy of Revolution.* New York: Norton.

Calmer, Alan. 1937. "Portrait of the Artist as a Proletarian." *Saturday Review of Literature* 16: 3-4, 14.

Coser, Lewis. 1965. *Men of Ideas.* New York: Free Press.

Farrell, James T. 1936. *A Note on Literary Criticism.* New York: Vanguard.

Fineberg, Jonathan. 1979. "Theater of the Real: Thoughts on Christo." *Art in America* 67: 92-99.

Freeman, Joseph. 1936. *An American Testament.* New York: Farrar and Rinehart.

Giddens, Anthony. 1973. *The Class Structure of the Advanced Societies.* New York: Harper & Row.

Gilbert, James B. 1968. *Writers and Partisans.* New York: John Wiley.

Glazer, Nathan. 1961. *The Social Basis of American Communism.* New York: Harcourt, Brace and World.

Gold, Michael. 1929. "Go Left, Young Writers." *New Masses* 4 (Jan.).

——. 1930. "Notes of the Month." *New Masses* 5 (Sept.).

Gouldner, Alvin W. 1979. *The Future of Intellectuals and the Rise of the New Class.* New York: Seabury Press.

Howe, Irving, and Lewis Coser. 1957. *The American Communist Party: A Critical History.* Boston: Beacon.

Kunitz, Stanley J. 1955. *Twentieth Century Authors: First Supplement.* New York: Wilson.

Kunitz, Stanley J., and Howard Haycraft, eds. 1942. *Twentieth Century Authors.* New York: Wilson.

Marcuse, Herbert. 1972. *Counterrevolution and Revolt.* Boston: Beacon.

Mungo, Raymond. 1971. *Mungobus.* New York: Avon.

New Masses. 1929-39. Davis: University of California. Microfiche.

Oberschall, Anthony. 1973. *Social Conflict and Social Movements.* Englewood Cliffs, N.J.: Prentice-Hall.

Pells, Richard H. 1973. *Radical Visions and American Dreams.* New York: Harper & Row.

Rahv, Philip. 1939. "Proletarian Literature: A Political Autopsy." *The Southern Review* 4: 616-28.

Rideout, Walter B. 1956. *The Radical Novel in the United States, 1900-1954.* Cambridge, Mass.: Harvard University Press.

Russak, Martin. 1929. "Jack London: America's First Proletarian Writer." *New Masses* 4 (Jan.).

Schachner, E. A. 1934. "Revolutionary Literature in the United States Today." *Windsor Quarterly* 2: 27-64.

Thompson, William Irvin. 1967. *The Imagination of an Insurrection.* New York: Oxford University Press.

Trotsky, Leon. 1957. *Literature and Revolution.* New York: Russell and Russell.

Weiss, Henry George. 1929. "Poetry and Revolution." *New Masses* 5 (Oct.).

Willener, Alfred. 1970. *The Action-Image of Society: On Cultural Politicization.* London: Tavistock.

7 Beat Politics: New Left and Hippie Beginnings in the Postwar Counterculture

Paul S. George and Jerold M. Starr

Modern bohemia can be traced to the production of Victor Hugo's play *Hernani* in Paris in 1830. Amid shouts of "shock the bourgeoisie," "Hugo's 'romantic army' of wild-haired, funkily-dressed artists was born." These first bohemians had rejected their bourgeois families to make art and live freely among the city's poor. The bourgeoisie called them *buozingo*—a derogatory reference to their fondness for booze.

In the late 1840s Henri Murger wrote several stories about four bohemian comrades that he called *Scènes de la vie bohème*. The lines include: "Where will we eat today? We'll know tomorrow." In 1849 he put them together into a surprisingly popular play, and in 1896 the play became the opera *La bohème*, by Puccini. All of this notoriety "drew young people aspiring to the life, along with bourgeois voyeurs" (Miller 1977, pp. 44–58; Graber 1958). Malcolm Cowley (1951, p. 13) credits Murger with creating the myth of bohemia as a territory and a way of life.

Through the years bohemian communities have grown up at different times all over the world. San Francisco, a lusty, brawling city immersed in the feverish California gold rush and settled recently by "lunatic miners, whores, pirates, Latins and Asians," became an early haven for bohemians (McNally 1979, p. 201). An explosion of interest in the arts in the 1880s gave the city the claim to be America's first true bohemia. From the turn of the century through the 1920s, New York and Chicago also had flourishing bohemias. They were located in older, poorer neighborhoods where food and lodging were inexpensive. Bistros and restaurants served as important social centers (Howard 1974, p. 181).

Wherever they lived, bohemians expressed certain Romantic ideals in their art and life-styles. These included the notion that every human's potential should be allowed to develop freely; adoration of the "primitive"; the celebration of fraternity; the beauty of nature; wanderlust and the lure of the exotic; the transformative power of art; free love; the quest for intense experience; and, above all, living uncorrupted by bourgeois materialism and unrestrained by bourgeois convention (Mannheim 1971; Gouldner 1973).

The materialist and nationalist preoccupations of the Great Depression and World War II proved inhospitable to the survival of a bohemian alternative in the United States. By the end of the war none was visible. Soon after, however, small numbers of dissident artists and intellectuals began seeking escape from bourgeois society in New York's Greenwich Village and San Francisco's North Beach.

Over the next several years, American society became increasingly militarized. For the first time in its history, the federal government forced its young men into peacetime military training. It raced with the Soviet Union to develop and stockpile nuclear weapons even larger than those which had leveled Hiroshima and Nagasaki. And it sacrificed 50,000 lives in Korea in what it called a "police action."

On the home front, patriotic conformity was enforced by the carrot of Madison Avenue consumerism and the stick of McCarthyite repression. The principles of Nuremberg were left to the Existentialist philosophers. In the midst of all this, those few bohemian alternative communities grew rapidly, each in its own way. In the early 1950s, some of the New York bohemian writers traveled to San Francisco and made contact with their brothers. Within the next five years, they started a countercultural rebellion. The Beat Generation was born.

HIPSTERS BEGET BEATS

The tone of New York bohemian life after World War II was profoundly influenced by the cultural rebellion in the black ghetto.

Recalling the spirit of the Harlem Renaissance of the 1920s, many residents sought to re-create the culture of their community. Renouncing Uncle Tomism, they declared their independence of whites through a new language, dress, and music. A restrained "cool," referred to these days as "style," replaced the earlier image of a child-like, excitable "darkie" who humbled himself before whites.

These new blacks, aggressively independent, were called "hip." Some claimed the term referred to someone who lived dangerously and carried "a bottle or bankroll or, more likely, a gun on his hip" (Miller 1977, pp. 238–39). Others suggested the term came from "a much earlier phrase, 'to be on the hip,' to be a devotee of opium smoking—during which activity one lies on one's hip" (Polsky 1969, pp. 145–46). In either case, the term "hip" was associated with drugs, violence, and crime. Daring and defiant, the "hipster" was a person "who could take care of himself in any situation."

The patois of the hipster, called "jive" talk, was a secret code language, laced with poetic metaphor to conceal illegal drug traffic. For music, the hipsters "dug" blues or hot jazz that gave expression to the sorrow of their oppression and the transcendent joy of their togetherness (McNally 1979, p. 82; Mailer 1969).

As early as the late 1920s, white big-band musicians, such as Mezz Mezzrow and Bix Beiderbecke, were smoking marijuana and talking jive with their black brothers (Nuttall 1968, pp. 3–9; Miller 1977, pp. 237–38). By the 1940s other disaffiliated whites used drugs and took up the outlaw life-style of the black hipster. In recalling his youth in the 1940s, Malcolm X reflected, "A few of the white men around Harlem, younger ones whom we called 'hippies,' acted more Negro than Negroes" (Miller 1977, p. 239).

THE CENTRAL CHARACTERS

It was on the edge of Harlem, around Columbia University, that the New York wing of the Beat Generation first formed. Around Christmas of 1944, Lucien Carr introduced his fellow Saint Louisan Bill Burroughs to Allen Ginsberg, whom he had met in his Columbia dormitory the previous year. Carr also had introduced Jack Kerouac, another Columbia undergraduate, to Burroughs, and it was Burroughs who brought Ginsberg, then a sophomore, and Kerouac together (Cook 1971, pp. 40–41).

Ginsberg was very impressed with Kerouac, who had come to Columbia four years earlier on a football scholarship. "I remember being awed by him, because I'd never met a big jock who was sensitive and intelligent about poetry." Kerouac was at first less taken with Ginsberg, who was five years his junior and had a reputation as a mad genius who would argue any position for the sport of it. Before long, however, Kerouac was charmed by Ginsberg's passion for ideas and total candor (Cook 1971, pp. 40–41).

Within a year the three grew to be close friends. Ginsberg was 21; Kerouac, 26; and Burroughs, 32. Ginsberg and Kerouac were impressed with Burroughs, who put them on a reading regimen of literary works by such "renegades of high culture" as Céline, Rimbaud, Spengler, Kafka, Gogol, Yeats, and Gide (McNally 1979, p. 66; Kostelanetz 1970). Burroughs also conducted psychoanalysis with each, on the couch in his back room, for about a year (Cook 1971, p. 41).

By that time Burroughs was addicted to heroin. He introduced Ginsberg and Kerouac to one of his friendly connections, Herbert Huncke. A homosexual, drug addict, intellectual, and part-time researcher for the original Kinsey Report, Huncke was "an authentic professor of hip" (Tytell 1976, pp. 37–40). He led the three on a personal tour of the hipster underworld of Times Square, turned them on to several drugs, and introduced them to "a steady succession of petty and not-so-petty criminals, sex deviates and desperate men" (Cook 1971, p. 42). From these experiences Ginsberg and Kerouac saw that there were others, like themselves, who were different, and came to identify with the defiance of the outlaw rather than the shame of the outcast (Tytell 1976, p. 57).

Around the beginning of 1947, Kerouac met Neal Cassady through former roommate Hal Chase. Cassady and Chase were both from Denver and knew each other through their common mentor, high school teacher Justin Brierly. Chase called Cassady "a self aware representative of the American underclass, a reform school punk with an eye for poetry." Soon after meeting Cassady, Kerouac introduced him to the group in New York. All of them were impressed with young Neal, who had served time in prison and also wrote poetry (McNally 1979, pp. 89–93; Gifford and Lee 1979, p. 85).

Cassady was a skillful, tireless automobile driver and mechanic with a passion for speed. Referred to in print as "Superman," the "fastestmanalive," and "the Holy Goof," Cassady is fictionalized as

"Hart Kennedy" in the first Beat novel, John Clellan Holmes's *GO*, as "Dean Moriarty" and "Cody Pomeray" in Kerouac's *On the Road* and *Visions of Cody*, and as "Hicks" in Robert Stone's *Dog Soldiers* (later made into a film called *Who'll Stop the Rain*).

Cassady was a man of enormous energy, a nonstop talker, handsome, muscular, and bursting with intelligent curiosity. He had affairs with countless women and also with Allen Ginsberg and a few other men, apparently as part of his insatiable quest for new experience.

Many considered Cassady to be the most authentic Beat of all because he never acquired money or national reputation from the movement (Hills 1979; Cook 1971, p. 198). Yet in the late 1960s Kerouac was to claim: "I'm not afraid to admit that Neal made me a better writer. His letters, his philosophy, his whole existence was a treasure to me. Neal Cassady was the greatest writer of the bunch. Better than Ginsberg, Holmes, Corso" (Jarvis 1973–74, p. 132; Gifford and Lee 1977, p. 115).

It was Cassady who put the Beat's Romantic wanderlust in high gear. By the summer of 1947, with Cassady behind the wheel, Kerouac, Burroughs, Huncke, and Ginsberg crisscrossed the continent in search of adventure. Burroughs' homes in Louisiana and, later, Mexico were frequent stops, as were Denver and San Francisco.

Despite their limited success—none of the Beats really made any money from their writing until 1957—all of them thought of themselves as men of letters. In his introduction to Burroughs' autobiography, *Junky*, Ginsberg admits that, by the beginning of the 1950s, both he and Kerouac considered themselves "poet/writers in Destiny" (Burroughs 1979, p. v).

According to Ginsberg, "it was Kerouac who encouraged Burroughs to write," first involving him in a "big detective book" in which they alternated chapters, imitating the style of Dashiell Hammett (Clark 1970). By the beginning of the 1950s, Burroughs had completed *Junky* and Ginsberg "began taking it around to various classmates in college or mental hospitals who had succeeded in establishing themselves in Publishing—an ambition which was mine also, frustrated; and thus incompetent in wordly matters, I conceived of myself as a secret literary agent" (Burroughs 1979, p. vi). At the time, Ginsberg also was carrying around "Kerouac's Proustian Chapters from *Visions of Cody* that later developed into the vision of *On the Road*." He met Carl Solomon, a poet and bohemian celebrity, while both were patients at the New York Psychiatric

Institute. Soloman later became an editor under his uncle at Ace Books, and Ginsberg persuaded him to publish *Junky* and advance Kerouac $250 for a prose novel (Burroughs 1979, p. vii; Clark 1970, p. 133).

Although many interesting women passed through their lives, they all were kept outside of this tight circle of "junkies and geniuses" who met frequently to discuss literature, philosophy, and social change, experiment with drugs, and party raucously. Carr believed the circle was creating a "New Vision," a heightened awareness of man and society (McNally 1979, pp. 62–67; Gifford and Lee 1979, p. 45; Kramer 1968, p. 77).

THE GENERATIONAL VISION

Kerouac has left a fascinating account of the emergence of this postwar counterculture. Toward the end of the war, he observed hipsters around Times Square who "looked like criminals" and spoke a language sprinkled liberally with such phrases as "crazy, man" and "man, I'm beat" (Kerouac 1959). He also heard them articulate "long lines of personal experience and vision, nightlong expressions full of hope that had become illicit and repressed by War, stirring rumblings of a new soul" (Plummer 1979). "Rising from the under-ground," Kerouac (1957, p. 46) wrote in *On the Road*, was "the sordid hipster, a new beat generation that I was slowly joining."

Kerouac told John Clellan Holmes (1958) of a vision he had of crazy, illuminated hipsters roaming America. In a conversation with Cassady in 1951, he pictured an America where at "a Ritz Yale Club party [which he attended] . . . there were hundreds of kids in leather jackets instead of big tuxedo Clancy millionaires . . . cool, and every-body was smoking marijuana, wailing in a new decade in one wild crowd." According to Kerouac (1972, pp. 36–37), this second gen-eration of hip replaced the original black hipsters, who, by 1950, had "vanished into jails and madhouses, or were shamed into silent con-formity. . . ." This new, post–Korean War "Beat Generation" con-sisted of white youth who slouched around in T-shirts and jeans, wore long sideburns, took drugs, "dug" bebop, and talked like the original hipsters.

The term "Beat" was taken from the jive talk of the jazz musi-cians. It was introduced to Kerouac by Huncke, who used it to describe a person "exhausted, defeated, depressed, but full of internal conviction" (Kramer 1968, p. 77). In the first Beat novel, *Go*, author John Clellan Holmes (1967, p. 107) quotes Kerouac's definition of Beat:

> It's a sort of furtiveness, like we're a generation of furtives. You know, with an inner knowledge there's no use flaunting on that level, the level of the "public," a kind of beatness—I mean being right down to it, to ourselves, because we all really know where we are—and a weariness with all the forms, all the conventions of the world. . . . It's something like that. So I guess you might say we're a beat generation.

Holmes added that the "Beats" felt like Negroes caught in a square world that wasn't enough for them.

SAN FRANCISCO BEAT

In 1952 Ginsberg and Kerouac moved to Berkeley, where they met Kenneth Rexroth and, over the next three years, many young San Francisco poets. By the time Kerouac and Ginsberg arrived, San Francisco had been a center for political and cultural radicalism for years. During World War II the War Resisters League and Fellowship of Reconciliation were actively supported. San Francisco was within hitchhiking distance of all of the conscientious objectors' camps in America; most passed through and many stayed. Rexroth recalls:

> All of this led immediately after the war to the founding of the Anarchist Circle, a very important group while it lasted. Talk about your intellectual fellowship—well, you really could sense it in those meetings . . . you could say damned near anything there and not get sneered at or put down. It was all open in a way that real political discussion never is. This was ideas beyond factions and politics. (Cook 1971, p. 60)

In 1947 Ruth White founded the San Francisco Poetry Center. Along with Rexroth, Philip Lamantia, Robert Duncan, and Lew Welch gathered there regularly. A radical conscientious objector named William Everson came to town and started writing poems for *Catholic World* under the name of Brother Antoninus. Michael McClure came from the Midwest, Philip Whalen and Gary Snyder from the Northwest, and Lawrence Ferlinghetti from New York.

Ferlinghetti established the City Lights Bookstore, perhaps the first paperback bookstore in the country. It became a favorite hangout for many local poets and, at their urging, Ferlinghetti started the City Lights Press in 1956 to publish their works.

Ginsberg introduced Kerouac to poet Gary Snyder, who had a profound impact on the Beat movement. First, he introduced the Beats to a love of nature and more natural ways of living (Seelye 1974). A student of the American Indian, Snyder was deeply concerned about the destruction of the environment. In his collection *Earth House Hold*, Snyder (1969, p. 90) writes: "The conditions, The Cold War, has turned all modern societies—Communist included—into vicious distortions of man's true potential. . . . The soil, the forests, and all the animal life are being consumed by these cancerous collectivities; the air and water of the planets are being fouled by them."

Snyder's second major contribution to the Beats consisted of "his anecdotes and poems of the wandering Zen Buddhist monks," which "gave a sense of intellectual, even religious justification to the beats' deep natural impulse to freedom, their wish to stay unattached and on the move" (Cook 1971, p. 29).

Under Snyder's influence Kerouac learned to camp in the mountains and commune with nature. He abandoned the desperate activity of his previous escapes from boredom and began an inward search for his roots. Written in 1956, *The Dharma Bums* "replaces the hysteria of *On the Road* with quietly contemplative retreat toward meditation" (Tytell 1976, p. 25).

The philosophy of Zen Buddhism enjoyed widespread popularity through the 1950s. Polsky (1969, p. 172) calls it perhaps the first major bohemian cultural importation in America that traveled from west to east. Many of its themes were compatible with the Beats' Romantic, bohemian outlook, including the focus on inner consciousness and the fleeting present, the political quietism, the idea of the wandering quest, the holiness of the personal impulse, and the significant role of the Zen lunatic, the holy madman.

THE IDEOLOGY OF BEAT

Kerouac's encounter with Zen reinforced the Catholic mysticism of his youth. Snyder chided him, "You old son of a bitch. You're going to end up asking for the Catholic rites on your death bed"

(Cook 1971, p. 84). And, in fact, it was in a church in Lowell in 1954 that Kerouac had had the religious experience that led to his redefinition of "Beat": "I went one afternoon to the church of my childhood (one of them), Ste. Jeanne d'Arc in Lowell . . . and suddenly with tears in my eyes I had a vision of what I must have really meant with "Beat" anyhow when I heard the holy silence in the church . . ." (Rigney and Smith 1961, pp. 34–35).

When *On the Road* was published in 1957, it contained a new definition of Beat: "He was BEAT—the root, the soul of Beatific." In other comments Kerouac disavowed the label of bohemian for the Beats and emphasized the religious dimension of their philosophic quest. In a 1958 article, "The Philosophy of the Beat Generation," Holmes concurred with Kerouac: "The Beat Generation is basically a religious generation . . . [it] means beatitude, not beat up." In May 1959 several North Beach poets launched a magazine that they called *Beatitude* (Rigney and Smith 1961, p. 32).

On the other hand, while "a few of the beats" studied by Rigney and Smith (1961, pp. 34–38) in North Beach "professed to be Orientalists, the majority were 'irreligious' avowedly professing no belief in anything." Neither did many see themselves as Beat "in the sense of beatitude or 'holiness' or mysticism." Instead, they saw themselves as "beaten down" but not "entirely 'out'" (Rigney and Smith 1961, p. 28). Through the years both the black/hipster and the religious meanings of Beat persisted, the former more compatible with the New Left of the early 1960s, the latter with the New Age movement of the early 1970s.

THE SOCIAL PSYCHOLOGY OF IDEOLOGY

In *Young Man Luther*, Erikson (1959) applies Freudian theory to the analysis of Martin Luther's biography in order to identify the psychological sources of his religious ideology. In Erikson's view, it was Luther's intense need "to be justified" in relation to his father that drove him to his revolutionary work. His historical success was due to the fact that, in working through his personal problems on the symbolic level, he developed an ideological solution to historical problems confronting vast numbers of his contemporaries. Thus, he was able "to lift his individual patienthood to the level of a universal one and to try to solve for all what he could not solve for himself alone" (Erikson 1959, p. 67).

The personal lives of the original Beats were marked by conflict, deprivation, failure, and disorder. They all suffered miserable early childhoods and, throughout life, found normal institutional regimentation an impossible burden to bear. As a consequence they became gifted misfits—refusing to fit into what they perceived to be an unfit fitness. Through the years they never stopped believing in their destinies as great writers. They burned with the need to justify themselves to the world and, through their writings, they gave voice to many others.

Ginsberg's mother, Naomi, a schoolteacher and Communist Party worker, suffered numerous nervous breakdowns, beginning in 1919, even before Allen was born. As Allen and his brother Eugene grew up,

> They watched her deteriorate before their eyes. One breakdown followed another, put her in and out of hospitals, and left her in a more or less permanent state of paranoia. . . . Her feelings of persecution were tied in the most twisted knots to her background in radical politics. Nothing was clearcut. Everyone was against her. (Cook 1971, pp. 113-14)

Allen and Eugene lived with their mother separately for extended periods of time. Ginsberg was certain that his homosexuality had roots in his adolescent repulsion toward his mother. His profoundest memories of that period "are of his mother's gross carnal reality— dresses hitched to the hips, pubic hair exposed, the smells of the body. Yes, always the body, her body" (Cook 1971, p. 114). All of this is revealed in his poem "Kaddish." A later poem, "The Change," resolves this conflict. In Cook's view, "The Change" should be read "as the missing final movement of 'Kaddish,' Resolution: To forgive the body that Naomi had made him hate was to forgive the body principle, woman, Naomi herself" (Cook 1971, p. 116).

Perhaps Naomi influenced Allen's politics, from his sustained opposition to all establishments to his later preoccupation with a mammoth drug ring conspiracy involving the CIA, the police, and organized crime (for which, it must be said, more than a little evidence exists). However, given the complexities of human character, Ginsberg's politics might better be considered an expression of his personality. Dickstein (1977, p. 20) comments:

> In his *Playboy* interview, Ginsberg described how his homosexuality . . . contributed to his political consciousness by making him sensitive to

the element of hyper-masculinity and aggressiveness in the American mentality. He revived Whitman's version of a society whose communal ties are based on a renewal of personal tenderness. And of course he was delighted at the "reappearance in the form of long hair and joyful dress of the affectionate feminine in the natural Adamic man, the whole man, the man of many parts."

Although a brilliant student, Ginsberg had numerous confrontations with the dean of Columbia College "due to his sloppy appearance and eccentric behavior" (Cook 1971, p. 41). It sometimes took the intervention of such an esteemed Columbia scholar as Lionel Trilling and Mark Van Doren to get him off the hook with the Columbia administration. All of this must have made some impression, however, because the dean later got Ginsberg out of a threatening criminal situation by intervening with District Attorney Frank Hogan, a Columbia graduate (Tytell 1976, p. 94).

From 1945 to 1955 Ginsberg made five separate attempts at psychoanalysis. The first was with Burroughs; the second, for three months, with "a Reichian who is no longer a Reichian." In 1950 his association with Huncke, caught leaving Ginsberg's apartment with stolen merchandise, landed him in the New York State Psychiatric Institute for eight months with "dreary Freudians." This was followed by two and a half years with a doctor formerly attached to the institute. His final bout with therapy was his most successful. In 1955 Ginsberg spent a year with a follower of Harry Stack Sullivan in San Francisco. This doctor "urged Ginsberg to abandon the square life of a market researcher for Peter [Orlovsky], poetry, and pleasure," advice that apparently brought him greater peace of mind (Kostelanetz 1970).

Kerouac was born Jean Louis Kerouac, the son of French-Canadian parents in the old New England mill town of Lowell, Massachusetts. His alcoholic father died of stomach cancer when Jack was twenty-four. His mother was protective and domineering. In early childhood Jack witnessed the death of his brother Gerard of rheumatic fever. Gerard was the family saint, and he made a lasting impression on Jack both in life and in death. Charles Jarvis, an English professor, Lowell neighbor, and biographer of Kerouac, claims that Kerouac's glorification of his "holy brother" Neal Cassady in *Visions of Cody* and *On the Road* has roots in his spiritual longing for Gerard (Jarvis 1973–74, p. 128). Indeed, in *On the Road*, Kerouac (1957, p.

10) says Dean (Cassady) "reminded me of some long-lost brother."
Five years after *Visions of Cody*, Kerouac wrote *Visions of Gerard*.

According to Jarvis, Kerouac grew up "sexually inhibited" and
"very straight as a kid." He endeared himself to his gang of friends
by his remarkable ability to recall the intimate details of their esca-
pades, a service he was later to perform for the Beats. In Lowell they
called him "memory babe" (Jarvis 1973–74, pp. 142–43, 162).

Kerouac's college career started with great promise. A star running
back in high school, he received a scholarship to play football at
Columbia. Within two years he had broken his leg during a game,
decided to drop football, lost his scholarship, and enlisted in the
navy. It was 1942, but the navy soon discharged him as "a schizoid
personality," and he drifted into the merchant marine. In 1944 he
got married during one of his weeks in port. He took his wife back to
Columbia, determined to "get himself an education and become a
great writer. But neither marriage nor his pass at education lasted
long. His wife left him after six months, and shortly afterward he
dropped out of Columbia" (Cook 1971, p. 41). He underwent psychoanalysis with Burroughs at the same time as Ginsberg, but it
apparently failed to give him peace of mind.

In Jarvis' (1973–74, p. 208) view, Kerouac "was a man at war
with himself. If his Beat novels shriek for the desire to burn, burn,
burn, his Lowell novels lament for a lost innocence, an unfulfilled
grace." While his Beat novels strove to achieve absolutely unedited
spontaneity, his Lowell novels were censored so as not to offend his
mother. Tytell (1976, p. 24) describes him as "brooding, lonely,
seized by moments of self-hatred."

Visions of Cody was written between the fall of 1951 and the
spring of 1952, while Kerouac lived with Neal Cassady and shared
the affections of his wife, Carolyn. In her sentimental account of
that period, Carolyn Cassady says she has "never known a man with
such a tender heart, so much sweetness." However, he "was far too
moody, his feelings too touchy, too wrapped up in himself." Although
he was a brilliant observer, Kerouac's efforts to participate fully in
life around him were "generally disappointing; he felt threatened and
alone." Even his lovemaking "had an air of apology. I didn't feel that
he ever gave or received completely." Only 31 at the time, Kerouac
already "was never far from a bottle of wine." His alcoholism grew
progressively worse (Cassady 1976, pp. 116–17). Kerouac vigorously
denied being a "fag," but his association with Ginsberg, Burroughs,

and Huncke caused rumors that disturbed him. (The most publicized was Gore Vidal's boast of having seduced him.) After two bad marriages and the shock of his sudden celebrity in the late 1950s, Kerouac returned to Lowell to marry a high school girlfriend and take care of his widowed mother. He remained a recluse during the final years of his life, his mother turning away the visits of Ginsberg, Burroughs, and others, until he succumbed to cirrhosis of the liver in 1969, at the age of 47 (McNally 1979, pp. 322–24, 344; Charters 1973, pp. 362–67).

Kerouac's companion Neal Cassady grew up in poverty in Denver. His father, a skid row alcoholic, separated from his mother when Neal was just a toddler. As early as age six, Neal remembers living with his father in flophouses, taking his meals at a nearby mission, begging his father to stop drinking, and riding the rails east to Kansas City and west to Los Angeles. His mother had nine children from her two marriages and was "simply too much harassed" to show him "her affection adequately . . . I still can't remember her ever kissing me." Still, he recalled her as "the kindest and most gentle of women" (Cassady 1971, p. 53).

Two older stepbrothers, as strapping adolescents, used to beat his father bloody when he came home drunk every Saturday night and, after his separation from their mother, whenever their paths crossed. Another stepbrother, a few years older and larger than Neal, was a jealous, sadistic bully who enjoyed beating him and imprisoning him inside a wall bed for hours on end.

A compulsive car thief, Cassady refers, in a letter to Kerouac dated July 3, 1949, to already having been arrested 10 times, and convicted 6 times, and to having served 15 months (Cassady 1971, p. 129). Some of these arrests may have been for marijuana, which brought him a two-year sentence on a California prison farm in 1957–58 (Cook 1971, p. 198). Shortly thereafter, he met Ken Kesey and over the next few years became one of Kesey's Merry Pranksters, graduating from pot and peyote to LSD and speed. In the mid-1960s he drove Kesey's Dayglo colored bus up and down the California coast and across the country (Wolfe 1968).

Cassady's father disappeared sometime during Neal's youth. As late as age 24, while on the road with Kerouac, Neal still searched for him, but in vain. Despite his awesome manic energy, Cassady has been described as unhappy, even suicidal, for most of his adult life (Berriault 1972). He was married three times, but was alone at the end. He died of exposure in rural Mexico in February 1968, rumored to have been depressed at growing old. He was 42.

William Burroughs was born to wealthy parents in St. Louis in 1914. His father owned and ran a lumber business. His grandfather had started the Burroughs machine empire and left him a trust fund that provided $150 per month for life. Still, life was anything but easy for young Bill. In his autobiography, *Junky*, Burroughs confesses that his "earliest memories are colored by a fear of nightmares. I was afraid to be alone, and afraid of the dark, and afraid to go to sleep because of dreams where a supernatural horror seemed always on the point of taking shape." Even when awake, Burroughs suffered from recurring hallucinations (Burroughs 1979, pp. xi–xvi).

Burroughs went to a "progressive school," where he was "timid with the other children and afraid of physical violence." In high school he became a "chronic malingerer" with fantasies of a life of crime, given to acts of petty vandalism to combat the "dullness of a Midwest suburb where all contact with life was shut out" (Burroughs 1979, p. xii). One episode cost him his only friend, and he then found himself "a good deal alone," drifting into "solo adventures" of breaking into private homes (but not taking anything) and reckless driving.

At Harvard, Burroughs "knew no one," "was lonely," "hated the University," and "hated the town it was in." For a time he associated with "some rich homosexuals of the international queer set," but decided they were "jerks" and went his own way. However, his desire for young males was now established. He was graduated from Harvard "without honors" and "drifted around Europe for a year or so."

Back in the United States, Burroughs underwent three years of psychoanalysis that "removed inhibitions and anxiety" regarding his homosexuality. Somewhere along the line he was put into a "nut house" and diagnosed "schizophrenic, paranoid" after cutting off a finger joint as a gesture of love for a friend. This record was sufficient to have him released from military service after a short stint during the war.

Burroughs then drifted along, holding a variety of jobs, such as private detective, exterminator, bartender, factory worker, and office worker, also engaging in occasional petty crime. Burroughs writes, "It was at this time and under these circumstances that I came in contact with junk, became an addict, and thereby gained the motivation, the real need for money I had never had before" (Burroughs 1979, p. xi). His nightmarish addiction to heroin was to last for 15 years. Married for many years, he accidentally killed his wife, Peggy, while demonstrating his prowess with a pistol. Urged on by friends, although too drunk to aim straight, he missed the apple and put a bullet through her head.

The last of the principal New York Beats to join the circle was Gregory Corso. Ginsberg met Corso at a bar in 1950. Corso had grown up a street kid, his Italian immigrant father a hazy figure of his childhood and his mother having died young. He spent some time in the children's observation ward at Bellevue Hospital and was in and out of trouble. At 16 he was sentenced for robbery and spent the next three years in prison. Corso, just released, had written some poems while in prison that he showed to Ginsberg at his urging. He soon became the "bad boy" of the Beats, a role he gloried in (Cook 1971, pp. 133–49).

In sum, all of the Beats suffered childhoods troubled by parents who were disturbed, alcoholic, domineering, or unloving, or siblings who were jealous and sadistic. Whatever resources they developed within themselves to cope with these situations somehow rendered them unfit for conventional life. They had confrontations with school authorities or the law, they dropped out, were imprisoned, placed in an asylum, or became addicted to heroin. None of them desired any vocation in life other than writing, so they took only temporary jobs to support their literature. They lived in barely furnished, run-down apartment buildings, in neighborhoods that trafficked in all sorts of crime. They wore old clothes and made most of their own entertainment. They were shunned by the "square" world and scorned by many of the prominent critics of their day as untalented "know nothings."

What distinguished them from ordinary deviants or malcontents was their talent, their inner conviction, and the historical circumstances that made it possible for them to communicate with the growing constituency of youth and bohemians they came to represent. In so doing, they turned their stigma into a blessing, their shame into defiance. In the process they set the pattern for the black, youth, women's and gay revolutions to follow. Each of these groups stopped trying to justify its failure to meet white, adult, middle-class male standards, and instead accepted the dominant stereotype of themselves and declared it superior. They inverted the values by which such judgments were made and such prestige hierarchies sustained. The Beats were the first to put down the "squares," ridicule the authorities, debunk the myths, expose the hypocrisies, and, thus, delegitimate the culture of domination. Writing about Cassady (Dean Moriarty) in *On the Road*, Kerouac (1957, p. 11) declares, "His 'criminality' was not something that sulked and sneered; it was a wild yea-saying overburst of American joy. . . ."

BEAT WRITING: THE ROMANTIC CHALLENGE

The main characteristics of Beat writing are the juxtaposition of opposites, presenting a picture of the world in all its beauty and terror; a sense of the absurd; the importance of the clown or holy fool; and insistence on the nonrational as a way of knowing (Lipton 1959, pp. 238–44). This orientation is reflected in the Beat writers' lists of their favorite poets and authors: almost entirely nineteenth-century French and English Romantics and American transcendentalists such as Hugo, Baudelaire, Rimbaud, Blake, Shelley, Keats, Byron, Thoreau, and Whitman (Kostelanetz 1970; Clark 1970).

Ginsberg and Kerouac, in particular among the Beats, attempted to achieve Romantic form in their writing. In Ginsberg's view, the "trouble with conventional form is it's too symmetrical, geometrical, numbered and pre-fixed unlike my own mind which has no beginning and end, nor fixed measure of thought [of speech writing] other than its own cornerless mystery" (Kostelanetz 1970).

Kerouac's challenge was to break down the distinction between the frank content of personal conversation between friends and the formality of conventional literary subject matter. Ginsberg comments,

> That was Kerouac's great discovery in *On the Road*. The kinds of things that he and Neal Cassady were talking about, he finally discovered were *the* subject matter for what he wanted to write down. That meant, at that minute, a complete revision of what literature was supposed to be. (Clark 1970, p. 135)

The special form the Beats attempted to effect in their writing was that of black urban bebop jazz. Bebop was first played in a Harlem nightclub called Minturn's Playhouse in 1942. The group consisted of Thelonious Monk (piano), Dizzie Gillespie (trumpet),

Charles Christian (guitar), and Kenny Clark (drums), and featured Charlie Parker (saxophone) (Hodeir 1956, p. 99). It carried jazz radically further in its movement away from the tight symphonic arrangements of the white "swing" bands and toward group and solo improvisation and an emphasis on rhythm and feeling (Hodeir 1956, pp. 99–104; Willener 1970, pp. 231–32; Bjorn 1980). Bebop was played everywhere in the post-World War II period.

The Beats embraced jazz with a passion. Holmes (1958, p. 38) stated:

> In the arts, modern jazz is almost exclusively the music of the Beat Generation . . . because jazz is almost exclusively the music of the inner freedom, of improvisation, of the creative individual rather than the interpretative group. It is the music of a submerged people, who *feel* free, and this is precisely how young people feel today.

Lipton (1959, p. 212) added, "To the Beat generation, jazz is also a music of protest. Being apolitical does not preclude protest. There are other solutions besides political solutions."

Ginsberg's poems "Howl" and "Kaddish" are said to be "saxophone inspired" (Nuttall 1968, p. 110). Indeed, in his Paris interview Ginsberg explains that his "organic" approach to poetry allows the source of the meter to come "from a source deeper than the mind," from "the breathing and belly and the lungs" (Clark 1970, p. 130). Ginsberg says the organization used in "Howl," "a recurrent kind of syntax," is based on the "myth of Lester Young as described by Kerouac, blowing 89 choruses of *Lady Be Good* say, in one night, or my own hearing of Illinois Jacquet's *Jazz at the Philharmonic* Volume 2; I think *Can't Get Started* was the title" (Clark 1970, p. 131).

Kerouac was the Beat most obsessed with the jazz ethos. Cook (1971, p. 221) writes, "It was not just in the occasional scene that Kerouac would try to inject something of the jazz feeling; he attempted rather, to infuse all his work with the urgency and continuous flow of music." It was the "furious abandon and overwhelming spontaneity of Charlie Parker" that for Kerouac "became the model for unfettered, immediate creativity . . . Kerouac wanted to let go into an almost biological form of writing—to write spontaneously, outwards from a burning center, until details and words pile up into a fluid frenzy of notes and rhythms."

His method was to type his prose onto a continuous roll of tele-type paper (provided by Lucien Carr), writing as fast as possible, never stopping to choose the "proper" word, concentrating only on the subject in his imagination, and never revising: to seek "deep form, poetic form, the way consciousness *really* digs everything that happens" (Cook 1971, p. 74). In this manner the original manuscript of *On the Road* was completed in three weeks of almost nonstop typing. Ginsberg called it "spontaneous bop prosody" (Cook 1971, p. 221; Tytell 1976, p. 17).

Most literary critics were hostile to the Beats. Writing in *Partisan Review*, Norman Podhoretz (1960) called the Beats "know nothing bohemians" who were "hostile to civilization." In fact, the Beats aroused such intense antipathy from some of the gatekeepers of high culture that Cook (1971, p. 87) commented, "There were people who made a career out of attacking the Beats."

The reaction was predictable. The literary scene in the 1950s was dominated by the New Critics of the colleges and universities and those New York intellectuals, like Podhoretz, known as the *Partisan Review* crowd. The former were academic elitists who delighted in making small points. For them, a poem was to be analyzed as an object that was independent of the author's life and background, an object that employed particular means to achieve particular effects (Bush 1978, p. 167). The latter were political polemicists. Thus, the norms were either classicism or abstract political moralizing. Neither approached literature in a spirit of play (Cook 1971, pp. 11–12).

Needless to say, the aggressively Romantic Beats loomed as a wild, shaggy menace to these establishments. Seymour Krim observed that the New Criticism started out as a "worthy effort" to "lift American experience and intellectual standards, but had become enslaved by its own criteria" until it became just an effort "to impose European standards on American experience." As such, "the Beat thing was healthy, organic, unstoppable. It had to happen" (Cook 1971, pp. 52–53).

BEAT COMES OF AGE AND BECOMES THE RAGE

In 1955 the interaction of the New York and San Francisco Beats began to give off sparks. In the words of Rexroth, Ginsberg "was impatient for the revolution to begin" (Cook 1971, p. 62). Sensing the time was right for the inaugural event, he organized a reading at the

Six Gallery in San Francisco, bringing together the area's best young poets for a full evening of poetry. Participants included Philip Lamantia, Michael McClure, Gary Snyder, Lew Welch, Philip Whalen, and Ginsberg himself. Writing about the reading in *The Dharma Bums*, Kerouac called it "the birth of the San Francisco Poetry Renaissance."

The climax of the evening was Ginsberg's half-drunk, wildly rhythmic recitation of "Howl." He had written the poem two weeks earlier, "during a long weekend spent in his room under the influence of various drugs—peyote for visions, amphetamine to speed up, and Dexedrine to keep going." Ginsberg's delivery electrified the audience, bringing forth chants of "Go! Go! Go!" (Cook 1971, p. 64). Later, Rexroth was to say, "It was different from anything he had done up until then—hell, it was different from what anyone had done until then" (Cook 1971, p. 61).

"Howl" begins with an allusion to the hipster experience that has become one of the most widely quoted passages in American poetry:

> I saw the best minds of my generation, starving hysterical naked, drag-
> ging themselves through the negro streets at dawn looking for an angry
> fix, angelheaded hipsters burning for the ancient heavenly connection.
> . . . (Ginsberg 1956, p. 3)

It concludes with a series of indictments of the corporate America of the 1950s that seethe with controlled rage:

> Moloch . . . whose love is endless oil and stone! Moloch whose soul is
> electricity and bands! Moloch whose poverty is the specter of genius!
> Moloch whose fate is a cloud of sexless hydrogen. . . . (Ginsberg 1956,
> p. 27)

In 1957 Ferlinghetti's City Lights Books published the poem in a collection entitled *Howl and Other Poems*. Publication was blocked immediately by an obscenity suit. Ferlinghetti noted that the trial was "not only a forum on the meaning of obscenity and the right of free speech but also a platform for ideas that would be of widespread concern" in the years to follow (Cherkovski 1979, p. 109). The trial brought the book widespread notoriety and the judge upheld the defendants' rights of free press. Ginsberg' scathing denunciation of materialism, militarism, and conformity, his adulation of the primitive, and his tribute to sex, drugs, and other taboo literary subjects would be read.

Ginsberg soon found his public. Within a dozen years the City Lights edition of *Howl* sold over 150,000 copies in 20 printings (Kostelanetz 1970). The most immediate impact was on the hundreds of kindred bohemian souls who migrated to North Beach, Venice West, and Greenwich Village in those last three years of the decade.

With the publication of Kerouac's *On the Road*, also in 1957, the movement gained national attention. Based on the adventures of Kerouac (Sal Paradise) and Cassady (Dean Moriarty), who rambled around the country in the late 1940s and early 1950s, *On the Road* is filled with vivid vignettes of the underside of affluent America. The novel became an instant best seller, especially among the restless young, for whom Dean Moriarty became a modern romantic hero.

Gilbert Millstein (1957), writing in the *New York Times*, hailed its publication as a "historic occasion" and predicted that just as *The Sun Also Rises* was a testimonial to the Lost Generation, so would *On the Road* become a monument to the "Beat Generation." *On the Road*, Millstein concluded, was "the most beautifully executed, the clearest and most important utterance yet made by the generation Kerouac himself named 'beat'. . ." For Holmes (1958) the Beats were a generation "groping toward faith out of an intellectual despair and moral chaos in which they refuse to lose themselves."

The popularity of *On the Road* triggered a wave of national publicity for the Beat Generation. Kerouac, Ginsberg, and Corso were interviewed by representatives from all the mass media. The term "beatnik" was fastened to members of the movement by *San Francisco Chronicle* columnist Herb Caen, who explained that he had invented it in the wake of Sputnik because beatniks were "equally far out" to him (McNally 1979, p. 253; Cook 1971, p. 199).

Holmes believed the Beat Generation was an international phenomenon, sharing many traits with Britain's Teddy Boys, Japan's Sun Tribers, and even some underground youth in Russia. At a party to celebrate the publication of *The Beats*, editor Seymour Krim proclaimed, "It's a posture of rebellion. It's for anybody unwilling to put up with the older compromises" (*New Yorker* 1960a).

Obviously there were many such rebels in waiting because, as Cook (1971, p. 10) reports, the movement "attracted thousands—tens of thousands—of young people in a very short time." Beat symbols and styles found a fertile climate in the burgeoning college campuses of affluent America. After World War II and through the 1960s, the number of college students grew to encompass over half of the 18- to 21-year-old cohort. Such youth represented a new social category created by a number of factors, including the need to delay the assimilation of the "baby boom" cohorts into the economy, the growing reliance of private industry on universities for low-wage, high-skill labor (graduate students) for research and development, larger federal subsidies to higher education (especially through the military), a credential inflation in the job market, and rising status competition in the expanding middle class (Starr 1980; 1981).

All of these factors resulted in a delayed entry into marriage and the labor market, a prolongation of adolescence into what had been young adulthood (Starr 1981). Erikson's (1953) popular *Childhood and Society* introduced his concept of the "identity crisis." Through the decade many youth learned to conceptualize "their quite understandable anxieties about an uncertain future" as a problem of "identity." According to this developmental norm, one is obliged to continue "searching for" one's identity "until one's commitments to and immersion in family, community, and career result in the disappearance of the identity problem—whereupon one may be told that the identity crisis has been resolved" (Berger 1971, p. 90).

The appeal of the Beats to such youth obviously resided in their burning existential quest. As Holmes (1957–1958, p. 17) insisted:

> Everywhere the Beat Generation seems occupied with the feverish production of answers . . . to a single question: how are we to live? . . . This generation cannot conceive of the question in any but personal terms, and knows that the only answer it can accept will come out of the dark night of the individual soul.

In a short time dress and grooming among the young reflected the new style: beards, blue jeans, sandals, berets, and sweatshirts for the men; long hair, beads, and leotards or black stockings for the women. From the late 1950s until the mid-1960s, there were Beat coffeehouses in every city of over 100,000 population (Cook 1971, p. 92). As an important consequence poetry, jazz, and Abstract Expressionist art gained new followings.

The major centers—Greenwich Village, North Beach, and Venice West—were all studied by social scientists. Titillated by their reports, "squares" crammed into buses offering tours of the bohemian sections. Motion picture and television producers moved quickly to capitalize on public interest in the beatniks. Kerouac's *The Subter-raneans*, a 1953 novel about his unhappy love affair with a black Indian woman (he loses her to Corso), was made into a movie. The insipid cinema version claimed to tell the shocking "truth" about the sex, drugs, and music of the new bohemians. A television producer approached Kerouac about writing episodes for a weekly series based on *On the Road.* Kerouac declined, but the series went on the next year under the title "Route Sixty-Six." It featured Martin Milner and a young actor, named George Maharis, who bore a close resemblance to Kerouac (Cook 1971, pp. 72–73). Perhaps the most famous beatnik was Maynard G. Krebs, the scrawny, shaggy sidekick of television's "Dobie Gillis."

The publicity given to the Beats was quite mixed. The Luce publications made the movement sound both ridiculous and dangerous (Cook 1971, p. 91). Paul O'Neil (1959) of *Life* magazine dismissed the Beats as dirty, noisy rebels. *Time* denounced them as "mendicants of marijuana and mad verse" and "oddballs who celebrate booze, dope, sex, and despair." Ginsberg later returned the compliment by calling *Time* "the whore of Babylon" (*Time* 1959a; 1959b).

GROWTH OF THE BEAT COLONIES

Despite, or perhaps because of, the criticism of the conservative media, young people migrated in large numbers to expand the Beat colonies in North Beach and Greenwich Village. As mentioned, social scientists soon showed up on the scene to record their views. Rigney and Smith (1961) sampled 51 out of an estimated 180 to 200 Beats living in North Beach, and Polsky (1969) did in situ interviews with an estimated 300 Beats in the Village.

The Rigney and Smith sample consisted of 33 men, whose average age was 27 years, and 18 women, whose average age was 24 years. Most had come to North Beach from big cities like New York, Los Angeles, or Chicago. Less than a fifth came from rural areas. Two-thirds came from middle-to-upper-middle-class homes, in contrast with only about one-third in the general population. Polsky's estimates are quite comparable: about 5 percent upper-class, 60 percent middle-class, and 35 percent lower-class.

More than 70 percent of the North Beach Beats started college, most going for two years and about a fifth graduating. Three had master's degrees in music. However, only about half a dozen Beats (less than one in eight) had white-collar jobs. Over a third were dependent on the government, partners, or parents as their primary means of support. Most Beats worked at low-paid clerical, sales, or personal service jobs that required little formal education or training and offered very limited opportunities for advancement. Less than half had steady employment of any kind.

Polsky reported that the anti-work ethic was so strong that many took jobs away from the scene so as not to be seen by other Beats. Some would have preferred to starve rather than take work they considered demeaning. In Polsky's view, this refusal was ideological: "Sensible of America's inequitable distribution of income *and* its racial injustices *and* its Permanent War Economy, the Beats have responded with a Permanent Strike" (Polsky 1969, pp. 159–60). Goodman (1960, p. 68) points out that the humble jobs taken by the Beats could be justified in that they perform useful service, "no questions asked and no beards have to be shaved." They were jobs that were easily taken and left, jobs that fit a life committed to art and movement.

Of the 51 Beats surveyed by Rigney and Smith (1961, p. 178), 46 said they had "some sort of artistic outlet." These included two composers, two jazz men, three painters, one writer, and four poets (altogether about one-fourth of the sample) who were considered "better than 'good,' even near 'great'" by their peers. Polsky (1969), much more critical, estimated only one-sixth were "habituated to reading" and less than one-tenth were concerned with writing. While this latter proportion compares with that of earlier bohemias, Polsky complained it was "godawful stuff," marred by anti-academicism, anti-historicism, and a consequent lack of technical skills.

Goodman (1960, p. 68) also denigrated the Beats' lack of standards, doubted they really cared about the bomb, and suspected that their rejection of competition and achievement was just a defense against a deeply felt sense of inferiority and fear of failure. Nevertheless, Polsky and Goodman both conceded that aesthetic values occupied a much more important place in the Beat community than in "square" society. Indeed, Goodman (1960, p. 179) observed that "everybody engages in creative acts and is likely to carry a sketchbook." He acknowledged that "such creative activity sharpens the perceptions, releases and refines feelings, and is a powerful bond."

Of course, there were occasions when Beats would compromise their principles of eschewing money and "squares." Ted Joans, a black Village poet, rented himself out as a Beatnik for "square" parties so that he could make enough money to take a cruise around the world. Around the same time a Beat woman contacted a "Rent-a-Beatnik" agency in the Village for work similar to Joans's. She insisted that she found the idea of displaying herself at a "square" party "faintly nauseating" but she needed the "bread," and "for that, almost anything is worth it . . ." (Millstein 1960, pp. 3, 28, 30).

Such instances can fit within the Beat ethic if one distinguishes between a "gig" (gainful employment) and a "hustle" or "scuffle." The latter involves deceiving, swindling, or, in these two cases, putting somebody on. In putting on the timid "squares," Beats provided a cheap thrill, kept their cool, and remained in control of the situation (Rigney and Smith 1961, pp. xiii–xvii).

About half the North Beach Beats were single. A fourth were married, and another fourth were divorced. Ten had children. Although there was no gay subculture in North Beach, 12 of the 33 men had had homosexual experiences. However, all but one of the 12 considered themselves actively bisexual. Although many failed "to establish deep and lasting sexual relationships," there was a "very high tolerance of sex-role ambiguity" (Polsky 1969). Sexual freedom for Beats on both coasts included liaisons with blacks, typically between black men and white women, although these were not approved by all.

Many in the North Beach group had emotional problems. Seven had been in mental hospitals, five were undergoing psychotherapy, and five were taking medication regularly. However, Rigney and Smith (1961, p. 39) cautioned that sickness certainly was "not a requirement for membership in the group." Many were emotionally stable. What was distinctive about the community was its tolerance for eccentric behavior based on an appreciation of a common humanity that was missing in polite bourgeois society.

All the North Beach Beats experimented with a wide variety of drugs. Four-fifths had tried marijuana, half had taken peyote, and a fourth had used heroin. Of the 13 who had tried heroin, 7 had become addicted, but 5 had kicked the habit before coming to North Beach. The favorite drug in North Beach was alcohol. Almost all had taken a drink, and eight (about one in six) had become addicted. Polsky reported marijuana, hashish, peyote, synthetic mescaline, and heroin use among the Village Beats. He estimated that while about 10 percent of the Beats over 20 years of age were heroin addicts, about 90 percent were mairjuana users.

Drugs were advocated to overcome one's cultural conditioning, to liberate the mind from false concepts and the body from deeply implanted self-repression. To get high, one had to suspend one's rational defenses and submit to the total experience. Once launched on one's inner trip, one could search for the holy primitive within, the authentic nature that had been repressed and distorted by the demands of bourgeois society.

Drugs also were used as aids to creativity. A North Beach painter claimed that peyote helped him to see "new colors hidden from my conscious mind" (Rigney and Smith 1961, p. 39). In Venice West a Beat insisted that he "never really *heard* the music until (he) started listening with pot" (Lipton 1959, p. 172).

Thus, in social background, current circumstances, and ideology, these Beats closely resembled the original New York group. Many came to North Beach because they viewed it as a retreat from "square" society where they could devote themselves to art. Other enticements included low rents, inexpensive food, friendly bistros, and the area's reputation for tolerance.

THE POLITICS OF ROMANTICISM: RADICAL AND CONSERVATIVE BEATS

As pointed out in the introduction to this volume, Romanticism can lead in antagonistic political directions. Both versions reject bourgeois Rationalism with its abstract analysis and positivistic-utilitarian philosophy. Instead, they champion holistic thinking, personal intuition, devotion to higher principles, and individual heroism.

The rejection of any objective method or standard of truth soon leads to the problem of order. One solution is to reject a common order and allow each person his or her individual expression. Another is to invest all authority in a charismatic leader with claims to a higher truth. One solution offers freedom but threatens chaos; the other offers security but threatens repression. Thus, one version of Romanticism is radically progressive, extending the democratic imperative toward anarchism. The other version is reactionary, reaching back to an idealized premodern past, exalting the virtues of blood and soil, patriarchal religion, patriarchal family, and nationalism—that is, neofascism.

As long as Romanticism is confined to culturally radical expression, its implicit political foundations may not be apparent. Because the Beats avoided politics through the 1950s, differences in philosophy remained covert. As Michael Harrington (1972, p. 100) reflected on the late 1940s bohemia around the University of Chicago: "As long as there was an iconoclastic regard for standards and a contempt for a middle class utilitarianism, Bohemia could assimilate any content, the revolutionary as well as the conservative, the romantic and realist. . . ."

The dynamics of this ideological diversity can be illustrated vividly by tracing the public careers of the original Beat brothers, Allen Ginsberg and Jack Kerouac, as the politics of the 1960s brought them to a fork in the long and winding road they had traveled together. In 1960 Ginsberg began to get involved in radical politics. He signed ads in support of the pro-Castro Fair Play for Cuba Committee and traveled to Cuba to view the revolution first hand. The following year he pronounced Beat "dead" and left America for spiritual study in India, which took up most of the next four years (Dickstein 1977, p. 8).

While in New York in 1964, Ginsberg joined with many other Lower East Side poets to protest the *New York Daily News* editorial attacks on the Mobilization for Youth program. A writer covering the event asked: "Is it not possible that the same Poet-prophet who warned us with a terrible negation of our emptiness—might now be one, if not *the* one, to find us a challenge of spiritual and social affirmation? . . ." (Hahn 1966, pp. 293–94).

Ginsberg became an active participant in many pro-pot demonstrations. He served as a witness at congressional hearings and wrote "one of the most elegantly written pro-pot polemics in print, 'The Great Marijuana Hoax.'" The essay was published in *Atlantic Monthly* and reprinted in *The Marijuana Papers* (Kostelanetz 1970). During the period 1964–66 Ginsberg also supported the activities of a free-love cult called Kerista, seeing "political overtones" in the new family structures and life-styles (Gruen 1966, p. 54).

As he surveyed the radical movement in the mid-1960s, Ginsberg saw the political radicals as having a "real vision of the material and social ills of the society," but little insight into personal consciousness. His objection to confrontational tactics was that "certain kinds of political action deform the agent more than they change society" (Dickstein 1977, p. 21). He was seeking a creative synthesis of means and ends, a strategy of oppositional politics that would liberate the participants as it effected change in the system. A proven publicist, he felt that any attempt to change public opinion would have to involve the mass media.

From 1966 to 1968, Ginsberg emerged as a major public figure, a patient, charming, and conciliatory "guru to the new generation" who lent "his magnetic spiritual presence to so many of the most obscene and solemn moments of the 1960s" (Dickstein 1977, p. 6; Cook 1971, p. 205). Wherever he went, he preached his new philosophy of cultural politics, a radical synthesis to achieve the final transformation.

Ginsberg's ideological solution was to advocate a "politics of exorcism, celebration and public joy rather than violent confrontation," to seduce rather than debate those undecided or opposed (Dickstein 1977, p. 22). In 1966 he wrote a poem called "How to Make a March/Spectacle" that advised demonstrators to "lay aside their usually grave and pugnacious quality in favor of a festive dancing and chanting parade that would pass out balloons and flowers, candy and kisses, bread and wine to everyone along the line of march—including to the cops and any Hell's Angels in the vicinity" (Roszak 1969, p. 150).

Ginsberg's approach restored the affirmative implicit in the original meaning of protest—to "witness for" something. It allowed for a demonstration of radical cultural values as a basis for radical politics. It showed peace and love.

In January 1967, Ginsberg joined with Gary Snyder to stage "A Gathering of Tribes for a Human Be-In" on the polo fields of Golden Gate Park. The "Be-In" was partly a demonstration of solidarity with Haight-Ashbury Beat/hippies weary from their community battles with "square"/straight adversaries and partly an elaboration on the Free Fairs put on by the Artists Liberation Front and the Trips Festivals sponsored by Ken Kesey and the Merry Pranksters (Wolfe 1968, pp. 13–14; Cook 1971, pp. 199–201; Kramer 1969, pp. 189–91; Cherkovski 1979, p. 184–85). Also participating in the event were a diverse group of hipsters and radicals, including Dizzie Gillespie, Dick Gregory, Jerry Rubin, and Tim Leary. Called to celebrate the New Age, the "Be-In" attracted widespread media coverage, created the myth of the hippie, and triggered the migration of 100,000 youths to San Francisco for the "Summer of Love" (Miller 1977, p. 251).

In 1968 Ginsberg attended the Democratic National Convention in Chicago as a correspondent for the now defunct *Eye* magazine. As commotion raged on the convention floor, where Mayor Daley controlled all the microphones, Ginsberg chanted mantras from the balcony—apparently hoping to calm the multitude and chase the evil vibrations from the convention. He was picked up by the Chicago police, and the Secret Service took his press pass away. Ginsberg commented later, "Every reporter got the same treatment. The police were working hand in hand with the government men, Daley and Hoover . . . I suddenly realized that I was living in a police state then and there." In Ginsberg's view it was all done to keep Eugene McCarthy from being nominated because he also was afraid of the authoritarian police state (Cook 1971, p. 242).

By the end of the decade, Ginsberg spoke hopefully about the political possibilities of the themes of the 1967 "Be-In." He insisted that "anything communal is thus political," that the genesis of political movement lies in communal energy. He felt that the "one sort of spontaneous movement" that had come out of the commune movement was "the sudden awareness of the menace to ecology" (Cook 1971, p. 240). This, he felt, was facilitated by the new world view of the 1960s generation, "a cosmic consciousness, an awareness of being in the middle of the cosmos instead of this town or that valley or city" (Cook 1971, p. 243). And this cosmic consciousness was nurtured by LSD: "It was necessary and inevitable in a highly rigid and brainwashed civilization such as ours to help us find what was always there. To us the LSD thing was just as important as the trip to the moon. LSD equals the moon in terms of the expansion of human possibilities" (Cook 1971, p. 245).

In Ginsberg's view, the intellectual heart of the Beat movement was "the return to nature and the revolt against the machine," and the "getting out from under the American flag and marching to a different drummer in the Thoreauvian sense that one can find one's own self here," that is, Romantic anarchism (Cook 1971, p. 104). In 1969, looking back on the last quarter-century, Ginsberg saw "many elements of continuity from the Beats to the present," "including the first serious experimentation with altered states of consciousness," the "movement from jazz and rhythm and blues in *On the Road* to rock today," the "whole rediscovery of the Body of the Land," and "the Eastern elements that interest young people today" (Cook 1971, p. 104).

On the other hand, the road Kerouac traveled in the 1960s took him far away from Ginsberg and his Beat comrades. In fact, "as his friends gained widespread recognition as radicals, he raged at them for not being like him, American Patriots." Through the decade Kerouac denounced Ginsberg for his "socialist ideals," Holmes for his "leftism," and Ferlinghetti and Lipton as "Communists." He put down liberalism as a sham for the middle class and adamantly declared his support for William F. Buckley, Jr., the leading spokesman for the Romantic conservative Libertarian right (Charters 1973, p. 344; Tytell 1976, p. 62).

Kerouac was vehemently critical of black militants, the politicized evolution of his early hipster heroes. In conversation one evening, Corso challenged his attitude toward blacks, reminding him of the passage in *On the Road* that reads: "At lilac evening I walked with every muscle aching among the lights of 27 and Welton in the Denver section, wishing I were a Negro, feeling that the best the white world offered was not enough ecstasy for me, not enough life, joy, kicks, darkness, music, not enough night" (Kerouac 1957, p. 148).

> Kerouac protested, "Nobody is going to tell me how to live, or come into my house, or insult my own people because they're not Negro."
>
> Corso: "Ah, then that's where it's at, Jackie. How could you mean what you wrote when you feel that way?"
>
> Kerouac: "I felt that way, then, *that night*."
>
> Corso: "But you weren't looking inside the Negro. You weren't seeing him, his misery, his isolation."
>
> Kerouac: "I wanted to have a good time, the way the Negroes can."
>
> Corso: "But they didn't really feel that way. They didn't want to be that way."
>
> Kerouac: "I will never take back one poetic statement I've ever written." (Jarvis 1973-74, pp. 157-58)

Kerouac also rejected the hippies. He had been willing to break down conventional literary and social barriers in his quest for authenticity, but he was shocked and repelled by the blatancy of those who carried the movement forward. Jarvis (1973-74, p. 106) reports, "In my talks with him about hippies, he kept coming back to one term, 'loud-mouthed fags.' He had no use for them, said they were assuming a stature they had not earned, said they were playacting, said they hadn't produced any real literature and never would."

Looking back on his Beat days, Kerouac denied that he was trying "to create any kind of consciousness or anything like that. We didn't have a whole lot of abstract thoughts. We were just a bunch of guys who were out trying to get laid" (Cook 1971, p. 89). Indeed, in *On the Road*, Kerouac finds Cassady, the mad conman, superior to the "tedious intellectualness" of all his other friends. Kerouac (1957, p. 11) adds, "Besides, all my New York friends were in the negative, nightmare position of putting down society and giving their tired bookish or political or psychoanalytical reasons, but Dean just raced in society, eager for bread and love. . . ." Later in the novel, Kerouac observed with contempt, "The arty types were all over America, sucking up its blood."

In Cook's (1971, p. 85) view, those who knew Kerouac in the old days weren't surprised by his later conservatism. Michael McClure "recalls that he shocked all his friends in San Francisco in 1956 by insisting that if he were voting that year he would vote for Eisenhower. 'It just seemed a weird idea to us then,' he said. 'Not voting we could understand, but *wanting* to vote for Eisenhower!'" Burroughs explains, "His father was a real old French peasant anti-Semite, Catholic rightist, and Jack got a lot of his basic attitudes from him. And his mother! Talk about your old peasant types!" (Cook 1971, p. 181).

It seems clear that Kerouac's strong Catholic and smalltown roots were the basis for his Romanticism. At one point in *On the Road* Kerouac (1957, p. 82) goes with a Mexican woman and her son and becomes a migrant worker, picking cotton for very low pay until his fingers bleed. Still, he rejoices, "I was a man of the earth, precisely as I had dreamed I would be." In Jarvis' (1973–74, p. 193) view, Kerouac preferred a "romanticized America which, in the context of current events, makes him an arch conservative." "Few men," Jarvis (1973–74, p. 99) states, "loved America as Jack Kerouac did; and in this abiding love there was no room for criticism—especially of its political institutions." Tytell agrees, characterizing Kerouac's Romantic visions as nostalgia for the rural frontier, the rugged individualist, the outlaw (Tytell 1976, pp. 52, 63, 65, 140–42, 160–61). With its rolling landscapes and boozathons, *On the Road* is much more the romance of a trucker than an artist or intellectual, a good ol' boy on the run, a melancholy Rabelais on wheels.

When confronted by Cook in 1968, Kerouac insisted that his politics had not changed, explaining: "Everybody just assumed I thought the way *they* wanted me to think. What really bothered me a lot, though, was the way a certain cadre of leftists among the so-called beats took over my mantle and twisted my thoughts to suit their own purpose" (Cook 1971, p. 88).

The misrepresentation of Kerouac's private convictions in his public image wasn't due solely to the company he kept. In any literary movement there may emerge commentators who succeed in shaping its political meaning and, perhaps, its public effects. One common strategy to influence public perception of a movement is to attribute certain unspoken intentions to the author(s) of certain works or events. The role of hip commentator on the Beats was played by none other than Norman Mailer. In 1957 Mailer wrote an essay called "The White Negro," published in *Dissent*. The essay begins with references to the Holocaust, the bomb, and the "collective failure of nerve" that paralyzes American life. Mailer (1969, pp. 198–99) introduces his savior thus:

> ... the American existentialist—the hipster, the man who knows that if our collective condition is to live with instant death by atomic war ... or with a slow death by conformity with every creative and rebellious instinct stifled ... then the only life-giving answer is to accept the terms of death, to live with death as immediate danger, to divorce oneself from society, to exist without roots, to set out on that uncharted journey into the rebellious imperative of the self.

In America, Mailer wrote, "The source of Hip is the Negro, for he has been living on the margin between totalitarianism and democracy for two centuries." As such, in certain places, such as Greenwich Village, the black, the juvenile delinquent, and the bohemian have come together around marijuana, jazz, and the special argot of hip to form a common culture. Because there were whites who had come to embrace so much of black culture, they are best described as "white Negroes."

Mailer's essay created a stir and, when the Beats gained sudden popularity that year, he put himself forward as their public supporter. Mailer argued that the Beats, as well as all those who were alienated or angry, embodied an authentic critique of bourgeois society. In attempting to impose this interpretation on Kerouac, Mailer provided perhaps the most amusing example of such ideological reinterpretation:

> There is a sort of instinctive sense in them that they should stay away from politics—or make their remarks on politics surrealistic. For exam-

ple, when Kerouac says, "I like Eisenhower, I think he's a great man. I think he's our greatest president since Abraham Lincoln." Well, you know that's not a serious political remark at all. I don't think he even believed it, except, perhaps when he said it. It's a surrealistic remark. He's mixing two ideas that have absolutely no relation to each other—one of them is greatness and the other is Eisenhower. (Cook 1971, p. 96)

Of course, Kerouac had twisted his own thoughts to serve his purpose by redefining Beat from beat-up to beatific. But while the beatific was related to Kerouac's roots in Catholic mysticism, this didn't stop Ginsberg from appropriating the new term for the acid hippie movement of the late 1960s. In a 1969 interview with Cook he stated, "LSD equals the moon in terms of expansion of human possibilities. The moon thing is a technological manifestation of cosmic consciousness. . . . It was what we meant when we used to tell them that Beat was short for Beatific" (Cook 1971, p. 245). Moreover, despite Kerouac's obviously superficial understanding of blacks, Corso credited him with predicting the black revolution in his novel *The Subterraneans* (*Newsweek* 1963). Neither could Kerouac escape having his thoughts twisted to others' purpose long after he left the Beats—indeed, even after his death.

In 1968, after Kerouac had slipped deep into alcoholism, pledged himself to Jesus, returned to Lowell, married his high school sweetheart, become outspokenly archconservative, and refused to see his former Beat buddies, Ginsberg still commented, "It seemed that he was so horrified by the police state he saw taking shape around us that he decided to stay as far away from it as possible. He practically went underground! So in a way he took it more seriously than any of us" (Cook 1971, p. 85). Even in death, Kerouac's public image was fashioned to fit the new radicalism. In Corso's poetic eulogy he was joined finally with the hippies he held in such profound contempt:

> And you were flashed upon the old and darkling
> day a Beat Christ-Boy . . . bearing the gentle
> roundness of things
> Insisting the soul was round not square
> and soon . . . behind there came
> A–Following
> the children of flowers. (Corso 1970)

Romanticism does have a Janus face. Mussolini was able to harness the Futurists' muddled anarchism to his program of fascism (Wohl 1979; Shapiro 1976). Such co-optations are more common than what befell Kerouac. Perhaps turnabout is fair play.

In the final analysis, the movements of the 1960s embodied the principles of both of these men. Certainly, the Romanticism they shared was widely in evidence. Kerouac's themes of alienation and the search for identity, fraternity, travel, and adventure described the orientation of the youth generation. And, certainly, active sexuality, drugs, wanderlust, mysticism, openness, freedom, and spontaneity were countercultural values they both could claim (Spates 1971; Ebner 1972; Hodges 1974, p. 509).

THE RELATION BETWEEN CULTURAL AND POLITICAL RADICALISM

Like Kerouac and Ginsberg in earlier days, Beats in the 1950s rejected electoral politics. Lipton (1959, p. 306) noted, "All the vital decisions [the Beats] will tell you, are beyond the control of the electorate, so why go to the polls?" For most Beats the ballot was meaningless because it did not represent "such vital issues as war and peace to the voter." Other Beats insisted that all political parties used lies and manipulations: "Elections are rigged . . . the whole political game is a big shuck, the biggest shuck of all." Polsky said the Beats were not just apolitical but "anti-political," because they rejected not only the major political parties but the opposition movements as well. As Romantics, most Beats did not believe it possible for one person to represent another.

On the other hand, Goodman (1960, pp. 187–88) proposed that the very existence of the Beat community constituted an important political statement: *"People can go it on their own*, without resentment, hostility, delinquency, or stupidity better than when they move in the organized system and are subject to authority." Indeed, Willener (1970, p. 259) has distinguished "two senses" in which "the notion of politics may be understood: (a) institutional/organizational, or explicit; and (b) cultural, a latent force of conservation or transformation." Politics of the latter type would include creating a bohemian counter to bourgeois culture.

Berger has discriminated political from cultural radicalism according to the ends pursued—whether change is sought in the structure of political and/or economic institutions or in the practice of life-styles and the arts. Of course, this leaves open the possibility that political radicals may employ cultural innovation as one means to achieve their ends and that, conversely, cultural radicals may employ overtly political tactics in order to achieve their ends.

The latter is most likely to occur when the liberty to practice life-style and artistic innovation is denied by state intervention. Such intervention may take various forms, such as police raids on parties, drug busts, harassment of interracial couples and gays, or the shutting down of important community institutions (such as coffeehouses or communes) by agencies of the state (such as the fire department, the zoning commission, or the liquor control commission) (Hahn 1966, pp. 266–68; Smith and Luce 1976, p. 80; Rigney and Smith 1961, pp. 5–10).

In their ongoing "war" with bourgeois society, Beats frequently found their social life, art, and morals the target of state regulation and police violence. In the late 1950s and early 1960s, many Beats abandoned their disengagement to commit themselves to the struggle for cultural freedom. They responded with rallies, demonstrations, legal challenges, and other weapons of political protest (*San Francisco Chronicle* 1960a; Rigney and Smith 1961, p. 164).

Until the media "discovered" North Beach in 1957, the Beats there lived in virtual anonymity. Soon sensational stories of alleged Beat orgies, depravity, and violence brought seemingly endless invasions of tourists, youthful adventurers, and police. Especially damaging to the North Beach colony were three exposés in the Hearst-owned *San Francisco Examiner* in May 1958, which caused more police to be sent to the area. Called "distorted" and "sensational" by many, these articles were soon followed by the accidental death of a young man from Chicago who fell from the roof of a Beat bistro while drunk, and the murder of his girlfriend that same evening by an "alcoholic, drug addicted Negro seaman out near Golden Gate Park." Neither the murderer nor the victims were locals or even Beats, but the *Examiner* featured front-page coverage of the "beatnik deaths," and the "police crackdown" on what Police Captain Charles Borland had now decided was a "notorious problem section" (Rigney and Smith 1961, pp. 159–60; Hahn 1966, pp. 267–68).

Public outcry led to police raids on Beat hangouts. Many were arrested on charges of drunkenness and vagrancy. When some protested that they were being denied their constitutional rights, they were slapped with additional charges of "obscenity," "resisting arrest," or "interfering with justice." Several arrests were accompanied by name-calling, shoving, handcuffing, and brutality. A cop asked one club owner, "Why do you allow so many commies and jigs to patronize this place? After all, if you give 'em an inch, they'll take a mile." In another incident, a policeman called a white woman with a black man a "nigger-lover." She was threatened with a vagrancy arrest usually reserved for suspected prostitutes and warned: "Don't let us catch you around here again with a Negro . . . [or] we'll run you in" (Rigney and Smith 1961, pp. 161–64).

In February 1959 several Beats organized the North Beach Citizens' Committee with the charge to fight police harassment, explain their civil rights to members of the colony, and provide bail and instruction on how to behave when arrested. One member announced: "Our job will be to protect our group from the police" (Rigney and Smith 1961, pp. 165–66). Beats began watching the police, hanging around during interrogations, bearing witness to misconduct.

Relations between Beats and police worsened. In August 1959 black poet Bob Kaufman had to have his toenail removed after police stomped on it while arresting him. Kaufman's experience is described in his subsequent "Jail Poem" (Rigney and Smith 1961, pp. 164–65). In January 1960 there were several marijuana raids, including one in which police destroyed books on Communism and ripped paintings off the walls while arresting all of the occupants of a Beat "pad."

One week after the raid, the Beats held a rally in North Beach's Washington Square that drew 325 persons, including a reported 25 plainclothes cops. North Beach Beats accused police of violating their civil rights, blamed the area's newspapers for increasing tensions, and criticized members of their own group for failing to defend themselves against these assaults. Chester Anderson, editor of *Beatitude* and *Underhound* (*sic*), exhorted the audience to use every legal means available to protect themselves. "If you are falsely arrested," he shouted, "say so and sue. If you are roughed up by the police, say so and sue. Don't cover up. Fight back in every legal way" (*San Francisco Chronicle* 1960a).

Jerry Kamstra, bearded owner of a book and art shop in North Beach, shouted that he was "'tired of being persecuted for not supporting any razor company . . . tired of being persecuted for not sharing the same social point of view as [the police].'" Kamstra equated police "repression" in North Beach with Nazi Germany.

Kaufman complained that he had "'spent World War II fighting for democracy'" and now received only "'2% of it [in North Beach].'" One unidentified speaker declared that the rally was the beginning "'of a great American general strike.'" She called for an alliance of artists and writers with the "'workingmen who have no democracy'" (*San Francisco Chronicle* 1960a).

By the fall of 1959, many Beats had left embattled North Beach for Greenwich Village. After publication of Lawrence Lipton's study of Venice West, another 500 to 1,000 Beats moved there. The sudden immigration divided the Venice West community. Many protested. One irate resident complained: "They're a dirty bunch of people. They drink and are every night in debauchery. They make free love practically in the streets, play bongo drums, and none of us can get any sleep after 2 AM." In contrast, sympathetic residents organized the Venice Citizens and Property Owners Committee for Cultural Advancement to support the Beats, stressing their potential cultural and commercial contributions to the community (*Newsweek* 1959).

The North Beach pattern was repeated in Venice West and Greenwich Village. As each community grew, media coverage became more sensational, bringing citizen pressure upon city officials to constrain Beat activities. After Venice officials closed the Gas House, a popular coffeehouse, the community's bohemians contacted the local chapter of the American Civil Liberties Union for assistance (*Newsweek* 1959; *Time* 1959b).

In 1960 Village Beats marched in demonstration after the fire department closed two prominent coffeehouses for purported violation of department regulations. One was allowed to reopen at half of its former capacity. A committee of several coffeehouse owners was organized to conduct a legal defense against the closing and to rally community support for their businesses (*New York Times* 1960a; 1960b). The manager of the Figaro coffeehouse proclaimed with proud defiance: "We don't permit the weekend tourist beatnik in here. Our beatniks are the real, true, old-fashioned wonderful bohemians" (*New Yorker* 1960b).

In Fort Worth, Texas, concern with community protection and improvement led Beats to try electoral politics. Two bearded coffeehouse poets and helpers ran for two Democratic Party precinct chairmanships under the slogan "Kick the Cows out of Cowtown and Let the Cats in to Swing." Their program called for cleaning up government, slum clearance, and better flophouses for winos (*Life* 1960).

Beat involvement in community politics finally led to collaboration with political radicals. A few months after the Beat rally in Washington Square, hundreds of students and Beats protested outside San Francisco's city hall against the House Committee on Un-American Activities (HUAC) hearings on subversives in the Bay area. Jerry Kamstra was arrested and dragged away from the building after attempting to gain entry to the hearing (*San Francisco Chronicle* 1960b). Police turned fire hoses on seated demonstrators, dragged many all the way down the steep concrete steps, and arrested 68. In response, some 5,000 showed up to picket city hall the next day.

This event received tremendous publicity over the next year and has often been cited as a milestone in the founding of the New Left. In its zeal HUAC impounded enough television news film to produce a highly biased and inflammatory film, entitled *Operation Abolition*, which claimed that the students had provoked the violence and were Communist dupes in a plot to discredit HUAC. For the next year and a half, the film "was a staple item on the rightwing banquet and camp meeting circuit." The Bay Area Student Committee for the Abolition of HUAC was formed in response and

> ... sent speakers and literature around the country pointing out the distortions and inaccuracies in the film. The American Civil Liberties Union made a film of its own, supporting the student version and calling for the Committee's abolition. On campuses where both sides of the story were heard, the Berkeley students emerged a clear winner. (O'Brien 1968, pp. 3-4)

"Local Committees to Abolish HUAC were organized in many areas," and a "federation of local civil liberties and anti-HUAC student groups was organized which provided speakers and literature to local groups, and coordinated the showing of films on campuses throughout the country." These civil liberties campaigns "laid the groundwork for more widespread and politically focused activities" (Altbach 1974, pp. 181–82).

Beat political activism in the early 1960s was almost always anarchist in orientation. Except for a brief flirtation with the Fair Play for Cuba Committee following Castro's successful revolution, we have not been able to find any instances of Beats supporting socialist causes. Even in this case, it is worth noting that Ginsberg was expelled from Cuba for protesting Castro's discrimination against homosexuals. This same issue provoked his expulsion from Czecho-slovakia in 1965, reinforcing his conviction, expressed in his 1960 poem "Death to Van Gogh's Ear," that there is "no human answer" in "dogmatic Leninism-Marxism."

As cultural radicals, Beats condemned power as inherently cor-rupting of the individual spirit. They were not interested in seizing the state to promote equality, especially if such a program required the bureaucratic regulation of social life. On the contrary, they were concerned with opposing the state in order to maximize individual liberty. Their anarchist ideology was consistent with causes like draft resistance, repeal of drug restrictions, and freedom of speech and the press. Robert McGrath, a Beat artist and one of the few who ignored his draft summons in 1960s, charged that military service was de-grading to the human personality and the state had no moral authority to induct him against his will. He was given a one-year jail sentence (Adams 1980; Ross 1961).

Whatever their intention, the Beats had a powerful impact on the politics of the 1960s. Michael Harrington (1972–1973, p. 137) re-flects, "It seemed obvious enough that the cultural rebellion in North Beach and the political beginnings at Berkeley [late 1950s] were of a piece." In Jessica Mitford Treuhaft's (1961) view, "The beats may have helped crystallize for students a concept of what they are against." Altbach (1974, pp. 216, 219) proposes that the Beats and their hippie followers "helped to infuse the student community with a certain style of activism through their attacks against the achieve-ment orientation of the broader society and a concomitant emphasis on noncompetitive values and experiments with new life styles." Jacobs and Landau (1966, p. 13) describe some of the flavor of that new style:

> As the apolitical "beats"—almost alone as symbols of protest in the 1950s—turned their concern to concrete issues of racial equality and peace, their style, dress and decor affected the activists. Arguments about politics began to include discussions of sexual freedom and marijuana. The language of the Negro poet-hipster premeated analyses of the Cuban Revolution. Protests over the execution of Caryl Chessman ultimately brought together students and some bohemians—the loose and overlapping segments of what was to become known as The Move-ment.

Beat enclaves, typically located near urban college campuses, provided many recruits for protest causes in the early days of the New Left Movement (Jacobs and Landau 1966, p. 13; O'Neil 1959; Altbach 1974, pp. 112, 115, 210). Yippie leader and Chicago 8 defendant Abbie Hoffman was one of those clubbed by police in the anti-HUAC protest in San Francisco. He promptly joined the ACLU tour of college campuses calling for the abolition of HUAC. Also, in 1960 Robert Allen Haber (1966, p. 49), cofounder of the Students for a Democratic Society, acknowledged that "the Movement has drawn heavily, if not always reliably," on the Beat group. Haber's SDS cofounder, Tom Hayden, revealed in his 1972 *Rolling Stone* interviews that his political education started only in 1960, at which time he "was an editor, very influenced by the Beat Generation. My thing was to hitchhike all over the country in different directions—the Latin Quarter of New Orleans and Miami and New York, Greenwich Village . . ." (Findley 1972, p. 38). Bob Dylan, a balladeer of the protest movement in the early 1960s, recalls that after reading the Beats, he realized "there were other people out there like me" (McNally 1979, p. 307). In fact, the style of Dylan's early protest songs clearly reflects the influence of his friend Allen Ginsberg.

By the late 1960s, there were millions of youth "out there" like Dylan, practicing life-styles and supporting causes introduced by the small circle of New York and San Francisco bohemian artists whose own youth was long past. Ironically, the retreatist, apolitical Beats played a critical role in the rise of both the hippies and the New Left, movements that together significantly altered a society most Beats believed was beyond redemption.

REFERENCES

Adams, William R. 1980. Interview with Paul S. George. St. Augustine, Fla., Sept. 7.

Altbach, Philip. 1974. *Student Politics in America: A Historical Analysis.* New York: McGraw-Hill.

Ball, Gordon, ed. 1977. *Allen Ginsberg, Journals: Early Fifties, Early Sixties.* New York: Grove Press.

Berger, Bennett. 1971. *Looking for America: Essays on Youth, Suburbia and Other American Obsessions.* Englewood Cliffs, New Jersey: Prentice-Hall.

Berriault, Gina. 1972. "Neal's Ashes." *Rolling Stone*, Oct. 19, pp. 32, 34, 36.

Bjorn, Lars. 1980. "The Evolution of Jazz—The Artist's Effects." Paper Presented at American Sociological Association Meeting, New York.

Brown, Bernard O. 1968. "An Empirical Study of Ideology in Formation." *Review of Religious Research* 9: 79-87.

Burroughs, William S. 1979. *Junky.* New York: Penguin Books.

Bush, Douglas. 1978. "Literature, the Academy, and the Public." *Daedalus* 107, no. 4 (Fall): 165-74.

Cassady, Carolyn. 1976. *Heartbeat: My Life with Jack and Neal.* New York: Pocket Books.

Cassady, Neal. 1971. *The First Third and Other Writings.* San Francisco: City Lights Books.

Charters, Ann. 1973. *Kerouac.* New York: Warner Paperback Library.

Cherkovski, Neeli. 1979. *Ferlinghetti: A Biography.* New York: Doubleday.

Clark, Thomas. 1970. "Interview with Allen Ginsberg: 'The Art of Poetry.'" In *The Radical Vision: Essays for the Seventies*, edited by Leo Hamalian and Frederick R. Karl, pp. 129-65. New York: Thomas Y. Crowell.

Cook, Bruce. 1971. *The Beat Generation.* New York: Charles Scribner's Sons.

Corso, Gregory. 1970. "Elegiac Feelings American (for the dear memory of John Kerouac)." In *Elegiac Feelings American*, edited by Gregory Corso. New York: New Directions: 3-12.

Cowley, Malcolm. 1951. *Exile's Return.* New York: Viking Press. Reprinted in *Writers at Work: The Paris Review Interview*, edited by Malcolm Cowley, pp. 279-320. New York: Viking Press, 1967.

Dickstein, Morris. 1977. *Gates of Eden: American Culture in the Sixties.* New York: Basic Books.

Ebner, David Y. 1972. "Beats and Hippies: A Comparative Analysis." In *Society's Shadow: Studies in the Sociology of Countercultures*, edited by Kenneth Westhues. Toronto: McGraw-Hill.

Erikson, Erik H. 1959. *Young Man Luther.* New York: W. W. Norton.

——. 1953. *Childhood and Society.* New York: W. W. Norton.

Findley, Tom. 1972. "Tom Hayden: Rolling Stone Interview, Part I." *Rolling Stone*, Oct. 26, pp. 38-39.

Fromm, Erich. 1941. *Escape from Freedom.* New York: Avon Books.

Gifford, Barry, ed. 1977. *As Ever, The Collected Correspondence of Allen Ginsberg and Neal Cassady.* Berkeley: Creative Arts Book Co.

Gifford, Barry, and Lawrence Lee. 1979. *Jack's Book: An Oral Biography of Jack Kerouac.* New York: Penguin Books.

Ginsberg, Allen. 1956. *Howl and Other Poems.* San Francisco: City Lights Press.

Goodman, Paul. 1960. *Growing up Absurd: Problems of Youth in the Organized Society.* New York: Vintage Books.

Gouldner, Alvin. 1973. "Romanticism and Classicism: Deep Structures in Social Science." In *For Sociology: Renewal and Critique in Sociology Today*, edited by Alvin Gouldner, pp. 324-53. New York: Basic Books.

Graber, David. 1978. "Bohemia in Revolt." *Human Behavior*, June, p. 8.

Gruen, John. 1966. *The New Bohemia: The Combine Generation.* New York: Grosset and Dunlap.

Haber, Robert. 1966. "From Protest to Radicalism: An Appraisal of the Student Movement." In *The New Student Left: An Anthology*, edited by Mitchell Cohen and Dennis Hale, pp. 41-49. Boston: Beacon.

Hahn, Emily. 1966. *Romantic Rebels: An Informal History of Bohemianism in America.* Cambridge, Mass.: Riverside Press.

Harrington, Michael. 1972-73. *Fragments of the Century.* New York: Simon and Schuster.

——. 1972. "We Few, We Happy Few, We Bohemians." *Esquire*, Aug., pp. 99-103, 162-64.

——. 1962. "The American Campus: 1962." *Dissent*, Spring: 164-68.

Hills, Ruts. 1979. "Introduction." In Ken Kesey, "The Day After Superman Died." *Esquire*, Oct., pp. 42–44.

Hodeir, André. 1956. *Jazz: Its Evolution and Essence.* New York: Grove Press.

Hodges, Harold, Jr. 1974. *Conflict and Consensus: An Introduction to Sociology*, 2nd ed. New York: Harper & Row.

Holmes, John C. 1967. *Nothing More to Declare.* New York: Dutton.

——. 1958. "The Philosophy of the Beat Generation." *Esquire*, Feb., pp. 35–38.

——. 1952a. *GO.* New York: Charles Scribner's Sons.

——. 1952b. "This Is the Beat Generation." *New York Times Magazine*, Nov. 16, pp. 10, 19, 20, 22.

Howard, John. 1974. *The Cutting Edge: Social Movement and Social Change in America.* New York: Lippincott.

Jacobs, Paul, and Saul Landau. 1966. *The New Radicals: A Report with Documents.* New York: Vintage Books.

Jarvis, Charles. 1973–74. *Vision of Kerouac.* Lowell, Mass.: Ithaca Press.

Kerouac, Jack. 1972. *Visions of Cody.* New York: McGraw-Hill.

——. 1959. "The Origins of the Beat Generation." *Playboy*, June, pp. 31–32, 42, 79.

——. 1957. *On the Road.* New York: Signet.

Kostelanetz, Richard. 1970. "Allen Ginsberg: Artist as Apostle, Poet as Preacher." In *Representative Man: Cult Heroes of Our Time*, edited by Theodore L. Gross, pp. 257–75. New York: The Free Press.

Kramer, Jane. 1969. *Allen Ginsberg in America.* New York: Random House.

——. 1968. "Profiles: Allen Ginsberg." *New Yorker* 44 (Aug. 24): 77–79.

Life. 1960. "Politics: Beat in the Hip of Texas." Mar. 7, pp. 48–51.

Lipton, Lawrence. 1959. *The Holy Barbarians.* New York: Julian Messner.

Mailer, Norman. 1969. "The White Negro: Superficial Reflections on the Hipster." In *Voices of Dissent*, pp. 197-214. Freeport, N.Y.: Books for Libraries Press. Originally published in *Dissent* 4 (1957): 276-93.

McNally, Dennis. 1979. *Desolate Angel: Jack Kerouac, the Beat Generation and America.* New York: Random House.

Mannheim, Karl. 1971. "Conservative Thought." In *From Karl Mannheim*, edited by Kurt Wolff, pp. 132-222. New York: Oxford University Press.

Miller, Richard. 1977. *Bohemia: The Protoculture Then and Now.* Chicago: Nelson-Hall.

Millstein, Gilbert. 1960. "Rent a Beatnik and Swing." *New York Times Magazine*, Apr. 17, pp. 26, 28, 30.

——. 1957. "Books of the Times." *New York Times*, Sept. 5, p. 27.

Myerhoff, Barbara. 1972. "The Revolution as a Trip: Symbol and Paradox." In *The New Pilgrims: Youth Protest in Transition*, edited by Philip Altbach and Robert Laufer, pp. 251-66. New York: David McKay.

Newsweek. 1963. "Bye Bye Beatnik." July 1, p. 65.

——. 1959. "Heat on the Beatniks." Aug. 17, p. 36.

New Yorker. 1960a. "The Talk of the Town: Movement Party to Celebrate Publication of *The Beats*." Apr. 16, pp. 36-37.

——. 1960b. "Life Line: The Figaro in Greenwich Village." Aug. 6, pp. 21-23.

New York Times. 1960a. June 11, p. 23.

——. 1960b. June 13, p. 32.

Nuttall, Jeff. 1968. *Bomb Culture.* New York: Delacorte Press.

O'Brien, James. 1968. *A History of the New Left, 1960-1968.* Boston: New England Free Press.

O'Neil, Paul. 1959. "Only Rebellion Around." *Life*, Nov. 30, pp. 114-16, 119-20, 123-24, 126, 129-30.

Plummer, William. 1981. *The Holy Goof: A Biography of Neal Cassady.* Englewood Cliffs, N.J.: Prentice-Hall.

——. 1979. "The Beat Goes on." *New York Times Magazine*, Dec. 30, p. 41.

Podhoretz, Norman. 1960. "The Know Nothing Bohemians." In *The Beats*, edited by Seymour Krim. Greenwich, Conn.: Fawcett. The essay originally appeared in *Partisan Review* 25 (Spring 1958): 111-24.

Polsky, Ned. 1969. *Hustlers, Beats, and Others.* Garden City, N.Y.: Anchor Books.

Richardson, Derek. 1979. Review of *Desolate Angel. In These Times*, Dec. 5-11, p. 12.

Rigney, Francis, and Douglas Smith. 1961. *The Real Bohemia.* New York: Basic Books.

Ross, Tim. "Rise and Fall of the Beats." *The Nation*, May 27, pp. 456-58.

Roszak, Theodore. 1969. *The Making of a Counterculture: Reflections on the Technocratic Society and Its Youthful Opposition.* Garden City, N.Y.: Doubleday/Anchor.

San Francisco Chronicle. 1960a. Jan. 31, p. 1.

——. 1960b. May 15, pp. 1, 4.

Schjeldahl, Peter. 1976. Review of John Tytell's *Naked Angels: The Lives and Literature of the Beat Generation. New York Times Book Review*, May 9, p. 4.

Seelye, John. 1974. "The Sum of '48." *The New Republic* 171 (Oct. 12): 23-24.

Shapiro, Theda. 1976. *Painters and Politics: The European Avant-Garde and Society.* New York: Elsevier.

Siske, John P. 1959. "Beatniks and Tradition." *Commonweal*, Apr. 17, pp. 75-78.

Smith, David E., and John Luce. 1976. *Love Needs Care: A History of San Francisco's Haight-Ashbury Free Medical Clinic and Its Pioneer Role in Treating Drug Abuse Problems.* Boston: Little, Brown.

Snyder, Gary. 1969. *Earth House Hold.* New York: New Directions.

Spates, James. 1971. "Structure and Trends in Value Systems in the 'Hip' Underground Counterculture and the American Middle Class, 1951–1957, 1967–1969." Ph.D. dissertation, Boston University.

Starr, Jerold. 1981. "Adolescents and Resistance to Schooling: A Dialectic." *Youth and Society*, Dec., pp. 189–228.

——. 1980. "New Directions in the Study of Youth and Society." *Current Sociology*, Winter, pp. 341–72.

Time. 1959a. "Manners and Morals, Fried Shoes." Feb. 9, p. 16.

——. 1959b. "Bang, Bong, Bing." Sept. 7, p. 80.

Treuhaft, Jessica Mitford. 1961. "The Indignant Generation." *The Nation*, May 27, pp. 451–56.

Tytell, John. 1976. *Naked Angels: The Lives and Loves of the Beat Generation.* New York: McGraw-Hill.

Willener, Alfred. 1970. *The Action-Image of Society: On Cultural Politicization.* New York: Pantheon Books.

Wohl, Robert. 1979. *The Generation of 1914.* Cambridge, Mass.: Harvard University Press.

Wolfe, Tom. 1968. *The Electric Kool-Aid Acid Test.* New York: Farrar, Straus and Giroux.

8 Cultural Politics in the 1960s

Jerold M. Starr

The 1960s embodied the most recent wave of Romantic resistance to Rationalism in the dialectic of Western history (see Chapter 9). It was a period in which many of the themes and practices of earlier Romantic movements were self-consciously recalled and many new ones introduced. Especially manifest over the years 1957–73, the movement of the 1960s further elaborated the tactics of radical cultural resistance, explored their possibilities, and exposed their limitations. It left in its wake several important lessons for later generations of American activists.

THE LEGACY OF THE "OLD LEFT"

In order to understand the New Left of the 1960s, it is first necessary to review the legacy of the Old Left of the 1930s. The Old Left gained a following with the Great Depression and Roosevelt's election in 1932, and persisted as a force in American politics until the post-World War II prosperity and the defeat of Progressive Party presidential candidate Henry Wallace in 1948.

The Old Left had a large immigrant component and embraced a range of labor advocacy groups including the trade unions, the Communist Party U.S.A. (CPUSA), and a diversity of socialist parties.

They all shared the general goal of ending the exploitation of labor and inequalities of class. The Marxist-Leninist groups were headed by party ideologists who enforced rank-and-file discipline in organizing industrial workers into militant labor unions.

The enemies of the Old Left were the owners and bosses of industry and the politicians who represented their interests. The major battlegrounds were the industrial work places: the mines, docks, and factories. The dominant strategy was nonviolent direct action, including such tactics as strikes, boycotts, and picketing, with occasional sabotage and disruption (Mauss 1971).

By the mid-1930s the CPUSA had reacted to the threat of fascism and the increasing popularity of the New Deal by abandoning its prohibition on "class collaboration" and adopting a reformist position (see Chapter 5). This Popular Front strategy was used to promote such New Deal programs as full employment, tax reform, and welfare relief for the poor.

Following the Leninist line, the Old Left was culturally conservative. It aimed at institutional change and did not concern itself with changes in life-styles or personal relationships. The Popular Front strategy was accompanied by an attempt to "Americanize" Communism. This typically meant staging patriotic celebrations, beauty pageants, and other conventional rituals to counter accusations of Soviet control.

Through the years of the Great Depression and World War II, the Roosevelt administration pursued a social control strategy of co-opting Old Left programs into the New Deal while using repressive legislation, such as the Smith Act, to harass left leaders and strain organizational resources. Despite this opposition, the Old Left achieved many reforms. It made an enormous contribution to establishing the trade union movement. It also provided leadership and ideals to a growing Democratic Party that, in turn, significantly expanded the welfare functions of the state.

In the final analysis, however, important criticisms of the Old Left remain. The CPUSA and other democratic centralist organizations used their "moral authority" to impose "authoritarianism" and "secrecy," to the detriment of the "independence of mind and spirit of the individual" (Gornick 1983, p. 18). This vanguard elitism with its ideological dogmatism exacerbated sectarian hostilities and undermined coalition building on the left. It also isolated many party workers from the local cultures of their potential constituencies and impeded effective communication and organizing. Finally, even when adopted, Old Left-inspired reforms had the effect of expanding the managerial authority of the capitalist state, rather than advancing the principles of workers' socialism.

THE DEMISE OF LEFT POLITICS IN THE 1950s

In 1948 Congress overrode a presidential veto to pass the Taft-Hartley Act. This act placed serious restrictions on the rights of unions to require membership as a condition for employment, to strike, and to elect Communists to union office. The Truman administration co-opted the unions by bringing them into the corporate-liberal Cold War program of larger budgets for national defense and social welfare. Socialist goals, such as worker ownership and/or participation in management, were abandoned to collective bargaining and increments of fringe benefits. Within a decade most workers had given up the dream of a labor party despite reservations about the influence of corporate industrial interests in the Democratic Party (Peck 1963). They had grown cynical about the intentions of even their own leadership and had withdrawn into consumer escapism and fantasies about life after the factory (Hodges 1962).

Throughout these years the state and certain private corporations waged a massive campaign of political repression and economic discrimination against private citizens from all walks of life. This period has come to be known by the name of its most zealous proponent of "anti-Communist" persecution, Senator Joseph McCarthy. Antagonized by their earlier factional struggles within the Popular Front and responsive to the xenophobia in high places, social democratic groups, such as the League for Industrial Democracy, became anti-Communist apologists for American imperialism around the world. The left was dealt another blow when the Soviet invasion of Hungary in 1956 incited a massive exodus of younger members from the Communist Party.

By the mid-1950s radical politics was "nearly dead" in the United States. The "trade unions were no longer crusading, many once radical anti-communists had become supporters of the Establishment, and the Socialists were barely distinguishable from liberal democrats" (Jacobs and Landau 1966, p. 8). Moreover, not even those few young dissidents who carried on the struggle by seeking a more democratic and American form of Communism displayed any interest in "the questions of cultural and sexual politics that would soon be raised by the New Left" (Isserman 1980, p. 5).

Taking the cue from their elders, college students in the 1950s came to be labeled the "Silent Generation." Students were afraid to sign petitions or join political organizations (Lee 1970). Only about a dozen colleges or universities had radical student groups with anywhere near 50 members (Altbach 1974). Even by the beginning of the 1960s there were no more than 50 campuses in the country where civil rights or peace-oriented activism was common. The biggest political rallies and demonstrations drew no more than 500 or 600 people (O'Brien 1972).

THE RISE OF CULTURAL RESISTANCE

This retreat from oppositional politics was reflected in the social science of the period. Concern with changing society gave way to criticism of the lack of "quality" in middle-class life. Social commentators lamented the loss of ethnic folk culture through rapid assimilation, the surrender of rugged individualism to anxious conformity, the striving for status, the consumerism, and the general "massification" of American society (Riesman 1953; Whyte 1956; Wheelis 1958).

Given the historical situation, it was to be expected that any opposition to the status quo would appear first in the realm of culture, not politics. By 1957 the most visible challenge to the conventional orthodoxy was spearheaded by the bohemians in Greenwich Village, North Beach, and Venice West who called themselves "Beats." The Beats challenged "the conservative and suburban values" of the American consumer paradise and were soon "widely publicized as rebels against the system" (Cook 1971, p. 10). In their art and in their personal lives the Beats mounted a "great refusal" against the establishment that justified the repression of dissent in the name of freedom from Communist repression of dissent. They ranted against militarism, racism, materialism, and conformity in American society, and raved about free love, mind-expanding drugs, and creative expression. They shunned "square" society and adamantly demanded the right to be different.

The national publicity given to the Beats in the late 1950s and early 1960s attracted many settlers and stimulated the commercial development of the primary Beat colonies. Over the period 1963–67 these colonies underwent a transformation in composition that culminated in the emergence of the hippie counterculture.

Beginning in 1963, "rising rents, police harassment, and the throngs of tourists, thrill-seekers, and hoodlums on Grant Avenue" pushed many young Beats out of North Beach and into the Haight-Ashbury section of San Francisco, about two miles away. Instead of "living as couples in pads," many "rented larger flats and entire houses that they turned into urban communes." Sensing an opportunity to cash in, landlords raised their rents to provoke the flight of retired people and poor black families. For this reason "a small subculture took root in the Flatlands and spread slowly up the slope of Mt. Sutro. By 1963 the Haight-Ashbury was the center of a small and unpublicized bohemian colony" (Smith and Luce 1971, p. 76). There beatnik artists and intellectuals in their thirties mingled with younger West Coast bohemians.

The city's plan to build a freeway that would cut the neighborhood off from nearby Golden Gate Park catalyzed the founding of the Haight-Ashbury Neighborhood Council. The long fight to keep the freeway out lasted until 1966. By that time, not only had the community become solidified, but it had changed in the process. Much younger newcomers then outnumbered the old-timers. They "were colorfully and outlandishly dressed in hand-me-downs" and "lounged around in bunches." In an article published on September 5, 1965, *San Francisco Examiner* writer Michael Fallon revived the term "hippies." For the next couple of years this term was used interchangeably with "beatnik," until it replaced the older term completely (Cook 1971, p. 199).

In most respects the hippie counterculture was continuous with that of the Beats. In San Francisco the Beats settled the community that spawned the hippies, and in Greenwich Village, Polsky (1961, p. 341) observed, "The attitudes of beats in their thirties have spread rapidly downward all the way to the very young teenagers (13–15). . . ." Appropriately, Beat celebrities promoted those very events that heralded the coming out of the new hippie counterculture. Allen Ginsberg, Gary Snyder, Timothy Leary, Richard Alpert, and other old heads were behind the Tripps Festival of January 1966, the Love Festival of October 1966, and the "be-in" at Golden Gate Park in January 1967. Also in attendance were such Beat stalwarts as Hugh Romney (a.k.a. Wavy Gravy when he traveled with Ken Kesey's

Merry Pranksters), Eric "Big Daddy" Nord, Tom "Big Daddy" Dona-
hue, and Francis Rigney.

The basic orientation of both Beats and hippies was to reject
"instrumental" in favor of "expressive" values (Spates 1971). Both
movements urged people to drop out of a society hung up on materialism and militarism (Howard 1969). Both rejected unhappy pasts
and goal-directed futures, and used drugs or alcohol to immerse themselves in "a quasi-mystical present" (Ebner 1972). Hodges (1974, p.
509) characterizes both movements as "existential, romantic and
anarchistic. More fundamentally still, both were dialectical reactions
against middle-class values, goals, and styles of life."

Despite such common roots and themes, however, there were several features of the hippie counterculture that differed visibly from
that of the beats. The original post-World War II Beat scene was
New York City at night, Harlem and the Village, cellar jazz clubs,
coffeehouse poetry readings, cool blacks, and white Negroes. As this
scene spread to the West Coast, it changed its coloration. Anarchist
poet Gary Snyder and others made two significant contributions to
the philosophy of Beat in the mid-1950s. The first was the introduction of Zen Buddhism and other Far Eastern religious concepts,
which "gave a sense of intellectual, even religious justification to the
Beats' deep natural impulse to freedom" (Cook 1971, p. 29) and
added a "quietly contemplative" dimension to the Beat spirit (Tytell
1976, p. 25). This change was reflected in the new construction of
Beat to mean "beatific" rather than "beat-up."

The second contribution was to take the movement to the great
outdoors. While the Beats had frequently hit the road, they were city
boys who knew little of America's mountains, fields, and streams.
The effect of this change of scene was to teach an appreciation of
nature that was to emerge as a major value of the counterculture of
the late 1960s. As part of this development, the American Indian
replaced the black as the "holy primitive" who exemplified the spirit
of the romantic counterculture. (Smith and Luce 1971, p. 95; see
also Wolfe 1968).

Probably the most significant difference between the Beats and
hippies was in their attitude toward the movement. Emerging in reaction to a period of political repression and social conformity in
American life, the Beats were pessimistic about the future. Frequently

threatened by "squares" and authorities, they were naturally suspicious of strangers. Oriented toward artistic creativity, they only wished to be left alone.

The hippies, on the other hand, were active during a period of exploding college enrollments and rising opposition to the war in Vietnam. They were optimistic about the future of their movement, and used drugs and music to proselytize potential recruits. In some communities they practiced a kind of Utopian communism in which lodging, food, and clothes were provided free to those in need.

The counterculture took concrete form in the many writings and social experiments of the 1960s. The counterculture rejected a political system organized around mass bureaucracies and proposed either no government or a government based on the direct participation of equals. It refused militarism as a method of resolving disputes, and called for universal peace and love. The counterculture turned away from an economy organized around the mastery of nature and the mass production of commodities for sale and profit. Instead, it called for a respect for nature, the ideal of individual craftsmanship, and production for human needs.

The counterculture declined interpersonal relations based on competition, deceit, calculation, and conformity. Instead, it embraced those based on cooperation, openness, spontaneity, and self-expression. The aesthetic of the counterculture rejected the artificial and the mechanical in favor of the authentic and the natural. The epistemology of the counterculture denied science, objectivity, analysis, and Western logic, and accepted mysticism, subjectivity, synthesis, and paradox. And the morality of the counterculture dissented from work, materialism, striving for the future, Oedipal love, and violence, electing instead pleasure, spiritualism, living for the moment, communal love, drug-induced states of ecstasy, and active sexuality (Starr 1974).

This personal vision synthesized the best of the preindustrial community with the best of industrial society. It combined the respect for nature, personal craftsmanship, and cooperative and sharing relationships of the former with the greater personal autonomy and self-expression of the latter. The alternative society sought by the hippies was a cosmopolitan community of equals living in solidarity but with a respect for individual differences; a tribe of peoples, each doing their own thing; a jazz band of soloists in perfect harmony.

COUNTERCULTURE ON THE CAMPUS

Throughout the decade the larger universities provided a setting especially hospitable to a radical bohemian opposition. Between 1960 and 1966 the number of students enrolled in college more than doubled, topping 7.3 million. This extension of schooling for almost half of those 18–21 years of age meant a further delay of marriage and entry into the wage-labor market. Keniston (1970) labeled this new postadolescent, preadult stage of life "youth."

Although their situation is temporary, college youth, like bohemians, live unmarried and in voluntary poverty. These conditions underlie a process Lofland (1972) calls the "niggarization" of youth. The trend toward large educational institutions has created "cities of youth," many ranging beyond 40,000 in number. Such youths must live crowded together in high-density ghettos. Faced with uncertain employment and a transient status, they rent rather than buy. They have low incomes and lack the resources necessary to repair and improve their places of habitation. They also fail to develop a significant identification with the institutions of the larger community, preferring to "stay with their own kind."

The low information flow between the ghetto and surrounding territories contributes to mutual "suspicion, fear, and distrust," and permits the development of a "discrediting or defaming" imputed personality that is believed to be characteristic of ghetto dwellers—in brief, a youth, particularly student, stereotype. This stereotype resembles the "classic portrait of failings attributed to ghetto dwellers," including the "elements of laziness, irresponsibility, hedonism, lack of pride in property or personal appearance, promiscuousness, deviousness, and family and employment instability." Under these circumstances, many such youth come to feel like objects of discrimination, marginal to middle-class society (Lofland 1972, pp. 243–47).

As higher education was expanded to include youth from diverse class and ethnic backgrounds, the traditional "collegiate" subculture came under criticism. Originated at the turn of the century, when college life was restricted to a small elite, customs like freshman hazing and beanies, social clubs, and big-time intercollegiate sports now seemed frivolous at best, undemocratic at worst. Social fraternities were pressured to cease racial and religious discrimination (Lee 1970).

It wasn't just vocationalism. Many students had learned from their parents' generation that money didn't guarantee happiness. Besides, the economy was booming and there was a general optimism about opportunities. In this context the Beat challenge had a powerful appeal to youth. Many resonated with the Beats' existential quest for an authentic identity. Voluntary poverty means improvising on the margins while you search for a place worthy of commitment, a place where you can be your "true self." Many became anxious, even indignant, that there might not be any such places for them. In the view of Aronowitz (1973, p. 331), "The perception of the banality of existence became the core of the youth revolt of the 1960s."

By the late 1960s, inspired by the Romantic revolution in culture and aroused by historical crises such as the black movement, the "discovery" of poverty, and the war in Vietnam, the intellectually oriented academics and expressively rebellious hippies came to have a significant impact on student culture, especially on the more elite campuses where the luxury of choice often presented the dilemma of commitment.

The diffusion of the counterculture was accelerated greatly over the period 1965–68 by the development of FM radio stations for youth and the proliferation of alternative newspapers. Ray Mungo (1970), cofounder of the Liberation News Service, estimates the number of such papers in the United States soared from 50 to 300 in 1967 alone. Circulation ranged between 10,000 and 160,000 readers each. Estimates of overall readership ranged between 2 million and 30 million (Lewis 1972).

The radical cultural opposition to the industrial welfare state was so pervasive among youth in the 1960s that it gave the impression of more consensus on political issues than actually existed. In fact, the complex nature of Romanticism allowed it to be assimilated to a diversity of political orientations.

While it can not be proved, as the Scranton Commission (Scranton 1971, p. 61) claims, that a "change in the culture of students" was the basic "cause" of student protest, it certainly was an integral part of much of it. The most distinctive characteristics of the New Left were its rejection of ideology and its open organizational style. It rejected the ideology of the Old Left and embraced an orientation best characterized as "the morality of openness, of antidoctrine, of a 'way of life' and a crusading style" (Horowitz and Friedland 1970, p. 107). In the view of Roszak (1969), this "extraordinary personalism" of the New Left constituted a "sensibility" that made them allies with the hippies. Altbach (1974, p. 216) states that it was precisely "this mixture of culture and politics" that "was a key element in the popularity and strength of the New Left."

On the other hand, it is critical to acknowledge that cultural radicalism in the 1960s took politically reactionary and quietistic forms as well. This was a source of much confusion both inside and outside the movement.

ROMANTIC CONSERVATISM: THE POLITICS OF POT AND ROCK

Even many conservative students were infused with a spirit of Romantic individualism. Young Americans for Freedom (YAF), the largest of such groups, claimed 20,000 members on about 200 campuses. Founded by William F. Buckley, Jr., in 1960, the YAF campaigned for Barry Goldwater in 1964 and, later, for a military victory in Vietnam. Conservative in its support for capitalism, nationalism, and militarism, the YAF nonetheless shared with the radical Students for a Democratic Society (SDS) a concern for the "essential worth" and "dignity" of the individual struggling for freedom against an institutional world that "denies freedom and self-realization." YAF's passionate advocacy of rugged individualism through unrestrained capitalism clearly marked it as Romantic Conservative in ideology (Westby and Braungart 1970; Schweitzer and Eldon 1971).

The YAF brand of Romantic Conservatism was reactionary in thrust and had little influence on the student movement of the 1960s. Another form of Romantic Conservatism, quietistic in thrust, however, played a major role in the development of the counterculture of the period.

The two most salient features of the counterculture—drugs and rock music—were both co-opted by Romantic Conservative strata in the "movement." According to the Gallup Poll, the use of marijuana by U.S. college students soared from 5 percent in 1967 to over 50 percent in 1971. While the more powerful hallucinogens, such as LSD, were used by only 3–5 percent of students, the mythology surrounding their effects had a tremendous impact on the art and music of the counterculture.

Because such drug use was punishable by severe penalties, it often acquired a kind of "conspiratorial magic" (Hinckle 1967, p. 17).

Writing about the New Left, Dick Cluster (1979, p. 124) reflects: "It is . . . impossible to convey the spirit of my own experiences or of politics among white youth in the '60s in general without conveying the atmosphere of grass, acid, hitchhiking trips, Janis Joplin, Rolling Stones, and 'We Are All Outlaws in the Eyes of America' in which they floated." In its first communiqué, the Weather Underground claimed, "Dope is one of our weapons, the laws against marijuana mean that millions of us are outlaws long before we actually split. Guns and grass are united in the youth underground."

Although drug use had some relation to cultural rebellion for most youth, there is no evidence that it implied any radical political content (Clarke and Levine 1971). Many ignored politics altogether. Many others espoused a politics that was quietistic in its implications. The high priest of drugs was Dr. Timothy Leary, who delivered drug sacraments while wearing white cotton pajamas, burning incense, and espousing an idiosyncratic amalgam of Far Eastern religions, especially Zen Buddhism.

For Leary and the millions of Aquarian Youth who followed his example, drugs were not just part of the revolution, they *were* the revolution. In his best-known book, *The Politics of Ecstasy*, Leary declared that "lighting a joint is a revolutionary act" and urged everyone to "turn on, tune in, and drop out." When Leary called upon youth to drop out, he did not mean just out of "straight" society. He also urged young people to "drop out of politics, protest, petitions, and pickets" and to join his "new religion," in which "you have to be out of your mind to pray" (Hinckle 1974, p. 149). In Leary's view, liberals and Marxists were opposed to the individual freedom that the psychedelic revolution represents. To become an "ecstatic saint" was to become a "social force" defending "individual internal freedom" and subverting the materialistic urban empire from below. For Leary, it was necessary to change your head before you changed the world, and acid was the only path to this new future.

Leary's efforts to make a political ideology out of mere drug use had its parallel in the efforts of others with respect to rock'n' roll music. In the mid-1960s the San Francisco scene was exploding with many new bands introducing the psychedelic sound experience of acid rock: "shrill feedback guitar, tremendous volume, heavy crescendoes, and electronic sound for its own sake" (Cook 1971, p. 228). Miller (1977, p. 252) writes: "Just as poetry was the art axis for the romantics of 1830 and as poetry/fiction was that of the Beats, so was music the art-axis of the Haight community. The bands were its central institutions."

The drugs, sexuality, and youthful rebellion associated with the new music alarmed institutional authorities and spokespersons for the older generation. Political conservatives, from the John Birch Society to Vice-President Agnew, mirroring the puritanical authoritarianism of their Soviet counterparts, blamed the music industry for promoting a youthful decadence that made America vulnerable to foreign influence. The politicians exerted pressure on the main radio stations, which refused to play such outspokenly critical musicians as Country Joe MacDonald, the Fugs, and Phil Ochs. In fact, it was only the expansion of local FM programming in 1967 that allowed such musicians to find their own audiences.

The commercially successful performers, such as Bob Dylan and the Beatles, were closely supervised. Promotional people in the industry kept the pressure on the Beatles' manager, Brian Epstein, to restrict "the group's freedom in talks about 'controversial' subjects, such as war and revolution." Such control, coupled with his own ambivalence, influenced John Lennon to reverse the lyrics on his single "Revolution" from "count me in" on violence to "count me out" (Kopkind 1971, p. 55).

Of the many thousands of songs commercially released in the 1960s, there probably were fewer than 50 or so that had an explicitly political message. Of these, only a handful were performed at political rallies, most notable of which were Country Joe MacDonald's "Fixin' to Die Rag" and John Lennon and Paul McCartney's "Give Peace a Chance." Neither of these was as popular as the more traditional songs, such as Pete Seeger's "Blowin' in the Wind" or the classic "We Shall Overcome," a black spiritual adapted for the labor movement in the 1930s, again for the civil rights movement of the 1950s, and, finally, for the peace movement of the 1960s.

By the end of the decade, with the previously noted exceptions, rock music had been co-opted completely by the Romantic Conservatives. Rock music critic Ralph Gleason and his partner, *Rolling Stone* editor Jann Wenner, proclaimed that rock music *was* the revolution, and any attempt to mix it with politics would only pollute its purity. Gleason (1967) rejected the politics of the "Square Left," charging it with being imprisoned in the same rationalist assumptions as the political establishment. In fact, he saw no difference between the far left and the far right. According to Gleason, neither of these alternatives had any appeal for the "New Youth," which was "finding its prophets in strange places—in dance halls and on the juke box." The New Youth, Gleason declared, would be changed "by poetics and not by politics."

The Romantic Conservatives confidently advised people desiring change to just lie back and groove, and in time the revolution would come to them. The great symbolic event of this crusade was the Woodstock music festival. On August 15–17, 1969, between 300,000 and 400,000 young people gathered in a small village in New York to listen to the music of several of the nation's top rock bands. The festival organizers were not prepared for such a large turnout. The supply of food ran out and garbage piled up. Many people had no place to sleep. There was practically no security. As if things weren't bad enough, it rained almost continuously. Bad drugs were sold and there was little medical help available.

By the end of the three days, 4,000 people had been treated for injuries, illness, or an overdose of drugs. There were three reported deaths, numerous hospitalizations, over 30 cases of poisoning from impure LSD, at least 15 miscarriages, and 80 drug arrests. Only the movement groups were able to organize themselves adequately to provide food and medical care to their numbers, and they were cut off from the main gathering on the opposite side of a small woods (Gabree 1969). This isolation of the political left was more than territorial. Abbie Hoffman was clubbed off the stage by Peter Townshend of The Who for trying to mobilize support for White Panther Party leader and MC-5 manager John Sinclair's legal defense fund.

However, what could easily have been condemned as a disaster was celebrated as a beacon of the coming age. Defenders pointed out that there was very little violence, let alone any riots. People shared food, dope, and cover from the rain, and Monticello's police chief saluted the festival crowd as "the most courteous, considerate and well-behaved group of kids" he had ever managed. The police chief's statement lent credence to participants' reports about the feeling of communion that made the weekend so special (Howard 1969). Since the organizers of the festival also made arrangements for albums and a feature film, Woodstock soon became a romantic myth of the possibility of instant community, the kind of instinctive fellowship that Charles Reich waxed lyrical about in *The Greening of America.*

What was ignored, of course, were the casualties, the rip-off intentions of the promoters, the passivity of most of the audience, and the brevity of the event—three days does not a society make. Nevertheless, *Life*, *Time*, *Newsweek*, and the *New York Times* all heralded the discovery of a "free, dope-smoking, cooperative, non-violent, anti-political—though potentially culturally revolutionary—counter-community of youth which was cemented together by rock music, but retained enough good middle-class manners to clean up after itself"—a "Woodstock Nation" (Stern 1970, p. 113).

This Romantic Conservative myth of community without politics was so compelling to the media that they completely ignored not only the painful lessons of Woodstock but also the music festival four months later that would expose the shallowness of this dream and the dangers it held for the naive—Altamont.

On December 6, 1969, the Rolling Stones offered a free, all-day concert at Altamont Racetrack in California. Its promoters billed it as "Woodstock West." The Stones' decision to hire the Hell's Angels as crowd marshals was praised by Gleason as "a different kind" of politics. The Stones, who refused to appeal for funds for the beleaguered Black Panthers, apparently also practiced "a different kind" of politics.

On this occasion the Angels ran rampant. They tore into the crowd, mauling and bloodying over 100 people. When a young black drew a pistol to defend himself, he was ritually stabbed to death by several of the Angels. This murder occurred just 25 feet from the stage as Mick Jagger sang "Sympathy for the Devil." Rather than stop the performance and call for order, Jagger moved right into a rendition of "Street Fighting Man." Three others were killed accidentally and at least 100 had to be treated for "nightmarishly bad acid trips" (Stern 1970, p. 114). Significantly, neither *Time* nor *Life* carried any coverage of Altamont. Robert Stone, author and early Merry Prankster, speculated that the business media were "relatively kind to the hippies because their dream-dope environment renders them 'safe' in the eyes of the Establishment" (von Hoffman 1968).

ROMANTIC RADICALISM:
THE EMERGENCE OF THE NEW LEFT

Maverick sociologist C. Wright Mills (1960) introduced the idea that the "young intelligentsia" constitutes a "new left" that could revitalize the movement for "reason, freedom, and justice" that had been thwarted by the American and Soviet political establishments. His *New Left Review* article made a strong impression on young Tom Hayden, who published his own "Letter to the New (Young) Left" and saw to it that Mills's article was reprinted as an SDS pamphlet in 1961.

The New Left was born in 1960 with organizations such as the Student Peace Union, the Student Nonviolent Coordinating Committee (SNCC), and SDS. These student political groups were the first in American history that "had no formal adult ties and were organizationally independent" (Altbach 1974).

The membership base of the New Left consisted of black youth, college students, and radical, university-based intellectuals. The goals of the New Left were to advocate liberty and end the repression of the state, and to organize community to combat alienation. In the late 1960s certain Marxist-Leninist sects, Progressive Labor in particular, tried to mobilize students and blacks around the issue of economic equality, but they were never able to gain much of a following. Specific objectives of the New Left included putting an end to racial discrimination, the draft, and legal restrictions on personal expression.

The enemies of the New Left were the "Establishment," or what Mills called the "power elite," an unofficial triumvirate of corporate leaders, military officials, and key politicians. The battlegrounds of the New Left were mainly the campuses and black ghettos. Although these communities were peripheral to the dominant economic sector, many hoped the university could be made into a base for a larger revolution of youth, racial minorities, and poor whites.

The essential ethos of the New Left was Romantic Radicalism. This ethos encompassed a rejection of formal ideology, a neoanarchist conception of organization, a countercultural life-style, and a "pluralistic socialism" that combined advocacy of the "unrepresented" with a respect for cultural relativity (Wood 1975).

The principal strategy of the New Left was nonviolent direct action, including civil disobedience (such as sit-ins, building occupations, demonstrations) and passive resistance (such as class strikes and boycotts). Despite the accusations of enemies and sensationalism of press accounts, violence was rarely used (Long and Foster 1970; Astin et al. 1975; Yankelovich 1972).

Achievements for which the New Left deserves credit are the decline of the House Un-American Activities Committee (HUAC), the Nuclear Test Ban Treaty of 1963, the termination of *in loco parentis* on college campuses, the Civil Rights Act of 1964, the Voting Rights Act of 1965, and the end of segregation and increasing political power of blacks that followed.

WE SHALL OVERCOME:
CIVIL RIGHTS TO BLACK POWER

It is not possible to understand the ideological tensions and trans- formations in the white radical youth movement from 1964 to 1968 apart from that experienced within the black movement over that same period. Momentum gained with the establishment of Martin Luther King, Jr.'s, Southern Christian Leadership Conference (SCLC) in the mid-1950s was accelerated rapidly after the widely publicized lunch counter sit-in by black students in Greensboro, North Carolina, in 1960 (Zinn 1964).

With help from the SCLC, black youth were organized into a new group, SNCC. Many white youth joined the cause. In fact, most of the leaders of the white New Left received their basic training in oppositional politics in the civil rights movement. Tom Hayden, Abbie Hoffman, Mario Savio, and many others were graduates of the Southern campaigns. SNCC was an organization of organizers, not a mass-membership association. At its peak it had only about 250 paid staff, 250 volunteers, and a budget of $800,000. In the first couple of years SNCC sponsored Freedom Rides and sit-ins to desegregate public accommodations in the South. Over 50,000 people staged such demonstrations in over 100 cities. In 1961–63 it shifted to a longer-term strategy of organizing rural communities around voter registration. The principal tactic was to establish Freedom Schools to teach literacy to adults and racial pride to children. The Civil Rights Act of 1964 and the Voting Rights Act of 1965 represent the crown- ing achievements of this liberal civil rights coalition, and are a tribute to the sacrifices of thousands of idealistic black and white youth.

From 1964 to 1968 the civil rights movement underwent a radi- cal transformation. The movement of the early 1960s was largely middle-class, interracial, and reform-oriented. Duberman (1968) states that SNCC's staff was "chiefly concerned with winning the right to share more equitably in the 'American Dream' . . . and optimistic about the possibility of being allowed to do so." The movement used legal petitions and nonviolent direct action to "appeal to the national conscience" to remove the legal barriers to integration in the South. It looked to the federal government for support.

The basic cultural orientation of the early civil rights movement was rooted in the church, specifically the ministers in the SCLC. Influenced by the philosophy of Gandhi, King preached a doctrine of redemptive love to members of the dominant group. This emphasis on nonviolence and faith also reassured King's followers of their moral superiority and final victory. Most meetings took place in churches. New lyrics were adapted to old Negro spirituals to give collective vocal expression to the faith and hopes of those in the movement.

In contrast, the new movement of the late 1960s turned away from the white liberal coalition and the federal government. It reached out to lower-class blacks, concentrated on developing black leadership, and called for local control of community institutions. Centered more in the urban ghettos of the North and West, the new movement raised a more general protest against institutionalized racism and a demand for equality on all fronts. It turned away from the church and the philosophy of nonviolence, stressing self-defense and liberation by any means necessary. To bond these new factions in solidarity, it was necessary to create a new ideology of black nationalism. This historical development provides one of the most interesting examples of cultural politics in the 1960s.

Several factors combined to bring about this transformation: the unwillingness of the Justice Department and the FBI to provide adequate physical protection from racist violence for civil rights workers in the South, the unwillingness of the liberal coalition to move beyond constitutionalism in its advocacy of black interests, the surge of ghetto riots in the large cities of the North and West and their violent repression, and the rapid escalation of the Vietnam war. I will examine these factors in turn.

We Shall Not Be Moved

In the early 1960s civil rights workers were subject to shootings, beatings, and jailings under brutal conditions. "SNCC's short history has literally been written in the blood of its staff and supporters" (O'Brien 1968). Local authorities permitted, and sometimes took part in, these assaults. FBI agents frequently were present, but just took notes. Worse yet, recently uncovered evidence reveals collusion among the FBI, Birmingham police, and Ku Klux Klan to ambush Freedom Riders during this period, Repeated telegrams to Attorney General Robert Kennedy failed to bring the needed protection.

In early 1964, under the direction of Robert Paris Moses, SNCC workers "issued a call for a thousand northern college students to spend a summer in Mississippi—helping with voter registration, teaching in improvised 'freedom schools,' and sharing the physical danger that is part of every black person's life in Mississippi" (O'Brien 1968, p. 8). Eight hundred students answered the call. During the course of the year, more than 20,000 civil rights demonstrators were arrested.

The "Mississippi Summer" had two goals. One was to force the federal government to offer more protection to civil rights workers. The other was to build a movement called the Mississippi Freedom Democratic Party (MFDP), open to both blacks and whites, with delegates elected at grass-roots caucuses. Over 60,000 were registered, and a full delegation was chosen and sent to the Democratic National Convention in Atlantic City. With legal representation from Americans for Democratic Action leader Joseph Rauh, Jr., the MFDP challenged the legality of the "regular Mississippi delegation" and demanded that they be seated instead. It was a direct appeal to Northern liberals to join them in opposing racist politics.

Despite the regular delegation's preference for Goldwater over Johnson, the Democratic leadership wished to avoid a confrontation with its "Dixiecrat" colleagues. They proposed a compromise by which the regular delegation would retain its seats and the MFDP would get two of its leaders seated as delegates at large. Responding to pressure from Walter Reuther and the United Auto Workers, Rauh, King, Bayard Rustin, and other leaders urged SNCC to accept the offer. Moses and James Foreman called for a stand on principle, and were strongly backed by the MFDP. James O'Brien (1968, p. 9) comments:

> More than any other single event, this dramatized the readiness of militants in the civil rights movement to break away from the liberal coalition of the Johnson administration. Pleas that unity was needed to keep Barry Goldwater from being elected president meant less than their just claim to the seats.

The MFDP challenge was defeated by a margin of almost 2–1. In 1965, Bob Moses led another challenge. The MFDP demanded that

Congress seat Fannie Lou Hamer of Ruleville, Mississippi, in place of Representative Jamie Whitten, "on the grounds that more than half of the residents of his district were black but less than 3% of these had been allowed to register" (Reagon 1979, p. 27). Again they were defeated. These several months of persistent reform efforts further alienated liberal whites in the civil rights coalition from SNCC. In fact, many stopped contributing to SNCC programs.

Racial tensions increased within SNCC as well. Because it was easier for whites to adjust to office work than to field visits, they wound up making a lot of the decisions (Lynd 1969). The harder many whites worked to show their commitment, the more it looked to some like they were trying to take over (Marx and Useem 1971). By the time of the Mississippi Freedom Summer of 1964, many blacks, especially those from lower-class backgrounds, expressed resentment about having to take orders from "bossy" white organizers. Lauter and Howe (1970, p. 46) report, "By the winter, local people were commenting that whites smoked in church sanctuaries, dressed shabbily, came and went." The erosion of white liberal support further exacerbated these tensions. By the summer of 1965, whites were discouraged from volunteering in Mississippi. Only about one in 15 whites who went south in the summer of 1965 remained during the fall (Demerath, Marwell and Aiken 1971). The validity of black concerns about the commitment of many white civil rights volunteers has been confirmed by the research of Demerath, Marwell and Aiken (1971). After finding that the white volunteers' social and political attitudes were very little changed by their summer experience, the authors propose that their orientation was essentially romantic; an emotional commitment always vulnerable to later "cooling."

The Voting Rights Act of 1965 was proving to be an empty victory. White resistance in the South stiffened. Registering black voters continued to be a lengthy and complicated process. The Loundes County, Alabama, Black Panther Party campaign of 1965–66 failed to elect a single black candidate. Civil rights workers in the South began to despair.

The Move North

In the North over the period 1950–70, an estimated 11 million whites moved out of the cities and millions of jobs followed. Just between 1960 and 1965 the proportion of blacks in the inner cities increased by 23 percent while the proportion of whites declined by 9 percent. Nevertheless, movement workers in the North frequently were disappointed by the unwillingness of white sympathizers to move beyond constitutional advocacy to support concrete demands for more jobs or better schools (Dizzard 1970, p. 204).

The race riots in Harlem in 1964 and Watts in 1965 brought attention to their depressed economic conditions and accelerated changes within the movement. The riots revealed a greater depth of frustration and rage among the black urban underclass than had been realized. Research on ghetto rioters found them to be younger, more educated, more likely Northern-born, and more sensitive to white racism than nonparticipants (Sears and McConahay 1970; Caplan and Page 1968).

In reaction to the movement's gains over the years 1963–65, the incidents of anti-rights demonstrations and violent attacks on civil rights supporters increased sharply (McAdams 1981). Many blacks were killed, some 36 during the Watts riot of 1965. After Watts, local blacks formed a community action patrol to monitor police conduct during arrests (Skolnick 1969, p. 152). In Oakland the following year, some blacks organized armed patrols to reduce the community's dependence on and vulnerability to the police. This small group grew into the Black Panther Party, a national organization with chapters in several cities and a ten-point program for social change.

The commitment to nonviolence was tested frequently in the early 1960s. The question of whether violence was necessary to obtain civil rights was debated in Freedom Schools during the Mississippi Summer. The continued failure of the federal government to protect civil rights workers from racist violence, the collapse of the liberal-civil rights coalition, the ghetto riots and their violent repression, and the subsequent rise of black civilian defense patrols all tipped the scales toward armed self-defense.

The war in Vietnam constituted the final historical development contributing to this ideological transformation. Having passed two major civil rights bills, Congress shifted its attention to the war and other matters. As the war escalated, it took media coverage and public attention away from the issue of civil rights. Prosecution of the war demanded more and more of the government's resources. Black youth were being drafted in disproportionate numbers.

Black Power and Community Control

In 1966, Sammy Younge, Jr., a student at Tuskeegee Institute, was killed while trying to use a "whites only" restroom at a gas station in Alabama. Three days after his murder, SNCC issued its first official statement opposing the war in Vietnam. The statement pointed out that Younge's murder had taken place at a time when the United States was sending black youths as well as white to Vietnam to fight for the "freedom of others, while in our country, many government officials openly avow racism." The march organized to protest Younge's murder revealed how far the movement had come toward a position of black nationalism and self-defense. James Foreman (1968, pp. 252–53) describes it thus:

> We had no form, which was beautiful. People were just filling the streets, and they weren't singing no freedom songs. They were mad. People would try and strike up a freedom song, but it wouldn't work. All of a sudden you heard this: "Black Power." People felt what was going on. They were tired of this whole nonviolent bit. They were tired of this organized demonstration-type thing. They were going to do something.

In an all-night meeting held near Nashville, Tennessee, in May 1966, Stokely Carmichael seized the leadership of SNCC from John Lewis. Carmichael did not share SNCC's commitment to nonviolence and gradually repudiated its philosophy, changing the group's name to the Student National Coordinating Committee.

The following month, despite the presence of FBI and Justice Department officials and television cameras, James Meredith was gunned down while on a well publicized march through Mississippi. Roy Wilkins and Bayard Rustin refused to join this march for fear of endangering white congressional support for new civil rights legislation, but King and Carmichael rushed down to finish it. Carmichael argued publicly with King about the limitations of nonviolence and began to popularize the slogan "Black Power." A few months later the *New York Times* published a controversial letter in which blacks in SNCC (1967) attacked their white co-workers for their attitudes of "superiority" and "paternalism" and for being "symbols of oppression to the Black Community." The SNCC blacks proposed that the organization "should be black-staffed, black-controlled, and black-financed," in order to develop the "indigenous leadership" the long-term struggle would require.

Focusing on the external political and economic control of black inner-city ghettos in the North, Carmichael and Charles V. Hamilton (1967) formulated a program of "Black Power" to promote "group solidarity" among blacks, develop indigenous community leadership, and bring about a "transformation of American institutions."

As early as 1965 many SNCC leaders had come to the conclusion that Vietnam and segregation were "part of the same system." In June 1966, SNCC boycotted a White House conference on civil rights supported by the NAACP and the Urban League, on the ground that "an administration that was obliterating human rights in Vietnam could not further them within the United States." Core leader Lincoln Lynch explained that to support the war, so "suffused with conscious racism, is to support the racism on which it feeds." Julian Bond gave up his seat in the Georgia state legislature rather than disavow SNCC's staunch opposition to the war. By then, despite severe admonitions from national leaders, Martin Luther King, Jr., had begun linking the two issues.

Several developments during this period culminated in the emergence of a new analysis of race relations in the United States, organized around the model of colonialism. Between 1945 and 1965 the number of independent African states in the United Nations grew from 4 to 36. Black militants increasingly viewed the United States as a colonial power and themselves as part of a world majority of peoples of color. After his break with Islam in 1963, Malcolm X (1965) gained national attention by calling on "African-Americans" to expand their struggle "from the level of civil rights to human rights" and, thus, to join with their "brothers and sisters in Africa and Asia." In 1965, Frantz Fanon's *The Wretched of the Earth* was published in the United States. California students Huey Newton and Bobby Seale read Fanon's ideas about the functional importance of violence and the rebirth of native culture in liberating oppressed people and credit him with inspiring them to organize the Black Panther Party. In 1966 blacks in SNCC compared paternalistic whites in their movement to civil servants and missionaries in the colonial countries, and concluded that "the reality of the colonial people taking over their own lives and controlling their own destiny must be faced."

With the publication of Carmichael and Hamilton's *Black Power* in 1967, the paradigm of "internal colonialism" was given widespread attention. This paradigm linked support for the Vietnamese war for national liberation with the decolonization of the new African states and the black struggle for community control of the Northern ghettos. By 1967 black protest had come to reflect three major themes: political autonomy and community control, self-defense and the rejection of nonviolence, and cultural autonomy, racial pride, and the rejection of white values.

By and large, the goal of community control was frustrated by the opposition of professional organizations, such as the American Federation of Teachers, and co-opted by the Nixon administration's skillful promotion of the chimera of "black capitalism." The rhetoric of self-defense, on the other hand, was taken all too literally and triggered a white backlash, led by the police and national guard, that took a heavy toll in black lives. SNCC concentrated on organizing student power fights on black campuses and black student unions on white campuses. Carmichael was forced to flee the country and his successor, H. Rap Brown, was railroaded into prison. By 1969 SNCC was reduced to "merely a group of 150 wandering, homeless, hard-core militants" (Shoben, Werdell and Long 1970, p. 218).

Police Brutality

The Black Panthers, in particular, became a symbol of rebellion that challenged the authority of the state. Between 1968 and 1970 police in cities all over the country conducted a virtual war on the Panthers. They staged numerous unannounced raids on Panther head-quarters in which they destroyed property, beat Panthers, and arrested many on charges ranging from inciting to riot, murder, and arson to purse snatching and possession of marijuana. Bail typically was high ($20,000–$50,000) and trials long delayed (Worthy 1969; Chrisman 1971).

When cases finally came to trial, they usually ended either in dismissals for lack of evidence, mistrials due to tampering by the state, or hung juries. Panther leaders such as Huey Newton, Bobby Seale, and Erika Huggins spent years in prison awaiting trial before a mistrial was declared or charges were dropped after their juries failed to convict them. The most shameful episode in this national campaign to eradicate the Panthers took place in Chicago in December 1969, when police riddled the apartment of Panther Fred Hampton with 82 bullets, killing 2 people and wounding several. The survivors were charged with capital offenses, later dropped when a grand jury investigation found evidence of "purposeful malfeasance" by the police laboratory.

The Panthers' recklessly courageous resistance to police repression set a standard of bravado that, along with that of the Viet Cong, inspired elements in the white radical movement to more physical confrontation with the police. At the 1969 SDS convention, a representative of the Black Panther Party challenged white radicals to "pick up the telephone and call Chairman Mao Tse-tung" if they doubted the Panthers were the vanguard organization in the United States (O'Brien 1978, p. 9). The martyrdom of Panther leaders earned the Panthers much deference from white radical youth and had more than a little to do with the rise of the Weatherman Underground and its campaign of terrorist bombings in the early 1970s.

Black Is Beautiful

In the final analysis, the most significant achievement of the Black Power movement was its rejection of white values and development of cultural nationalism. From almost the beginning of the decade, activists argued that schools whose curricula were dominated by white values and images socialized black youth into acceptance of their status as victims. Freedom Schools in the early 1960s had some success in raising the consciousness and increasing the racial pride of black children in the South. The Panthers and other groups continued such programs in the North throughout the decade.

In the late 1960s, elaborating on a strategy developed by the Black Muslims, militants argued that a cultural revolution was prerequisite for establishing the unity necessary to achieve liberation from white oppression and exploitation. Therefore, it was first imperative to convert the oppressed from their slave-descended identity of "Negroes" to one based on racial pride and solidarity. As part of this program, a buried history of African cultural heritage, resistance to slavery, and contributions to the welfare of mankind was unearthed and publicized.

The high school was chosen as the main target of militant action for lower-class urban youth and for a significant segment of middle-class youth as well. More black teachers and black studies programs were demanded to help "Negroes" learn to become "blacks." Even at the college level, the assassination of Martin Luther King, Jr., provoked movements on campuses all over America "to establish Afro-American history courses and Afro-American majors, to increase the number of black professors, and to enroll greater numbers of black students" (Lee 1970, p. 144). In 1969 "black recognition" became the principal theme of campus protests.

All of this was accompanied by a cultural renaissance that featured African dress, hair styles, music, and other cultural forms that persisted well through the next decade. Rejecting a past of chemically aided attempts to look more white, blacks promoted a new aesthetic based on pride in one's natural appearance: "black is beautiful." For many blacks, African fashions, such as the dashiki, symbolized a feeling of nationhood with all African peoples and a new attitude of militant assertion of rights. Verbal expressions (such as "Tell it like it is!" and "Power to the people!") and physical gestures (such as the raised fist) were developed as part of this new presentation of self.

The emphasis on blackness created a vital symbolic link between the middle and lower classes, and signaled a shift away from integration and toward the basic economic reforms needed to raise all black people out of poverty. Even civil rights objectives typically beneficial only to the middle class (such as increased university admissions) were couched within an ethic of social responsibility to serve the entire black community with one's education and skills. Finally, a mystique of "soul" was invoked to symbolize the collective racial identity of all blacks, regardless of class, and their isolation from whites, regardless of intentions (Hannerz 1970).

The general effect of this cultural assertion was to hasten the demise of de jure segregation and to change the norms of black-white encounters. Whites are now free to associate with, but not to demean, blacks in public. Within much of the white middle class, even private expressions of prejudice are censured. For the first time in American history, whites are expected to treat blacks as equals in society. Clearly, more radical economic reforms are needed to make these new liberties into concrete freedoms. Most blacks remain mired in poverty, with no immediate prospects for improvement. What changed in the 1960s was the prestige accorded to blacks of achievement. For them, basic human respect has become a right, not a privilege.

STUDENTS FOR A DEMOCRATIC SOCIETY:
THE HEART OF THE NEW LEFT

SDS was the principal organization of the New Left throughout the 1960s. Many of the early members came from urban, professional families and thought of themselves as young intellectuals with possible futures in organizational politics. Some had their first experience with political activism in the civil rights movement. In the summer of 1964, having completed their educations, they took the movement off campus to promote "grass roots insurgency" through the Economic Research and Action Project (ERAP). From 1964 to 1966 ERAP ran projects in ten urban ghettos of the North. ERAP organizers built "community unions" to mobilize neighbors around local issues such as garbage removal or jobs, better schools, and traffic lights, hoping that, eventually, they would become alternative centers of power. There was an even greater Romantic fantasy of such actions leading to a chain reaction of structural changes throughout the whole system (Kopkind 1970, p. 285).

On most domestic issues, the early members of SDS shared the Social Democratic positions of their first sponsor, the League for Industrial Democracy. However, consistent with the principles of Romantic Radicalism, SDS rejected formal ideology, bureaucratic organization, and strategic politics.

With its "top-down" structure emphasizing hierarchy and control at the expense of collective participation and change, bureaucratic organization was seen as antithetical to the spirit of a democratic society. In the spring of 1965, SDS leaders Tom Hayden, Norm Fruchter, and Allan Chaise rejected a proposal by a group of young Marxist intellectuals to establish a "radical center" to build a new ideological analysis, explaining: "What we seek . . . is a thoroughly democratic revolution, in which the most oppressed aspire to govern and decide, begin to practice their aspiration, and finally carry it to fulfillment by transforming decision-making everywhere . . ." (Jacobs and Landau 1966, pp. 267–69). Winni Breines (1982, pp. 15–16) calls this "bottom-up" kind of politics "prefigurative." It is concerned with building a community that embodies "a sense of wholeness and communication in social relationships," so as to "develop the seeds of liberation and the new society prior to and in the process of revolution."

During this period SDS members in ERAP tried many experiments in everyday life within their project of seeking to transform the community in which they lived. These included experiments in communal living and cooperative child rearing that had two purposes: to free participants from many of the demands of everyday life, so as to be able to engage in historical action, and "to make history directly by creating actual change in the culture, the social structure and personal character from the bottom up" (Flacks 1974).

Before ERAP was terminated in 1966, many organizers could testify to valued personal growth while making concrete contributions to the community. However, they "were never able to find a strategy for mobilizing masses of people to restructure 'the institutions which control their lives' . . ." And, needless to say, they were never able to start the "chain reaction" that would transform the whole system (Kopkind 1970, p. 285).

By the end of 1964, SDS membership stood at only about 2,000 students on some 75 campuses. Within four years it would reach its peak of an estimated 40,000–100,000 members on 350–400 campuses (Sale 1973). The turning point in the popularity of SDS was its decision to sponsor the first national demonstration against the Vietnam war in April 1965. The demonstration attracted 20,000–25,000 marchers, received national publicity, and brought a large number of applications for membership. In the process, the whole complexion of the organization changed.

The new generation of members came from lower-middle-class and working-class families from more culturally conservative areas in the Plains states and the South. They had little or no political education and were less articulate than the original members. They wore their hair longer, smoked pot, and were clearly more anti-intellectual, alienated, and anarchistic.

Most of the old guard were involved in ERAP, which, despite its difficulties, still had 300 full-time workers in over a dozen cities. They had left the campuses and wanted to broaden the base of the movement to include poor blacks and whites in the inner cities. They also wanted to be a critical influence on the Democratic Party and the liberal unions. Despite the large turnout for the 1965 demonstration, they either despaired of effective opposition to the war or felt it was better left to liberal youth with less ideological vision. They had experimented with more participatory forms of organization and, acknowledging its limitations, advocated more organizational responsibility and representative democracy. Some even looked back with appreciation on the effectiveness of parliamentary procedure in expediting debates and decisions.

The new "Prairie Power" faction had joined SDS in response to its media image as a student anti-war organization. For them, as for the millions of students who were to follow, "the war created a nexus between the individual student's concern for himself, his future and his personal self-interest, on the one hand, and his concerns for the condition of society on the other" (Horowitz and Friedland 1970). They argued for abolition of the national office, little or no structure, and expanded activism against the war on the campuses. Running on a platform of "student syndicalism," Nick Egelson was elected president at the August 1966 national convention in Clear Lake, Iowa. After that, SDS became committed to an ideology of "direct democracy and spontaneous direct action politics" (Breines 1982, p. 87; Gitlin 1980). While Progressive Labor directed many of its young members into SDS that year, they were never able to change the basically decentralized and unplanned character of the organization. At best, they hastened its final breakup during 1968–69 by forcing confrontations over divisive issues at national conventions.

The praxis that united theory and action, means and ends for SDS was "participatory democracy." Hentoff (1965, p. 145) explains, "Participatory democracy means that every member should share in the decisions of any organization or government to which he belongs." Leadership was viewed with much ambivalence. Openness and tolerance were stressed at meetings. No speaker was silenced, no matter how irrelevant or repetitious. Voting was rejected in favor of decision making by consensus.

Participatory democracy had been developed in SNCC and ERAP over the period 1963–65 as a way of bringing poor blacks and whites of the community into the decision-making process. It stood opposed to bureaucratization, charismatic leadership, and any form of elitism that prevented the rank and file from learning the political skills they needed to lead themselves (Flacks 1966).

By the end of the decade, the Scranton Commission (Scranton 1971, p. 66) found that "participatory democracy" had to come to characterize the meeting behavior of all student activist groups: "The new culture decisional style is founded on the endless mass meeting at which there is no chairman and no agenda, and from which the crowd or parts of the crowd melt away or move off into actions."

While the intention of this open organizational style might have been to open up participation to less articulate members, it did not prevent those more skilled in passionate oratory from seizing the initiative in many meetings. In fact, the movement's emphasis on Romantic individualism made it especially vulnerable to charismatic leadership. In a universe where individual actions can affect events, personal heroism becomes possible. Horowitz and Friedland (1972, p. 117) state: "In the movement the 'hero' is restored to an honored place, whether as martyr or leader. This opportunity to perform heroically further justifies rejection of small-minded, timid bourgeois society." The moral injunction of the movement was to "put your body on the line"; to risk confrontations with authorities, racists, the police, the military; to bear active moral witness to injustice; and to demonstrate one's commitment to the cause.

ROMANTIC RADICALISM AND THE DILEMMAS OF ORGANIZATION

Unfortunately, SDS's success was its own undoing. By all accounts its fragile organization could not absorb the flood of new members in 1965. Ironically, the experiment with prefigurative politics was reintensified just as the organization was growing large enough to be politically effective. At the base of SDS's dilemma was its Romantic aversion to rational organization, leadership, and "representative" politics. Wishing to avoid centralization, it minimized communication between the national staff and local chapters. Consequently, it was never able to devise and implement a national strategy necessary to influence federal policies.

Wishing to be as open as possible, SDS refused to enforce delegate credentials for voting at meetings of its National Council. This had the effect of "undermining the chapter as the basic unit of the organization" (Breines 1982, p. 60). There were two further consequences: there was less incentive for members to be active in building local chapters, and there was no authority to disavow the extremist tactics of some members when the demands for more militancy were raised (often by government agents provocateurs) in the late 1960s.

As the organization and its national meeting attendance grew in size, mass consensus was no longer a workable procedure for making decisions. A report from the Newark ERAP reflected, "Although many of us regard voting as undemocratic, there is a real question about whether we can afford to take 8 hours to attain consensus on every issue." Nevertheless, no procedure was adopted for delegating decision making. This had two consequences: meetings tended to be long and unproductive, and collective solidarity frequently gave way to bitter factional strife. In time, positions became rigidified and compromise impossible.

Wishing to combat bureaucracy, SDS limited the number of offices and rotated incumbents at least once a year. However, it neglected to establish any mechanisms for socializing new leaders into the skills and responsibilities of their positions. As a result, much executive experience was lost and organizational continuity was disrupted. In this context, the paid national staff "became crucial to the maintenance of the organization." However, the staff was not elected and definitely "not formally responsible to the membership" (Breines 1982, p. 60). Moreover, it was guided by an informal elite who used their prestige to influence policy decisions. As a consequence, measures intended to broaden participation in decision making tended to narrow it to personal cliques that were not accountable to the formal membership. This absence of accountable representation was exploited further by the media, which arbitrarily promoted various individuals to national celebrity as spokespersons for the movement (Gitlin 1980). Needless to say, this further exacerbated rivalry and dissension within the organization.

The anti-authoritarian bias within the organization also discouraged many of the most talented leaders from seeking or staying in important administrative roles. Few were willing to commit themselves to serving the organization when it meant sacrificing opportunities for their personal development while being vulnerable to ad hominem attacks from others (Flacks 1974; Gitlin 1980). As this anti-authoritarian principle became firmly entrenched by the end of the 1960s, even the "ambition to lead" was "a source of guilt" (Flacks 1974, p. 38). This rejection of structure fed the mystique of charismatic leadership and "more revolutionary-than-thou" militance that plagued the movement at the end of the decade.

An admirable attempt to avoid the elitism of democratic centralism and the inertia of bureaucracy, and to develop a more humanistic form of organization, participatory democracy was never able to surmount the problem of scale. As it grew in size, SDS's continued emphasis on individual participation prevented it from realizing its potential to be politically effective. As a result, it never developed a clear strategy for assuming power nor a viable alternative to the mass bureaucratic organization of the modern industrial state. In short, "it could not specify how to clothe and feed people" (Breines 1982, p. 59).

Organizations that were more explicitly anarchist in ideology than SDS had more serious problems of administration. In the Haight-Ashbury, the best-organized of such efforts was a group who called themselves the Diggers after the seventeenth-century English agrarian anarchists who advocated a radical concept of freedom that included equal access to resources (Tod and Wheeler 1978). The twentieth-century Haight-Ashbury Diggers were led by Emmet Grogan and Arthur Lisch. The Diggers rented crash pads for teenage runaways, supervised a number of free communes, opened stores that gave away clothes, and set up a free soup kitchen in the Panhandle. They even fed people nightly in the parks, begging, borrowing, or stealing whatever they gave away. All of this demonstrated their assertion of the right of people to life's essentials regardless of whether they had money. Their aim was to "create a totally cooperative community" (Hinckle 1967, p. 10).

The Diggers accepted the basic ethic of the hippies, described by Ron Thelin, proprietor of the nation's first "head shop," as "the inalienable right of each person to act upon his impulses, to work out his creativity, to pursue his trip so long as he doesn't lay it on another man. It's called doing your thing" (Miller 1977, p. 106). Although this ethic worked to legitimate experiments with different life-styles, it undermined institution building. By 1968 the Diggers had stopped passing out free food in the park. One of them explained:

> Well, man, it took a lot of organization to get that done. We had to scuffle to get the food. Then the chicks or somebody had to prepare it. Then we got to serve it. A lot of people got to do a lot of things at the right time or it doesn't come off. Well, it got so that people weren't doing it. I mean a cat wouldn't let us have his truck when we needed it or some chick is grooving somewhere and can't help out. Now you hate to get into a power bag and start telling people what to do. But without that, man, well! (Howard 1969, p. 47)

Spates (1971, p. 878) reports that as early as 1967, there were numerous reports in underground papers of "apartments being abandoned because no one bought the food, took out the garbage or paid the rent . . . of whole counterculture communities . . . and communes atrophying because even the minimal amount of attention required for survival could not be mobilized."

Such failures made apparent the limitations of Romantic Radicalism as the philosophical basis of building alternative institutions and movements. The error of Romanticism is not that it overestimates the human potential for cooperation and sharing. There is abundant evidence for this behavior in societies around the world and throughout history. Rather, the error is that Romantic Radicalism underestimates the need for organization to facilitate collective life. All formal groups must create mechanisms for communication, setting goals, dividing the labor, assigning tasks, recruiting and orienting new members, and controlling any deviance that threatens the general welfare. To ignore these collective needs is to invite conflict and/or apathy. As cohesion wanes, doing your own thing gains at the expense of tribal responsibility. Finally Romantic Radicalism degenerates into the "me first" narcissism of corporate capitalism. To recapitulate, it is not overly Romantic to expect people to be capable of better. That, in fact, is the primary virtue of Romanticism. However, it defeats its own purpose when it expects such behavior from people without their consciously attending to the norms of their ongoing relationships.

THE TACTICS OF ROMANTIC RADICALISM

The action emphasis of Romantic Radicalism made tactics a more important concern than organizational structure. Over the latter half of the 1960s, the New Left developed a new "prefigurative" style of protest, a style that fused means and ends by expressing the values of the protest in form as well as in content.

Beat poet Allen Ginsberg was the individual most responsible for developing this concept. Ginsberg was present at the October 1965 Vietnam Day Committee marches on the Oakland Army Base, which were attacked by police and the Hell's Angels. In the days that followed, another march on the base was discussed. In response to concerns about another hostile confrontation with the Angels, Ginsberg proposed making the demonstration into "an exemplary spectacle of how to handle situations of anxiety and fear/threat" (Rubin 1970, p. 45).

A few months later Ginsberg wrote a poem called "How to Make a March/Spectacle" to share his vision with others. In this poem he advised demonstrators to

> . . . lay aside their usual grave and pugnacious quality in favor of a festive dancing and chanting parade that would pass out balloons and flowers, candy and kisses, bread and wine to everyone along the line of the march including to cops and any Hell's Angels in the vicinity. The atmosphere should be one of gaiety and affection, governed by the intention to attract or seduce participation from the usually impassive bystanders— or at least overcome their worse suspicions and hostilities. (Roszak 1969, p. 150)

Dickstein (1977, p. 261) has likened this atmosphere to ethnic festivals where members come together to reaffirm their "common identity, a shared culture, shared values, shared music, and language, and a common feeling of special virtue and distinctness. . . ." This clearly was the spirit of comradeship expressed in the idea of "Wood-stock Nation" two years later. By the time of the May 1970 campus protests against the Cambodian invasion and the Kent State-Jackson State killings, this new unity of cultural and political radicalism had spread far and wide. In Myerhoff's (1972) view, the "revolution as a trip" fostered community and asserted a countercultural identity for the participants.

YIPPIES BLOW MINDS

The other side of Ginsberg's "exemplary spectacles" to "seduce" participation from bystanders was the use of unconventional, even blatantly deviant, behavior to blow people's minds. To blow people's minds was to confront them with a situation that could shatter their cultural assumptions and, perhaps, liberate them from ruling-class images. Such people might withdraw from participation in mainstream society ("drop out"), become active in the counterculture ("freak out"), or become active in oppositional politics ("radicalize").

Without question, the master mindblowers in the New Left were a scruffy band of self-described "anti-intellectual action freaks" who called themselves the Youth International Party (YIP). The Yippies and their star attractions, Abbie Hoffman and Jerry Rubin, had a special talent for self-advertisement and made-for-media pranks. In a style reminiscent of the Futurists and Dadaists, they practiced a kind of political theater scripted to mock the establishment and embolden youth to rebel against authority in the name of personal pleasure. Wood (1975, p. 44) has termed this ideology "hedonistic anarchism," an appropriate label, given Hoffman's position on pornography: that arousing prurient interest *is* its redeeming social value.

Hoffman and Rubin first teamed up in August 1967 in New York. After four years with the civil rights movement, Hoffman was alienated by the shift to Black Power, moved to New York, and began working with a Digger-like craft cooperative on the Lower East side who called themselves the Motherfuckers. Rubin had lived since 1964 in Berkeley, where he developed a reputation as the "P. T. Barnum of the left, organizing spectacular events such as marathon Vietnam Day marches, teach-ins, and International Days of Protest" (Lucas 1971, p. 386). In 1967 Rubin ran a losing campaign for mayor of Berkeley, then moved to New York at the request of Dave Dellinger of the War Resisters League, to help organize the October demonstrations at the Pentagon. Abbie comments on their meeting:

> We were two people who sensed the opportunity of blending the political and cultural revolutions. Jerry's forte was the political timing, mine dramatic. . . . We were anarchists, but even among anarchists there are not that many who can map out strategy and lead. Some anarchists are just more equal than others in that ability. (Hoffman 1980, p. 128)

In the fall of 1967, along with Paul Krassner, Stew Albert, Anita Hoffman, Nancy Kursham (Rubin), and others, they formed the YIP. It was conceived as a media event to attract demonstrators to the Democratic National Convention to nominate a pig for president as part of a "Festival of Life" to counter the Democrats' "Convention of Death," the expected nomination of Hubert Humphrey, and the continuation of the war in Vietnam. The concept of "party" was a play on words. Following Allen Ginsberg, what they intended to demonstrate at Chicago was a "spirit" of "young people having fun while they were protesting the system" (Hoffman 1972, p. 36).

As anarchists, the Yippies sought a "revolution" aimed at "the destruction of a system based on bosses and competition and the building of a new community based on people and cooperation . . . a society in which the people directly decide and control the decisions that affect their lives" (Hoffman 1969, p. 77).

Who were the people to make this revolution? At the 1967 SDS national conference, Sale (1973) reports, there were at least 20 proposals to politicize the hippies. Torn between whether to organize factory workers or the "new working class" of college-educated labor, SDS ignored the hippies as an agency of change. The Yippies took up the challenge. Operating without any explicit ideology, they proposed organizing young street people around a model of a "long-haired, crazy revolutionary" fighting for his own cultural liberation and producing a social transformation in the process (Rubin 1970, p. 39).

The Black Nationalists looked to peoples of color as the pivotal stratum for the revolution. The Marxists looked to the working class. Rubin envisioned an activated generation whose bond of age and history would be so powerful as to erase all other social divisions and usher in an age free of material conflicts, an age in which "machines could do most of the work" and "imagination reigned supreme" (Rubin 1969, p. 18; 1970, p. 251).

Lacking any theory or organization and with a narrow social base, the Yippies concentrated on tactics. They used dramatic irony to reveal absurd contradictions in a social order whose legitimacy depended on the appearance of rationality. The object was to provoke people into reacting, with the expectation that reflection might produce new insights and, possibly, new commitments. Rubin (1970, pp. 249–52) proclaimed: "America suffers from a great cancer; it's called APATHY. . . . Alienating people is a necessary process in getting them to move. . . . What breaks through apathy and complacency are confrontations and actions, the creation of new situations which previous mental pictures do not explain . . . persuasion follows the disruption."

The Yippies' first major prank was to shower dollar bills from the visitors' gallery onto the floor of the New York Stock Exchange. Hoffman (1980, p. 101) gleefully describes the reaction: "Pandemonium, the sacred electronic ticker tape, the heartbeat of the Western world, stopped cold. Stockbrokers scrambled over the floor like worried mice, scurrying after the money. Greed had burst through the business-as-usual facade." As if to make the Yippies' triumph complete, the stock market security organization reacted by installing bulletproof glass around the observation platform. Hoffman (1980, p. 102) assessed the action thus: "The system cracked a little. Not a drop of blood had been spilled, not a bone broken, but on that day, with that gesture, an image had begun. In the minds of millions of teenagers the stock market had just crashed."

This action was followed by many more theatrical assaults on the institutions and conventions of the establishment. A common game was to provoke authority into blowing its cool and overreacting. Once they lost control of their emotions, the targets of Yippie subversion were forced to act on impulse. Such behavior shattered the pretense of objectivity and presented onlookers with the image of a confused authority, vulnerable to attack. The Yippies appeared naked in a church; invaded university classrooms, where they stripped to the waist and French kissed; dressed as Keystone Kops and staged a mock raid on the (State University of New York) Stony Brook campus to arrest all the whiskey drinkers; planted trees in the center of city streets; dumped soot and smokebombs in Con Edison's lobby; and called a press conference to demonstrate a drug called "lace," which, when squirted at the police, made them take their clothes off and make love.

Their most widely publicized action was the October 21, 1967, "exorcism of the Pentagon," in which the Yippies dressed as "long-haired warlocks who 'cast mighty words of white light against the demon-controlled structure, in hopes of levitating that grim ziggurat right off the ground'" (Roszak 1969, pp. 124–25). It was this demonstration that convinced Rubin that

> We could build a movement by knocking off American symbols. We had symbolically destroyed the Pentagon, the symbol of the war machine, by throwing blood on it, pissing on it, dancing on it, painting "Che lives" on it. It was a total cultural attack on the Pentagon. The media had communicated this all over the country and lots of people identified with us, the besiegers. (Lukas 1971, pp. 388-89)

Many in the movement resented the Yippies' media attention. They felt that the Yippies gave a naive public the wrong impression of the movement. The Yippies rejected the rest of the movement in turn. As far as they were concerned, the liberals were hypocritical sellouts, SDS were sexually repressed organization men, Marxists were dogmatic pedants, and hippie leaders were self-indulgent exploiters.

The decision to challenge Mayor Richard Daley's armed forces of repression (such as barbed wire, tanks, troops armed with M-1 rifles) was opposed by all the other branches of the movement. Everyone feared for the safety of those who went and, as events have shown, with good cause. The warnings were effective. The Yippies had boasted of an expected 500,000, privately expected maybe 50,000, and got about 2,000–3,000. As described by Rubin (1972, p. 24), the protestors assembled in Chicago were, indeed, the hard core of macho rebel outlaws the Yippies demanded: "We were dirty, smelly, grimy, foul, loud, dope-crazed, hell-bent, leather-jacketed. We were a public display of filth and shabbiness, living-in-the-flesh rejects of middle-class standards." What wasn't known at the time, but could have been expected, was that about one out of six were police infiltrators.

The Chicago Study Team of the National Commission on the Causes and Prevention of Violence subsequently charged the Chicago police with "unrestrained and indiscriminate . . . violence on many occasions, especially at night." In the 1969 Chicago conspiracy trial, government witnesses were identified as agents provocateurs whose acts were used to justify the police brutality. It is also true, however, that the Yippies, apparently caught up in the mystique of revolutionary resistance, actively participated in the confrontation. Rubin (1972, p. 25) proudly reports:

> Yippies faced the big Machine until the last minute. Then we split into the streets, shouting joyously: "The streets belong to the people!" Yippies set fires in garbage cans, knocked them into the streets, set off fire alarms, disrupted traffic, broke windows with rocks, created chaos in a hundred different directions.

While the "battle of Chicago" shocked many television viewers into sympathy with the demonstrators, many more applauded the brutality of the Chicago police. The following year Hoffman and Rubin were tried by the federal government on charges of conspiracy, along with six other defendants from different branches of the antiwar movement. This obvious government "show trial," designed to make negative examples of the defendants, win public opinion to the side of the government, and drain the resources of the movement, brought the Yippies even greater celebrity and further polarized political forces in the country.

By 1970, according to Hoffman (1980, p. 263), the Yippies had branches in 70 cities and towns in the United States as well as Europe. Because they opposed formal organization, however, there were no membership records to document this claim, and certainly no central coordination between the various branches. In fact, the younger recruits called themselves "Zippies" and rebelled even against the founding generation, illustrating Rubin's (1972, p. 18) statement that "Yippies are leaders without followers."

In the absence of organization, the Yippies relied primarily on the mass media to reach their potential constituency. In this regard they were as naive about the power of commercial media to subvert the established order as were the conservatives they scorned. Rubin even argued that the students who demonstrated at Columbia in 1968 did so because they had been turned on by watching the Free Speech Movement on television four years earlier.

Hoffman capitalized on his new fame by making numerous television, radio, and campus appearances. He saw television as "an enormously successful vehicle for making statements to a mass audience." He prepared himself for such video agitation by "writing commercials for the revolution to learn the rhythm of the medium." Sometimes he would surprise his hosts with a prank that, when it worked, caused them to "lose . . . composure," "scream," or "explode." However, most of the time he'd "talk about the war or other social issues, using humor as a hook," as well as "advertise upcoming demonstrations" (Hoffman 1980, p. 113–17).

Although Abbie put on a good show, it was unrealistic to think he could use a business-controlled medium to make war on business and Hoffman knew it. Gifted community organizer that he was and is, Hoffman was keenly aware of the limitations of celebrity politics. Writing under the alias of George Metefsky (1970, pp. 14–15), Hoffman praised the underground press for its contribution to "the slow education of a mass constituency" and reflected: "Purely exemplary action is often nothing but 'doing your own thing' without relating to the community, and it can fail to organize the community, in spite of concrete, daily oppression."

Despite their success at manipulating the mass media, in the end, the Yippies' own myth was co-opted, distorted, and turned back on them by the Cyclops they sought to master. A fugitive Abbie Hoffman reflected during his *Playboy* interview:

> Yippie was a school of the streets, a school of protest and a technique for communicating through the mass media so that people would go to the demonstrations in Chicago. . . . It was a technique, not something I wanted as a movement. But the media image was so strong that it stuck. (Kelley 1976, pp. 80, 218)

The Yippies could be co-opted by the media because they shared their view of the American people as a passive mass to be manipulated into certain behaviors. But changing consumer brands is a lot simpler than changing political allegiances. Moreover, any attempt to resocialize people into a new politics that is based on converting the individual ignores decades of research on the vital role of primary groups in establishing, maintaining, and changing social norms. This research includes the work of Kurt Lewin and his students on the superiority of having groups, rather than individuals, as the target of persuasion attempts.

Even when effective, the Yippies' media tactics could not produce a concerned public capable of participating in the political process in any unified way. Rather, the Yippies' following fulfilled their image of a mass: "atomized, far-flung, episodic, not active politically except when mobilized in behalf of centralized symbols of revolt" (Gitlin 1980, p. 173). In Hoffman's own judgment, "Flashy exemplary leadership" was effective only in limited situations "like street-fighting"; a tactic that, like media politics, had been elevated to prominence in the movement with the failure of more conventional tactics to achieve necessary results (Metefsky 1970).

True to their Romantic anarchism, the Yippies rejected any theory, ideology, or program. Hoffman (1969, p. 39) explained that politics was "the way that you led your life, not who you supported." To be a Yippie meant a rejection of all authority—parents, teachers, police, politicians—and the substitution of impulse for institutions: "Cultural revolution requires people to change the way they live and act . . . the cultural view creates outlaws" (Hoffman 1969, p. 7).

Naturally, few were capable of such a total existential commitment. In the absence of any objective criteria of membership, attempts to confirm one's outlaw identity were reduced to acts of defiance that provoked repression by one's enemies. Indeed, such repression was the ratification such rebels needed. Rubin and Hoffman both took great pride in reciting their arrests and subpoenas (Rubin 1971, pp. 135–36). After the Chicago conspiracy trial, Rubin reports Hoffman was "down, quiet, moody" because "he had been sentenced to only eight months for contempt," less than rival Tom Hayden, who had consistently advocated "winning the jury through rational arguments and good behavior."

Yippie mind blowing was an imaginative demonstration of the subversive power of cultural politics. Unfortunately, however, the

Yippies were never able to identify reliable criteria for choosing tactics that would not only provoke authority but also educate and persuade their audience. Tactical debates tended to dissolve into personal aesthetic judgments. Hoffman (1980, p. 278) complained, "Zippies practiced street comedy that I thought was sick . . . their art got heavy-handed." During the Chicago trial the Weatherpeople came to town to demonstrate their opposition. Hoffman (1980, p. 246) claimed credit for the billing "The Days of Rage" but gave the show a bad review: "I castigated the street-fighters for smashing the windows of Volkswagens and mama-papa grocery stores." I personally consider Abbie Hoffman one of the funniest and most humane people I've ever had the privilege of meeting. Precisely because he's one of a kind, however, he's a very tough act to follow. Thus, the fact remains that, for want of any clear articulation of principles, the collective struggle foundered on what seemed to be issues of personal taste.

At the level of taste there were no constraints on Yippie Romantic excesses. As a consequence, tactical means often became ends in themselves, as blowing minds degenerated into vulgar display or hostile mocking. Foss (1972) observed, "A heavy air of sheer disgust permeates the freak consciousness, an impulse to be as obnoxious and raunchy as possible." For his book, *Do It!*, Rubin kicked out all the jams,* dedicating it to "The Weather Underground," getting confessed rapist and black militant Eldridge Cleaver to write the introduction, and devoting several pages to praising Charles Manson, with whom he says he fell in love during a visit in prison. Of course, all this poet-warrior posturing alienated almost everyone but the young toughs. Moreover, by Rubin's (1972, p. 215) own admission, it allowed "police undercover agents provocateur . . . to infiltrate the movement with plans of bombing and murder." In the end, the poetic vision of the postrevolutionary society was sacrificed to journalistic sensationalism.

---

*"Kick out the jams" is a rock musician's expression for playing all out, without reservation. It became generalized in the counterculture for any unrestrained behavior.

THINGS FALL APART

The New Left movement of the 1960s ultimately failed because it never was able to develop the ideology and program necessary to expand its political base much beyond college youth and young black militants. In fact, despite some modest efforts, it never established a foothold among middle-class professionals, many of whose socialization and formal education also made them resentful about their lack of participation in the decisions that controlled their lives (Haber and Haber 1967). Without such a base the New Left was limited in its tactical options to civil disobedience and anarchist disruption. Passive resistance and electoral and legal challenges required greater numbers and more cohesive organization than it was able to muster. In short, the New Left was never in a position to contest the power of the elite.

From 1966 to 1969 SDS in particular within the New Left searched constantly for an ideological analysis that would provide an adequate cognitive map of what had become a very problematic social reality, a map that could guide the creation of collective conscience, engender commitment, and motivate action for the necessary transformation of society (Geertz 1964; Mullins 1972). Various factions proposed different analyses—"students as a class," "the new working class," "Maoism"—in a futile attempt to find the strategy that would resolve the "conflict between the enormous scope of [the New Left's] ambition—to transform the whole society, root and branch—and the narrowness of its social and cultural base" (Gitlin 1980, p. 239).

In Gitlin's (1980, p. 239) view, that narrowness was a condition of "the absence of a radical tradition within a formative culture" and "the lack of social institutions of leftist continuity." Indeed, the two-party system had denied formal political representation to the left in the United States, and the New Left rejected the parties of the Old Left as either irredeemably compromised (for instance, League for Industrial Democracy) or too authoritarian, and ideologically sectarian (for instance, Socialist Workers Party). Reflecting on the dilemma of wanting "to make a socialist revolution in the United States" but "without a socialist tradition to rely on," Cluster (1979, p. 126) wrote that "[we] suffered from our need for everything to be new, experimental, an emotional high . . . we were quick to jump from conclusion to conclusion, from strategy to strategy . . . we were not experienced enough, not enough used to thinking historically, to see that revolution would be a long process."

The year 1968 was the turning point in the movement. The Tet offensive in February belied the Johnson administration's prediction of imminent victory and turned public opinion against the war. Facing a stiff challenge from Senator Eugene McCarthy, and then Senator Robert Kennedy, President Johnson ordered a partial halt to the bombing of North Vietnam, called on Ho Chi Minh to come to Paris for "peace talks" to end the war, and, most dramatically, announced that he would not seek reelection that year. He endorsed his vice-president, Hubert Humphrey. However, Humphrey continued to defend the war and to reject any proposal that recognized the right of the Viet Cong to participate in a negotiated settlement. Any movement in Congress to pressure the White House into making that essential concession was still two years off.

On April 14, 1968, Martin Luther King, Jr., was assassinated. Blacks rioted in 138 cities in 36 states. There were more national guard and federal troops called more times than in all of 1967. Tens of thousands were arrested. Frustration grew within the movement and, with it, despair that the conventional tactics of peaceful demonstrations, public education, and petitioning and lobbying Congress could end the war and bring justice to black and poor people.

Spearheaded by SDS, awareness grew on campus after campus of university connections with the defense establishment and indifference to the needs of minorities. The war was seen less as a mistake and more as an expression of American imperialism. The university was seen less as a retreat and more as an important cog in the war machine. Protests were organized for more black studies, students, and faculty, and against military research centers, ROTC programs and facilities, and recruiters for military contracters, especially Dow Chemical, the maker of napalm.

Many of these protests featured more militant tactics, such as blockading or occupying buildings, burning draft cards, and even "trashing" property. The police response to such incidents and to longhairs and youth generally became increasingly violent. The Skolnick Commission (Skolnick 1969) reports that, from 1968 on, there were "numerous instances where violence [was] initiated or exacerbated by police action and attitudes." Much research has demonstrated that the dominant effect of such attacks was to intensify the hostility of activists and to incite bystanders to moral outrage and sympathy for the protesters (Adamek and Lewis 1974; Armistead 1969; Shaw 1966; Wilson 1975).

As they became aware of this pattern, the more militant organizers adopted a confrontation strategy to provoke police overreaction and force fence-sitting students and faculty to take sides. There were protests at three out of four universities over the academic year 1968–69. Estimates of violence ranged between 6 and 25 percent of all schools. The Skolnick Commission (Skolnick 1969, pp. 67–68) confirmed that demonstrators and movement workers continued to be much more often the objects than the agents of violence. Indeed, Yankelovich (1972) found that less than one in ten students endorsed violence "as a general tactic."

On the other hand, Yankelovich also found that a substantial majority would "sometimes" justify such civil disobedience as blockading buildings, shielding political prisoners, resisting or disobeying the police, sit-ins, or giving ultimatums to those in authority. Just as the black movement had turned toward self-defense two years earlier, the mood of the white radical youth movement in 1968 was "confrontation, escalation, and protest" (Lee 1970, pp. 136–37).

The FBI, the Pentagon, and other agencies launched massive counterintelligence campaigns against anti-war groups and political dissenters, including illegal wiretaps, mail openings, break-ins, burglaries, harassment, and the extensive use of undercover agents provocateurs to entrap activists into using violent means that would justify further repression by the state (Perkus 1975). Legislatures all over the country passed tough new laws against campus demonstrations.

The most dramatic campus confrontation of the year took place at Columbia University. The ultimate goal of Columbia SDS leaders was to transform the university into a "revolutionary political weapon" to put an "end to war, racism, and the political system they considered responsible for both" (Scranton 1971, p. 34). The Cox Commission report, *The Crisis at Columbia* (1968), found the Columbia administration guilty of "authoritarianism and inviting distrust" and the police of using "excessive force." However, it also observed that "more than a few students" were motivated by Romantic fantasies in which they "lived gloriously like the revolutionary citizens of Paris."

Lasch (1969, pp. 181–82) proposes that the lack of a coherent political program and "the search for personal integrity could lead only to a politics in which 'authenticity' was equated with the degree of one's alienation, the degree of one's willingness to undertake existential acts of defiance." In the end, this obsession with authenticity, "when combined with the general moral anguish of the war in Vietnam," generated a "mystique of 'resistance'." One Romantic excess led to another. Speaking from his personal experience within SDS, Cluster (1979, p. 126) comments, "Leadership often took the form of being a star, a 'heavy,' more revolutionary-than-thou, rather than the form of being a learner and a teacher."

Over the period 1968–70 trashings escalated into bombings as the anarchist Weatherman split off from SDS and other underground groups sought to purge themselves of "white skin privilege" and demonstrate their revolutionary commitment to Third World peoples (Sale 1973). The increased repression by the FBI, local police "red squads," and the Nixon administration, designed to isolate militants within the movement, convinced many of them that armed struggle was becoming increasingly necessary to resist fascist repression in America. The ultimate effect of this spiral of violence was to frighten away a lot of the fence sitters and to discourage the older organizers from the routine base-building a long-term movement requires.

The hippies were helpless before the police backlash. When San Francisco was flooded with perhaps as many as 100,000 youth seeking a "summer of love" in 1967, the police "cracked down with a vengeance." Bruce Cook (1971, p. 203) relates that the police "shut off the old, reliable sources for acid and marijuana . . . and the kids . . . began to turn on with whatever was available." This "finally brought in the Mafia. Prices were upped. A heavy sociopathic element moved in. . . . The crime rate—strongarming, muggings, burglaries, and hold-ups especially—began to rise alarmingly. The district was no longer safe. . . ."

By 1968, Haight Street swarmed with violent predators and the original residents conducted a "funeral march down the street mourning the death of Hippie, the Devoted Son of Mass Media" (Miller 1977, p. 255). This symbolic gesture didn't put a stop to the community's degeneration. The nadir was reached on July 16, 1968, during a five-hour period that has come to be known as "the siege of Haight-Ashbury." From 6 P.M. until 11 P.M., over 100 patrolmen and members of the Tactical Squad from Park Station rampaged through the area, attacking and arresting anyone in their way. Scores of people were treated for broken bones and/or scalp lacerations, and scores more were jailed. Clergy and doctors who tried to restore calm were themselves assaulted or threatened by the police (Smith and

Luce 1971, pp. 277–81). "Love Street had changed into Desperation Row" (Miller 1977, p. 255).

Although the mounting violence of the state provoked many in the New Left to more extreme reactions, it convinced many in the counterculture of "the futility of political reform." The commune movement offered hippies both an escape from repression and a chance "to create a new society in microcosm, to plant the germ cells of a new organism" (Melville 1972, p. 80). Up until 1967 there probably were no more than a dozen or so rural communes in the United States. The outlawing of LSD and the siege of the Haight led to the founding of about 100 rural communes. After that, the number began to multiply exponentially. By 1970 estimates of the number of rural communes ranged between 3,000 and 10,000 with the number of urban communes even greater. Gardner (1978) estimates the total number of people involved in one form of communal living or another at something like a half a million. He calls it a "strategy of retreat" from a society perceived as "immoral and rotten throughout" (Gardner 1978, p. 4). Even Ray Mungo (1970), cofounder of the Liberation News Service, observed that "the movement was sour and bitter," abandoned his political work, and moved to the country to "live the post-revolutionary life." Resigned to the "lesson" that "ideals cannot be institutionalized," Mungo and friends simply "tried to enjoy life as much as possible, took acid trips, went to the movies. . . ."

The commercial media both reflected and amplified this growing separation of political and cultural radicalism among youth. First, responding to pressure from the Nixon administration, the press reduced significantly its coverage of campus protest. The American Council on Education surveys showed that "40 percent of the institutions experiencing severe unrest in 1968–69 received press coverage; in contrast only 10 percent of those experiencing severe unrest in 1970–71 were covered by the press" (Astin et al. 1975, p. 37). Even major national events, such as the 1970 march on Washington, were relatively ignored.

Instead, major news sources, such as CBS Television and the *New York Times*, presented much broader and more sympathetic coverage of those within the anti-war movement who were still willing to work within the political system (Gitlin 1980). That such youth also were more culturally conventional reinforced the traditional separation of those spheres. The willingness of campaigners for presidential candidate Eugene McCarthy to shave their beards and cut their hair in order to be more pleasing in their door-to-door canvassing ("Clean for Gene") became symbolic of the willingness of many youth to sacrifice their freedom of cultural expression in order to have a political effect. Their example was cited as justification for dismissing the political statements of the longhairs.

At the same time, the media gave extensive favorable coverage to counterculture events that eschewed politics, such as Woodstock, while it ignored the reactionary elements within the counterculture, such as the disaster at Altamont. The promotion of Charles Reich's *The Greening of America* (1970) may have been the media's most significant contribution to deradicalizing the image of the youth movement. The book was published first as a long article in the September 1969 issue of the *New Yorker* magazine. When the issue sold out and stimulated many letters, the *New York Times* treated it as a cultural event and gave it several pages of publicity (Starr 1970). The book quickly became a best seller.

The message of Reich's book was that the younger generation was endowed with a revolutionary new consciousness that would transform America. In contrast with the "rugged individualism" of Consciousness I or the "managerial liberalism" of Consciousness II, Consciousness III was "deeply suspicious of logic, rationality, analysis, and of principles." Reich's conception of "Consciousness III" was merely a synonym for the quietistic counterculture. He urged everyone to write off the political system as a means of significant change, and just wait until the anarchy of Consciousness III youth spread peacefully through the entire population. In Robert Eisner's (1970) caustic capsule of Reich's thesis: "As we all refuse to buy what we are told to buy, to work when and at what we are told to work, the whole corporate state with its acquisitiveness and repression will just wither away. It is that simple." Kopkind (1971b, p. 52) continues: "The new institutions will grow according to the new consciousness after everybody wears comfortable clothes, makes love not war, and takes dope instead of booze."

Like Henri Murger's extremely popular play *La vie bohème*, produced the year after the crushing of the Revolution of 1848, Reich's message was one many wanted to hear. The conservatives heaved a sigh of relief over the apparent waning of militant confrontation. The hippies took hope from the prophecy of a New Age. Revolutionary aspirations were reduced to a hazy vision of a coming Age of Aquarius in which "the problems of racism, sexism, poverty, war and waste" would "melt away like March snow" (Kopkind 1971, p. 52). What Christopher Lasch was later to criticize as the "new narcissism" of the 1970s was already conspicuous in the apolitical hedonism of the counterculture of the late 1960s.

The withdrawal from collective political action into individual life-style innovation persisted into the 1970s. For most this choice reflected a concession to conservative political forces. Some held out hope that such changes in life-style could bring about structural change through the power of example. The idea was that "if a few people perform an exemplary act"—organic gardening, vegetarianism, living collectively—"other people will be inspired to do the same thing." As the movement grows in this way, the older order, because it is increasingly "irrelevant to freshly perceived needs, will wither away" and "a new, simpler way of life . . . will take its place" (Rihn and Jezer 1977, p. 2). This anarchist principle has a distinguished history in American thought from Thoreau to Martin Luther King, Jr. However, while it might be able to inspire change in the moral conduct of individuals, such a strategy does not begin to address the complex problems of changing institutional relations.

In Ehrenreich's (1977) view, such life-style politics actually degrades the slogan "the personal is political" to mean "that whatever you happen to be doing is a form of political action." However, "a political morality demands consistency between the spheres of individual choice and the world order. It requires actions which go beyond exemplary forms of behavior—actions which are calculated interventions in human history." Such actions require knowledge of the larger social structure and the dynamics of social change. And they require a willingness and ability to make the linkage between that structure and one's personal milieu. Without such linkage, any choice of tactics becomes merely a matter of taste and convenience.

WOMEN'S LIBERATION

In closing, I must note that the year 1968 also marked the emergence of perhaps the decade's most enduring effort to synthesize radical innovations in both culture and politics—the women's liberation movement. The movement grew out of the New Left, where women had opportunities to develop their organizing skills and to

establish their personal networks, enhancing their feelings of effectiveness and self-esteem in the process.

Women in the New Left confirmed their commitment to social
equality and developed "a language to describe oppression and justify
revolt" (Evans 1975). Their personal discontent grew as they applied
this awareness to their position in the movement. To a great extent,
the men were the policy makers and media stars while the women
were relegated to supportive roles: housekeeping, typing, and clerical
work. In addition, the sexual freedom experimented with by the
counterculturally influenced men of the New Left too often reduced
the women to mere sex objects, not sexual beings with their own
needs and desires (Freeman 1973; Evans 1979).

In 1964, provoked by conflicts between black and white women
over sexual relations with black men, a group of women in SNCC
met to consider their role in the organization. Ruby Doris Smith
Robinson presented a paper, "The Position of Women in SNCC,"
based on this discussion. Stokely Carmichael quipped, "The only
position for women in SNCC is prone." The following year Casey
Hayden and Mary King wrote "A Kind of Memo" which described
the second class status of women in SNCC. It also was ignored.

Frustrated by the reluctance of men in SNCC and SDS to take
their protest seriously, the women in SDS organized their own workshops in 1966 and sent memos to the National Council for consideration. In June 1967 the Women's Liberation Workshop presented an
analysis of the women's position to the SDS National Council in
which female oppression was compared to oppression in the Third
World: "Our oppression is as real, as legitimate, as necessary to fight
against as that of blacks, Chicanos, or the Vietnamese." Many of the
men disputed the analogy as false, but the women would not allow
the men to debate their analysis and the meeting degenerated into
male hoots and catcalls.

Two months later, at the National Conference for a New Politics,
women again tried to take the stand to argue their case, but they
were brushed aside for another cause. One week later, in August
1967, the decision was made to form the women's liberation movement. Over the course of the next year, radical women's groups such
as Red Stockings, Witch, and Bread and Roses were formed, and
women's liberation became a nationwide movement and public issue.
The women gained national publicity at the 1968 Miss America
Pageant by throwing false eyelashes, padded bras, spiked-heel shoes,

steno pads, and other symbols of their exploitation and oppression into a "freedom trash can," announcing their new liberated identity by burning the props of the old. For women, the fusion of political and cultural radicalism was encompassed under the slogan "the personal is political." Ann Popkin (1979, pp. 220–21) explains:

> Issues that were once considered private—sexuality, the family, how you look and act—are now seen as political. Personal life does not merely reflect politics; it *is* politics. . . .
>
> The reflections of this changed consciousness—changed by the struggle we began—are all around us. They can be seen in some tiny reforms now taken for granted, such as the right of female teenagers to wear pants to school, in newer reforms such as increasing female participation in athletics; and in larger battles, such as the one over sex segregation in work and affirmative action.

The larger battles over sex segregation in work and affirmative action have extended the conflict between management and labor into new terrain. Like their brothers and sisters in the factories, women clerical workers have demanded the right to negotiate production standards, control over the conditions and pace of work, and rates of compensation in the office, frequently with success. In addition, they have made issues out of matters such as sexual harassment that have challenged assumptions about "women's place" deeply rooted in the culture of modern industrial capitalism.

As SDS degenerated into battles between Stalinists and militant anarchists, the women's movement became the principal setting for continuing the experimentation with prefigurative organization. For example, recognizing that most women were not yet comfortable in a public speaking role, Red Stockings developed a method for regulating and legitimating turn-taking in their discussions. Each woman was provided with a store of chips and had to give one up each time she talked. "When all her chips were gone, she could not make any more contributions that evening. Those women with chips took over the rest of the meeting" (Popkin 1979, pp. 202–03). Popkin acknowledges that the emphasis on feelings over structure sometimes led to a "tyranny of structurelessness" that "forfeited progress in planned discussions." Many women's groups continue to be plagued by this new dogmatism. Norma Becker (1984, p. 1) observes: "There is a drift toward the creation of a feminist orthodoxy in regard to group process. Specific methods like consensus, the lack of leaders, or small groups are extolled as sacrosanct." It still remains a hopeful sign, however, that such issues are discussed in the women's movements. Creative resolutions of the conflict between task and process are very much needed in radical political groups today. If such resolutions are forthcoming, the women's movement is as likely a source as any.

The women's movement also carried on the Yippie practice of political theater to expose cultural assumptions and provoke change. The women used what they called "zap actions," usually featuring "costumes or skits as well as leaflets," to "expose the sexism of an institution or activity." For example, Bread and Roses staged an "Ogle-In" in a busy shopping area, giving the men the women's traditional treatment of stares, whistles, catcalls, and pinches" (Popkin 1979, p. 203).

The efforts of the women's movement over the years have had a major impact in the marketplace as well as in the norms of heterosexual relations. From 1970 to 1980 women continued to grow as a proportion of the labor force. The percentage of women working full time almost doubled, from 18 to 35. Employment gains for women were recorded in all the male-dominated professions. By the end of the decade women accounted for 25 percent of the managers and administrators, 25 percent of the pharmacists, over 12 percent of lawyers, judges, and physicians, and almost 5 percent of dentists. However, these notable gains in the professions must be qualified by the persistent inequality for women generally. About 80 percent of all women in the labor force still are confined to the lower-paying fields in which women traditionally have been employed: clerical, sales, factory and plant work. According to the most recent government data, the median salary for women working full time continues to be only 59 percent that of men, a ratio that has held steady for many years.

Despite setbacks such as the failure of the ERA, the women's movement has grown in numbers, organization, finances, and experience, and should continue to do so. The National Organization for Women (NOW) currently has 250,000 members, and the National Abortion Rights Action League over 150,000. Even the new group Working Women has chapters in all 50 states and has joined with the 650,000-member Service Employees International Union in a campaign to organize the nation's nearly 20 million female office workers.

The women's movement has changed conventional attitudes toward the family and toward work. Women now outnumber men voters and, as analysts of the "gender gap" will testify, women are "softer" on the issues: more critical of militarism and racism, more supportive of social services (see Starr 1983). As feminist ideology has developed, it has begun to cement the critical links among the three issues with the largest national following: peace, human rights, and environmentalism. Certainly, concerns at the heart of the women's movement—for life, health, and community—can provide the moral basis for any future opposition to the excesses of capitalism and its amoral rationality.

REFERENCES

Adamek, Raymond J., and Jerry Lewis. 1974. "Social Control, Violence and Radicalization: Behavioral Data." Paper presented at the Annual Meetings of the American Sociological Association, Montreal.

Altbach, Philip. 1974. *Student Politics in America: A Historical Analysis.* New York: McGraw-Hill.

Altbach, Philip G., and Patti Peterson. 1972. "Before Berkeley: Historical Perspectives on American Student Activism." In *The New Pilgrims: Youth Protest in Transition*, edited by Philip Altbach and Robert Laufer. New York: David McKay.

Armistead, T. W. 1969. "Police on Campus and the Evolution of Personal Commitments: A Survey of Non-Strikers' Attitudes During a Berkeley Confrontation." *Issues in Criminology* 4 (Fall): 171-84.

Aronowitz, Stanley. 1973. *False Promises: The Shaping of American Working Class Consciousness.* New York: McGraw-Hill.

Astin, Alexander, Helen S. Astin, Alan Bayer, and Ann Bisconti. 1975. *The Power of Protest.* San Francisco: Jossey-Bass.

Becker, Norma. 1984. "Feminist Organizing in the Peace Movement: The Role of Women's Actions." *WRL News* 242 (May–June): 1, 7.

Blauner, Robert. 1969. "Internal Colonialism and Ghetto Revolt." *Social Problems* 16, no. 4: 393-408.

Breines, Winni. 1982. *The Great Refusal—Community and Organization in the New Left, 1962-1968.* New York: J. F. Bergin.

Brown, Michael E. 1969. "The Condemnation and Persecution of Hippies." *Trans-action*, Sept., pp. 33-46.

Caplan, Nathan, and Jeffrey Page. 1968. "A Study of Ghetto Rioters." *Scientific American* 219 (Aug.): 15-21.

Carmichael, Stokely. 1966. "What We Want." *New York Review of Books*, Sept. 22: 5-8.

Carmichael, Stokely, and Charles Hamilton. 1967. *Black Power: The Politics of Liberation in America.* New York: Vintage.

Chrisman, Robert. 1971. "The Black Panther Thrust in American Revolution." *Saturday Review*, July 24, p. 36.

Clarke, James W., and E. Lester Levine. 1971. "Marijuana Use, Social Discontent and Political Alienation: A Study of High School Youth." *The American Political Science Review* 65: 120-30.

Cluster, Dick. 1979. "Rebellions Outside Ourselves." In *They Should Have Served That Cup of Coffee*, edited by Dick Cluster, pp. 111-30. Boston: South End Press.

Cook, Bruce. 1971. *The Beat Generation.* New York: Scribner's.

Cox, Oliver. 1968. *Crisis at Columbia.* New York: Vintage.

Demerath, N. J. III, Gerald Marwell, and Michael Aiken. 1971. "Criteria and Contingencies of Success in a Radical Political Movement." *Journal of Social Issues* 27, no. 1: 63-80.

Denisoff, R. Serge, and Richard A. Peterson. 1972. *The Sounds of Social Change.* Chicago: Rand McNally.

Dickstein, Morris. 1977. *Gates of Eden: American Culture in the Sixties.* New York: Basic Books.

Dizzard, Jan. 1970. "Black Identity: Social Class, and Black Power." *Psychiatry* 33 (May): 195-207.

Duberman, Martin. 1968. "Black Power in America." *Partisan Review* 35 (Winter): 34-48. Also in *The Radical Vision: Essays for the Seventies*, edited by Leo Hamilian and Frederick Karl. New York: Thomas Y. Crowell, 1970.

Ebner, David. 1972. "Beats and Hippies: A Comparative Analysis." In *Society's Shadow: Studies in the Sociology of Counterculture*, edited by Kenneth Westhues. Toronto: McGraw-Hill.

Ehrenreich, Barbara. 1977. "Toward a Political Morality." *Liberation*, July–Aug., pp. 21–23.

Eisner, Robert. 1970. "Review of *The Greening of America.*" *Saturday Review*, Dec. 5, pp. 29–36.

Evans, Sara. 1979. *Personal Politics: The Roots of Women's Liberation in the Civil Rights Movement and the New Left.* New York: Alfred A. Knopf.

Evans, Sara. 1975. "The Origins of the Women's Liberation Movement." *Radical America*, 9(2).

Flacks, Richard. 1974. "Making History vs. Making Life: Dilemmas of an American Left." *Working Papers* 2, no. 2 (Summer): 56–76.

——. 1966. "On the Uses of Participatory Democracy." *Dissent* 13 (Nov.): 701–08.

Foreman, James. 1968. *Sammy Younge, Jr.: The First Black College Student to Die in the Black Liberation Movement.* New York: Grove Press.

Foss, Daniel. 1972. *Freak Culture.* New York: New Critics Press.

Freeman, Jo. 1973. "The Origins of the Women's Liberation Movement." *American Journal of Sociology*, 78(4): 792–811.

Gabree, John. 1969. "Woodstock: They CAN Bust Our Music." *Guardian*, Aug. 23, p. 5.

Gardner, Hugh. 1978. *The Children of Prosperity.* New York: St. Martin's Press.

Geertz, Clifford. 1964. "Ideology as a Cultural System." In *Ideology and Discontent*, edited by David Apter. London: The Free Press.

Gitlin, Todd. 1980. *The Whole World Is Watching: Mass Media in the Making and Unmaking of the New Left.* Berkeley and Los Angeles: University of California Press.

Gleason, Ralph. 1967. "Like a Rolling Stone." *The American Scholar* 36 (Autumn): 555–63.

Gornick, Vivian. 1983. "To Be Young, Gifted and Red." *Mother Jones* 8(8): 16–22, 51.

Haber, Al, and Barbara Haber. 1967. "Getting by with a Little Help from Our Friends." *Our Generation* 5, 2. Reprinted in *Radical Sociology*, edited by J. David Colfax and Jack L. Roach, pp. 388–405. New York: Basic Books.

Hannerz, Ulf. 1970. "The Significance of Soul." In *Black Experience: The Transformation of Activism*, edited by August Meier. New Brunswick, N.J.: Transaction Press.

Hayden, Thomas. 1961. "A Letter to the New (Young) Left." *The Activist*. Reprinted in *The New Student Left*, edited by Mitchell Cohen and Dennis Hale, pp. 2–9. Boston: Beacon Press, 1966.

Hentoff, Nat. 1965. "We're Happening All over." *Playboy*, vol. 13, no. 3 (March): 82–83, 98, 144–46, 149–51.

Hinckle, Warren. 1974. *If You Have a Lemon, Make Lemonade.* New York: Bantam.

——. 1967. "The Social History of the Hippies." *Ramparts*, Mar., pp. 9–12, 17–26.

Hodges, Donald. 1962. "Cynicism in the Labor Movement." *The American Journal of Economics and Sociology* 21, no. 1: 29–36.

Hodges, Harold M., Jr. 1974. *Conflict and Consensus: An Introduction to Sociology*, 2nd ed. New York: Harper & Row.

Hoffman, Abbie. 1980. *Soon to Be a Major Motion Picture.* New York: G. P. Putnam's Sons.

——. 1972. "Testimony of Abbie Hoffman" (from Chicago trial). In *Counterculture and Revolution*, edited by David Horowitz, Michael Lerner, and Craig Pyes. New York: Random House.

——. 1969. *Woodstock Nation.* New York: Vintage.

——. 1968. *Revolution for the Hell of It.* New York: Dial.

Horowitz, Irving L., and William Friedland. 1970. *The Knowledge Factory: Student Power in Academic Politics in America.* Carbondale: Southern Illinois University Press.

Howard, John R. 1969. "The Flowering of the Hippie Movement." *The Annals of American Academy of Political and Social Science* 382 (March): 43–55.

Hughes, H. Stuart. 1961. *Consciousness and Society: The Reorientation of European Social Thought 1890–1930.* New York: Vintage. Reprinted. New York: Octagon, 1976.

Isserman, Maurice. 1980. "The 1956 Generation: An Alternative Approach to the History of American Communism." *Radical America* 14, no. 2 (Mar.-Apr.): 43–51.

Jacobs, Paul, and Saul Landau. 1966. *The New Radicals: A Report with Documents.* New York: Vintage.

Kelley, Ken. 1976. "Playboy Interview: Abbie Hoffman." *Playboy*, pp. 57–80, 218–20.

Keniston, Kenneth. 1970. "Youth: A 'New' Stage of Life." *The American Scholar* 39: 631–54.

Kopkind, Andrew. 1971a. "I Wanna Hold Your Head: John Lennon After the Fall." *Ramparts*, Apr., pp. 19, 55–56.

——. 1971b. "The Greening of America: Beyond the Valley of the Heads." *Ramparts*, March, pp. 51–52.

——. 1970. "Going Down in Chicago." In *Weatherman*, edited by Harold Jacobs. New York: Ramparts Press.

Lasch, Christopher. 1971. "From Culture to Politics." In *The Revival of American Socialism*, edited by George Fischer. New York: Oxford University Press.

——. 1969. *The Agony of the American Left.* New York: Vintage.

Lauter, Paul, and Florence Howe. 1970. *The Conspiracy of the Young.* New York: World.

Lee, Calvin. 1970. *The Campus Scene, 1900–1970: Changing Styles in Undergraduate Life.* New York: David McKay.

Lewis, Roger. 1972. *Outlaws of America: The Underground Press and Its Context.* Baltimore: Penguin.

Lofland, John. 1972. "The New Segregation: A Perspective on Age Categories in America." In *Youth and Sociology*, edited by Peter Manning and Marcello Truzzi. Englewood Cliffs, N.J.: Prentice-Hall.

Long, Durwood, and Julian Foster. 1970. "Levels of Protest." In *Protest: Student Activism in America*, edited by Julian Foster and Durwood Long. New York: Morrow.

Lukas, J. Anthony. 1971. *Don't Shoot—We Are Your Children.* New York: Delta.

Lynd, Staughton. 1969. "The Movement: A New Beginning." *Liberation*, May 14, pp. 7–20.

Marx, Gary, and Michael Useem. 1971. "Majority Involvement in Minority Groups: Civil Rights Abolition, Untouchability." *Journal of Social Issues* 27, no. 1: 81–104.

Mauss, Armand. 1971. "The Lost Promise of Reconciliation: New Left vs. Old Left." *Journal of Social Issues* 27, no. 1: 1–20.

McAdams, Doug. 1981. "The Generation of Insurgency and the Black Movement." Paper presented at the Annual Meetings of the American Sociological Association, Toronto.

Melville, Keith. 1972. *Communes in the Counterculture.* New York: Morrow.

Metefsky, George (a.k.a. Abbie Hoffman). 1970. "Right On, Culture Freaks!" In *Hip Culture: 6 Essays on Its Revolutionary Potential.* New York: Times Change Press, pp. 5–18.

Miller, Richard. 1977. *Bohemia: The Protoculture Then and Now.* Chicago: Nelson-Hall.

Mills, C. Wright. 1961. "On the New Left." *Studies on the Left* 2, no. 1. Reprinted in *The New Radicals*, edited by Paul Jacobs and Saul Landau, pp. 101–14. New York: Vintage, 1966.

Mullins, Nicholas. 1972. "On the Concept of Ideology in Political Science." *American Political Science Review* 66, no. 2: 498–510.

Mungo, Raymond. 1970. *Famous Long Ago: My Life and Hard Times with the Liberation News Service.* Boston: Beacon.

Myerhoff, Barbara. 1972. "The Revolution as a Trip." In *The New Pilgrims: Youth Protest in Transition*, edited by Philip Altbach and Robert Laufer, pp. 251–66. New York: David McKay.

O'Brien, James. 1978. *American Leninism in the 1970s.* Boston: New England Free Press.

———. 1972. "The Development of the New Left." In *The New Pilgrims: Youth Protest in Transition*, edited by Philip Altbach and Robert Laufer. New York: David McKay.

———. 1968. *A History of the New Left, 1960–68.* Boston: New England Free Press.

Peck, Sidney. 1963. *The Rank-and-File Leaders.* New Haven, Conn.: College and University Press.

Perkus, Cathy, ed. 1975. *COINTELPRO: The FBI's Secret War on Political Freedom*, intro. by Noam Chomsky. New York: Monad Press.

Polsky, Ned. 1961. "The Village Beat Scene: Summer 1960." *Dissent* 8, no. 3: 339–59.

Popkin, Ann. 1979. "The Personal Is Political." In *They Should Have Served That Cup of Coffee*, edited by Dick Cluster, pp. 181–224. Boston: South End Press.

Pyes, Craig. 1972. "Rolling Stone Gathers No Politix." In *Counterculture and Revolution*, edited by David Horowitz, Michael Lerner, and Craig Pyes. New York: Random House.

Reagon, Bernice Johnson. 1979. "The Morning Struggle: The Civil Rights Movement." In *They Should Have Served That Cup of Coffee*, edited by Dick Cluster, pp. 1–40. Boston: South End Press.

Reich, Charles. 1970. *The Greening of America.* New York: Random House.

Riesman, David, with Nathan Glazer and Ruel Denney. 1953. *The Lonely Crowd.* New York: Doubleday/Anchor.

Rihn, Shoshana and Marty Jezer. 1977. "Which Way to the Revolution?" *WIN*, March 10.

Rosenfeld, G. 1965. "Generational Revolt and the Free Speech Movement." *Liberation* 10: 13–17.

Rossi, Peter, ed. 1970. *Ghetto Revolts.* Chicago: Aldine.

Roszak, Theodore. 1969. *The Making of a Counterculture: Reflections on the Technocratic Society and Its Youthful Opposition.* Garden City, N.Y.: Doubleday/Anchor.

Rubin, Jerry. 1972. "Songs of Innocence." In *Counterculture and Revolution*, edited by David Horowitz, Michael Lerner, and Craig Pyes. New York: Random House.

——. 1971. *We Are Everywhere.* New York: Harper & Row.

——. 1970. *Do It! Scenarios of the Revolution.* New York: Ballantine.

——. 1969. "A Yippie Manifesto." *Evergreen Review* 13 (May): Reprinted in *The Radical Vision: Essays for the Seventies*, edited by Leo Hamalian and Frederick Karl. New York: Thomas Y. Crowell, 1970: 41-43, 83-92.

Sale, Kirkpatrick. 1973. *SDS.* New York: Vintage.

Schweitzer, David, and James Eldon. 1971. "New Left vs. Right: Convergent Themes of Political Discontent. *Journal of Social Issues* 27, no. 1: 141-66.

Scranton, William (chairman). 1971. *The Report of the President's Commission on Campus Unrest.* New York: Avon.

Sears, David, and John McConahay. 1970. "Racial Socialization, Comparison Levels and the Watts Riot." *Journal of Social Issues* 26, no. 1 (Winter): 121-40.

Shaw, Nancy Stoller. 1966. *The Ins and Outs of SNCC.* Waltham, Mass.: Studies in Brandeis Sociology.

Shoben, E. Joseph, Jr., Philip Werdell, and Durwood Long. 1970. "Radical Student Organizations." In *Protest! Student Activism in America*, edited by Julian Foster and Durwood Long, pp. 202-22. New York: Morrow.

Skolnick, Jerome H. (director). 1969. *The Politics of Protest: A Task Force Report Submitted to the National Commission on the Causes and Prevention of Violence.* New York: Simon and Schuster.

Smith, David, and John Luce. 1971. *Love Needs Care: A History of San Francisco's Haight-Ashbury Free Medical Clinic and Its Pioneer Role in Treating Drug Abuse Problems.* Boston: Little, Brown.

SNCC Staff. 1967. "The Basis of Black Power." *New York Times*, Aug. 5, pp. 1-4. Also in *The American Left: Radical Political Thought in the Twentieth Century*, edited by Loren Baritz. New York: Basic Books.

Spates, James. 1971. "Structure and Trends in Value Systems in the 'Hip' Underground Counterculture and the American Middle Class, 1951-1957, 1967-1969." Ph.D. dissertation, Boston University.

Starr, Jerold. 1983. "Sex Role and Attitudes toward Institutional Violence: A Test and Reconceptualization." Humanity and Society 7 (2): 127-48.

———. 1974. "The Peace and Love Generation: Changing Attitudes Toward Sex and Violence Among College Youth." *Journal of Social Issues* 30, no. 2: 73-106.

Starr, Roger. 1970. "The Counter-culture and Its Apologists: 2." *Commentary*, Dec., pp. 46-54.

Stern, Sol. 1970. "Altamont: Pearl Harbor to Woodstock Nation." In *Counterculture and Revolution*, edited by David Horowitz, Michael Lerner, and Craig Pyes. New York: Random House, 1972.

Tod, Ian, and Michael Wheeler. 1978. *Utopia.* New York: Harmony.

Turner, Ralph. 1969. "The Theme of Contemporary Social Movements." *British Journal of Sociology* 20, no. 4: 390-405.

Tytell, John. 1976. *Naked Angels: The Lives and Loves of the Beat Generation.* New York: McGraw-Hill.

von Hoffman, Nicholas. 1968. *We Are the People Our Parents Warned Us Against.* New York: Fawcett.

Weather Underground. 1970. "Communiqué #1." *The Berkeley Tribe*, July 31. Reprinted in *Counterculture and Revolution*, edited by David Horowitz, Michael Lerner, and Craig Pyes. New York: Random House, 1972.

Westby, David. 1976. *The Clouded Vision: The Student Movement in the United States in the 1960s.* Lewisburg, Pa.: Bucknell University Press.

Westby, David, and Richard Braungart. 1970. "Activists and the History of the Future." In *Protest! Student Activism in America*, edited by Julian Foster and Durwood Long, pp. 158-83. New York: Morrow.

Wheelis, Alan. 1958. *The Quest for Identity.* New York: W. W. Norton.

Whyte, William H. 1956. *The Organization Man.* New York: Doubleday.

Wilson, John. 1975. "The Effects of Social Control on Movements." Paper presented at the Annual Meetings of the American Sociological Association, San Francisco.

Wolfe, Tom. 1968. *The Electric Kool-Aid Acid Test.* New York: Farrar, Straus and Giroux.

Wood, James. 1975. *New Left Ideology: Its Dimensions and Development.* Beverly Hills, Calif.: Sage.

Worthy, William. 1969. "The Decline of the Black Militants." *Boston Sunday Globe*, July 13, pp. 7–16.

X, Malcolm. 1965. "The Black Revolution." In *Malcolm X Speaks*, edited by George Breitman. New York: Merit. Originally a speech delivered on Apr. 8, 1964.

Yankelovich, Daniel. 1974. *The New Morality: A Profile of American Youth in the '70's.* New York: McGraw-Hill.

——. 1972. *The Changing Values on Campus.* New York: Washington Square Press.

Zinn, Howard. 1964. *SNCC: The New Abolitionists.* Boston: Beacon.

9 Cultural Politics and the Prospects for Radical Change in the 1980s

Jerold M. Starr

A pattern emerges from the study of the diverse radical movements that have arisen since the early nineteenth century. I call this pattern the dialectic of Rationalism and Romanticism. The eighteenth-century transition from rural, agrarian monarchies to industrial, capitalist republics created a crisis in cultural authority. Rationalism was one response. Romanticism followed soon after.

Both Rationalism and Romanticism were attempts to establish a new cultural basis to replace the "waning traditions and discredited authority of the old regimes." The cultural authority of the old regime resided in the church. In their earliest formulations both the Rationalists and the Romantics "wanted to be modern without relinquishing religion." The Rationalists sought the basis for the new cultural authority in the method of the natural sciences and "sought to accommodate religion to science by creating a religion of humanity." Its "new priests would be scientists, but its scientists would also be priests" (Gouldner 1973, p. 325). The Romantics sought the new authority in "the certitude of inner feeling and artistic imagination." They "identified the modern with the emancipation of the sentiments or feeling, not of reason or science, and defined sentiment as near the core of religion."

Both movements represented attempts to facilitate the reorientation from a society organized around the principles of hierarchy and tradition to one organized around the principles of individualism and change. In fact, one can find qualities of each mode of thought co-existing peacefully in the writings of such important eighteenth-century philosophers as Montesquieu and Rousseau.

Over time, however, Rationalism and Romanticism were re-formulated into ideologies for movements led by competing social and intellectual strata. As a consequence, their similarities were obscured, their differences exaggerated. Rationalism "was a movement led by a new technological elite whom the new industrialization had almost immediately advantaged." Conversely, Romanticism "was the product of the older, culture-creating elites—artists, dramatists, poets, musicians—who at first were squeezed aside and had no place in the new world of business, industry, and science" (Gouldner 1973, pp. 334–35).

The dominant mode of thought in preindustrial society regarded all knowledge as embedded within the context of concrete relationships and common understandings. Communication, logic, and morality were circumscribed by community. This mode gave way to Rationalism wherever industrial capitalism established itself.

The method of Rationalism is to abstract knowledge from its social context in order to subject it to a type of proof that may be demonstrated to everyone as universally valid. The prototype is mathematics. Rationalism is clearly the logic of free agents in the impersonal marketplace, not of members of a community. Under the logic of capitalism, even man is reduced to a commodity, "his labor-power a calculable magnitude with which one reckons as with all quantities" (Mannheim 1971, p. 145).

The growth of industrial capitalism featured the increasing centralization of the state, monopolization of production, specialization of labor, rise of bureaucratic administration, rapid technological change (including mass transportation and communication), and growth and concentration of the population. From the assembly lines to the board rooms, industrial capitalism has been expressed culturally through secularism, impersonal social relations, managerialism, professionalism, routine work procedures, technical discipline, and the practice of mastery through calculation. Coming to rest on its own "mechanical foundations," industrial capitalism shed all concern with the realm of faith and spirit (Weber 1930). Success in the marketplace required that the head rule the heart.

In the areas of life demarcated as private, however, the traditional modes of experience and expression have survived. In the privacy of home or neighborhood, one can still participate in communal sentiments, spiritual experiences, spontaneous play, artistic imagination, and erotic fantasies. Moreover, these values have remained salient in those strata marginal to the dominant institutions of industrial capitalism: the peasants or subsistence farmers, the urban underclass, women and youth, and artists and craftsmen. These strata occupy the "free spaces" within modern society where human feeling counts and traditional loyalties provide a supportive framework for personal expression.

In the 1960s blacks, youth, and women shared the cultures of traditional institutions that have become marginal to the dominant order. One reason these institutions have survived is that they are a necessary complement to the political economy. Family, church, and university are all preindustrial institutions based on the value of community and personalistic in orientation. The ideal of the church is "a community of worship," hostile to the empiricism, materialism, and impersonality of the corporate sector. The university dates back to the twelfth century and, for most of its history, provided scholastic training for the elite and monastic training for the priesthood. Its ideal is a "community of scholars."

Although they have evolved from an earlier historical period, such institutionalized communities have been critical to the survival of industrial capitalism. During periods of market contraction, even collapse, these organized networks of family and fellows compensate by expanding the systems of informal exchange that supplement the contract-based formal economy. People swap goods and services, make loans and gifts, and help each other out in a spirit of loyalty or sympathy. In so doing, ironically, they help the recovery of a system that, by its nature, is indifferent to traditional loyalties.

THE NEW SOCIAL MOVEMENTS:
FROM ALIENATION TO IDENTITY

The rebellion of these strata poses a challenge to the dominant order that is quite different from those of the past. Past revolutionary movements were concerned exclusively with political reforms to achieve liberty or economic reforms to reduce inequality and provide relief from poverty. In contrast, the social movements of blacks, women, and, especially, youth in the 1960s also were indignant about "the fact that people lack a sense of personal worth—that they lack an inner peace of mind which comes from a sense of personal dignity or a clear sense of identity" (Turner 1969, p. 590). Certainly, alienation is most poignantly the problem of a youthful generation with more education and leisure than ever before but without opportunities to create or contribute. Ralph Turner (1969, p. 593) states: "The sense of alienation is distinctively the sense of a person who realizes great expectations for himself yet must live in a nonstatus."

While these strata seek participation in the dominant order, they prefer to do so on familiar terms. Many are unwilling to sacrifice their individuality or their personal commitments in order to fit into the bureaucratic structures of the corporations and the state. For example, research on the occupational criteria of college students in the late 1960s and early 1970s showed that many more preferred "meaningful" work that provided "opportunities for freedom of action," a "chance to make a contribution to society," and the "ability to express oneself" before such factors as "security of job," "money you earn," and "chance to get ahead" (Bayer et al. 1973; Yankelovich 1972).

The Marxist-oriented labor movement of the Old Left sought to take over the institutions of the capitalist state in order to expropriate their profits for the common welfare. In contrast, the marginal, largely middle-class strata of the New Left sought to decentralize that institutional order and melt its cold rationality by reintegrating work and community life. In short, the New Left sought to "put a more human face" on the institutions of the modern welfare state. In this quest they shared a deep affinity with the peoples in Czechoslovakia, Poland, and other Communist industrial societies. When such marginal strata have challenged the dominant order, Romanticism typically has served as their ideological statement. Karl Mannheim (1971, p. 147) comments:

> The sociological significance of romanticism lies in its function as the historical opponent of the ... philosophical exponents of bourgeois capitalism. ... Romanticism took up just those spheres of life and behavior which existed as mere undercurrents to the mainstream of bourgeois rationalism. It made it its task to rescue these elements, to lend them new dignity and value and to save them from disappearance.

Whenever and wherever Romantic movements have erupted, they have promoted a complex of traditional values to counter those of bourgeois Rationalism: community against contract, intuitive certainty against logic, spiritual experience against material observation, imagination and fantasy against calculation, the unique against the uniform, the natural against the mechanical.

The epistemological position of Romanticism has been that the world is complex and, especially during periods of rapid change, does not lend itself to neat analytic distinctions and rational formulas. Instead of stable identities and clear-cut boundaries, one find objects blending into one another and being transformed into something else. This position has led to new aesthetic doctrines stressing the importance of symbolism and irony, and to a major language breakthrough that occurred with the development of the non-Aristotelian dialectical logic of Hegel and, later, Marx.

The political content and functions of Romanticism, like those of Rationalism, have varied significantly with sociohistorical context. Certainly, some forms of Romanticism have been reactionary. In the aftermath of the French Revolution, Romantic Conservatives such as Burke, deMaistre, and Schlegel advocated a counterrevolutionary theory of the state that denigrated reason and celebrated hierarchy, tradition, and prejudice. This form of Romanticism has surfaced at many times and in many places since then, as a form of resistance against modernism among populations in transition.

There also is a radically progressive expression of Romanticism that has an even longer history. From the eighteenth century to the present, Romantics have championed the rights of the downtrodden: women, youth, peasants, and the other oppressed classes. It must be noted that these are precisely the marginal strata that have served as reservoirs of Romantic values. Moreover, it is this cultural stereotype that has been used by elites to justify their subordination. Hans Speier (1950, p. 104) reports that, in contemplating the further extension of the American democratic revolution to include women, the poor, and the "lower orders" in general, the ruling bourgeoisie expressed concern about the "irrational" aspects of human nature. They called for government programs of political indoctrination, newspaper censorship, and patriotic spectacles in order to ensure the loyal obedience of "those who did not think."

In contrast, Romantics have maintained that even the social worlds of the lowly and the neglected are uniquely valuable and worthy of study. Moreover, they propose personal immersion in these worlds as the only adequate way to learn from them. Thus, Romantics reject the elitism of depending on official accounts and invite "each order to give testimony concerning its own condition."

Certainly, Romanticism has had an explicitly democratic emphasis in the history of arts and letters. From its beginning it was "a revolt of intellectual and artistic elites against their own cultural establishments, and against the standards that have been conventionally used to govern their own specialized spheres of cultural activity" (Gouldner 1973, p. 327).

Finally, and this goes to the heart of the matter, Romantic Radicalism has stood for the value of the individual over class and society. Its advocacy of the individual has been even more adamant than that of bourgeois Rationalism. It refuses to judge human value by status of birth or value of property. It is concerned with the developmental potential of all persons. It rejects the imposition of uniform programs and standards, and celebrates the unique creativity of each human spirit.

THE CONTRADICTION OF ROMANTIC INDIVIDUALISM

The political problem with the Romantic concept of the individual is that, ultimately, it is quietistic. The soldier of fortune, the gypsy given to wanderlust by the lure of the exotic, the poet-warrior all deny the principle of human community. They all represent forms of individual freedom, but none of them is civic freedom.

This Romantic concept of the individual is deeply engrained in American culture, despite the spread of capitalist rationality. America was built on a "rags to riches" myth that lured millions of European immigrants to fuel the Industrial Revolution. In its progressive aspect this concept underpins a cultural value on fairness and respect for the rights of the individual, regardless of social standing.

On the other hand, the vision of success for those who seek to "strike it rich" does not embody a concept of civic freedom, but of special privilege attained through material wealth. It is the vision of the "house on the hill," far removed from the hassles of everyday life among the common people. In such a vision freedom is not a value to be attained through the organization of institutionalized relationships, but a sort of commodity to be procured by those few individuals with the means to do so. Of course, such freedom, if it can be called that, also has been and is available for those willing to give up the dream of riches and to withdraw from institutionalized relationships altogether.

The great movement balladeer, Pete Seeger, once said, "Directly or indirectly I have always hoped my music could help build a new socialist world society." But he added ruefully, "I feel strongly now that Woody [Guthrie] and I either praised the traveller too much, or didn't praise the stay-at-home enough," because the task of the people's revolution is to "save each neighborhood of the world," a task that requires people willing to stay at home and work at it (Miller 1977, p. 236).

In the hippie experiments of the late 1960s, it is clear that the injunction to "do your own thing" conflicted with the ethic of tribal responsibility and undermined efforts at cooperative organization. While I applaud the value that Romantic Radicals have put on human potential and individual creativity, it must be understood that such individuality is not opposed to social organization, but dependent on it. Max Horkheimer (1974, p. 135) explains:

> The absolutely isolated individual has always been an illusion. The most esteemed personal qualities, such as independence, will to freedom, sympathy, and the sense of justice, are social as well as individual virtues. The fully developed individual is the consummation of a fully developed society. The emancipation of the individual is not an emancipation from society, but the deliverance of society from atomization, an atomization that may reach its peak in periods of collectivization and mass culture.

All Romantics understand that authentic individuality is threatened by a society that holds that the value of everything can be reduced to a common cash standard, and whose dominant form of organization is based on the interchangeability of officeholders. What Romantics don't seem to understand is that personality is not innate in the genes or the soul, but is a product of the social environment. A highly differentiated, pluralistically tolerant society will provide the stimulation and support for the development of many "individual" personalities. A primitive retreat from the curse of modernism, although perhaps more loving, will not develop many "individuals." In fact, Horkheimer (1974, p. 135) warns, "Individuality is impaired when each man decides to shift for himself. As the ordinary man withdraws from participation in political affairs, society tends to revert to the law of the jungle, which crushes all vestiges of individuality." Without the protection of community, individuals become vulnerable to elite pressures to obey and conform. Many longhairs learned this the hard way at the hands of scissors-wielding police. At the same time, attempts to achieve individual growth outside of a stable community context have proved illusory. In the 1960s and 1970s the middle-class preoccupation with actualizing one's human potential in "strangers' labs" was finally co-opted by "hip capitalists" who packaged ephemeral new experiences for mass consumers.

THE CONTRADICTION OF
ROMANTIC ANTI-RATIONALITY

The other major flaw in contemporary Romanticism is that it misperceives the nature of contemporary Rationalism and uncritically adopts a posture of diametrical opposition that is self-defeating. Hugh Gardner (1978, p. 14) describes this logic of "alternatives" thus:

> If industrial technology brought trivial jobs, waste, plastic goods, and materialistic greed . . . then a good alternative was craftsmanship, doing more with less, and idealizing subsistence living and preindustrial technology. . . . If urbanization meant fouled, congested cities, overstimulation, freeways, anonymous and lonely living, sterile suburbs, and imprisoning ghettos, then the alternative was the rural countryside, clean air, green grass and trees, relaxation, and small, face-to-face communities.

This logic of alternatives also was applied to the principle of reason. Since the destruction of rolling meadows to build shopping malls was justified as good business sense, the counterculture escaped into voluntary poverty and drug fantasies. Since the manufacturers of nuclear missiles cloaked themselves in the mantle of science, the counterculture embraced magic. And when Lyndon Johnson unctuously implored his Vietnam critics to "reason together" with him, the counterculture celebrated madness. By the mid-1960s even many within the New Left had rejected reason as hopelessly corrupt and had embraced anti-intellectuality as the only pure attitude. Paul Jacobs and Saul Landau (1966, p. 14) observed:

... While the older ones among them had been able to articulate their views in a speech or a pamphlet, some of the younger ones, those who came into the Movement later and rejected politics—a small but growing number of middle-class youth—made a virtue of their inability to articulate and analyze coherently. They talked "from the gut," stumbling, haltingly, using the language of the new folksingers, deliberately adopting a style that was the antithesis of what they had heard from their professors.

What such youth did not understand is that this contemporary formulation of Rationalism as a legitimation for elite domination is not at all the ideal of reason that inspired our forefathers to establish a democratic society. To advise the public that matters of life and death, prosperity and poverty, are the preserve of experts and beyond the understanding of common people is to demean reason. It is a "paternalism of expertise" more compatible with monarchy than with democracy. In fact, as Theodore Roszak (1969, p. 142) points out, the power elite in modern society actually appeals to Romantic Conservative impulses to justify its authority:

> Expertise—technical, scientific, managerial, military, educational, financial, medical—has become the prestigious mystagogy of the technocratic society. Its principal purpose in the hands of ruling elites is to mystify the popular mind by creating illusions of omnipotence and omniscience—in much the same way that the pharaohs and priesthood of ancient Egypt used their monopoly of the calendar to command the awed docility of ignorant subjects.

Roszak (1969, p. 297) concludes:

> The general public had to content itself with accepting the decision of experts that what the scientists say is true, that what the technicians design is beneficial. All that remained to be done to turn such an authoritative professionalism into a new regime of bad magicians was for the ruling political and economic elites to begin buying up the experts and using them for their own purposes.

The Rationalism of the contemporary power elite is both undemocratic and unreasonable. It excludes consideration of human values or feelings on principle. Objectivity is supposed to be "dispassionate" and "value-free." Contemporary Rationalism refers only to a method of calculating the most efficient means to achieve given ends. These ends are not inherent in the process but are given by those in authority—the ones who, for example, determine that electric toothbrushes and nuclear missiles shall be the end products of technology. And they would rather not have to debate the value of these ends with an aroused public. In fact, many of them haven't developed the faculty of mind or strength of character to confront their own assumptions even if it were demanded of them.

Max Weber (1956) called this kind of rationality "formal rationality." He contrasted it with "substantive rationality," in which all choices are rooted consciously within some scheme of values that are subject to reflection. Like the eighteenth-century Rationalists and Romantics, Weber didn't believe that true reason precluded ethics or morality.

In Weber's view, the diffusion of formal rationality accompanied the expansion of industrial capitalism and was the dominant, all-embracing trend in Western history. Formal rationality is the basis for the culture of bureaucracy, which Weber identified with "mechanism, depersonalization, and oppressive routine [which are] adverse to personal freedom" (Gerth and Mills 1953, p. 50). Weber considered capitalism, the "alienation" of workers from the means of production, and the European socialism of the period, even more rationally organized to suppress individuality, also to be major manifestations of this process. In short, formal rationality is only the rationality of the marketplace, the cash nexus, the bureaucracy. It is not the reason of society or community. Believing that freedom is founded on "substantive rationality," Weber worried about the destiny of the West, imprisoned in its "iron cage" of bureaucracy, increasingly detached from human values and, thus, without spiritual direction.

C. Wright Mills (1959a; 1959b; 1956), whom many consider the father of the early New Left, was self-consciously in the Weberian tradition. He was scornful of the formal rationality of the American power elite, with its refusal to examine the assumptions upon which its calculations are premised. He called it "crackpot realism." For a contemporary example consider President Reagan's dark warnings about the "evil empire" of Godless Communism as the premise for the Defense Department's "objective" calculation of our military requirements.

HUMANIST REASON IN THE MAKING OF DEMOCRACY

Formal rationality is the classical ideal of reason stripped of any concern for values or human experience. It is a rationality of "body counts," "kill ratios," and "technological unemployment," a method of calculation that takes no account of the human cost. The effective response to rationality deficient in moral community is not anti-rationality deficient in moral community. It is substantive rationality (what Horkheimer calls "objective reason") or what I shall call humanist reason, a union of both rationality and moral community. Humanist reason rejects the false dualism of formal rationality and anti-rationality, and strives for a dialectical synthesis of facts and values, science and morality, cognitions and feelings, head and heart.

Humanist reason is what is needed if we are to achieve the revolution in both culture and politics that will democratize our institutions and our personal relationships. In the remainder of this essay I will examine the cultural political strategies of domination employed by today's ruling elite and suggest reasonable responses that those in the movement should consider in their efforts to make the revolution in the 1980s.

The Politics of "Public Opinion"

By definition, a movement that seeks a more fundamental democratization of both culture and politics must develop strategies for increasing public participation in institutional life. In fact, the political theory of democracy requires that the electorate actively discuss public affairs and rationally consider community interests. The concept of public opinion is celebrated in the Constitution and is at the heart of democratic theory.

Public opinion must have its setting in society and be a function of that society in operation. A society "is composed of diverse kinds of functional groups" that differ in terms of special interest, prestige, and power. Such groups are organized and have leaders who act on their behalf. When such groups act, they do so through available channels in an attempt to influence those "key people" who are strategically located in the society's important institutions. Since key individuals are subjected to many points of view, they can be expected to respond on the basis of the groups presenting the different views.

Thus, public opinion "occurs in large measure through the inter-action of groups" who differ in function, interest, power, and prestige (Blumer 1948, pp. 198–202; Wirth 1948).

To repeat the point: Public opinion is produced by the interaction of organized groups, not by individuals. For Robert Wolff (1969, p. 45) this principle is so basic to the pluralist theory of American politics that "Any policy urged by a group in the system must be given respectful attention, no matter how bizarre. By the same token, a policy or principle which lacks legitimate representation has no place in society, no matter how reasonable or right it might be."

Clearly, the popular meaning of public opinion today is funda-mentally different from that articulated in the theory of democratic politics. What goes under the label of public opinion today is the commercially published results of a polling procedure administered by an agency specializing in market research. Questions designed by survey researchers are put by paid interviewers to a statistically repre-sentative cross section of the population. The individual subjects are asked to choose from among a set of prestructured response alterna-tives, then these choices are tabulated and broken down into such sociodemographic categories as sex, age, and region of residence. Given the entertainment function of the mass media and their as-sumption about the limited attention span of their audience, there typically are few if any interpretations proposed for these tabula-tions (Diamond 1976).

In addition to government agencies, universities, and newspapers, there are about 1,000 commercial concerns active in the polling busi-ness, with an estimated revenue of $500 million a year (Reinhold 1975). The founder of this huge industry, George Gallup, started out in the 1930s doing market research for commercial products. In 1935, wanting to sound like a scientific academy, Gallup set up shop as the Institute of Public Opinion. He persuaded President Franklin D. Roosevelt to purchase his services and was credited with helping him win the 1936 election (Fleming 1971). Thus, as Friedrich Pollock (1976, p. 226) points out, opinion research "tacitly posits the universe of the customer as that of mankind as a whole," a con-ception that invites an attitude of manipulation. Newspapers and radio and television stations purchase these polls for the entertain-ment of their readers and viewers, who are themselves organized by merchandising territories rather than geographic boundaries. Mills (1956, p. 304) states, "In a mass society, the dominant type of communication is the formal media, and the publics become mere *media markets*: all those exposed to the content of a given media."

Despite their disclaimers, there is evidence to suggest that the major pollsters are not just the neutral fact finders they claim to be. In 1969 George Gallup appeared in a USIA film in which he documented the claim of a "silent majority" by reporting that a large majority supported President Nixon and that a Vietnam moratorium protest gave no help to the purpose of ending the war. A few years later his rival, Lou Harris, reported enthusiastically to a large group of Democratic state governors that a recent poll that showed greater public confidence in state, compared with federal, government offered a "ray of hope" upon which to build greater public support of state government.

Most authorities agree that it is impossible to tell what actually is measured by public opinion polls. Typically, there is no concern with whether the subject has any knowledge or information about the issue, how central it is for him/her, or with what intensity the opinion is held. Most people, not wishing to appear ignorant, will give an opinion when the interviewer demands it. As Leo Bogart (1967, p. 337) suggests, obviously "The first question to ask is: Have you thought about this at all? Do you *have* an opinion?" On many issues, most people really don't.

Ironically, one of the most consistent findings of public opinion researchers over the years is that opinions on the most important world issues—issues of war and peace—are the least rational. They show much less interest, information, temporal stability, and internal consistency than opinions on topics that are more simple and close to home (Scott 1958/59; Prothro and Grigg 1960; Converse 1962, 1964; Hero 1965; Caspary 1970; Hennessey 1972). As Fisher and Belknap (1952) explain:

> Not only are foreign affairs questions ordinarily less immediately con-
> sequential for the individual than such questions as employment, recre-
> ation, and family life, but they are also less real . . . this situation makes
> the usual role of the ordinary citizen more one of customer than a pro-
> cess participant. He can "buy" a point of view, or several of them; and
> if these viewpoints are logically in conflict, he need only avoid using
> them simultaneously.

Because they are so shallow, opinions on the most significant issues have been shown to vary widely by question phrasing and to be highly susceptible to influence by political authorities. Poll results have been known to shift overnight by as much as 25 percentage points after an announced change of presidential policy (Schuman and Converse 1970, p. 7). Erikson and Luttberg (1973, p. 325) explain:

> Because most political events are remote from people's everyday lives, people willingly view these events through the interpretation of their leaders. Also, since people want to believe that their political system is benign rather than corrupt or evil, they readily find reassurance from optimistic interpretations of the existing order and resist voices that tell them otherwise.

It seems clear that public opinion polls are primarily weapons in the hands of those in power. When poll results disagree with the policy of the administration, they are routinely disregarded. For example, since 1939 at least two-thirds of those polled have supported federally guaranteed employment, and since 1956 at least three-fourths have supported a national health care plan (Erikson and Luttberg 1973). These appear to be rather large and constant constituencies for what are basically socialist programs. But they are safely ignored because the elite knows that such opinion can have no effect on policy unless and until it becomes real public opinion, organized and active in the political process. The National Rifle Association teaches this lesson to the suburban middle class every year. Despite this benign neglect, when the poll results agree with their policy, elites often try to use them to intimidate any real opposition from forming. Until 1968 President Johnson carried press clippings of favorable Vietnam war polls in his pockets and would quote them in an effort to impress critics. Presidents Johnson and Nixon, basing their foreign policy on the "doctrine of credibility," used the polls to criticize anti-war demonstrators for misleading our enemies into underestimating our national determination to continue the war. Horkheimer (1974, pp. 30–31) states:

> The majority principle, in the form of popular verdicts on each and every matter, implemented by all kinds of polls . . . has become the sovereign force to which thought must cater. It is a new god . . . a power of resistance to anything that does not conform. The more the judgment of the people is manipulated by all kinds of interests, the more is the majority presented as the arbiter of cultural life . . . the

greater the extent to which scientific propaganda makes of public opinion a mere tool for obscure forces, the more does public opinion appear a substitute for reason.

For those concerned with moving people to change society, the most critical deficiencies of public opinion polls are the lack of evidence that anyone is expressing an opinion in behavior and whether and what effects such behavior is having on policy makers. In fact, an awful lot of what passes for electoral politics today consists of a "scientized" administration using its "bureaucratized" power to sponsor campaigns to sell a "mediatized" electorate its opinions. The official public realm is confined to periodic "spectacles and acclamation" (Habermas 1971, pp. 75–76). Or, as Shroyer (1973, p. 240) puts it, "Politics today means the creation of pseudo-issues that can legitimate one administration over its opponent—without involving any of the system's priorities."

This salesmanship occurs within the context of a system of communication that is organized like a monopoly, not an open marketplace of free competition between different points of view. There are 91,000 government units, 10,000 national associations, 320,000 churches, 121,000 schools and colleges, and 2.5 million business firms in the United States and, on any given day, many of these are trying to "make the news." Molotch and Lester (1975, p. 111) point out, however, that "those who seek to create public events by promoting their activities" must have access to the news assemblers. Theirs and other studies conclude that routine access is available only to high government officials, major corporate figures, and, to a lesser extent, certain glamorous personalities (see also Tuchman 1972, 1973, 1974, 1978; Fishman 1980; Gans 1979; Molotch and Lester 1974).

Real publics face physical obstacles in their efforts to communicate with other publics in the nation. The typical strategy has been to stage a crowd event that departs from the normal routine. When the news media cover such events, however, they frame it like a crime story, focusing on police estimates of crowd size, reports of damage and arrests, and pictures of the attendant scuffle, no matter how unrepresentative it might be of the general participation. The opinions of the demonstrating public are reduced to mere background. As a consequence, mass audiences are fed images of political authorities calmly responding to images of public disorder. This tends to reinforce the stereotypic connection in our cultural memory between the physical expression of public opinion and the Romantic Conservative horror of the "swinish multitude" destroying society's most precious institutions.

This is easily explained. Establishment newspapers are big businesses that depend on advertising revenue to make a profit. While many of their reporters may entertain liberal opinions privately, the publishers determine editorial policy—and they have endorsed the Republican candidate for president in the last four elections by margins of five to one or better. Certainly the commercial mass media lagged well behind the movement in criticizing the Vietnam war. A 1967 Associated Press survey of newspaper editors found that, although critical of President Johnson's management of relevant information, 79 of 103 editors expressed "generally enthusiastic support for the administration's policies in Vietnam."

Television networks are even bigger businesses and make their profits from selling audiences to advertisers. This is done, as former FCC Commissioner Nicholas Johnson tells us, "at a cost per thousand, like cattle" (Brown 1973). Seeking to reach audiences of up to 100 million, the nation's 100 largest advertisers account for over 80 percent of the $10 billion in advertising revenue collected by the major networks. The network journalist is allocated only 5 percent of television's prime-time schedule, and the average station allocates barely 10 percent of an 18-hour day to the news. Despite this, television critic John O'Connor notes that newscasts have proven to be both profitable and an important source of prestige for the television business.

Those responsible for manufacturing news daily must cultivate the most common sources of news. People in the government know this, and have staffs that routinely dispatch self-serving press releases. Occasionally they call news conferences to announce important developments. Reporters who too often ignore or criticize government officials' routine press releases may find their names missing from the list of guests invited to the important news events.

Despite their ability to influence the determination of what's news, there is no hard evidence that political elites have been able to use the media to get people to do what they want them to do. In fact, even at the height of his popularity, President Nixon had to mobilize his entire reelection committee and thousands of dollars to manufacture evidence of public support for his mining of Haiphong Harbor (Woodward and Bernstein 1973).

Unlike the situation with family, peers, or church, the media cannot reward or punish someone for conforming or not. In fact, people often don't pay attention to television sets and radios that are turned on. People choose the communications they expose themselves to on the basis of their backgrounds and predispositions. Moreover, research has shown that any content considered important is modified by local opinion leaders in friendship circles where it is discussed (Katz 1957; Brouwer 1964; Gerson 1966; Greenberg and Dominick 1969). Finally, despite the calculated "objectivity," it should be recognized that news programming "must compete with a whole machinery of amusement within a marketing context of distrust" (Mills 1956, p. 336). In the final analysis, the primary social control function of the media for the elites may only be to reinforce the acquiescence of a subdued public.

We don't know what the social potential of popularly accessible media might be. However, as long as the media remain under the control of the government and the communications industry, we are not likely to get much more than each season's version of the "vast wasteland." The obvious lesson for radical activists is to minimize the commercial media as a factor in any strategy. The activists' most powerful appeals are to reason and participation, and there is little time or space for that within the profit and entertainment orientation of the commercial media.

Of course, the rapid development of new home communications technology brings film and video productions within reach of any organization. In addition, community access television and public radio provide channels of mass communication that can be used by movements for any number of purposes. It is only the confining commercial network media that should be ignored, not the many other forms of decentralized electronic communications between groups and publics.

The Problem of Participation in Modern Society

It is clear that the elite, wishing to appear in control, would prefer not to deal with real publics. It would be much more comfortable presiding over masses—anonymous, physically separated individuals, with so little organization they are unable to act with any unity. Members of a mass are likely to be confused and uncertain, and to make selections based on vague impulses (Blumer 1966, p. 43). Such people would be highly susceptible to manipulation through the mass media. If American society consisted of no more than such masses, this would be a very efficient strategy of control. As Raymond Williams (1958, p. 319) proposes, however, "there are in fact no masses; there are only ways of seeing people as masses":

> If our purpose is art, education, the giving of information or opinion, our interpretation will be in terms of the rational and interested being. If, on the other hand, our purpose is manipulation—the persuasion of a large number of people to act, feel, think, know, in certain ways—the convenient formula will be that of the masses. (Williams 1958, p. 322)

From the "revolt against positivism" at the end of the nineteenth century to the present, critics have warned against potential destruction and enslavement by a mass society (Hughes 1961; Halebsky 1976; Walter 1964). The most common dystopian image is that of *1984*, a population atomized into lonely individuals subject to direct manipulation by remote elites through the mass media. Well, 1984 is past and, although the technologies of communication and surveillance have grown formidable, community still survives. In fact, as mentioned, the managers of the political economy depend on local reciprocity systems to cushion the shocks of disturbances in the marketplace.

Despite a steady increase in the divorce rate, almost everyone marries. And, although new forms are emerging, the family remains a very strong institution in American society (Masnick, Bane et al. 1980). It also is apparent that, in many areas, neighbors relate actively to each other. And community religious institutions are widely supported through frequent attendance and financial contributions.

The problem of American society today is not that the people have become cheerful robots who jump to the commands of Big Brother. Neither is it that people are selfish and indifferent to the needs of others. These are implicitly elitist images of the masses. Neither is the problem that people are hostile to the ideas that radicals espouse. Numerous surveys from 1968 to the present demonstrate majority endorsement of what once were only countercultural and New Left positions on civil liberties, civil rights for minorities and women, support for environmental protection, opposition to militarism, and loss of confidence in the leaders of almost all dominant institutions. Writing for the conservative American Enterprise

Institute magazine *Public Opinion*, Lipset and Schneider (1978, p. 46) are forced to conclude: "The Vietnam involvement, the explosion of antiwar protests, and the rise of militant social movements concerned with the status of various minority groups—blacks, Hispanics, and particularly, a nonminority group, women—seemingly changed the perception which Americans had of their country." As we have seen, however, this radical shift in the opinion polls has had little effect on government policies in these areas, especially militarism.

The problem of American society is that the people are isolated from the great bureaucracies of formal government. What is missing is the public sphere, the intermediate institutions and channels of communication through which groups can compel the decision makers to serve their human needs. Only about a fifth of the labor force is represented by a union, and until recently most of the white churches have not engaged in political issues. Studies conducted over the period 1929–71 show large majorities not involved with any other groups, especially among the poorer and less educated, who are least served by government (see Lynd and Lynd 1929; Lundberg, Komarovsky and McInerny 1934; Komarovsky 1946; Foskett 1955; Axelrod 1956; Scott 1957; Greer 1958; Wright and Hyman 1958; Hyman and Wright 1971).

As a consequence of this general situation, many people have come to think of government as something beyond their control—"you can't fight city hall." Such resignation is most apparent when only about half of the adult population even bothers to vote for president or, as Milbrath (1965) found, only about one in seven adults engages in any political activity beyond voting.

While citizens in other industrial countries have much higher rates of union representation and electoral participation (75–95 percent), there is no evidence of more active public participation generally. It seems to be in the nature of mass welfare states to pacify the citizenry with commodities while it encloses the public sphere within giant bureaucracies run by managers and technocrats. On the other hand, effective social movements don't require the participation of everyone. The most famous revolutions in history are estimated to have directly involved no more than 10 percent of the concerned population. And, according to Hersh (1983), a demonstration of 500,000 in the nation's capital in 1969 dissuaded President Nixon from ordering the use of nuclear weapons near the Chinese border during the Vietnam war.

The challenge for radical activists is not to turn the polls around but to move people to action. Activists shouldn't care what randomly chosen individuals tell a pollster. What activists need to know is whether people care about an issue and what they are willing and able to do about it. By maintaining a focus on collective behavior rather than private opinion, activists not only would be true to the spirit of their goal of generating popular participation in government, but also more effective in reaching it. For example, activists could make better use of the social survey method to do their own applied research relevant to their own informational needs. They could design interview schedules to find out what the people themselves care about, as well as to collect information about local groups and personal networks. Such knowledge of salient community issues and resources could then be used to evaluate organizing strategies.

Simple sociometric techniques could yield data that could be processed on an inexpensive microcomputer to identify informal opinion leaders who could be used as consultants, and even sponsors, to counteract the prestige of elite leaders. Through such means one could also identify obstacles to people's participation and gain a fuller picture of the various social forces in the setting. Such surveys could be carried out in conjunction with any other canvassing activity in which literature is distributed, contributions are solicited, or whatever. In fact, recapturing the pedagogical spirit of Marx and Engels' social surveys of the poor, the interviews could be designed in such a way as to educate people about the structure of their social world at the same time that information is collected on their experiences and perceptions. This is not the place to discuss this technique in detail. We should observe, however, that local activists usually know too little about the people they aspire to influence and that the techniques for collecting and processing such information are readily and cheaply available.

The goal of a popular democratic movement should be to help give power to the people. The most efficient means to that end is to help active publics link with one another to gain mutual access to key people in society's important institutions. Since real publics emerge from activated functional groups, organizers should start by finding out what local groups already exist (block clubs, the PTA, and so on) in the community.

The advantages of such a strategy are threefold. First, you meet people already active in groups. Active people have overcome whatever social or psychological obstacles prevent others from taking a public role and are more likely to act on their opinions. Second, you tap into existing communication networks and can more easily identify and contact potential recruits. Finally, any effort to socialize people to new behaviors is more likely to be effective (and, of course, efficient) when aimed at groups rather than individuals. This principle goes back to Kurt Lewin's research for the government during World War II and was demonstrated again in the women's movement.

Another major lesson learned in the 1960s is that any political movement must solve its problem of organization before it can challenge the power elite. All organizations must devise processes for recruiting and socializing new members, making decisions about goals and strategies, dividing the labor, assigning people to roles, establishing norms and controlling deviance. At the risk of oversimplification, groups have to know how to attract new members and how to involve the ones they get. There are many models to choose from. To the extent the social environment will permit, the model should be one that facilitates actualization of the group's values. A group that values individual autonomy and participation must organize itself in such a way as to support these commitments.

Some groups don't adequately attend to these functional prerequisites, either out of ignorance or because of a naively Romantic opposition to rational authority. Not only does such inattention not promote individuality but it invites conflict, withdrawal, and a general inability to act collectively. Often such ignorance is perpetuated by blaming the failure of organization on the weakness of "human nature" or on the character defects of certain individuals. When people begin speculating on other people's motives, it's a clear sign that moral consensus has broken down. The next step usually proposed to save the group is to purge some members and/or to demand greater conformity of expression as a condition for future participation.

On the other hand, groups that approach the task of organization building with an attitude of humanist reason actually can create much greater opportunities for the development and expression of individual differences. And they can do this while establishing the organizational solidarity needed for effective collective action.

I have studied the personal accounts of people who became "radicalized" in the 1960s and have been deeply impressed with the diversity of reasons or motives people have offered as explanation. Some mention purposive incentives such as belief in the cause, a need to feel justified, or a desire to express certain values in action. Others mention solidaristic incentives such as the friendship of like-minded people and the chance to gain personal recognition, clarify one's sense of self or enhance one's self-esteem. Others refer to expressive incentives such as feeling more in control of one's life, exploring one's potential for growth, seeking fun and excitement, even the ecstasy of making history. Still others cite instrumental incentives such as gaining power through greater numbers, finding sources of material support, learning personal techniques for handling the problems of everyday life, and developing organizational skills in research, writing, public speaking, and demonstration planning.

Effective recruitment amounts to persuading people that they can satisfy these various needs and develop these different skills through participation in the group. They should be helped to understand that, as a consequence of such group participation, they actually will become more individual, not less. Such differences also can be a source of group cohesion. They constitute the basis for interdependence that strengthens the group's integration, and they also increase the group's pool of resources to draw on when confronted with new challenges. Robin Williams (1957) has hypothesized that the greater the functional interdependence within a system, the greater the divergence of values that can be tolerated without disruption of the system. Reciprocal dependencies are the essence of group solidarity, and groups with high solidarity can be politically effective without demanding consensus on such intangibles as personal motivation.

The Movement for a Democratic Society in the 1980s

I have argued that the most effective recruitment strategy is one organized around already existing friendship networks, neighborhood groups, and local community institutions. The possibilities for growth here actually are better than ever. In contrast with the situation at the beginning of the 1960s, many observers in the 1980s (such as Herbers 1982) have noted a dramatic upsurge in citizen activism at the community level on a variety of issues.

The Office of Neighborhoods, Voluntary Associations, and Consumer Affairs of the U.S. Department of Housing and Urban Development estimates that there are about 15,000 consumer and citizen organizations active today (see Perlman 1978; Emmons 1979). Organizations such as Massachusetts Fair Share, the Pennsylvania Public Interest Coalition, and the Illinois Public Action Council have been remarkably effective in controlling the rates and services of public utilities in the absence of effective government regulation. The National Commission on Neighborhoods has identified more than 8,000 neighborhood associations in the United States, with over 10,000 block clubs in New York City alone. By 1980 coalitions of tenants had "forced politicians to enact legislation insuring fairer treatment for tenants" in a majority of states (Atlas and Dreier 1980, p. 16). One of these groups, the New Jersey Tenants Organization, has 50,000 members.

The neighborhood movement also shows how commonplace the protest tactics of the 1960s have become in the 1980s. In seeking to promote their interests, tenants have used "rent strikes, court strikes, lobbying, mass rallies, picketing, and sit-ins" (Atlas and Dreier 1980, p. 16).

Another major focus of New Left cultural politics in the 1960s was the development of organizational alternatives to bureaucracy. Such alternative organizations, including communes, cooperatives, and collectives, are personalistic, moralistic, holistic, and egalitarian. There is an emphasis on role rotation, teamwork or task sharing, internal education, and minimal pay and benefit differentials. A high value is placed on community (Rothschild-Whitt 1979).

Since about 1970 such organizations have been proliferating at a remarkable rate. The number of outside-the-system free schools multiplied from 30 to 800 between 1967 and 1973. This figure doesn't include "the countless open classrooms and free schools within public systems that by then were developed" (Rothschild-Whitt 1976). Gardner (1978) has estimated that during the mid-1970s, alternative institutions were being created at the rate of about 1,000 a year. A survey at the end of the 1970s found more than 100 alternative publications still serving 34 of the nation's 50 largest cities and another 49 smaller communities (Watson 1979).

The 1980 Food-Co-op Directory lists nearly 2,300 preorder co-ops and estimates there are 1,100 more. Total sales are estimated at $170 million annually. In 1979 there were 700 storefront co-ops, with total sales of over $220 million. By 1980 many of these co-ops were organized into 56 federations and 69 warehouses that provided technical and financial assistance (*Dollars & Sense* 1981).

There also are hundreds of small groups organized to oppose nuclear power and advocate safer forms of energy, such as solar power. The Abalone Alliance on the West Coast and the Clamshell Alliance on the East Coast each claim about 70 groups. Over the past few years, demonstrations involving civil disobedience have been staged at nuclear power plants in dozens of states. In some cases the protests have prodded government investigations. Certainly all the publicity the movement has attracted has heightened the awareness of the dangers of nuclear power, turned many against it, and compelled more careful government supervision of such plants (Pector 1979; Darnovsky 1979).

Probably the fastest-growing movement in the country is concerned with an immediate, mutually verifiable, bilateral freeze on the production, testing, and deployment of nuclear weapons. This goal is a relatively modest step toward total disarmament, but it is endorsed by millions and would require a critical change of policy by the militaristic elites of both superpowers. Most impressive has been the passage of resolutions by hundreds of town councils calling for the freeze. It is a notable attempt to compel national-level policy makers to respond to initiatives from grass-roots democratic institutions.

At the national level there are scores of mass-membership organizations with tens of thousands of dues-paying members each. Some number in the hundreds of thousands. Another extremely important development is the tremendous increase in activism by the churches. Their organizational and financial resources constitute significant contributions to the movement of the 1980s. Also, their traditional moral concerns with individual conscience and community welfare challenge the formal rationality of the state where it is most vulnerable.

The major national issues are human rights, including civil liberties and equal opportunities for minorities and women; peace, including nuclear disarmament, draft resistance, and opposition to military intervention in other countries; and environmentalism, including regulation of the food and drug industries, occupational safety and health, and protection of the natural environment. Such organizations have professional staffs that include research scientists, economists, attorneys, and lobbyists.

These various organizations have done quite well in the areas of research, publication, and congressional lobbying. They even have been able to organize temporary coalitions to stage rallies that in the

1980s have drawn as many as 800,000 people. In a more recent development, several of these groups have organized coalitions of their respective political action committees to elect candidates with a progressive position on human rights. So far, however, most haven't addressed, let alone solved, the problem of how to build local organizations that can participate in a sustained, decentralized, collective campaign to change national policy. Yet this is what is needed if we hope to create a democratic revolution in both culture and politics.

This problem has organizational, ideological, and strategic dimensions. First, we need to find ways to disseminate valid knowledge about and techniques of organizational development to people who can use them. The sad truth is that there are a great many well-intentioned people who just don't know how to organize themselves for public action. In fact, a 1971–72 survey by the National Assessment of Educational Progress found that only 44 percent of American adults knew how to use a ballot correctly. Some excellent work is being done by Heather Booth at Chicago's Midwest Academy, by George Lakey at Philadelphia's Movement for a New Society, by Boston's South End Press, and by other groups, but the effort needs to be expanded considerably.

When we consider the complex problem of scale, we still know very little. How do we build an organization small enough to allow satisfying member participation and yet large enough to be able to influence state and national authorities? How do we prevent a growing organization from becoming a mass association in which, as Mills has noted, "its leaders come to organize the opinions they represent?" In short, how do we organize the numbers and resources necessary to challenge the policies of the national elite without reproducing its relations of domination?

We also have not learned how to preserve democratic processes in the context of repression. Thus far, the power elite has been able to militarize popular revolutions at home and abroad by using systematic violence to provoke a defensive reorganization that destroys trust and elevates the militants to greater power within the movement. The elite may not succeed in actually conquering the revolution, but they do kill the dream and discourage other such attempts at liberation. How can we ensure our physical survival without sacrificing our cultural freedom?

Much work needs to be done in the area of ideological development so that the various issue-oriented movements can identify their conceptual and practical links, pool their resources, and work together to their mutual benefit. Many in the movement have neglected this need, either because of a Romantic aversion to intellectual work or because of the dominant prejudice against ideology as a self-serving distortion of the real world.

It must be appreciated that, historically, ideologies have performed vital cognitive and motivational functions for groups with diffuse boundaries, especially during periods of rapid change. Geertz (1964) explains that ideological construction is symbolic activity that allows a group to represent itself to itself in the total context of society and history in order to establish a project of collective action to maintain or transform society for the future. An ideology links the present to the future, engenders commitment, and motivates action in a way that "objective" science cannot. In the process of its application, an ideology defines or obscures social categories, stabilizes or upsets social expectations, maintains or undermines social norms, and relieves or exacerbates social tensions.

Many people in different single-issue movements have come to realize that their own power to affect events would be amplified significantly if they were to join forces with groups representing the same general values or interests. Conferences sponsored by the American Friends Service Committee, the Coalition for a New Foreign and Military Policy, the Committee for a SANE Nuclear Policy, and the Institute for Policy Studies to explore the "deadly connections" between the Cold War arms race and military intervention in the internal affairs of smaller countries are a start in this direction. So also are rallies, such as the AFL-CIO-sponsored "Solidarity Day" against Reagan administration policies, which brought together the presidents of almost all the country's major unions with the heads of 200 nonunion groups, including civil rights, women's, gay, senior citizen, educational, environmental, peace, and socialist organizations.

Disarmament advocates are beginning to realize that nuclear confrontation is most likely to occur in what begins as a local dispute triggered by outside intervention. Both peace movements are seeing links between militarism and racism. They need to understand that both greater minority participation in the peace movement and any plan for a durable peace will require a program for economic justice. Real peace means replacing threats and fears with harmonious relations, not just the momentary stoppage of violence. Such peace is not possible without economic justice.

Anti-nuclear power activists now make the obvious connection between their cause and the nuclear arms race. Environmentalists generally are realizing the need for more civilian constraint on the power of the military, from poison gas and nuclear waste disposal to the damming of rivers and displacement of communities by the Army Corps of Engineers.

All of the above movements may come to realize that advocacy of a demilitarized economy will require a conversion plan to ensure employment for all workers. Some unions are beginning to understand that social programs produce more jobs than military spending, that military aid to foreign dictatorships prevents unionism abroad and weakens it at home, and that the environmental movement could be an ally in improving the occupational safety and health of workers. However, none of these groups has sufficiently developed an analysis that forges these links into a coherent program that could attract the support of such a broad coalition (see Albert and Dellinger 1983 for an important attempt to explicate these connections).

Finally, we need to critically evaluate the dynamic relation between our goals and objectives and the strategic and tactical alternatives available to us. We need to know what is possible and what means are likely to succeed under what conditions. We need to study the decision process and the key situations that reproduce the dominant order, and ascertain the points of effective intervention. Successful movements, such as the Montgomery Improvement Association's bus boycott in 1955–56, were based as much on shrewd tactical calculation as on the inspiration of heroic individuals such as Rosa Parks and Martin Luther King, Jr. It should be obvious that people who want to make a difference would make better use of their time and energies by ignoring those who disagree with them and teaching those who do agree how to be more effective politically.

There should be a place for every tactic, depending on the situation, target, and intended effect. In the disarmament movement, peace groups whose goal is to recruit large numbers from all sectors of the population to work within the political system have relied on more conventional "legal tactics such as referenda and campaigns for the establishment of nuclear free zones." On the other hand, "activists from more pacifist and grass-roots 'action' groups," either because of their lack of confidence in the political system or because of the structural constraints of their situation, have chosen to "speak the truth" through the direct moral confrontation of civil disobedience.

Advocates claim that civil disobedience creates a "situation of crisis" that gives its practitioners a "sense of empowerment" at the same time that it forces others "to face the magnitude and urgency of the problem" (Peacock 1983). Within the broader movement, these should not be seen as antagonistic approaches.

USING ART TO MAKE POLITICS

The starting point for the analysis of the political potential of radical art must be the recognition that sociocultural continuity depends on people being socialized by authorities into a sense of reality that serves to rationalize and justify the status quo. In this context, radical art can function to "derealize" or dereify that which is taken for granted (Willener 1970). For example, Surrealist derealization, such as Dali's "melted" timepieces, sabotages the apparent concreteness of the products of modern technology. Such derealization of the dominant culture can lead to the awareness of the possibility of change—what some people have produced, other people can change.

A work of art may be judged radical with respect to its content or its form. Radical content would include images that expose the structures of power and privilege, and protest the exploitation and oppression of the victimized. Radical art also may celebrate the virtues of the common people, inspire them with images of the power that can come from solidarity, and show them the "future they can create for themselves" (Rocamora 1980, p. 3).

Radical form erases the barriers between the artist and his or her audience, between the world of art and the world of everyday life. In literature, radical form may subvert social hierarchies by making ordinary people into heroic characters. Or it may violate conventional boundaries by putting the language of frankly private conversation into public print. In this context, Marcuse (1977) suggests that invoking the sexual and other repressed spheres of reality can desublimate people's perceptions of the dominant culture, and thus liberate them from the symbols of authority. Certainly, the use of obscenity and profanity in literature constitutes "an assault on decorum" that suits the purpose of the revolutionary (Bliven 1981, p. 97).

In theater, radical form tears away the curtain that separates the performers from the audience, sending performers out into the audience or inviting members of the audience to participate in the play. Street theater breaks the boundaries of institutional theater completely, undermines people's sense of public order, and provokes them to reflect on what is real and what is fantasy (Willener 1970).

Radical painting, drawing, or sculpture uses surfaces or materials from the everyday world of ordinary people, as in the Dada or Cubist montages, the "ready-mades" of Duchamp or the "found objects" of the Pop artists. Radical art also includes forms that are more accessible to the public than elite institutional art. For example, in the 1930s anti-war artist Käthe Kollwitz, wishing to make art that was politically "effective," produced posters, prints, and woodcuts because they were "direct," "simple," and within easy reach of common people. Other popular forms are murals, wall paintings, illustrated leaflets, and banners.

The Democratic Socialist *In These Times* has reported that since the 1960s the New Left and countercultural groups have increasingly used comic books to provide popular introductions to imperialism, ecology, sexism, radical history, and the lives of revolutionary leaders. In the words of political cartoonist Jules Feiffer, cartoons are "sharp," "direct," "simplistic," and "black and white." Because of these features, the cartoon form "radicalizes the reader's sensibility." Also, it can be mass-produced for a broad and heterogeneous audience.

Today, many agree with play and screen writer Trevor Griffiths (*Reds*) that the movement should use film and television more, in order to reach "the widest possible audience" (Quart and Auster 1982, p. 24). Others argue that such conservative forms blunt the thrust of radical drama by assimilating it to conventional assumptions and habitual patterns of response. They propose that the audience can be provoked out of its apathy only by modernist devices such as "shock effects, discontinuities of narrative, abrupt changes of level, and the comprehensive undermining of illusionism" (Murdock 1981, p. 8). However, there are disagreements about whether popular audiences are willing to tolerate and/or able to cope with such modernist devices.

As an increasing number of artists have become involved with the nuclear disarmament movement, they have begun to reflect on what qualities of art can move people to political action. Many feel that politically effective art, although necessarily critical of the status quo, must communicate an optimism about the possibility of change in order to be effective. Media Network director Marc Weiss points out that "A good film can have a terrible result . . . if it doesn't help people get beyond a numbing or shocking effect and move them to action" (Demeter 1983, p. 24). One example of how that might be accomplished is offered by dramatist Paul Zimet, who chose to approach the subject of extinction by turning it around and showing "what is precious in life . . . what was worth preserving" (Rizzo 1983, pp. 20–22).

Many also feel that, despite its political objectives, effective political art must be true to its own standards and not be reduced to obvious propaganda. Left film maker Saul Landau says, "All my films try to teach people without preaching too hard" (Demeter 1983). Lawrence Lasker, one of the producers of the anti-nuclear war film *War Games*, feels that one of the reasons for the film's popularity is that "it doesn't barrage you with propaganda" (Labaco 1983, p. 15). Activist poet Kathy Engel explains, "I don't write poetry thinking: 'I hope someone reads this and then has a sit in at the Pentagon!' Poetry is offering your version of the truth. You can't tell people what to do. You just hope it moves them" (Barry 1983, p. 31). Others have objected that the nuclear threat is too grave and the need for action too imperative to rely on art, with all of its complex ambiguities, to convey a political message.

While these controversies over perception and attitude are important, we must keep in mind that no aesthetic experience can lead to political commitment unless it occurs in the context of political organization. One of the principal values of art is that its presentation creates the occasion to reconstitute the public sphere. Since our mediatized society has lost the traditions of the coffeehouse, salon, and cabaret, this creation of social space for public interaction is vital to the health of any democratic movement. The function of art within this public sphere is to personalize the collectivity while it collectivizes the personal. Art represents a dynamic mediation between the private and the public, the individual and the group. On the one hand, it helps individuals to perceive their personal troubles as shared by others, and thus promotes the formation of a community of interest. On the other hand, the complexity of the artistic experience ensures a diversity of responses that reinforces the importance of individual differences to social creation and re-creation. A society without art is one without imagination, and a society without imagination is limited to reproducing the present, no matter how unfulfilling it may be. A society that values art is not likely to mistake sameness for equality, a distinction fundamental to the vital combination of social justice and cultural pluralism.

SUMMARY AND CONCLUSION

In summary, bourgeois rationalism is the ruling ideology of the capitalist elites. It is undemocratic because it legitimates bureaucratic decision making and deliberately excludes human values and costs from its planning and accounting. Historically, many opposition movements have lost their radical thrust by gravitating toward the extremes of dogmatic authoritarianism (such as Stalinism) or quietistic individualism and anti-rationality (such as Romanticism).

To create a democratic and effective alternative, movements in the 1980s must adopt a position of humanist reason, reason based on the principle that individual freedom and rational social planning must be rooted in democratically organized social relationships and concerned with ultimate ends or values. Humanist reason strives for a dialectical synthesis of rationality and moral community, individual creative freedom and collective solidarity, head and heart.

Modern elites use the mass communications and public opinion industries to simulate democratic participation to legitimate their rule. In response, real publics often feel compelled to adopt crowd tactics that give them visibility but make them appear unreasonable. Radical activists must remember that their challenge is not to get on commercial network television or to influence the mass opinion polls, but to move people to effective action. The shortest route to success is to help already active publics link up with one another to gain mutual access to decision makers in key institutions.

To do this, activists must develop organizational structures that combine opportunities for individual expression with the collective solidarity needed for effective action; formulate an ideology that identifies the theoretical and practical links between the major contemporary movements for peace, human rights, and environmental protection; and study the social structure and our own actions to discover what tactics are most likely to succeed in what types of situations and with what consequences for the movement's ideals.

The urgency and ambiguity of these questions make one thing clear: we in the movement need conferences, workshops, and newsletters devoted to the sharing and evaluation of our organizing experiences. This would provide us with the possibility of authentic praxis in which political actions can be chosen on the basis of theoretical knowledge, and the lessons learned from such actions used to modify and develop that knowledge.

The problems of organization, ideology, and strategy that confront movements for change today will not yield to the imposition of authoritarian discipline and antiquated dogma, and they will not dissolve in the euphoria of Romantic fantasy. Only a concerted application of value-committed humanist reason can deliver us from these self-defeating extremes and provide a sound, humane, and popular alternative to the status quo.

REFERENCES

Albert, Mike, and Dave Dellinger, eds. 1983. *Beyond Survival: New Directions for the Disarmament Movement.* Boston: South End Press.

Atlas, John, and Peter Dreier. 1980. "The Housing Crisis and the Tenants' Revolt." *Social Policy*, Jan./Feb., pp. 13-24.

Axelrod, Morris. 1956. "Urban Structure and Social Participation." *American Sociological Review* 31 (Feb.): 13-18.

Barry, Daniel. 1983. "Well-Versed Activists Speak Out." *Nuclear Times*, July, pp. 30-31.

Bayer, A. E., J. T. Royer, and R. M. Webb. 1973. *Four Years After College Entry.* Princeton, N.J.: American Council on Education Research Reports, 8.

Bliven, Naomi. 1981. Review of James H. Billington. "Fire in the Minds of Men: Origins of the Revolutionary Faith." *The New Yorker*, January 12, pp. 97-102.

Blumer, Herbert. 1966. "The Mass, the Public, and Public Opinion." In *Public Opinion and Communication*, edited by Bernard Berelson and Morris Janowitz. 2nd ed. New York: Free Press.

——. 1948. "Public Opinion and Public Opinion Polling." *American Sociological Review* 13 (Oct.): 542-49.

Bogart, Leo. 1967. "No Opinion, Don't Know, and Maybe No Answer." *Public Opinion Quarterly* 31, no.. 3: 331-45.

Brouwer, Martin. 1964. "Mass Communication and the Social Sciences: Some Neglected Areas." In *People, Society and Mass Communications*, edited by Lewis Dexter and David Whites, pp. 547-66. New York: The Free Press.

Brown, Jud. 1973. "Nick Johnson's Blues." *The Free Drummer*, Apr. 10, p. 1.

Caspary, William R. 1970. "The 'Mood Theory': A Study of Public Opinion and Foreign Policy." *American Political Science Review* 64 (June): 536-47.

Converse, Philip E. 1964. "The Nature of Belief Systems in Mass Publics." In *Ideology and Discontent*, edited by David Apter. New York: The Free Press.

——. 1962. "Information Flow and the Stability of Partisan Attitudes." *Public Opinion Quarterly* 26, no. 3: 578-99.

Darnovsky, Marcy. 1979. "A Strategy for the Anti-Nuclear Movement: A Response to Pector." *Socialist Review* 9, no. 3 (May-June): 119-28.

Demeter, John. 1983. "Movement Passes Screen Test." *Nuclear Times*, July, pp. 23-24.

Diamond, Edwin. 1976. "Political News Showed up Show Biz on TV." *New York Times*, June 13, sec. 2, p. 1.

Dollars & Sense. 1981. "Can Coops Keep up with the Competition?" 64 (Feb.): 13-15.

Emmons, David. 1979. *Neighborhood Activists and Community Organizations: A Critical Review of the Literature.* Evanston, Ill.: Northwestern University Office for Urban Affairs.

Erikson, Robert S., and Norman R. Luttberg. 1973. *American Public Opinion: Its Origins, Content and Impact.* New York: John Wiley and Sons.

Fisher, D. R., and G. Belknap. 1952. *America's Role in World Affairs.* Ann Arbor: University of Michigan Survey Research Center.

Fishman, Mark. 1980. *Manufacturing the News.* Austin: University of Texas Press.

Fleming, Donald. 1971. "Attitude: The History of a Concept."

Foskett, John M. 1955. "Social Structure and Social Participation." *American Sociological Review* 20 (Aug.): 433-38.

Freedman, Ronald, and Morris Axelrod. 1957. "Who Belongs to What in a Great Metropolis?" In *Readings in General Sociology*, edited by Robert W. O'Brien, Clarence C. Schrag, and Walter T. Martin, pp. 112-18. Boston: Houghton Mifflin.

Gans, Herbert. 1979. *Deciding What's News.* New York: Pantheon.

Gardner, Hugh. 1978. *The Children of Prosperity: Thirteen Modern American Communities.* New York. St. Martin's Press.

Gardner, Richard. 1976. *Alternative America.* Published privately.

Geertz, Clifford. 1964. "Ideology as a Cultural System." In *Ideology and Discontent*, edited by David Apter. New York: The Free Press.

Gerson, Walter. 1966. "Mass Media Socialization Behavior: Negro-White Differences." *Social Forces* 45 (Sept.): 40-50.

Gerth, Hans H., and C. Wright Mills. 1958. "Introduction" to *From Max Weber: Essays in Sociology*, translated and edited by H. H. Gerth and C. Wright Mills. New York: Oxford University Press.

——. 1953. *Character and Social Structure.* New York: Harcourt, Brace and World.

Gouldner, Alvin. 1973. "Romanticism and Classicism: Deep Structures in Social Science." In *For Sociology: Renewal and Critique in Sociology Today*, edited by Alvin Gouldner, pp. 324-53. New York: Basic Books.

Greenberg, Bradley, and Joseph Dominick. 1969. "Racial and Class Differences in Teen-agers Use of Television." *Journal of Broadcasting* 13: 3331-44.

Greensfelder, and Nicole Hollander. 1982. *In These Times.*

Greer, Scott. 1958. "Individual Participation in Mass Society." In *Approaches to the Study of Politics*, edited by Roland Young. Evanston, Ill.: Northwestern University Press.

Habermas, Jurgen. 1971. *Toward a Rational Society: Student Protest, Science and Politics.* Translated by J. J. Shapiro. London: Heinemann.

Halebsky, Sandor. 1976. *Mass Society and Political Conflict: Toward a Reconstruction of Theory.* New York: Cambridge University Press.

Hennessey, Bernard. 1972. "A Headnote on the Existence and Study of Political Attitudes." In *Political Attitudes and Public Opinion*, edited by Dan D. Nimmo and Charles M. Bonjean. New York: David McKay.

Herbers, John. 1982. "Citizen Activism Gaining in Nation." *New York Times*, May 16, p. 1.

Hero, Alfred O. 1965. "Foreign Aid and the American Public." *Public Policy* 14: 71-116.

Hersh, Seymour. 1983. *The Price of Power*. New York: Summit.

Horkheimer, Max. 1974. *Eclipse of Reason*. New York: Seabury Press.

Hughes, H. Stuart. 1961. *Consciousness and Society: The Reorientation of European Social Thought 1890-1930*. New York: Vintage. Reprinted New York: Octagon, 1976.

Hyman, Herbert H., and Charles R. Wright. 1971. "Trends in Voluntary Association Membership of American Adults: Replication Based on a Secondary Analysis of National Sample Surveys." *American Sociological Review* 36, no. 2: 191-206.

Jacobs, Paul, and Saul Landau. 1966. *The New Radicals: A Report with Documents*. New York: Vintage Books.

Katz, Elihu. 1957. *Personal Influence*. Glencoe, Ill.: The Free Press.

Komarovsky, Mira. 1946. "The Voluntary Association of Urban Dwellers." *American Sociological Review* 11 (Dec.): 686-98.

Labaco, Gina. 1983. "How Hollywood Learned to Play War Games." *Nuclear Times*, July, pp. 14-15.

Lipset, Seymour M., and Eugene Schneider. 1978. "How's Business? What the Public Thinks." *Public Opinion*, July/Aug.

Lundberg, G. A., M. Komarovsky, and M. A. McInerny. 1934. *Leisure: A Suburban Study*. New York: Columbia University Press.

Lynd, Robert S., and Helen M. Lynd. 1929. *Middletown*. New York: Harcourt Brace.

Mannheim, Karl. 1971. "Conservative Thought." In *From Karl Mannheim*, edited by Kurt A. Wolff, New York: Oxford University Press, pp. 132-222.

Marcuse, Herbert. 1977. *The Aesthetic Dimension.* Boston: Beacon.

Masnick, George, Mary J. Bane, et al. 1980. *The Nation's Families: 1960-1990.* Boston: Auburn House.

Milbrath, Lester. 1965. *Political Participation: How and Why Do People Get Involved in Politics?* Chicago: Rand McNally.

Miller, Richard. 1977. *Bohemia: The Protoculture Then and Now.* Chicago: Nelson-Hall.

——. 1956. *The Power Elite.* New York: Oxford University Press.

——. 1951. *White Collar.* New York: Oxford University Press.

Molotch, Harvey, and Marilyn Lester. 1975. "Accidental News: The Great Oil Spill as Local Occurrence and National Event." *American Journal of Sociology* 81, no. 2: 235-60.

——. 1974. "News as Purposive Behavior: On the Strategic Use of Routine Events, Accidents and Scandals." *American Sociological Review* 39, no. 1: 101-12.

Murdock, Graham. 1981. *Radical Drama, Radical Theatre.* Red Feather, Colo.: Institute for Advanced Studies in Sociology.

Peacock, Joe. 1983. "Catching the King's Conscience." *Nuclear Times*, June, pp. 14-15.

Pector, Jeff. 1979. "Further Thoughts on the Anti-Nuclear Movement: Response to Darnosky and Bayer." *Socialist Review* 9, no. 3 (May-June): 119-28.

Perlman, Janice. 1978. "Grassroots Participation from Neighborhood to Nation." In *Citizen Participation in America*, edited by Stuart Langton. Lexington, Mass.: D. C. Heath.

Pollock, Fredrich. 1976. "Empirical Research into Public Opinion." In *Critical Sociology*, edited by Paul Connert. New York: Penguin. Originally published in German in 1955.

Prothro, James, and Charles Grigg. 1960. "Fundamental Principles of Democracy: Bases of Agreement and Disagreement." *Journal of Politics* 2 (May): 276-94.

Quart, Leonard, and Al Auster. 1982. "Stage Left." *In These Times*, Apr., pp. 7-13.

Reinhold, Robert. 1975. "Polling Encounters Public Resistance: Decision-Making Process Is Threatened." *New York Times*, Oct. 26, p. 1.

Rizzo, Renata. 1983. "On the Road for Disarmament." *Nuclear Times*, July, pp. 20-22.

Rocamora, Nancy. 1980. "The Transformation of Underground Art in the Philippines." *Southeast Asia Chronicle* 70-71 (March-Apr.): 3-12.

Roszak, Theodore. 1969. *The Making of the Counterculture: Reflections on the Technocratic State and Its Youthful Opposition.* Garden City, N.Y.: Doubleday/Anchor.

Rothschild-Whitt, Joyce. 1979. "The Collectivist Organization: An Alternative to Rational-Bureaucratic Models." *American Sociological Review* 44 (Aug.): 509-27.

——. 1976. "Alternative Institutions as Collectively Controlled Workplaces: Some Dilemmas." Paper presented at the Annual Meetings of the American Sociological Association, Chicago.

Scott, John C. 1957. "Membership and Participation in Voluntary Associations." *American Sociological Review* 22 (June): 315-26.

Scott, William A. 1958/59. "Correlates of International Attitudes." *Public Opinion Quarterly* 22, no. 4: 464-72.

Schuman, Howard, and Philip E. Converse. 1970. "'Silent Majorities' and the Vietnam War." *Scientific American* 22, no. 6: 3-11.

Shayon, Robert L. 1969. "The Tip of the Iceberg." *Saturday Review*, Nov. 29, p. 24.

Shroyer, Trent. 1973. *The Critique of Domination: The Origins and Development of Critical Theory.* Boston: Beacon.

Speier, Hans. 1950. "Historical Development of Public Opinion." *American Journal of Sociology* 55 (Jan.): 376-88.

Tuchman, Gaye. 1978. *Making News.* New York: The Free Press.

———. 1974. *The TV Establishment.* Englewood Cliffs, N.J.: Prentice-Hall.

———. 1973. "Making News by Doing Work: Routinizing the Unexpected." *American Journal of Sociology* 79, no. 1 (July): 114-31.

———. 1972. "Objectivity as Strategic Ritual: An Examination of Newsmen's Notions of Objectivity." *American Journal of Sociology* 77, no. 4: 660-79.

Turner, Ralph. 1969. "The Theme of Contemporary Social Movements." *British Journal of Sociology* 20, no. 4: 390-405.

Walter, E. V. 1964. "'Mass Society': The Late Stages of an Idea." *Social Research* 31 (Winter): 391-419.

Watson, Francis, Jr. 1979. *The Alternative Media.* Rockford, Ill.: Rockford College Institute.

Weber, Max. 1956. *The Theory of Social and Economic Organization*, translated by A. M. Henderson and Talcott Partsons, edited by Talcott Parsons. Glencoe, Ill.: The Free Press.

———. 1930. *The Protestant Ethic and the Spirit of Capitalism*, translated by Talcott Parsons. New York: Scribner's.

Wheeler, Michael. 1976. *Lies, Damn Lies and Statistics: The Manipulation of Public Opinion.* New York: Laurel.

Willener, Alfred. 1970. *The Action Image of Society: On Cultural Politicization.* New York: Pantheon.

Williams, Robin M. 1957. "Unity and Diversity in Modern America." *Social Forces* 36, no. 1: 1-8.

Williams, Raymond. 1958. *Culture and Society 1780-1950.* New York: Columbia University Press.

Wirth, Louis. 1948. "Consensus and Mass Communication." *American Sociological Review* 13 (Feb.): 1-15.

Wolff, Robert Paul. 1969. "Beyond Tolarance." In *A Critique of Pure Tolerance*, edited by Robert Paul Wolff, Barrington Moore, Jr., and Herbert Marcuse, pp. 3-52. Boston: Beacon.

Woodward, Bob, and Carl Bernstein. 1973. "Was Nixon's Support on Haiphong Mining 'Fixed'?" *Washington Post* News Service, Apr. 25.

Wright, Charles. 1960. *Mass Communications: A Sociological Perspective.* New York: Random House.

Wright, Charles R., and Herbert Hyman. 1958. "Voluntary Association Memberships of American Adults: Evidence from National Sample Surveys." *American Sociological Review* 23 (June): 284-94.

Yankelovich, Daniel. 1972. *The Changing Values on Campus.* New York: Washington Square Press.

Index

Aaron, Daniel, 180-181
activism, 1
activists, 314-315, 321
Aiken, Michael, 253
Altamont, 248, 280
Altbach, Philip, 226
American Workers Party, 161
American Writers' Congresses, 163-164
anarchism, 122-123
Anderson, Chester, 223
Aquarian Youth, 245
Arbeitsrat für Kunst, 101
"Arcadian illusion," 26
Armory Show, 63-64
Aronowitz, Stanley, 243
Arp, Hans, 90-91, 111
art: to make politics, 322-325; movements
    in, 82-83; and politics, 173-175; pro-
    letarian, 102, 122; for revolution (*see*
    Leninists); and World War I, 87
artists: and Depression, 177-178; and
    nuclear disarmament, 323; as rebel
    prophets, 81-86
Association of American Painters and
    Sculptors, 63-64, 71

Baader, Johannes, 103, 106-107
Baargeld, Johannes, 97, 111
Ball, Hugo: and break with Dada, 99; and
    exile to Zurich, 89; and "sound
    poems," 92-93
Bamber, Linda, 120
Barrès, Maurice, 114
Beard, Charles, 56
Beatles, 246
beatnik, 208
Beat politics: and Beat colonies, 210-213;
    and bohemia, modern, 189-190; char-
    acters of, central, 191-194; and genera-
    tional vision, 194-195; and hipsters,
    190-191; ideology of, 196-197; popu-
    larity of, 206-210; and relation between
    cultural and political radicalism, 221-

227; and Romanticism, 213-221; and
    San Francisco Beat, 195-196; social
    psychology of ideology of, 197-204;
    writings of, 204-206
Beats: activism of, 225-226; and commer-
    cialization of colonies, 238-239; con-
    servative, 213-221; and cultural free-
    dom, 222; and electoral politics, 221;
    and hippies, 239-241; ideology of, 196;
    impact of, on politics, 226; media
    coverage of, 222-224; popularity of,
    206-210; radical, 213-221; recruits for
    protest causes, 227; and resistance to
    orthodoxy, 238-241; in San Francisco,
    195-196; term for, 194-195; writing
    of, 204-206
Bebop, 204-205
Becker, Norma, 283-284
Belknap, G., 307
Berger, Bennett M., 140, 174, 221-222
Berlin Dada Fair, 108-109
Berlin Dadaists: and art of politics, 108-110;
    exhibitions of, 105-107; original, 103-
    105; and politics of art, 107-108; pub-
    lications of, 105-107; scandal of, 105-
    107
Berlin League for Proletarian Culture, 101
"Beulah," 4
black migrations, 134-135
Black Panther Party, 254, 256-258
Black Power, 256
black power: and civil rights movement,
    250-251; and community control,
    255-257; and cultural nationalism,
    258-259; and Garvey, 131; and MFPD,
    252-253; and migration north, 253-
    254; and police brutality, 257-258;
    and SCLC, 250-251; and SNCC, 250;
    and themes of protest, 257; violence
    against, 251-252; and voter registra-
    tion, 252-253
Blake, William: groupings of, 28-29; ideology
    of, 4; and Industrial Revolution, 1; life

About the Editor and Contributors

FRANK T. EDGAR is professor of history, political science, and sociology at Culver-Stockton College, Canton, Missouri. He has taught at Utica College of Syracuse University, San Francisco State College, and Northern Illinois University.

Dr. Edgar has written and published in the areas of short fiction, biography, and the one-act drama, as well as scholarly articles. His *Sir Ralph Hopton: the King's Man in the West* was published (1968) by the Clarendon Press, Oxford. Dr. Edgar holds a B.A. from the University of Denver, an M.S. in education from Northern Illinois University, and a Ph.D. from the University of California.

ARTHUR FERRARI is associate professor of sociology at Connecticut College in New London. He has taught there since 1970, except for a two-year visit at the University of Arizona (1978–80). Dr. Ferrari has been a consultant to the Yale University School of Medicine and has published in *Sociology and Social Research* and *The Encyclopedia of Sociology*. He holds a B.A. from the State University of New York at Albany and an M.Phil. and Ph.D. from Yale University.

PAUL S. GEORGE teaches in the history department at the University of Miami. His articles and reviews have appeared in *Florida Historical Quarterly*, *Tequesta*, *New River News*, *Corrections Today*, and *Community College Frontiers*. Dr. George holds a B.A. from the University of Miami and an M.A. and Ph.D. from Florida State University.

DOUGLAS B. GUTKNECHT is assistant professor of sociology at Chapman College, Orange, California, where he coordinates both the social science B.A. and the M.S. degree in organizational and human resource development. He is chief coordinating editor of *Family, Self: Emerging Issues, Alternatives and Interventions* (University Press of America, 1983) as well as the author and editor of two recent texts: *Developing Organizational and Human Resources Toward the 21st Century* (University Press of America, 1984) and *Meeting Organizational and Human Resource Challenges in an Era of Change: Issues, Perspectives, and Strategies* (University Press of

America, 1984). Dr. Gutknecht holds a Ph.D. from the University of California, Riverside.

IRWIN MARCUS is professor of history at Indiana University of Pennsylvania, Indiana, Pennsylvania. Until 1965 he was assistant professor of history at Harrisburg Area Community College in Pennsylvania. His articles and reviews have appeared in *Labor History*, *Pennsylvania History*, and *Negro Bulletin*. Dr. Marcus holds a B.A. from the Pennsylvania State University and an M.A. and Ph.D. from Lehigh University, Bethlehem, Pennsylvania.

CONSTANCE ASHTON MYERS lives in South Carolina, where she teaches history at the university level. Her publications include reviews and articles in *Studies in Comparative Communism, Mid-Continent American Studies Journal, Journal of American History, American Historical Review*, and *Notable American Women: The Modern Period*, Barbara Sicherman and Carol H. Green eds. (Belknap, 1980), as well as a book, *The Prophet's Army: Trotskyists in America, 1928–1941* (Greenwood, Press, 1977). She is currently completing a history of the National Women's Party, to be published by the University of North Carolina Press. Dr. Myers holds a B.A. from California State University, an M.S. from Claremont Graduate School, and a Ph.D. from the University of South Carolina.

JEROLD M. STARR has been on the faculty of sociology and anthropology at West Virginia University since 1976. He taught at the University of Pennsylvania, from 1969 to 1976 and at the University of Hawaii in 1980. Dr. Starr is author of *Social Structure and Social Personality* (Little, Brown, 1974) and coeditor and contributor to *Technology, Power, and Social Change* (D. C. Heath, 1972). He has published many papers on human development, social movements, and research methods in such journals as *Qualitative Sociology, Journal of Social Issues, International Journal of Aging and Human Development, Youth & Society, Current Sociology*, and *Humanity & Society*. A book titled *Generational Politics: The Interaction of Biography and History* is scheduled for release in 1985.

At present, Dr. Starr is a participant in preparations for the United Nations International Year of Youth 1985. He has been active in movements for peace and human rights since the early 1960s. Dr. Starr holds a Ph.D. from Monteith College of Wayne State University and a Ph.D. from Brandeis University.

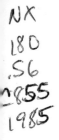